New Jersey: America's Main Road

Books by John T. Cunningham

RAILROADING IN NEW JERSEY

THIS IS NEW JERSEY

MADE IN NEW JERSEY

GARDEN STATE

THE NEW JERSEY SHORE

THE NEW JERSEY SAMPLER

NEW JERSEY

America's Main Road

JOHN T. CUNNINGHAM

Maps by Homer Hill

Doubleday & Company, Inc.

GARDEN CITY, NEW YORK

For Lloyd M. Felmly

With enduring appreciation for giving
me the time and the opportunity to know
New Jersey—and to tell its story.

Contents

CONTENTS

List of Illustrations

Following page 26

Following page 122

Following page 170

Preface

Fifteen years ago, when I first became genuinely interested in New Jersey—despite the fact that I am a native—those experts whom I met in the course of my wanderings as a newspaperman kept insisting that the state's prime need was an attractive, readable one-volume history. Samuel J. Smith wrote such a work in 1765 but since then no author has tackled the task. Good histories have been written: Francis Bazley Lee's four-volume work presented in 1902 is lively, attractive, and accurate; Irving S. Kull's four-volume history published in 1930 is satisfactory, if at times tedious; and, finally, William Starr Meyers' 1945 set of five volumes is generally well written and useful, although its high cost caused its publication in limited quantities.

The need has persisted. As the years have passed, an outpouring of books on New Jersey's counties, its folklore, its regions, its people, and its government has served to underscore the absence of a work pulling together the state's extremely varied historical threads.

This book is written to meet a need, but it is also written to satisfy my hope that many people—in New Jersey and elsewhere—can come to know the excitement and importance of the state and its more than 350 years. This has been a state of colonization, of colonists' struggles against tyranny, of Revolution, of transportation and industrial vigor. This has been a state of varied peoples, a pot which has melted, melded, and certainly always bubbled through all its recorded time. It is a state unquestionably as vital to American life as New England or Southern states, for all the volumes written about those regions.

Now it is clear to me why this history had not been written. New Jersey's story, often brushed aside as simply a matter of real estate between the great cities of New York and Philadelphia, is so complicated, so varied, so far-reaching, that it is difficult to capture in a single book. Few of the major elements of American history are missing, from the Revolution to the Gold Rush, from development of the steam engine to immigration, from Indians to exploration of outer space.

I am fully aware of the omissions necessary in any such history of any region. Writing history is, after all, a work of selection and interpretation; I have chosen to interpret New Jersey's past essentially in terms of those people who have moved constantly along the teeming roads from New York to Philadelphia. This is a story of their achievements and mistakes, of their pride and self-abasement.

Obviously the state has not existed in a vacuum, but while I seek here to place New Jersey in the mainstream of American history, my basic purpose is to tell of happenings within the land between the Hudson and Delaware rivers. If this seems chauvinistic, I have not meant to write a series of provincial essays. Within these pages are the accounts of blunders and misery as well as the details of heroism and conquest. A state, like a person, evolves as much through failures as through successes.

Perhaps this will be called a journalist's history, and indeed I would be proud of that. I am a journalist, trained as a newspaperman, filled with a newspaperman's awareness that nothing is all black or all white, and that everything, whether it be history or the United Nations, needs interpretation and analysis before it can be understood.

Many people have aided and encouraged me. I am grateful to those thoughtful admirers of New Jersey who began urging me to write this book at least a decade ago. I recall a debt to Dr. Frederick M. Raubinger, State Commissioner of Education, who once told me that he felt such a volume will fill a need in the schools and encouraged me to write it. I bow to those hundreds of teachers who have shown keen interest since I first began to admit idly that I contemplated a history of New Jersey.

The interest has been wide in scope. As I have lectured across the state, to women's clubs and historical societies, to PTAs and civic clubs, countless people have asked about the possibility of getting a broad picture of New Jersey's history in concise form. Now I can say, here it is.

General acknowledgments only set a background for specific debts. Miss Miriam Studley, dedicated and exceptionally knowledgeable head of the New Jersey division of Newark Public Library, read the original manuscript and made scores of useful comments and suggestions. Dr. Hubert G. Schmidt, professor of history at Rutgers University, also read the complete original manuscript and pointed out critical gaps. Dr. Frank B. Stover, Superintendent of Schools in Bloomfield, and Dr. Fred D. Cranse Jr., head of the social studies department in Bloomfield, read each chapter in the manuscript and suggested revisions and changes in emphasis. Those four people helped develop whatever soundness this book possesses. I acknowledge their aid, but I assume full responsibility for these words as they now appear.

I am appreciative of aid from many others—to Robert M. Lunny, Howard W. Wiseman, Mrs. Edith May, and others of the staff of the New Jersey Historical Society; to Mrs. Arlene R. Sayre for encouragement and suggestions; to the special collections section of Rutgers University Library; to many in the academic community at Rutgers who offered criticisms of specific chapters, to many libraries for materials; to W. Irving Tuttle for pictures. My last reserved acknowledgment goes to Tom Mackin for editorial aid.

Here it is, then: New Jersey's first one-volume history since Samuel Smith's monumental work in 1765. Whether or not it is the "attractive, readable" book called for is for others to say. Most of New Jersey's history has happened since 1765; much is happening now. May my state not have to wait 200 years for the next!

JOHN T. CUNNINGHAM

Florham Park, New Jersey
October, 1965

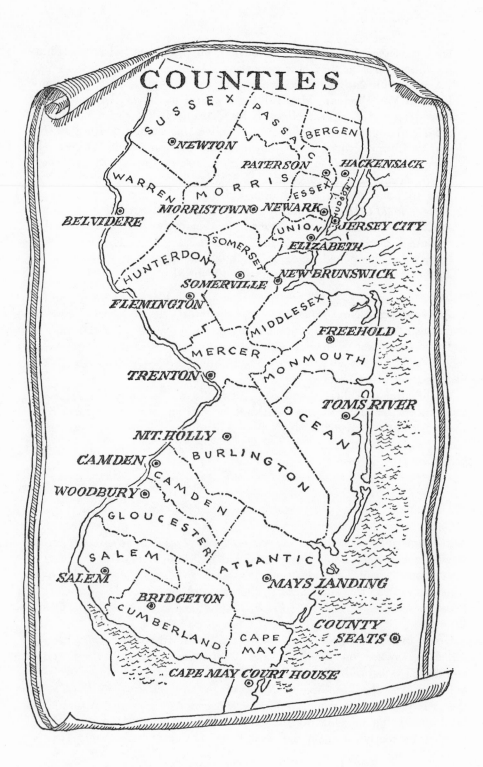

COUNTIES

SUSSEX
NEWTON
PASSAIC
BERGEN
WARREN
MORRIS
PATERSON
HACKENSACK
ESSEX
BELVIDERE
MORRISTOWN
NEWARK
HUDSON
UNION
JERSEY CITY
SOMERSET
ELIZABETH
HUNTERDON
SOMERVILLE
NEW BRUNSWICK
FLEMINGTON
MIDDLESEX
FREEHOLD
MERCER
MONMOUTH
TRENTON
TOMS RIVER
OCEAN
MT. HOLLY
CAMDEN
BURLINGTON
WOODBURY
CAMDEN
GLOUCESTER
SALEM
ATLANTIC
SALEM
MAYS LANDING
BRIDGETON
COUNTY
CUMBERLAND
CAPE
MAY
SEATS
CAPE MAY COURT HOUSE

Introduction: America's Main Road

Wedged between two broad rivers, lodged between New York and Philadelphia, halfway between Massachusetts to Virginia, mid-point between Maine and Florida: that is New Jersey. That is both the vigor and the effacement of the state, the reason why New Jersey has played such dramatic roles in America's history—and, paradoxically, why that history is so often ignored.

Washington slept here, hundreds of times, perhaps more than in any state except his own Virginia. Thomas A. Edison came from Ohio to spend his mature inventive years. Both Telestar and Tiros originated in New Jersey laboratories. The transistor and streptomycin won Nobel prizes for their New Jersey perfectors. For a century and more no state has carried a greater volume of traffic on its transportation arteries, whether that traffic be rail or motor.

Truly, New Jersey is America's main road.

Geology set the pattern. The last of the great glaciers to spread over North America reached halfway across New Jersey, then stopped and slowly inched back home, leaving behind the wide rivers that civilized man came to call Delaware and Hudson. The Lenni-Lenape Indians who first settled the land were mediators, seeking peace and harmony between warring tribes to the extent that others called them "The Old Women."

Henry Hudson touched New Jersey's coast in 1609 and would have sailed northward on the Delaware except that his *Half Moon* ran aground. He backed off, sailed the Hudson instead, and quite by accident led to the founding of New Amsterdam on the east bank of the river bearing his name. William Penn seriously considered placing his Philadelphia on New Jersey soil but decided instead to build the City of Brotherly Love on the west bank. Ordinary luck should have placed at least one of those two cities in New Jersey, but that was not the whim of history.

Time meant the state to be a tale of two cities—but possessor of neither. Sections of it revolve around New York on the one hand and Philadelphia on the other. Residents of Bergen County, across from New York City, know virtually nothing about Camden County, across from Philadelphia—and vice versa. The colonial Dutch houses of Bergen bespeak a heritage completely different from that which built the unique patterned brick houses of Salem County. Sussex County's rolling hills are as different from Cape May's sandy beaches as Kansas is different from Colorado.

If New York and Philadelphia have tended to throw their neighbor into the shade, they have also given New Jersey the spirit and excitement it has ever enjoyed. They have made it a common meeting ground.

Here came the Dutch to the Hudson, the Swedes to the Delaware, followed before the Revolution by English, Irish, Scotch, Germans, French, and others, all seeking living room by the pathways between emerging cities in neighbor states. Here came Puritans, the Dutch Reformed, the Presbyterians, and the Episcopalians to stamp their differing religious views on history. Here, in the fervor of religion's colonial Great Awakening were established Princeton and Rutgers universities, making New Jersey the only state to boast two colleges founded before the Revolution.

All of the passionate oratory of Virginia and the overt rebellion of New Englanders merged in New Jersey, mixed by travelers constantly on roads between North and South. Then, when Revolution burst, New Jersey became the key land—for whoever held New Jersey controlled both New York and Philadelphia. Thus Washington spent three of the first four winters of the war in the state and broke out of the fourth winter camp, at Valley Forge, to fight the monumental Battle of Monmouth. But hesitancy showed in the state; Tories in Monmouth and other counties nearly outnumbered patriots.

Firmly set on its midway course, New Jersey felt postwar bitterness when both New York and Philadelphia shunned her paper money and hampered development of her ports. Jerseymen thus readily joined those seeking a stronger federal government. In the showdown for a United States Constitution, they held so firmly for equal representation among states that compromise created two bodies of Congress and named the one devised from the "New Jersey Plan" as the United States Senate.

Transportation and industrial revolutions swept eastward and westward from the nation's two greatest early cities in the early nineteenth century. America's first railroad charter was granted Hoboken's John Stevens in 1812, and Stevens built and ran this nation's first steam locomotive in 1825. Railroads speedily took their course: long before the Civil War the greatest volume of rail traffic in the United States rolled across the little state.

Railroads made New Jersey what it is. They brought ever-expanding industry to Newark, Paterson, Trenton, Camden, Jersey City, and a score of other cities. They lured thousands of Irish immigrants to pour the ballast and to lay the tracks. The presence of the railroad between New York and Philadelphia prompted Thomas A. Edison to locate his first experimental laboratory on a high hill at Menlo Park, within sight and sound of the tracks, in 1876. Railroads created the mass of freight yards in Hudson and Essex counties. Railroads spawned the commuters of Bergen and Morris counties.

Ever at the mid-point, New Jersey played a strangely divided role in the Civil War, epitomizing to considerable extent the schism in all the land.

Newark industrialists bitterly opposed a war with the South, for the plantation states provided their best markets for jewelry, carriages, and shoes and clothing for both master and slave. Powerful Democrats in Bergen, Sussex, Hunterdon, and other counties opposed the war with such vehemence even beyond the Battle of Gettysburg that troops on Southern battlefields met to express indignation at the "Copperheads" in the legislature back home. Princeton University's student body split nearly evenly between North and South. Cape May's hotel proprietors mourned the loss of Richmond guests.

But when duty called, the state sent off considerably more than its quota of troops, turned out war material, and officially backed the war. That done, and the mourning for the assassinated Lincoln over, the legislature delayed embarrassingly long in ratifying the Thirteenth, Fourteenth, and Fifteenth Amendments.

History's march never ceased along this main road. Swarms of immigrants from Southern and Eastern Europe flocked into New Jersey's cities and to its farms between 1880 and 1920, for where better to settle than as close as possible to the docks, from where they had come and where their families and countrymen must arrive? The Italians, Poles, Russians, Ruthenians, Hungarians, and Slavs added their blood, their talents, their zeal, and their passion for America to the peoples who had come long before.

Two world wars, a nation gone mad for alcohol, and a nation sunk in depression: they left a mark. In this state of railroads and highways, troops came by the millions to train and to debark and the goods of war streamed to and from the docks. Between wars, rumrunners found the Jersey Shore to be one of the East's finest areas for clandestine landings. Depression struck hard at this state attuned to industry.

Now the land is filled with talk of Suburbia, the Negro, the conservation of water, the pollution of air and streams, the need for colleges, the alarm over expanding populations, the need to reapportion legislatures, the perplexing question of taxes, the nagging worries over deteriorating cities. These are problems or challenges, depending on point of view. Naturally, New Jersey is much involved, for its position as the most urban state in the land makes all of these matters agonizingly acute.

But the twentieth century vibrates with research and industry; these are the fiber of life. New Jersey has its share, and then some, of each. A state of Telestar, Tiros, transistor, and miracle drugs need not apologize for its role in a modern world.

Someone once asked if all of New Jersey's history is enchanting and romantic. It is not. Its flaws, its mistakes, its sordidness must be seen—as well as its glories, its claims to fame, its moments in the sun. History is not all engaging, all noble, all uplifting, but when one lives by America's main road he lives in perpetual drama—for this is a pike that time does not shun.

New Jersey: America's Main Road

1

Geology: Molder of Destiny

Geologic excitement eludes nearly all but geologists, and sometimes even they become so bogged down in terminology and time sequences as to miss the drama of the inexorable forces that shaped a land mass. Geologic time is not the heady moment—an Indian massacre, a battle, an impassioned speech—but it is the base on which all history rests.

Man depends completely upon land masses shaped for him by billions of passing years. He plows the fields in Cumberland County or he digs for iron near Dover. He uses millions of gallons of water for chemicals manufacture beside the Raritan River or he basks in the sand beside the rolling ocean. He raises dairy cattle near Newton or he settles in the Highlands of Morris County because of the view. Man may not know it, or acknowledge it, but he pays tribute constantly to geologic time—and seldom is the lesson of man's dependency on geology better taught than in New Jersey.

Eastward the deep river called the Hudson flows in a bed formed through millions upon millions of years. Westward, the Delaware River sweeps by the land in broad curves, its course set by geological aberrations. Between, a flat plain has been ground down by the forces of time; New Jersey's destiny as a pathway state is not hard to fathom. Most of the state's history is summed up in those neighborly cities and on the plains that link them.

Occasionally geologic time stands intimately exposed, as in 1961, when a pair of Livingston boys found a 190-million-year-old fossil in an excavation near their homes. Remains of prehistoric dinosaurs and strange sea beasts are often dug from greensand marl pits in Gloucester County. "Rock hounds" who find zinc at Franklin are indebted to mineral flows dating back a billion years. Remains of volcanic upheavals are visible in the trap rock quarries of the Watchung Mountains and in the Palisades of the Hudson River. Sand and gravel pits of northern New Jersey are calling cards of long-departed glaciers.

Passing eras have seen the land called New Jersey at times rise high, only to sink beneath the seas. The agonies of geologic growth have reared mountains here as high as the Andes and then eroded them away. Searing tropical heat has alternated with arctic cold. Tremendous beasts have come and gone, leaving their bones in marl pits and clay beds. Glaciers have gouged the land, and then returned to the far North, leaving lakes and swamps as mementos.

Here are all the elements of high drama. Unfortunately, it has taken so long for the action to unfold that sometimes a mere recital verges on tedium for most people. The fascination of geology for the average man is also lessened by the terminology: pre-Cambrian, Cambrian, Paleozoic, Mesozoic, Cenozoic, Triassic. Still, time and strange terminology notwithstanding, it is vital to go back two billion years or more.

THE OLDEST PART

In the beginning, about two billion years or so ago, a bit of blazing mass broke away from the sun and skimmed off into space. Like a flaming star it swirled, and as it cooled, moisture fell from its atmosphere and eventually formed seas. Within these waters on the new sphere, hot gases and lava from the cooling mass coursed within the steaming seas. The bubbling and boiling world gave way to cooling. Mountains would rise from the seas and land masses would be formed. Earth had begun.

Violence and instability marked the hundreds of millions of years that passed between the time that Earth broke loose and the time that geologists can measure and record with some degree of agreement. Land forms shifted constantly, but a measure of order began to evolve. One tiny spot on Earth, for example, rose from the sea in those formative years (which geologists call pre-Cambrian). This spot would be called New Jersey some two billion years later, and this is how it came to be.

Giant chunks of rock, torn by the waves from a far-off and now unknown land mass, began to build up beneath the surface. Higher and higher the rocks rose, tossed and twisted by the vagaries of tempestuous waters, until at last they reached a height of thousands of feet and finally they peeped above the surface of the ancient sea. The oldest part of New Jersey—the Highlands—had been formed.

Below the waves, meanwhile, minerals oozed through the sediment and the limestone mud that gathered in the rocks. They cooled slowly to bind the mass for durability and to form the zinc deposits near Franklin and Ogdensburg and the iron that threads through all the

Highlands between Hunterdon and Passaic counties. This was the beginning; on this Highland rock, New Jersey would grow. It would change drastically, but it would endure.

Pre-Cambrian time lasted more than a billion years, though who knows for sure how long it takes to change a blazing star into Earth?

INLAND SEAS AND ANCIENT PEAKS

Pre-Cambrian time ended some 550 to 600 million years ago. Since then, three long eras have been recorded to the point where Earth could sustain human life. The first era, the Paleozoic ("ancient life"), lasted about 400 million years. Paleozoic's first stage, or period, has been called Cambrian (hence, all that went before is pre-Cambrian).

As Paleozoic time started, New Jersey's topography was nearly the reverse of what it is today. Towering mountains lay to the east, on a land known to geologists as Appalachia. To the west, the long arm of a shallow sea reached northeastward from present-day Alabama and covered the area of New Jersey's modern mountains. Strange and primitive invertebrate marine life shared that ancient sea with sponges, corals, and mollusks. On the land itself, nothing lived.

Again and again that inland sea moved; at least three times within 300 million years the waters alternately covered and released the land, and at times probably covered all of modern New Jersey. Sediments continuously washed from the towering mountains to the east, coursing down streams that flowed to the west to fill the inland sea.

Finally, the southern sea retreated for the last time, and the shallow basin of the inland sea became land. Thick-trunked trees, lush ferns, and climbing vines covered the hot, moist valley swamps. These plants died and were submerged to form pockets of coal extending from Texas to Canada. New Jersey probably had its coal beds, too, but erosion removed them long ago.

It was a time of violence. Rock masses broke and thick belts of rock relentlessly slipped upward and westward to fold the ancestor of today's Appalachian Mountains. At the same time the eastward mountains began to sink slowly into the prehistoric seas.

Great peaks arose in what is now northwestern New Jersey. Many geologists think that those original Appalachians had peaks 30,000 feet above sea level—as high as the modern Himalayas. Others argue that counter forces of erosion kept the ancestral slopes to a height not much greater than today's Kittatinny Mountains. Regardless of height, the Kittatinnies are a lasting memento of that Appalachian revolution and the awesome writhings necessary to form a mountain are best revealed in Delaware Water Gap. Roadside cliffs in the Gap show rock layers crumbled and folded as if they had been soft batter for a marble cake rather than hard rock.

Paleozoic time came to an end about 225 million years ago. Great changes had been wrought: the shallow seas had passed from the northwest and mountains had risen in their place. Southeastward, the once proud peaks of Appalachia were nearly submerged beneath the rolling ocean.

RAIN, DROUGHT, AND FOSSILIZED FISH

Time moved from the Paleozoic era to the Mesozoic ("middle life"), an era that lasted 155 million years and radically altered Earth's physiognomy: huge cracks appeared and land blocks dropped downward, volcanoes erupted, lava flowed, and the peninsula that is New Jersey tilted like a giant seesaw. Tremendous reptiles came to roam over the land and to swarm in the deep seas which rolled again and again over the southern part of what is now New Jersey. Torrential rains poured down, followed by thousands of long dry spells.

Intense, scorching dryness—interspersed with violent rainstorms—pervaded the atmosphere as Mesozoic time began. There are indications that there were as many as 17,000 dry spells, some of them 100 years in length, during the early Mesozoic time. Drought would give way to overwhelming rain, which tore at the highlands to the west and spread eroded material south and east to build up the lower part of modern New Jersey.

Layers of fossilized fish found during an excavation for the Jersey City Reservoir at Boonton at the beginning of the twentieth century told the story of one here-again, gone-again Mesozoic lake and of a fish life which sought vainly to exist there.

Heavy rains would fill the depression near Boonton. Fish would appear, only to die when a century-long drought came. Sediment would cover the dead fish, only to have torrential downpours re-create the lake. Fish would reappear and the cycle of death and life would resume when dryness came again to be followed by rain. Within each successive layer, the fish became fossilized to await the reservoir diggers of the twentieth century.

Similarly, fish lived and died near Princeton, although these were in a salt bay rather than a fresh-water lake as at Boonton. Princeton University professors found hundreds of small fossilized fish in 1946 during the excavation for the Firestone Library. Students and professors alike "went fishing" in what they called "the old aquarium." More academically, curators of the American Museum of Natural History declared that the fossils were the best of their kind in the Western Hemisphere.

VOLCANOES, THE WATCHUNGS, AND THE PALISADES

While the fish came and went, recurring volcanic flows scorched the still-emerging New Jersey.

Waves of lava slid over parts of the northern New Jersey surface at least three times—and as many as a dozen times near Warren Township. The lava coursed from volcanic vents that extended from near Bernardsville to Boonton and northward to Oakland. Successive flows formed the several ridges of today's Watchung Mountains, which range south from Bergen County through Passaic, Essex, and Union counties and then west into Somerset County. In some places in the Watchungs the lava built up to a total thickness of 600 to 800 feet; at others, the lava is not more than 200 feet thick.

Eastward and southward from the vents which formed the Watchungs, other volcanic flows surged forth, but these moved a mile or more underground in the soft sandstone. The boiling "magma" (as differentiated from surface "lava") cut through the sandstone as if it were butter.

Magma and lava had the same chemical properties, but the rocks they created are different. Lava cooled "quickly" (in one to ten years) on the surface of the land. Magma, on the other hand, took anywhere from 10,000 to 100,000 years to cool in the subsurface sandstone. Thus lava hardened into what is now called basalt and magma into diabase. Today both are known as trap rock to contractors who blast them loose in quarries in the Watchungs or at Snake Hill on the Jersey Meadows.

Hundreds of centuries of erosion have revealed the underground magma flows. Most magnificent of these is the Palisades ridge overlooking the Hudson River from Hudson County northward into New York State. The diabase stands in columnar blocks, which from a distance resemble the logs of a colonial fortification—hence the name "Palisades."

Magma also is revealed to travelers crossing the Hackensack (or Jersey) Meadows on the Pennsylvania Railroad or the New Jersey Turnpike. Near Secaucus, the Turnpike cuts across the rugged base of Snake Hill (or Laurel Hill), a landmark created when the magma found a soft spot in the sandstone and shot suddenly upward from a mile or so underground to form a "pipe." Just east of Snake Hill is Little Snake Hill, a junior-grade magma hill formed the same way. Erosion of the soft sandstone which once buried them has made both Snake and Little Snake visible.

Now Little Snake Hill is a multimillion-year-old base for a billboard advertising a popular soft drink. Larger Snake Hill is said to have been the inspiration for the Prudential Insurance Company's Rock of Gibraltar trademark. It will not last as long as the Rock of Gibraltar, however, for quarrymen are gradually tearing down the trap-rock eminence.

DINOSAURS ON A SEESAW

For another concept of geologic might in Mesozoic time, imagine New Jersey as a geological seesaw, with the fulcrum on a line between the present cities of Trenton and New Brunswick. The southern part moved downward about 120 million years ago, making the once-towering mountains of Appalachia to the southeast disappear completely beneath the ocean. Correspondingly, the land to the northwest rose. Obviously this tilting was not confined to New Jersey: all of eastern North America tilted.

The ocean rose and fell in turn across that part of the seesaw south of the New Brunswick-Trenton fulcrum. At times all of southern New Jersey lay as much as 600 to 900 feet below the surface of the water. Proof of both the presence and the great depth of those ancient seas is found today in southern New Jersey's greensand marl beds, for greensand is found only in deep water—or where deep water once stood.

The crunching and folding of mountains and the tilting of tremendous land masses are difficult to comprehend. Perhaps more easily understood are dinosaurs—the "terrible lizards"—of the Mesozoic era. Dinosaur skeletons and bones are familiar in museums, and the movies have given numerous, fanciful versions of those lumbering, dim-witted monsters which lived on Earth seventy million to 200 million years ago.

New Jersey had at least four kinds of land-loving dinosaurs, but they were not the only giants of Mesozoic time. The seas swarmed with reptiles twenty to thirty feet in length, sharks up to seventy feet in length, and turtles as much as six feet in diameter. Tremendous crocodiles frequented the then semitropical swamps of New Jersey.

The late Dr. Henry B. Kummel, serious-minded geologist, used unusually colorful language when he wrote of those beasts in *The Geology of New Jersey:*

> Waters were dominated by huge reptiles which surpassed in size and strangeness the sea-serpents of fiction. There were the *Elasmosaurs,* 40 to 50 feet in length, of which 22 feet was neck, with swelling body, short flippers and long flattened tail; the *Mososaurs,* gigantic, scaled, carnivorous, marine lizards, some 30 feet in length with limbs modified into paddles and with ponderous jaws furnished with rows of great conic teeth; various species of crocodiles, whose abundance is shown by the frequency with which their remains have been found in the marl beds; turtles and tortoises of many kinds and sizes up to 6 feet in length.
>
> Besides the sea reptiles there were sharks, whose teeth found in large

numbers in the marl beds measure 4 to 5 inches in length and 3½ inches in width and indicate an individual 70 to 80 feet in length.

On land there were huge duck-billed, bipedal, plant-feeding dinosaurs, some of which were 28 to 30 feet in length, ponderous in body and probably slow in movement. A skeleton of the best known, *Trachodon* (Hadrosaurus), was discovered years ago near Haddonfield, Camden County, but portions of others have been found in at least eight other localities. It was a herbivorous animal of heavy proportions, short fore limbs, but very long and massive hind legs. Its great tail, long hind limbs and pelvic bones were an efficient support while it reached up to the limbs of trees on whose foliage it fed. Its forelimbs were used chiefly in drawing food to it, though it probably rested on them as it stooped to the ground to devour vegetable material there.

Trachodon probably found its mortal enemy in *Laelaps*, a slightly smaller, but more agile dinosaur of carnivorous habit, whose long curved claws, and knife-shaped teeth were splendid weapons of offense. It had shorter fore and longer hind legs than *Trachodon*, and like the birds, walked entirely on its hind limbs or leaped like the kangaroo. Remains of this ancient buccaneer were found many years ago in the West Jersey Marl Company's pits near Barnsboro.

But *Laelaps'* curved claws and knife-shaped teeth served him no better than rudimentary fins had served the fish that long before had died in the dried-up lake near Boonton. Climate changed, available food disappeared, and so did the dinosaur. That is the way of geologic time.

America's first major dinosaur discovery was that of the duck-billed *Trachodon* (Hadrosaurus), found near Haddonfield in 1858. The bones of the twenty-eight-foot-tall dinosaur went to the Academy of Sciences Museum in Philadelphia but a replica of the giant plant-eater is in the State Museum at Trenton. That dinosaur clipped off vegetation with his broad horny bill and lived a good life, *Trachodon* style, but he was prey for both the dinosaur on land and the great marine lizards in the water—a geologic version of being between the devil and the deep blue sea.

One of the mortal enemies of *Trachodon* was the sea-dwelling *Mososaur Maximus*, measuring up to fifty feet in length. One of these lizards was found in fossilized remains in 1961 in a sand pit at Sewell in Gloucester County. This skeleton scaled fifty feet, the largest *Mososaur* ever discovered. In 1948, the same sands had yielded a thirty-foot duck-billed *Trachodon*. Fossilized skeletons were first found in the Sewell pit in 1934 and are still being uncovered.

The Time to Assume a Shape

Mesozoic time flowed into the Cenozoic ("recent life") era about seventy million years ago. The time had come for the land to assume a shape to last for millions of years. This would be an era of erosion in some places and a filling in of others. Streams would make their beds and stay in them, except for a few changes that latter-day glaciers would force. Earth would swing full cycle: the old rocks of the pre-Cambrian Highlands would be uncovered in time for the coming of man.

One more warping had to take place in Cenozoic time to bridge ancient and modern topography. Once again the land tilted, the northwest rising and the southeast falling, although this tilt was quite mild compared to the violence of earlier upheavals. As the result of the tilt, streams tumbled rapidly southeastward, cutting deeper into the hard-rock ridges. This explains why so many New Jersey streams—the Delaware, the Rockaway, and the Pequannock, to mention only three—carved their way through hard-rock mountain passes in defiance of water's usual seeking of the paths of least resistance.

The tilting affected some old rivers adversely and they lost their waters to other streams. The best example was the Culvers Gap River in Sussex County. Today the Culvers Gap is simply a well-known indentation in the Kittatinny Mountains, through which Route 206 carries motorists bound for the Sussex County hills. For hundreds of thousands of years, though, a stream as mighty as the present-day Delaware River occupied that gap and cut a cleft downward some 700 feet. The opening is two-thirds of a mile wide at the top, in evidence that the river was magnificent. The river might have flowed eastward to form the headwaters of the modern Pequannock River or it might have flowed southward through a mountain pass in Scott's Mountain. Geologists are not certain.

During Cenozoic tilting, the Delaware took over the headwaters of the Culvers Gap River and then sliced its own way through the hard-rock ridge of pre-Cambrian times to form the deep cut known as Delaware Water Gap.

Other streams etched their beds down the valleys or gradually deepened their courses across the hard-rock Highlands. Atop the mountains, soft shale and soluble limestone eroded. Gradually the modern landscape appeared: southeastward from the upper reaches of the Delaware River were ranged the Kittatinny Mountains; the broad, fertile Kittatinny Valley, the Highlands with altitudes descending southeastward, the Piedmont Plain, and finally the Coastal Plain.

The ocean, rising and falling in Cenozoic time as it had since earliest eras, covered the Coastal Plain of New Jersey several times, but never again lapped higher than along a line from about Newark to Trenton. The last of those ocean highs (except for the seas affected by the glaciers) took place about one million years ago. At that time, the sea rose about 130 feet above southern New Jersey, its surface broken only by two prominent islands and scattered smaller islands. One of the islands would have comprised much of today's noted Pine Barrens; the other major land area took in higher lands in the eastern parts of modern Camden, Gloucester, and Salem counties.

Some historians and botanists have maintained that the wide range of unusual flora in the Pine Barrens probably is due to the onetime insular status. Recently, however, Dr. Horace G. Richards, chairman of the Department of Geology at Philadelphia's Academy of Sciences, emphasized that he did not believe this. He attributed the characteristic plants to localized soil and terrain peculiarities rather than to any insular origin.

A LAND GRIPPED BY ICE

Far to the north, incessant snows on the arctic ice cap set glacial masses in motion some 150,000 to 200,000 years ago. Four times glaciers advanced southward; four times they halted in North America and then moved northward again. The earliest glacial period (the Jerseyan) and the latest (the Wisconsin) definitely touched New Jersey, and another (the Illinoian) possibly reached this far, but nearly all evidence of glacial time in New Jersey stems from the Wisconsin period.

The Wisconsin glacier inched downward from the Arctic some 150,000 years ago. Its solid wall of ice, thousands of feet thick, advanced over all of the upper part of North America until finally its eastern edge came to a halt in New Jersey. Mountains slowed or weakened the glacial advance, but valleys in the Highlands and the flatlands between the Watchung Mountains and the Palisades encouraged the glacier's movement. Here in New Jersey the ice sheet slowed to a stop on an irregular line (called the terminal moraine) from Perth Amboy to Summit to Morristown and northwest to Dover, Hackettstown, and Belvidere.

Many things happened in the several thousand years that the glacier occupied this area. Waters impounded by the ice wall drastically lowered the ocean, until the shoreline stood about eighty miles east of where it is today. Streams such as the Passaic River, which once had flowed northward or eastward, had to seek new outlets to the south. Life ceased or migrated elsewhere as unending winter fastened an icy grip on the land.

Eventually the glacier retreated in a sort of ponderous tango, advancing a bit, only to retreat. The ice would melt, say ten inches for every nine inches it advanced, then twelve inches for every ten, then two feet for every one, and finally the Wisconsin glacier retreated all the way back from where it had come, 20,000 to 10,000 years ago.

The Wisconsin ice eroded the New Jersey surface not more than twenty-five feet, a relatively modest scraping, although traces of the implacable grinding of the ice sheet can still be seen in many places. The ice left its permanent mark in thick layers of glacial drift—boulders, gravel, sand, and clay now found over most of the northern region of the state. Less permanently but more spectacularly, it created several lakes by blocking valleys and holding waters in place until the drainage streams could break new exits through to the sea.

Relatively small glacial lakes filled the Wallkill Valley in Sussex County, the Black River Valley near Succasunna, and the Pequest Valley at Great Meadows. Today lettuce, celery, and onions grow in the black bottom soil of those onetime lakes.

LAKE PASSAIC AND LAKE HACKENSACK

Biggest and most clearly defined of the glacial lakes, however, were Lake Passaic and Lake Hackensack.

Information is plentiful on Lake Passaic. The Wisconsin ice choked off the original bed of the Passaic River by throwing a wall of ice and debris across the original river gap at Short Hills. As the Short Hills gap closed, a small lake, possibly ten miles in diameter, formed at the southern edge of the ice sheet and its rising waters forced a new river drainage south through a deep gorge near Far Hills. For a time the Passaic River flowed southward toward the Raritan Valley.

When the glacier slowly moved north, the lake waters followed, filling in the entire valley west of the Watchung Mountains. Lake Passaic emerged as something grand, if temporary. It stretched from Far Hills to north of Paterson, following the inner curves of the Watchung Mountains for thirty miles north and south. The lake reached widths of ten miles or more for most of its length, averaged 160 to 200 feet deep and in places was 240 feet deep. Lake Passaic couldn't last; the impounded waters at last broke through an ice remnant which plugged a gap at Little Falls, then plunged seventy feet over a cliff at Paterson, and rushed to the sea on a drastically different course from its original bed.

Behind, in the valley west of the Watchungs, the receding waters of Lake Passaic left a series of marshlands. Through these the Passaic River carved its present erratic path: it goes east, west, north, and south, without any pattern. The marshlands came to be called Great Swamp in one place, Troy Meadows and Great Piece Meadows in other areas. In twentieth-century times these "swamps" or "meadows" have become both problems and challenges, sought by engineers as places to be "modernized" with jetports or huge flood-control dams. Others revere the swamps as a link with quieter past. Great Swamp, the bed of glacial Lake Passaic, has been saved and is now a 3000-acre National Wildlife Refuge.

The other major glacial lake, Lake Hackensack, filled the valley from Perth Amboy to Hackensack, extending some twenty-five miles in length and as much as three to four miles in width. Lake Hackensack wasn't quite as large as Lake Passaic, but it lasted some 3000 years (as did Lake Passaic). When Lake Hackensack eventually drained seaward, it left behind the modern Jersey Meadows as an odoriferous, often troublesome—but highly valuable—stretch of marshland between Perth Amboy and Hackensack. The potential of that old bed of Lake Hackensack, within sight of New York City skyscrapers, is obvious.

With the disappearance of the glaciers, only one more major geological development remained: to get the sea back to where it belonged, or at least where twentieth-century man might *think* it belongs (geologic forces permit no set opinions on where *anything* belongs).

The melting ice cap released more and more water to swell rivers. As those torrents poured into the sea, the ocean level rose; it moved inland nearly 100 miles from where it had been when the glacier held sway. Soon much of southern New Jersey was once more awash. This ocean rise resulted partially from the released glacial waters and partially because the earth's surface lay depressed from the weight of the glacier, much as a soft rubber ball stays momentarily indented after a pressing thumb is removed.

But just as a rubber ball rebounds, so the earth's surface slowly resumed natural contours after the glacial "thumb" was lifted. The crust rose upward, and the seas leveled off at approximately their modern shoreline about 10,000 to 25,000 years ago.

THE DAWN OF TODAY

Geologic time had moved to within about 10,000 years of the present. Nothing of startling moment has since changed the area's physical outlines. Seas alter the coastline, riverbeds occasionally veer from course, rains erode the fields, but essentially the New Jersey of today is the land that lay in place as the Wisconsin glacier moved north.

New Jersey lay pristine and untouched. Forests stretched unbroken. Iron in the mountains, copper in the hills, clay in the plains, and clean sand in the south awaited only someone to need them. The rivers flowed clean and full. The bays knew no ships or coastal settlements.

Mighty animals roamed again after the ice age—not dinosaurs, but mammals such as the mastodon and the hairy mammoth. Six mastodon skeletons found in the 1850s on a farm near Hackettstown gave the first proof that the huge beasts were in this area. Soon after, in 1869, mastodon bones were found at Mannington in Salem County. Those remains were sadly mishandled as they made the rounds of carnivals, but enough remained to permit reconstruction in Rutgers University's Geologic Hall.

Possibly the best known and best preserved of New Jersey's mastodons is "Matilda," a remarkably complete skeleton found in 1954 at Ohberg's Pond near Vernon in Sussex County. Matilda was sighted during dredging operations at the pond (since renamed Mastodon Pond). Geologists surmised that the old lady mastodon had bogged down in a humus swamp as she followed the receding glacier northward. She sank deep into the swamp and died quickly, leaving her fossilized bones for a twentieth-century dredge to find.

Described by newspapers, affectionately if not scientifically, as "just a big shaggy elephant," she was donated to the State Museum. Matilda stands there now in bony eminence, causing youthful awe as thousands of schoolboys and girls file past her each year.

Matilda and other mastodons who disappeared with her were really the last link with the turbulence and the violence in which this peninsula called New Jersey had been born. Gone were the ice, the mastodons, the volcanoes, the awesome days of droughts and floods, the bubbling of the earth's crust. It had taken two billion years, plus or minus a few millions of years, but the future was clear: here, a civilization dependent on rivers and pathways would come to pass.

WHEN GEOLOGY BECOMES GEOGRAPHY

Geology becomes geography at that point where it begins to rule men's lives. Thus, New Jersey of today has four distinct physiographic regions: the Appalachian Valley, the Kittatinny ridge and valley in the extreme northwest; the Highlands, the pleasant hills in the north center; the Piedmont Plain, the foothills east of the Highlands; and the Coastal Plain, comprising the two-thirds of the state southeast of a line between Trenton and New Brunswick. The first three divisions all slant in a southwest to northeast pattern, strongly emphasizing the New York to Philadelphia pathway on the northern fringe of the Coastal Plain.

The so-called Appalachian "Valley" division contains New Jersey's highest level—1803 feet above sea level in the Kittatinny Mountains. Here is the state's most rugged land, wild and beautiful and eminently suited to parks and forests. Here, too, is the handsome dairyland of Sussex and Warren counties.

The Highlands roll across northern Hunterdon, Morris, and Passaic counties and the southeastern portions of Sussex and Warren. They rise as high as 1496 feet above sea level near Vernon, then level off southeastward in diminishing peaks. In these Highlands are most of the North Jersey lakes, all of the iron ore, the zinc of Franklin, the estates of millionaires, and the area of zooming population growth.

Of the four divisions, the Piedmont of New Jersey is the most vibrant, the most exciting, the most sought after. This is essentially a plain, broken by the volcano-formed Watchungs, Sourlands, and Palisades.

Here are all of the state's major cities except Camden and Atlantic City. Here is the seat of government, nearly all the major colleges and universities, the bulk of industry, the area where the state's most stirring historical happenings have taken place. Here occurs the "fall line," where rivers tumbling out of the mountains led to the early organization of big industry.

Southward is the Coastal Plain, the region encompassing 127 miles of the fabled Jersey Shore, the widespread Pine Barrens, and nearly all of the major Garden State vegetable farms. Many geographers also recognize a fifth zone—an inner coastal plain—as embracing a fifteen-mile-wide arc of highly fertile soil from near Freehold southwestward into part of Cumberland County. Geologists have no such division (although they readily agree that the rich marl beds underlying the region have made this the state's most fertile area).

Geologic forces still pick away at the state; a billion years of change can't stop. Rains wash sediment away (and since some of this is now valuable top soil, man worries). Stream beds widen and occasionally cut slightly new paths for themselves. Chunks of rock sometimes fall or slide. Fierce winds and pelting rains rearrange the Jersey Shore line, much to the indignation of entrepreneurs who think that humans can achieve ultimate control of their environment.

Control is impossible. It might be enough to be glad that after the ice age the earth had emerged from billions of years of geologic violence and made ready to welcome humans in serenity.

2

Before the White Sails Showed

Out of the northwest came those who would first settle New Jersey, leaving their homeland in Siberia and wandering across the frozen waters of the Bering Strait, through western Canada, and on to Lake Superior. Onward they walked through the centuries, journeying toward the sun, eastward to the great ocean that others would call Atlantic. There they stopped, 5000 years or so before the birth of Christ.

They were the Lenni-Lenape (le-nah-pay, with slight accent on the second syllable)—the Original People, as they proudly knew themselves. They had enduring traditions and they had a well-defined pattern of civilization long before colonists arrived, but they perished. Within a century after they encountered the disease, the alcohol, and the guns of first Europeans, the sad demise of these simple people was far along, for they were "savages" who stood in the way of another and more complex civilization.

Songs and legends handed down from generation to generation carried on the story of the Lenni-Lenape origins and heritage. The Indians knew that their ancestors somehow, sometime, had struggled overland from a country far off to find peace by the ocean. They told and retold the simple, legendary story as they gathered by their campfires.

THE WALUM OLUM OR RED SCORE

Echoes of Lenni-Lenape beginnings are found in the *Walum Olum* or *Red Score*, a hauntingly beautiful Indian epic that Constantine Samuel Rafinesque discovered and translated in the early 1830s.

Walum Olum means "painted records," with *Walum* more specifically meaning "painted red" and *Olum* implying a record painted or engraved on white bark. Some scholars remain skeptical about the authenticity of this migration legend of the Lenni-Lenape. Certainly it can't be viewed as "history," but at the very least Rafinesque's work has come to be considered a fine translation of a poetic Indian saga passed down through the ages.

At times the *Walum Olum* is reminiscent of the Old Testament, for it is the story of creation as seen by simple people, and it is a depiction of the struggles of humans against the difficulties of life and nature. There was a genesis:

> *At first, in that place, at all times, above the earth,*
> *On the earth, was an extended fog,*
> *And there the great Manito was.*
> *At first, forever, lost in space, everywhere,*
> *The great Manito was.*
> *He made the extended land in the sky.*
> *He made the sun, the moon, the stars.*
> *He made them all to move evenly.*
> *Then the wind blew violently, and it cleared,*
> *And the water flowed off far and strong.*
> *And groups of islands grew newly, and there remained.*

Thus it was in the beginning. But an evil being—a snake—brought wickedness and quarreling and unhappiness to the tribes. He brought bad weather, sickness, and death. He forced the Original People to leave their ancestral homes and they walked in floods and in shallow waters until finally the mighty snake departed.

Troubles constantly dogged their footsteps as they journeyed "To the sunrise." They sang: "A great land and a wide land was the east land, a land without snakes, a rich land, a pleasant land." Their footsteps took them there, to the edge of the sea, to the sunrise. Prophetically, the *Walum Olum* ended:

> *Watcher was chief; he looked toward the sea.*
> *At this time, from north and south, the whites came.*
> *They are peaceful; they have great things.*
> *Who are they?*

The time element in the birchbark saga is vague. Who were these "whites" borne on the water? They might have been very early Vikings, who possibly touched in New Jersey as early as the eleventh century (although proof of this has never been discovered). They might have been some of the crew of Giovanni da Verrazano, who looked in on the area in 1524. Or the "whites" might have been those who sailed in with Henry Hudson in September, 1609. Regardless of the exact time, to the watchers on shore these newcomers seemed impressive, even godlike. They were people to be welcomed, for that was the way of the Lenni-Lenape.

As Early Voyagers Saw Them

In return the seaborne adventurers called the natives Indians. The goal of these early fortune seekers was India, a land of silk and gold. Hence, those who came down to greet the ships just *had* to be Indians, if the dream was to be retained. Most who saw the Original People for the first time found them handsome, well built, friendly, and eager to please.

Verrazano, who explored this region in 1524, 252 years before the Declaration of Independence, wrote of the Lenni-Lanape:

> They came without fear aboard our ship. This is the goodliest people and of the fairest conditions that we have found in this our voyage. They exceed us in bigness, they are the colour of brass, some of them inclined more to whiteness, others are of yellow colour, of comely visage with long and black hair, which they are very careful to trim and deck up.
> They are black and quick eyed, and of sweet and pleasant countenance, imitating much the old fashion. . . . The women are of like conformity and beauty, very handsome and well favoured, of pleasant countenance, and comely to behold; they are as well mannered and continent as any women, and of good education; they are all naked save a cover of deer skin. . . ."

The Lenni-Lenape had not yet become "savages."

Eighty-five years later, Robert Juet, an office aboard Henry Hudson's *Half Moon,* recorded in his journal a visit of the Indians on September 4, 1609, shortly after Hudson's boat went aground in Sandy Hook Bay's "soft sand and ooze":

> This day the people of the country came aboard of us, seeming very glad of our coming, and brought green tobacco, and gave us of it for knives and beads. They go in deer skins loose, well dressed. They have yellow copper. They desire clothes, and are very civil.

Two days later the long boat of the *Half Moon* returned after an exploratory run through Newark Bay. In the bottom of the boat lay poor John Colman, an arrow through his lifeless throat. The *Half Moon's* crew buried him on Sandy Hook, first recorded victim of the American Indian wars. Now the pleasant host-guest relationship became tinged with suspicion. Natives came aboard on succeeding days and "made a show of love," but Hudson and crew watched them with distrust, although never so distrustfully that they couldn't accept piles of Lenni-Lenape gifts.

Sailorlike, the *Half Moon* crew had its fun with the natives. They took several of the "chiefe men" into the cabin on September 20 and "gave them so much Wine and Aqua vitae, that they were all merrie."

Lenni-Lenape tradition long remembered that forced intoxication—and in their innocence the Indians didn't see the humor. Mate Juet indicated a slight bit of shame: he wrote of an Indian wife who waited for her drunken husband and "sat as modestly as any of our Country women would doe in a strange place." One of the Indians became "drunke," and Juet wrote "that was strange to them, for they could not tell how to take it."

Mr. Juet's scribblings built up toward the inevitability of more bloodshed. It came on October 1 and 2 when seven or eight Indians fell before the booming guns of the *Half Moon.* Significantly, Juet now called them "Savages." Off sailed Henry Hudson two days later; the natives watched him go, possibly aware of a future soon to destroy them— whether it be by guns or alcohol.

THE ELEMENTS OF CIVILIZATION

The term "savage" often is a matter of misjudgment or avarice, of course; to dismiss the Lenni-Lenape with the colonial presumption that they were savages is to err. They had primitive ways and they were different, for they were simple people of the forests. Yet they had a definite form of government, a system of villages, a genuine religion, a devoted family relationship, a moral code, and a rudimentary educational system in which boys and girls learned what they needed to know to cope with their particular environments.

With all the advantages of hindsight, these things appear to be the elements of civilization. Captain Hudson, and all who followed him, might have been surprised if they had known, or cared to know, how carefully these Indians had preserved their identities and their traditions.

Three Lenni-Lenape subtribes inhabited the peninsula. To the north lived the Minsi, "the people of the stony country." Next, to the south, dwelled the Unami, "the people down the river" who ruled the central part. Southernmost were the Unilachtigo, "the people who lived near the ocean." Each subtribe had a sub-chief (*sakima*) and the Lenni-Lenape usually considered the Unami *sakimi* to be chief of all subtribes. He lived, interestingly, near where Trenton is today, as evidence that the geographical seat of government was as well suited to the Original People as it is to modern Jerseymen.

Each subtribe proudly identified itself with its totem emblems. The Minsi saw themselves symbolized in the wolf, or "round foot"; the Unami in the turtle or "*pokeungo* the crawler," and the Unalachtigo in the wild turkey.

Each subtribe had its own hunting and fishing grounds, respected the rights of others, and lived in peace. Every summer all of them, men, women and children, traveled well-defined trails across state to the sea-shore to fish and to gather shells for wampum. Their cross-state trails formed the basis of several colonial highways, and in some cases they even underlay the routes of modern roads. One major Lenni-Lenape trail, the Minisink, ran across state from ten miles south of Port Jervis to the Shrewsbury River, passing through such modern towns as New-ton, Chatham, Millburn, Westfield, Metuchin, and Matawan. Others ran from Trenton to Somers Point, from Camden to Tuckerton, and from Gloucester to Somers Point.

Back home, near the Delaware River, the Lenni-Lenape lived in scattered villages, usually placed on a forested bluff above a good stream. In the villages, their crude private houses were clustered about the long house, where tribal ceremonies were held. Building of a private home posed few problems: the Indians drove green saplings into the ground, two or three feet apart along the two long sides of a rectangle. The limber saplings were bent over, fastened at the top, and then covered with chestnut bark, skins, or grass mats. A hole in the roof let most of the smoke from interior fires escape. Platforms around the sides served as beds or seats. It wasn't elaborate, and it was smoky, but it was home.

The Lenni-Lenape, like all people close to nature, approached life as simply and directly as possible. Their dress consisted of little more than crudely tanned deer skins; in summer both men and women were naked above the waist. They ate whatever foods they found close at hand—animals shot with arrows or caught in traps, fish speared in streams, maize from their casually tended gardens, berries and nuts from the woods, and shellfish from the sea.

These Indians adorned themselves as they saw necessary, the men more than the women. Male vanity called for beads, earrings, and arm bands, but men also plucked out their hair except for a scalp lock down the center of their heads. Women, on the other hand, let their hair grow long, pulled it tightly back, and kept it in place with an ornamental stone given to them by a male Indian.

Naturally, such vanities, worn by man or by woman, usually were to please the opposite sex. When the right moment came for marriage, about age fourteen for the young squaw and about eighteen for the young brave, the female took a vigorous lead.

MARRIAGE, FAMILY, AND HOSPITALITY

The Lenni-Lenape teen-ager who had matrimony in mind worked long hours fashioning a beautiful dress from large wing and tail feathers of the wild turkey, tediously overlapping and working the feathers into a design that she hoped her choice of suitor couldn't overlook.

Donning her symbol of eligibility, she turned modest and sat chastely beside an understanding chaperon along the trail near her home. Except for the chaperon and the feathers, it all has a familiar tone, considerably like the mating intent of more modern times.

The chaperon entered into the game by nudging the young hopeful when the right male appeared. The sweetness of love began when young eyes met. If the exchange of looks from flashing black eyes proved exciting enough, eventually the two would walk together on the long trail of life. To seal the marriage bargain, the bridegroom gave his bride a bone, signifying that he would provide the meat for their home. She gave him an ear of corn, by way of saying that she would supply the grain.

After marriage the husband lived up to his gift of a bone, confining himself to hunting and fishing and things noble enough for a male. His wife, in turn, found that her ear of corn gave her not only the privilege of supplying grain but also the responsibility of rearing the children, tilling the fields, tending the home, and a wide variety of other tasks that no haughty brave would stoop to undertake.

Most recorders of Lenni-Lenape mores agree that Indian marriages usually lasted and that family relationships were very strong. However, in case of disagreement, divorce was as easy as the wife leaving with the children, never to return. The rigors of woodland life didn't make the Lenni-Lenape severe parents. Rather, their discipline was slight, for in their uncivilized way they felt example to be more powerful than a slap, and they taught their youngsters the lessons necessary for survival in their dangerous and uncompromising environment. The Lenni-Lenape also taught their children manners. Children never interrupted adults, and for that matter, adults also always waited for others to finish speaking. Hospitality was encouraged, and little girls helped mothers tend the ever-simmering pot, which signified that a Lenni-Lenape family would share whatever food it had with strangers.

One bit of Lenni-Lenape philosophy best summed up their live-and-let-live philosophy of life: Kill the rattlesnake that gives no warning; spare the one that does. Later both the Dutch and the English would know fully the literal meaning of this.

Other tribes in the Algonquin nation, of which the Lenni-Lenape were a part, scorned these New Jersey Indians. The Iroquois called them "The Old Women," looking upon them as weak and foolish and not worth the striking. The kindest interpretation of that nickname was that the Lenni-Lenape loved peace and served as intermediaries in the councils of war or after the intermittent trailside tomahawkings by other tribes. Undoubtedly the Lenni-Lenape believed in peace, and in their relationship with the first settlers, this proved most helpful —for the colonists rather than the Indians.

THE CLASH OF CIVILIZATIONS

Civilizations, European-style, ruined the Indians. The first Dutch trappers treated the natives with contempt, even looking upon them as possible slaves. Some occasional talk of converting the "squalid savages" to Christianity proved groundless. As long as the Lenni-Lenape exchanged pelts and furs for trifles, including such cultural advancements as rum and guns, most of the Dutch traders really didn't care if they stayed heathen.

Indian-colonist relations undoubtedly reached the lowest ebb during the Dutch rule in New York. One incredible slaughter at Pavonia (now Jersey City) rates mention in any reckoning of colonial infamy.

Minor Indian-Dutch troubles had begun as early as 1630, but on February 25, 1643, Indian blood flowed as never before. William Kiefft, director general of New Netherlands, resolved that night that he would make a large group of Indians encamped at Pavonia "wipe their chops." He ordered his soldiers to "drive away and destroy the savages." He might have thought his heart filled with charity when he added, ". . . spare as much as it is possible their wives and children."

Convinced of his righteousness, Kiefft experienced no qualms in concluding his order: "Our God may bless the expedition."

Several of Kiefft's aides bitterly warned him that such wanton action inevitably would bring retaliation on scattered and unprotected Dutch settlements across the Hudson. Captain David Pieterszoon DeVries admonished Kiefft as the soldiers marched off into the darkness. "Let this work alone," DeVries begged. "You will go to break the Indians, but it is our nation you are going to murder."

That night eighty Dutch soldiers fell upon the sleeping Indians in Pavonia, unleashing a horror that passage of time doesn't make less revolting. Across the river in New Amsterdam the sounds and screams of the midnight butchery sent chills of fear and disgust through Dutch homes. The berserk soldiers forgot to spare the women and children. One account describes children slain "while fastened to their little boards." Another tells of children being thrown into the river to drown; when parents waded into the water to save them, Dutch guns cut down both old and young.

"WORTHY OF OLD ROME"

Eighty Indians died that night at Pavonia, and in assessing this deed of one Indian death for each Dutch soldier involved, DeVries saw it as "a feat worthy of the heroes of old Rome." That, despite his original opposition to the massacre.

Eleven tribes quickly banded together for retaliation against the heroes of New Amsterdam and the emulators of old Rome. From the Raritan River to the Connecticut River not a settler was safe from the tomahawk and scalping knife, except those few clustered fearfully behind Fort Amsterdam's walls. Marauding bands of Indians killed, burned, looted, and laid waste to the farms in a dreadful, if probably justified, display of wrath. Nearly eighteen months of Indian terror ensued before a truce was secured in 1645.

Exactly ten years later the Indians again swarmed over the Dutch settlements along the Hudson River, this time in a warfare described by Charles H. Winfield in his *History of the County of Hudson.* Winfield aptly declared that the trouble "grew out of such a trifling fact that one almost fails to appreciate the wonderful stupidity which preceded it."

"The wonderful stupidity" involved a young Indian girl and a man described by Winfield as "a heavy-bottomed Dutchman" of New Amsterdam. The Indian girl climbed a tree in heavy-bottomed Hendrik Van Dyck's orchard at midnight to pluck a lovely peach. Van Dyck, relying on his musket rather than his fat legs, shot and killed the girl in the tree. As she fell dead, she symbolized the difficulty of enforcing "civilized" law on a carefree people.

Five hundred screaming Indian warriors swarmed across the Hudson River to New Amsterdam on September 15, 1655, unleashing vengeful anger outside the stern walls of the Dutch town. Frustrated there, they recrossed the river and "in the twinkle of an eye" all of Hoboken and Pavonia fell to the torch. Three days of raging attack from Pavonia to Staten Island took the lives of more than 100 of the Dutch, saw 150 of them carried into captivity, and more than 300 made homeless.

Eventually the captives were returned for ransom, including among other things substantial quantities of powder and lead. So, in writing an end to violence, the Dutch gave the Indians the basic means of beginning even worse war—and the Dutch were helpless to stop war if it came again.

EVERYTHING NEAT AND LEGAL

When England pushed Holland aside in 1664, the Indians were treated fairly, from the English viewpoint. Matters were handled in businesslike fashion, with Anglo-Saxon deeds and signatures and an exchange of commodity for land received. In complete justice to the English, this was how bargains were made across the sea; it was no fault of theirs that chiefs neither understood written documents nor knew that they were signing away a prized birthright for trinkets.

New Jersey history is filled with the extraordinarily fine real estate bargains driven by the English colonists. For example, Robert Treat, who founded Newark in 1666, bought a tract of land roughly equivalent to half of modern Essex County for fifty double hands of powder, 100 bars of lead, twenty axes, twenty coats, ten guns, twenty pistols, ten kettles, ten swords, four blankets, four barrels of beer, ten pair of breeches, fifty knives, twenty hoes, 850 fathom of wampum, about thirty-two gallons of liquor ("or something equivalent"), and three trooper's coats.

Elsewhere, local histories are replete with accounts of similar deals, and rarely, if ever, do such histories discuss the slight payments or the unquestionable fact that Indian chiefs didn't know they were selling anything other than *use* of the land. Indians didn't feel the right or the need to "own" property in the legalistic Anglo-Saxon sense. They merely bought and sold hunting and fishing privileges.

Sad days ensued. The proud Lenni-Lenape fell victim to governments which ruled them according to whim. The Indians succumbed to the throat-warming, mind-inflaming liquors of their new landlords. Smallpox, black measles, tuberculosis, and other civilized diseases of the settlers struck down the "savages," powerful men and little children alike. The love that the Indians had once freely offered the newcomers changed to smoldering, sullen disrespect and quiet hatred.

When a smallpox epidemic of the 1680s in Burlington County carried off Indians so fast that there was not even time to bury the dead, an aging chief declared that "In my grandfather's time the smallpox came, in my father's time the smallpox came, and now in my time the smallpox has come again." When the comet of 1680 emblazoned its pathway across the skies, a Lenni-Lenape *sakima* was asked what it meant. He replied:

"It means that Indians shall know the day when this country is inhabited by another people."

And so it came to pass.

The number of Indians living in New Jersey when the first Dutch arrived is estimated at about 2000. As the eighteenth century dawned, it is unlikely that a fourth of this number remained in New Jersey. Some had migrated north and west as early as 1690, seeking space, but most had perished here at home, victims of disease and want and indolence. The Original People grew ever weaker, ever more despised, ever more insecure, and ever more dependent on those who had succeeded them.

THE END OF THE LENNI-LENAPE

One more period of killing between 1755 and 1757 darkened the Lenni-Lenape record during the French and Indian War. This time Indians swooped without provocation through the northwestern hills, and twenty-seven killings were reported in West Jersey. One of the victims was Thomas Quick, Sr., who lived in a hamlet called Milford, just across the Delaware River in Pennsylvania.

Tradition says that son Tom Jr. vowed that before his own life ended he would avenge his father's death by killing 100 Indians. He lived long and he shot true and he slashed well, but he missed his goal. He killed only ninety-three, many along the Old Mine Road in Sussex County, before he died in 1795 or 1796. Tom's grisly feats (half fact, half legend) won him honors of a sort, but his paranoiac vendetta didn't make amicable relations with the Indians any easier to secure. Strangely, if the Tom Quick story can be believed, Tom killed far more Indians in death than in life. He died of smallpox; Indians dug up his body and cut it into small pieces for distribution among the tribes—and thereby spread the killing disease far and wide.

Peace came in 1758 when New Jersey Governor Francis Bernard and Lenni-Lenape leader named Teedyuscung met for an earnest discussion of problems at a conference at Easton, Pennsylvania. The Indians apologized for the murders committed by their hotheaded marauding braves (who, naturally, "had fallen under the influence of the French"). Governor Bernard in turn admitted that no doubt there had been some faulty land "purchases" from the Indians and agreed to reimburse the natives.

New Jersey's Assembly in 1758 established a permanent home in Burlington County for the last of the Lenni-Lenape. In return for this first Indian reservation in the New World, the Indians relinquished all rights to New Jersey, except for fishing and hunting privileges. About 200 or so Indians gathered at Edge Pillock in October, 1758, amid an enthusiasm inspired by the celebrated Indian missionary John Brainerd. Reverend Brainerd called the reservation Brotherton, in hopes that all men would be brothers.

That pitiful remnant of the Original People tilled the Brotherton fields, energetically fished the streams, and lackadaisically operated the grist and sawmills which gave the reservation its eventual name of Indian Mills (as the area is still known, although traces of the reservation disappeared long ago).

John Brainerd left the reservation in 1781 for another mission post. Indian affairs grew steadily worse. The countryside heard reports of "poor naked children," of "starving squaws," and of cold, hunger, and misery. Such tales traveled far, all the way to the land of the lakes in upper New York State.

Lenni-Lenape who had migrated to New Stockbridge, near Lake Oneida in New York, invited the New Jersey Indians to come to spread their mats before "our fireplace, where you will eat with your grandchildren out of one dish and use one spoon." The Indians of

Edge Pillock (Indian Mills) accepted the tempting offer in 1802 and petitioned the New Jersey legislature for the right to sell their lands to acquire funds for the move. Sale of the land paid all debts and left the Indians with $3551 invested in U.S. securities. Off went the Lenni-Lenape, now reduced to fewer than 200 people.

A CHANCE TO SALVE A CONSCIENCE

Northward, then westward, trekked the despairing Lenni-Lenape, back in the general direction from which *Walum Olum* said they had come. Then, in 1832, the Original People saw one more chance to permit New Jersey to favor them. Eastward came a poor, tired, old Indian with an English name: Bartholomew S. Calvin. Calvin's Indian name was Shawuskukukung, and it perfectly expressed both his plight and that of his people. It meant "Wilted Grass."

Princeton-educated Wilted Grass knew his manners and he knew his "place." The seventy-six-year-old Indian lost no time in getting to the heart of the matter as he spoke before the state legislature. Hunting and fishing rights had not been extinguished in past treaties, he insisted, and he touched only subtly on the possibility of using the courts ("It is not, however, our wish to excite litigation"). Still, his words were not without edge as he urged the legislators to look on the Indians with "an eye of pity."

Such a pity, he said gently but pointedly, had been shown by the Indians for the first European settlers who came to "our then extensive but uncultivated dominions." The Lenni-Lenape, he concluded with a sharp remark that is overlooked by those who wish to believe that the Indians were eternally grateful, had sold their land "for trifles in comparison as light as the air." He meant, to put it bluntly, that beads, trinkets, and alcohol scarcely constituted full payment for the land of the Original People.

The legislature felt a flush of generosity or a touch of conscience, or both, when they replied to old Wilted Grass. First praising themselves and all their New Jersey ancestors as people who always had acquired Indian lands "by fair and voluntary purchase and transfer," the legislators voted to pay the $2000, "as an act of voluntary justice, as a memorial of kindness and compassion to a once powerful and friendly people." It wasn't truly an admission of debt; it was viewed as a handout.

Money in hand, Wilted Grass on March 12, 1832, wrote the legislature a letter that forever eased the consciences of those who would brush off the Lenni-Lenape as savages lucky to get anything. His most-quoted paragraph declared:

Not a drop of our blood have you spilled in battle; not an acre of ground have you taken but by our consent. These facts speak for themselves and need no comment. They place the character of New Jersey in bold relief and bright example to those states within whose territorial limits our brethren still remain. Naught save benisons can fall upon her from the lips of a Lenni-Lenape.

Having written a quotation for those who demand justice, even in retrospect, Wilted Grass had at the same time composed an epitaph for New Jersey Indians. He took the $2000 and returned west to join the sadly decimated remnants of a once great people.

Only the Names Remain

Gone are the Lenni-Lenape, gone except for a variety of legends and numerous Indian arrow head collections. Yet their spirit lives in New Jersey, for their musical, poetic love of the land continues in names that they bestowed wherever they walked or camped.

Raritan, Passaic, Hackensack, Rockaway, Musconetcong, Rahway, Lopatcong, Assunpink, Pequest, and Yanticaw were their names for some of the streams, and these names serve yet. Manahawkin, Manasquan, Absecon and Navesink remain to remind shoregoers of a vanished group of red-skinned resort enthusiasts. Mountains that they called Kittatinny, Pohatcong, Watchung, and Ramapo are still so named. The greatest of New Jersey lakes they named Hopatcong. Elsewhere they passed and left their touch: Pompton, Hoboken, Amboy, Hacklebarney, Alloway, Whippany, Metuchen, Peapack, Matawan, Singac, Owassa, Parsippany, and a score of other stopping points in time.

Many Indian names are anglicized variations of the more melodic Indian language, it is true, but the free-flowing descriptive terms of the Lenni-Lenape live on, even in corrupted versions, to remind of the Original People.

Thus ends *Walum Olum,* updated.

3

New Amsterdam and New Sweden

Henry Hudson, an English sea captain sailing in the service of the Dutch, owes most of his enduring fame to a modest little journal that fellow Englishman and ship's officer Robert Juet kept during the voyage of the *Half Moon* in 1609. Juet possibly kept the diary to excuse himself lest he someday be tried on charges of mutiny, but small matter, for thanks to *Juet's Journal* the Dutch became interested in America—and Henry Hudson's name lives on.

The mutiny aboard the *Half Moon* is not a matter of conjecture. It is known that between May 5 and May 19, sailors aboard the *Half Moon* forced Hudson to change his course from northwest to south and west. The ship sailed south as far as present-day Virginia, then headed north off the Atlantic Coast. Juet may have been a ringleader in the 1609 mutiny, or at least a participant; a year later, when Hudson's subordinates again mutinied on Hudson's last voyage, Juet joined them, against his captain.

Ironically, therefore, it fell to *Juet's Journal* to keep green the memory of Hudson's exploration in and near New Jersey and to help excite the Dutch into settlement of New Amsterdam.

Juet first saw what is now New Jersey on the "eight and twentieth" of August, 1609, while Captain Hudson tried vainly to sail the *Half Moon* into "a great bay" (now Delaware Bay). The little ship encountered shoals "and once we strooke," before Hudson backed off to open sea and sailed north close to the coast. The next day Juet wrote in his journal: "Wee weighed at the breake of day, and stood toward the Norther Land, which we found to bee all Ilands to our sight." That was the long sandy stretch of islands between what are now Wildwood and Atlantic City.

Somewhere inland Juet saw a "great fire" on September 2, evidence that someone (the Lenni-Lenape) lived in the woods near the coast.

Wood engraving in Ballou's Magazine *for April 12, 1856, depicts Henry Hudson dealing with Lenni-Lenape on the river bearing his name.*

Set between two broad rivers, each destined to support a great city, New Jersey became a meeting ground from its first days. Here came Dutch, Swedish, and English colonists to establish the most varied settlements in the New World. Here they built contrasting homes and churches, introduced different ways of life, and used Old World talents to begin industry long before the Revolution. In the middle of the thirteen original colonies, New Jersey was a place where ideas crossed and armies clashed. Revolution touched the state often—at Newark, Trenton, Princeton, Monmouth, Morristown, Springfield, and scores of other spots.

1

ABOVE LEFT, *Johan Printz, greatest of the Swedes;* ABOVE RIGHT, *James, the Duke of York, who gave the colony its name; and* BELOW LEFT, *Peter Stuyvesant, mightiest of the Dutch, saw their fortunes meet within New Jersey.*

Still-standing buildings depict varied colonial architecture. OPPOSITE, *the 1751 Tennent Church in Monmouth County is "New England" in tone.* BELOW, *Bergen County's Von Steuben House, built in 1751, shows Dutch influence, and the 1754 brick Dickinson House in Salem County reveals a Quaker touch. These etchings, all by Earl Horter, are from the New Jersey State Library.*

New Jersey's iron mining began as early as 1685 and by 1710 had reached Morris County's Dickerson mine, shown here.

America's first successful glasswork started in 1738 at Wistarburg in Salem County.

When the College of New Jersey moved from Newark to Princeton in 1756, it built commodious Nassau Hall and a president's house, as shown in this noted Dawkins engraving of 1764.

Nassau Hall was a hotbed of revolutionists; many of them helped raise liberty poles in dozens of New Jersey towns.

One of the greatest of all military successes was Washington's crossing of the Delaware River on Christmas night, 1776, to attack the Hessians in Trenton.

He struck the next morning in a sleet storm, annihilating the defenders in the streets.

Then came Princeton, on January 3, 1777, and another victory for Washington as this colorful if highly imaginative lithograph by Nathaniel Currier portrays.

Seventeen months later Molly Pitcher, wife of an American soldier, won
attention on the scorched battlefield
of Monmouth on June 28, 1778, as
depicted in Harper's Magazine for
June, 1878.

Trenton turned out in April, 1789, to cheer Washington on his way to inauguration as first President. Currier's lithograph faithfully depicts the arched bridge and its slogan: "The defender of the mothers will be the protector of the daughters."

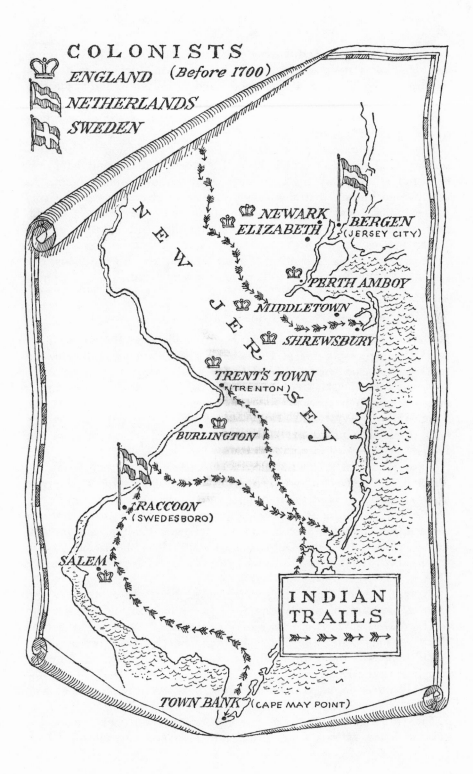

COLONISTS

(Before 1700)

ENGLAND

NETHERLANDS

SWEDEN

NEW JERSEY

NEWARK
ELIZABETH

BERGEN
(JERSEY CITY)

PERTH AMBOY

MIDDLETOWN

SHREWSBURY

TRENT'S TOWN
(TRENTON)

BURLINGTON

RACCOON
(SWEDESBORO)

SALEM

INDIAN
TRAILS

TOWN BANK (CAPE MAY POINT)

Late that day the *Half Moon* came within sight of "high Hills" (Navesink Highlands or possibly Staten Island). Mr. Juet concluded the day by writing: "This is a very good Land to fall with, and a pleasant Land to see." Thanks to seashore publicists, all of whom insist Robert Juet looked *directly* at their particular resort, that is the most widely quoted passage in *Juet's Journal*.

The *Half Moon* sailed into Sandy Hook Bay for a stop before Hudson explored the river which bears his name. The captain later maneuvered all the way north to near what is now Albany before he admitted to himself that this slowly narrowing river was not the way to the Indies. Meanwhile Juet wrote of the hills, the forests, the lushness of the lands, and the alternating timidity and boldness of the Indian natives.

Then, turning his ship about, Henry Hudson and his mutinous, disappointed crew sailed for Holland in late September.

THE WEALTH OF THE INDIES

Juet's Journal excited the greed of shareholders of the Dutch East India Company, sponsors of Hudson's voyage. They generally ignored Juet's enthusiastic words about the fine land, favoring such notations as "good furres," "skins of divers sorts," and the notes about copper ornaments worn by natives. Mr. Juet particularly intrigued them with a note about a "White green" cliff on the New Jersey side that perhaps held either a "Copper or Silver Myne." Riches! The wealth of the Indies!

Those visions of gold and silver that danced in sponsors' heads undoubtedly hurt Netherlands colonization. The first settlers to arrive after Hudson's voyage were trappers and adventurers, far more interested in beaver skins and gold prospecting than in the fertility of the soil. Several other Dutch explorers followed Hudson, but there is little likelihood that any Dutchman had settled on the island the Indians called Man-a-hat-ta, or anywhere else in the New World, before 1612.

Captain Samuel Argall of England looked briefly in on the bay and river at the south of present-day New Jersey in 1610 and named both for Lord De La Warr, governor of Virginia. Dutch and Swedes settled that river long before the Dutch, but the name De La Warr persisted. Argall happened by again in 1614, this time "subjugating" the three or four huts in the Dutch trading post on Man-a-hat-ta Island. The Dutch solemnly agreed to pay tribute to Virginia but forgot the promise as soon as Argall's sails disappeared southward beyond the horizon.

The Dutch of Man-a-hat-ta paid no tribute, and they also stayed close to home. It took Cornelius Hendrickson and Cornelius Jacobsen

Mey, flying the flag of the United Netherland Company, to extend Dutch claims with voyages between 1616 and 1621.

Hendrickson in 1616 piloted a thirty-eight-foot ship, the *Onrust*, built in Man-a-hat-ta in 1614, high up Lord De La Warr's River, or De Zuydt Rivier (South River), as the Dutch called it. He reached "The place of the tall pines," near modern Philadelphia. Later, in 1620, Mey maneuvered his ship closely along the coast, naming nearly everything in sight for himself; today only the lower bit of New Jersey acknowledges the Mey vanity—and even that has been anglicized to Cape May. Mey was a good explorer and he paid New Jersey the ultimate in Dutch compliments by declaring the climate to be "like Holland."

The basic clue to the casualness of Dutch colonization is found in the charter of the Dutch West India Company, incorporated in 1621 with two specific objects: to capture gold-laden Spanish galleons and to establish fur trade with the Indians—in that order. There was no talk of farming or villages or gardens; there was no thought of permanency.

West India Company stockholders stirred restlessly over poor returns from furs. One report showed furs brought in only sixty *thousand* guilders, compared with sixty *million* guilders from pirating Spanish vessels. Directors thereupon protested a possible peace treaty with Spain, scornfully referring to promises of peacetime colonization as a "trifling trade with the Indians."

TWENTY-FOUR MEN, TWENTY-FOUR DOLLARS

Captain Mey became Director General of New Netherlands in 1623 and the next year set twenty-four men ashore high up the Delaware River to establish Fort Nassau at what is now Gloucester. Eight years later a Dutch ship returned but found no life; the lonely little Dutch outpost had disappeared as completely as the Lost Colony of Roanoke. They might have been the victims of Indians, or they might have wandered elsewhere. There is lasting mystery.

Fur-trading posts passed for Dutch "settlements" on the North River (or Hudson River). It has been written that one of these was established as early as 1618 on the New Jersey side, although there is considerable doubt of this. Then, in 1626, Peter Minuit made his famed purchase from the Indians of the island of Man-a-hat-ta ("Heavenly Land") for trinkets worth twenty-four dollars (in currency of that time). Attention given to the real estate bargain usually overlooks Minuit's apparently sincere effort to deal fairly with the natives, the first Dutch awareness that colonization was more than a European paper claim to gold mines and furs.

West India Company directors soon recognized that they must either encourage colonization or get out of New Netherlands forever. Accordingly, in 1629 the company set up a system whereby patroons could establish agricultural settlements in the new land. A patroon could acquire a sizable tract of land simply by promising to transport fifty immigrants to his holdings, at his own expense, within four years. He had political, economic, and legal control over those people, in a feudalistic system of bondage worse than any in Europe.

Amsterdam Burgomaster Michael Pauw became patroon of a huge tract near what is now Jersey City in 1630 and in the best of egotistical traditions named it Pavonia (or "Land of the Peacock") for himself. Pauw failed to get the fifty persons "upwards of fifteen years old" for his feudal domain—and he never left Amsterdam himself— but in 1633 two houses had been built at Pavonia, the first homes on the New Jersey side of the river.

Settlement on the New Jersey side of the Hudson River depended entirely on good relations with the Indians. Scattered farms appeared, and soon after 1640, Aert Teunissen Van Putten and his family farmed an extensive acreage at Hoboken. Van Putten opened one of America's first brewhouses in 1642, on land which he leased for rent of "every fourth sheaf with which God almighty shall favor the field."

Southward in the present Jersey City region, Van Putten had heard of eight or ten "neighbor" families, all of them farmers. These Hollanders were not mere adventurers; they were here to stay and to prosper, and of them all, Jan Evertsen Bout prospered most. Bout spoke with both knowledge and love of his land when he wagered he could grow barley so high that he could tie it above his head. He won the wager by growing barley seven feet tall. These farm people —not the idle seekers of gold—provided the impetus for sound Dutch colonization. Time would prove that there just weren't enough of them eager to leave Holland for the uncertainties of an uncharted land.

Unfortunately the people on the "New Jersey" side of the Hudson also suffered most when eighteen months of Indian terror followed the senseless massacre of natives by Dutch soldiers in February, 1643. (See Chapter 2). Uneasy peace followed through all the 1640s, and, although Bout and a few others moved back to the Pavonia-Hoboken area in 1645, most of New Amsterdam's 800 persons preferred to dwell behind the solid walls of the fort on Manhattan Island.

NEW AMSTERDAM FINDS A LEADER

These first Hollanders deserved far better than they got in the way of leadership. Director General William Kiefft, the man who masterminded the incredibly stupid and brutal Pavonia massacre in 1643, busied himself more with such trivia as an evening curfew than with major colonial problems. Finally the burghers elected an advisory committee to "aid" Kiefft and his colony—and the committee contributed most notably to New Amsterdam when in 1645 it persuaded Kiefft to return to Holland.

Clearly, New Amsterdam and its scattered settlers to the west needed a leader both strong enough to control his people and sensitive enough to know that Indian rights must be protected—for selfish reasons of safety if not for humanitarian principles. That leader arrived on May 11, 1647, when a strong-willed, firm-acting tyrant named Peter Stuyvesant strode off a ship to become New Amsterdam's director general.

"I shall be as a father over his children," said Stuyvesant on his arrival. Unfatherlike, he promptly made his new constituents stand with bared heads to emphasize who gave the orders in New Amsterdam. Peter Stuyvesant made plenty of enemies, who called him "Old Peg Leg" behind his back as he limped about on his wooden leg. Some, paying mock homage to the silver studs in his peg leg, dubbed him "Old Silver Nails."

Stuyvesant bullied his people in autocratic fashion. He tapped his wooden leg violently when his councilors dared to oppose him and he could shout "in foul manner better befitting the fish market." Imperiously, he told protesting councilors: "We derive our authority from God and the Company, not from a few ignorant subjects."

Despite evident unwillingness to win friends, Old Silver Nails could influence people. He made New Amsterdam strong, forward-looking, and completely undemocratic. Stuyvesant brooked no debate: he told dissenters that if anyone wished to complain to the home authorities, "I will make him a foot shorter and send the pieces to Holland and let him appeal in that way."

Stuyvesant wasted neither time nor manpower in argument with the Indians. His job called for settling the land, not covering it with blood. Even when Simon Wallinges of Pavonia was found with an arrow in his head in March, 1649, Stuyvesant urged that "Christians carefully abstain from betraying any desire of revenge." The Indians, in turn, begged forgiveness and went away surprised and delighted with gifts handed them at New Amsterdam.

SWEDEN PLANTS ITS FLAG

Stuyvesant also needed strength and peace at New Amsterdam for reasons in no way related to humanitarianism, for down on the lower Delaware River a band of Swedes and Finns had come to pose a threat potentially greater than possible depredations by the Indians.

Stuyvesant decided that these colonists—who called their settlement New Sweden—must be disabused of their notions of grandeur.

New Sweden was an obvious extension of the power that Sweden had come to know at home; if other nations could be enriched by American colonies, Sweden decided to join them. The time was right, for Gustavus II, King of Sweden from 1611 to 1632, had driven his country from obscurity to first rank among Protestant countries in North Europe. He had forged Sweden, Finland, Estonia, and Latvia into one Scandinavian union, had pushed back Russia, and had begun to dream of conquests beyond the Baltic Sea.

When Sweden set out to dispute Dutch control on the Delaware River, they found their leadership among Dutchmen disenchanted with their homeland. William Usselinx, one of the founders of the Dutch West India Company, approached Sweden in 1624 to urge a colony on the Delaware. Two years later, Peter Minuit, just returned home from his twenty-four-dollar purchase of Manhattan Island, offered his services to Gustavus II to help found a colony "which might be named Nova Swedia."

Minuit estimated that he would need one vessel and a dozen soldiers for the American venture, but as a lure he held out the hope that investors would get "4500 or 6000 beaver skins, thus acquiring a large capital from so small a commencement." Tempting as the prospect seemed, Swedish involvement in the Thirty Years' War in Germany postponed sailing for a decade.

Eventually Minuit had his wish; on New Year's Eve, 1637, two little Swedish ships, the *Kalmar Nyckel* and the *Vogel Grip,* sailed west to found New Sweden. Both ships had Dutch captains, one of them being Minuit himself, but his strong belief in the wisdom of permanent settlement rather than fortune-seeking was not to get a fair test. Unfortunately, the "colonists" aboard his ships were all soldiers, never more noted than gold hunters as likely colonists.

Minuit guided the two ships into Delaware Bay in mid-March, 1638, to establish Fort Christina near what is now Wilmington, Delaware. He bought a thin strip of land from the Indians, then explored the river as far north as re-established Fort Nassau—where Dutch soldiers turned him back, despite Minuit's protests that Sweden had as much right to the Delaware valley as Holland. Before summer's end Minuit left twenty-five settlers in the log enclosure at Fort Christina, protected by cannon taken from the *Kalmar Nyckel*. He sailed for Sweden, filled with plans and dreams.

The Dutch dreamer perished in a violent hurricane on the way home, and when Minuit vanished, New Sweden lost its most enthusiastic promoter. Others picked up his plans, sent over some meager supplies, a few soldiers, a clergyman, and a new governor in 1640. The new governor was still another Dutchman in Swedish employ, Peter Hollander Ridder. New Sweden suffered from a lack of colonial enthusiasm at home; most Swedes loved their own land so much that they declined invitations to go west for a wilderness experience.

Ridder negotiated with the Indians in 1641 for a major piece of land on the east (New Jersey) side of the Delaware. A year later he joined with the Dutch in subjugating a small colony that New Englanders had established in 1634 at Varkens Kill (Salem Creek). Such a show of strength might have been impressive at Varkens Kill, but no one knew better than Ridder that New Sweden had no real might. Even the arrival of indentured Finns failed to make prospects bright, although the Finns at least recognized that this new world offered far better prospects for a future than they could find at home. At least they were here to stay.

JOHAN PRINTZ, MIGHTIEST SWEDE

Just as New Amsterdam got its Peter Stuyvesant in a time of trial, New Sweden received its mightiest leader when Governor Johan Printz landed on February 15, 1643. Described as "arrogant, choleric, and dictatorial"—and thoroughly capable—ex-army Colonel Printz loomed large in New Sweden for ten despotic years. He was doubly impressive; at 400 pounds the portly governor was the biggest colonist that the New World had seen. Johan Printz had none of the proverbial fat man's good humor; he raged when Indians dubbed him "Big Belly" and "Big Tub."

Printz quickly saw the military advantage of a piece of New Jersey land jutting out into Delaware River near present-day Finn's Point. He built Fort Elfsborg there and by late 1643 the fort was strong enough to force Dutch shipmasters to strike their colors as they tried to sail north to Fort Nassau. The uncertain little English colony at Varkens Kill also quickly swore full allegiance to New Sweden and Johan Printz in respect for Fort Elfsborg's guns. Printz cared little for any kind of respect other than that won by force; accused of brutality by some of his colonists, he hanged their spokesmen before denying the charges.

Faithful to the sword, the big, domineering governor swore that if he had more soldiers, "with the help of God not a single savage would be allowed to live on this river." Probably unaware of this scorn, those "savages" sold Printz enough grain to aid his troubled colony through the serious winters.

The stout governor's complaints mounted. Sweden sent no help; one stretch of five years elapsed without a ship from home. As another blow, fire in 1645 destroyed Printz's Tinicum Island mansion (said to be the finest house in the colonies between Virginia and New Amsterdam).

THE END OF NEW SWEDEN

Peter Stuyvesant decided in 1651 that the time had come to reclaim the river and valley for Holland. Strongly entrenched in New Amsterdam, Old Silver Nails challenged Big Belly for mastery of the Delaware River.

The Dutch sent 120 men overland to strengthen Fort Nassau in 1651 and the same year built Fort Casimir downstream from Fort Christina. Thus outflanked, Governor Printz withdrew his troops from Fort Elfsborg on the New Jersey side of the river. Tales had it that Jersey mosquitoes, not Dutchmen, drove the Swedes out of the fort (and Swedish soldiers *had* nicknamed it "Myggenborg" or "Mosquito Castle"), but the facts indicate that the Dutch sting far exceeded that of the winged marshland warriors. At any rate, Fort Elfsborg (or Myggenborg) lay useless and abandoned.

Frustrated and bitter, Johan Printz decided in 1653 that he could take no more. He had not seen a Swedish ship since 1648, so he walked his wife, four children, and twenty other settlers across the peninsula through the wilderness to New Amsterdam, where they sailed for home aboard a Dutch ship. New Sweden was about to fall; Governor Printz wisely decided to get back to Sweden before the demise.

Sadly, as New Sweden faded it got the only burst of genuine homeland enthusiasm that it had ever known. Some 260 colonists, four times the number already in New Sweden, embarked in 1654. New Governor Johan Rising sailed with them and on arrival abruptly made a fatal mistake: he took over the Dutch fort at Fort Casimir. Peter Stuyvesant swore to avenge "the violent usurpation of the Swedes." His reference to violence was symbolic; Fort Casimir had capitulated to the Swedes without a shot being fired.

One year later, in August, 1655, Stuyvesant put an end to New Sweden. Old Peg Leg personally led a fleet carrying 317 soldiers out of New Amsterdam, down the Atlantic Ocean, and into the Delaware River. This force, grand by early colonial standards, captured everything Swedish without so much as one cannon shot, in another silent battle in this least maiming of wars.

New Sweden's settlers had a choice between going home to Sweden or swearing allegiance to Holland. The Swedish leaders chose home; the majority of the settlers, many of them of lower class status in Sweden or Finland, chose to stay on under Dutch rule. A chance to better themselves, not allegiance to a particular flag, meant most to them. Adjusting readily to any rule, those Swedes and Finns later helped England's colonists through difficult early years along the Delaware.

The Swedes and Finns moved outward from the Delaware River through both Delaware and New Jersey. Completely at home in the forests, they spread across what are now Gloucester and Salem counties, ever seeking more space. They gave the American frontier its much-cherished log cabin (one of which has been reconstructed near the Hancock House in Salem County). This unique contribution to colonization is not usually associated with New Sweden or New Jersey; erroneously it is more often thought of as a Kentucky or Tennessee introduction.

THE DUTCH PUT DOWN ROOTS

Indian troubles at Fort Amsterdam forced Stuyvesant to hasten home after his victory on the Delaware in 1655. Furious at the renewed Indian warfare—and blaming his own people in large measure—Stuyvesant took strong measures at New Amsterdam. He ordered all inhabitants along the west (New Jersey) side of the river to band together in towns "like our neighbors of New England." Failure to do so meant double jeopardy—a potential scalping by the Indians or a certain fine of twenty-five Dutch guilders annually. Stuyvesant also forbade straw roofs and wooden chimneys as a precaution against Indian-lit blazes.

The Stuyvesant directives led to the establishment of Bergen (now Jersey City) in 1660 as New Jersey's first village. Settlers lived behind a wooden palisade, venturing out only to work in the *buyten tuyn* (outside gardens) or to drive cattle to and from the nearby salt meadows and watering places. A year later, in 1661, a *schout* (sheriff) was appointed at Bergen, and New Jersey's first courts were convened in the town.

Entrepreneurs at Communipaw (another section of modern Jersey City) opened a ferry in 1661, thus beginning the transportation emphasis that has always characterized what has become Hudson County. Out along the Raritan and Hackensack river valleys, restless Dutch settlers moved freely, always following the riverbeds. They rarely encountered trouble with the Indians, and New Amsterdam authorities considered such wanderers not worth the trouble of seeking out and fining twenty-five guilders annually for disobeying orders to live together in villages.

Dutchmen went well afield from New Amsterdam. Far to the west, in the valley beyond the last of New Jersey's rolling mountains, enterprising Dutchmen found copper in about 1650 on the west side of the Kittatinny Mountains overlooking the Delaware River. The intriguing thing is that the expedition did not come overland from New Amsterdam but rather followed a river valley leading through "a howling wilderness" southwestward from Esopus (now Kingston, New York).

The gaping entrance to that well-worked copper mine remains on the grounds of a Boy Scout camp at Pahaquarry, just north of Delaware Water Gap. Near the mine runs a macadamized road, the modernized version of the 140-mile "old Mine Road" built in the 1650s to take Pahaquarry copper to Esopus. This probably was the first improved road of any distance in America. That part of New Jersey is isolated even now; the dogged persistence of 1650 Dutchmen is best appreciated by visiting the section today, more than 300 years after they closed their mine.

As possible evidence that "Indian trouble" stemmed largely from unjust treatment of the natives by the newcomers, there is no recorded evidence of seventeenth-century trouble between Dutch and Indians in that far northwestern corner. This is noteworthy because those tree-covered slopes long had been the location of Minisink, the Lenapes' "Chief Town," and those northern Indians had earned a reputation as the most warlike of all Lenni-Lenapes. Surely, if Indian-settler trouble had been inevitable, it would have exploded there.

Copper mining in the upper Delaware Valley faded as a successful venture well before 1665, but in 1730 some English wanderers from Philadelphia found thriving Dutch homesteads near the abandoned copper mines. The Dutchmen who lived there had not the slightest awareness of Philadelphia or anything else that lay downriver. They still looked to Kingston (Esopus) as their prime port of call.

Inevitably the English decided to settle the nonsense of whether the Dutch or the Swedes owned the peninsula between the Hudson and Delaware rivers, for England long had claimed everything as a result of the voyages of the Cabots in 1497. King Charles II, the Duke of York, and court associates moved in 1664 to force stubborn, proud old Peter Stuyvesant to capitulate in August of that year. Both the Dutch and Swedish hopes faded before the British power.

Transfer of authority to the English meant little to people already on the land. Both Dutch and Swedes continued to live in harmony with their "conquerors," largely because no bloody battles preceded capitulation of Swedes to Dutch, and in turn, of Dutch to English. England ruled with a relatively tolerant hand; Dutch and Swedes fared as well as or better than new English colonists, and better than they had fared under their own rulers. In their own independent ways Dutch and Swedes already on the land continued the job of colonizing, as if Holland and Sweden had never pulled down their banners.

4

The Time of Two Jerseys

Hollanders and Swedes occupied New Jersey on borrowed time, awaiting the inevitable point when England would take over the only stretch of non-English territory between Massachusetts and Virginia. England certainly never intended to permit any other nation to occupy permanently the very middle of its colonies, and restoration of the Stuart monarchy to power in 1660 stepped up English interest in colonization.

King Charles II decided in 1664 that the time had come to colonize, or at least dispose of, the land between the Delaware and Hudson rivers. Charles summoned his brother, James, the Duke of York, on March 12, 1664, and with a flourish of his pen granted James all the region between the Connecticut and Delaware rivers. "Dearest Brother James" received not only the privilege to gain from the region whatever fortune he could, but also the absolute right to govern as "he shall thinke to be fittest for the good of the Adventurers & Inhabitants there."

The Duke knew that others already inhabited "his" property, and in May he dispatched Colonel Robert Nicolls westward to subdue the Dutch. Nicolls sailed with a fleet of four ships, an army of 450 soldiers, and a commission from James to rule as deputy governor. Nicolls took that commission seriously; later he seemed to be the only one of the principals who viewed colonization of New Jersey as something more than a royal whim.

With Nicolls still at sea, the Duke of York gave Sir George Carteret and John, Lord Berkeley, the territory between the Hudson and Delaware rivers, with boundaries essentially the same as present-day New Jersey. The lease signed on June 23, 1664, asked only ten shillings "in hand payd" and "the rent of a pepper corne upon the Feast of the Nativity of St. John Baptist next ensueing" (and even that only "if the same shall bee lawfully demanded"). Next day, in a deed of release,

James demanded in addition "Twentie Nobles of Lawfull money" per year.

On the twenty-third, the Duke of York also bestowed a name: he decreed that the "said Tract of Land hereafter is to be called by the name or names of New Cesarea or New Jersey." He thus showed sentimental gratitude, for Carteret had stoutly defended the Isle of Jersey for the Royalists in the British civil war that had temporarily unseated the Stuarts in the 1640s.

Berkeley and Carteret were enduring court favorites and both had been among the several proprietors granted the Carolinas in 1663. Carteret had by far the better temperament and loyalty of the two and "was much esteemed by all parties." Berkeley, called by Pepys "the most hot, fiery man in discourse, without any cause," was known to be "a passionate, and but weak man as to policy." Nevertheless, he had the esteem of King Charles and James—and that was enough.

Berkeley and Carteret acquired all the Duke's rights and powers in New Jersey, including not only the right to profit as they might from the land but also the full power to govern. Unwittingly and probably unconcernedly the Duke of York had fastened on New Jersey a cause for dissension and bitterness that would fester in the years to come.

CONQUEST AND COLONIZATION

Out on the high seas, Robert Nicolls knew nothing of the careless real estate transactions of James and his friends. He took his four ships in under the brooding guns of New Amsterdam in mid-August and demanded that the Dutch surrender. Peter Stuyvesant vowed that he would fight but ninety-three of the settlement's leading—and less stout-hearted—citizens begged him to desist. "Let it be so," Stuyvesant finally said, but he insisted on stalling for the best possible terms.

Stuyvesant's tactics delayed the British for more than a week before the stubborn old governor hauled down the Dutch flag in defeat on August 27. As the white flag of surrender rose, he was said to have muttered sadly, "I had rather be carried to my grave." He left the fort followed by his soldiers, with banners flying and a military band playing.

Nicolls promptly changed the colony's name from New Amsterdam to New York in honor of the Duke of York, and dispatched Sir Robert Carr to the Delaware to subdue the colonists there. Sir Robert found no opposition, but with an unnecessary show of strength he expended two barrels of powder and twenty shot, thereby killing several settlers at a time when live colonists of any nationality were the area's most crying need.

Carr's trigger-happy conduct did not reflect Nicolls' policies. Nicolls believed in amnesty, and under him the Dutch and Swedes enjoyed as many personal liberties as they had been accorded by their own nations. Dutchmen continued to push out along the Hackensack and Raritan rivers; downstate the Swedes and Finns probed inland on the creeks leading eastward from the Delaware River.

English settlers in other parts of America heeded Nicolls' generous invitations "to set out a town and inhabit together" in the domain west of the Hudson River (which he named Albania). Nicolls guaranteed new settlers the right to tax themselves—and thereby precipitated a misunderstanding that soon caused discord and violence. Nicolls also granted a somewhat limited freedom of worship, "provided such liberty is not carried to licentiousness or the disturbance of others in the exercise of Protestant religion."

Settlers who desired land in Albania needed only to apply to Nicolls and then purchase it "from the Indians of the projected location." That provision would tangle deeds and land claims and plague Berkeley and Carteret and all New Jersey proprietors who followed them.

Two groups of Long Islanders, transplants from New England, quickly accepted Nicolls' terms. One group of "Associates" from Jamaica, Long Island, applied on September 25, 1664, for permission to deal with the Indians. On October 28 they purchased a region that extended from the Raritan to the Passaic and some thirty miles inland, paying such miscellany as "twenty fathoms of trading cloth, two made coats, two guns, two kettles, ten bars of lead and twenty handfuls of powder." The Associates broke ground for the first permanent English settlement in New Jersey, naming it Elizabethtown in honor of Sir George Carteret's wife.

The other Long Island group received the Neversinks, or Monmouth, Patent on April 8, 1665. In granting them a tract twelve miles wide, vaguely described as running from Sandy Hook westward to the south side of Raritan Bay, Nicolls guaranteed complete liberty of conscience and the right to hold a representative assembly. The freedom-of-religion clause was attractive: Baptists from Rhode Island moved in to found Middletown and Quakers from Gravesend, Long Island, came to settle Shrewsbury.

PHILIP CARTERET: A SURPRISE ARRIVAL

Berkeley and Carteret knew nothing of Nicolls' land grants in that era of sailborne communications. The two absentee landlords commissioned Philip Carteret, a distant relative of Sir George's, as governor of New Jersey on February 10, 1665. They dispatched him to rule their peninsular holdings—and to spread the word that rents would soon be due. This began thirty-eight years of perplexing, and often turbulent, proprietary government.

Governor Carteret, twenty-six years old, arrived in New York late in July, 1665, to the complete surprise and anguish of Governor Nicolls. A few days later Philip guided his ship to the crude wharf where the Elizabethtown Associates worked blissfully to start a settlement. If Nicolls had been disconcerted, imagine the feelings in the village where Philip had chosen arbitrarily to establish the seat of government.

Philip made the best of an extremely difficult situation. The young governor greeted the Elizabethtown founders on behalf of Berkeley and Carteret. In turn, he read their Indian deed and Nicolls' patent with interest and amicably agreed to become one of the Associates. The amenities accomplished, Philip led his personal band of twelve new settlers in a pathetic little parade upward from the creek, shouldering a hoe to prove his approval of those who tilled the soil. Trailing behind were the eighteen servants of the twelve new settlers, evidence that a new and regal way of life had come to replace simplicity and diligence.

Governor Nicolls dispatched a furious letter to the Duke of York, sharply rebuking him for parting with Albania (not knowing or caring that the Duke had called it New Jersey). "All the improveable part" of the Duke's holding lay west of the Hudson River, Nicolls protested, adding that the region granted Berkeley and Carteret "could receive twenty times more people than Long Island" and had "the fair hope of Rich mines." Assuredly, such talk gained Nicolls no friends in court, and it availed him nothing in the New World.

Across the river in New Jersey, Philip Carteret gave Elizabethtowners a copy of "The Concessions and Agreements of the Lords Proprietors of the Province of New Cesarea or New Jersey," a document sent by Berkeley and Carteret. It guaranteed a reasonable measure of self-government in a popularly elected assembly to work with the governor and his appointed council. It accorded the right of each inhabitant to "freely and fully have and enjoy his and their judgements and con-sciences in matters of religion." Taxes could be levied only by the As-sembly. On paper, at least these appeared to be solid rights, and, as so often happens, the people took them seriously.

"The Concessions and Agreements" also provided that property holders must pay "one half-penny, lawful money of England" as annual rent for each acre held. Due every "five and twentieth day of March," the rents would go on "for ever." Berkeley and Carteret generously put the first payment off until 1670, giving Philip time to move ahead with coloniza-tion. However, even the thought of rents stirred resentment among those who understandably believed their grants from Nicolls and their purchases from the Indians freed them from such concerns.

Prospects of religious freedom lured a band of Branford and Milford, Connecticut, Puritans down to found Newark in 1666, and later they successfully bargained with the Indians for land (with Governor Philip Carteret's full approval, it is important to note). The Puritans went ashore to establish a hard-core theocracy in which religious freedom was granted to everyone—provided only that he was a Congregationalist. Political and religious activity was sternly controlled through town meetings limited to those maintaining "the purity of religion professed in the Congregational churches."

Late that year, in December, 1666, Governor Carteret also approved sale of the lower part of the Elizabethtown Tract to other New England Puritans, who divided their tract into settlements named Woodbridge and Piscataway.

Therefore, less than thirty months after Nicolls had forced down the Dutch flag, New Jersey had seven towns, including the Dutch town of Bergen that Stuyvesant had founded in 1660. All seven settlements following the typical New England pattern of compact towns stubbornly dependent on themselves for their own protection, government, and religious thought. Except for the Baptists in Middletown, the Quakers in Shrewsbury, and the Dutch Reformed in Bergen, the towns had strong Puritan overtones.

GOVERNMENT, TAXES, AND DISCONTENTMENT

Governor Carteret moved slowly in the face of such evident local independence, but early in 1688 he summoned the seven towns each to send "two able men" to New Jersey's first Assembly at Elizabethtown on May 26, 1668. These fourteen Burgesses, as Carteret called them in English fashion, were joined by two representatives from the Delaware Settlements.

Puritan philosophy dominated that brief first Assembly, which concluded business in five days. The Burgesses provided for uncompromising punishment of evil, including death for crimes ranging from witchcraft to acts by "undutiful children." They also instructed all men between sixteen and sixty to be ready for military duty, and ordered towns to appoint "fence viewers" (those who made sure that footloose cattle could not escape through poorly strung fences).

The Assembly also showed some sense of broader responsibility by levying an annual provincial tax of five pounds per town. Rebellious spirit stirred in the province of New Jersey over that levy; even taxation *with* representation offended settlers in 1668. Monmouth settlers openly refused to pay the tax and the second Assembly that met in November boldly protested Governor Carteret's "expectations that things must go according to your opinions." That session ended in discord—

and seven years would elapse before another legally called Assembly met.

The discord grew heated. Monmouth settlers refused to take oaths of fidelity to the proprietors, lest they jeopardize rights gained in the grant from Nicolls. Elizabethtowners fanned the embers of discord on March 25, 1670, when the first rents came due: they protested that their deed from the Indians ensured them against rents. Poor Philip Carteret, far from home and army, did his lonely best in the face of rebellion but he had no chance; on May 14, 1672, settlers called their own "assembly" and declared Carteret's post vacated. Filled with the heady spirit of independence, the leaders of this so-called Revolution of 1672 replaced Philip with James Carteret, dissolute second son of George. James gladly accepted the job and the title "President of the Country."

Horrified by this disobedience to himself, his office, the Proprietors— and in a direct line, even to the King himself—ex-Governor Philip Carteret hastened back to England "to endeavour to cure this wound by speedy medicine which delay may cause to gangrene." English authority, including King Charles, lined up solidly behind Philip, but before the governor could return with his "speedy medicine" another minor scene with the Dutch had to be played out in America.

Early in 1673 war broke out between England and Holland, and the sea-minded Dutch immediately dispatched a squadron of ships to the Hudson River. The Dutch fleet regained New York and environs in July with another of the strangely bloodless conquests that typified all Dutch "battles" in New Jersey. English Commander Manning faced a polite court-martial for his inept defense of New York and New Jersey. His peers ruled that Manning undoubtedly "deserved death," but they prudently observed that Manning "had seen the King and Duke," presumably talking them out of the death penalty. They let him off with merely having "his sword broke over his head."

England regained the territory—again without bloodshed—in the spring of 1674, and Philip returned to New Jersey a year later, more firmly entrenched than ever and apparently filled with a willingness to forgive. Good spirit prevailed; eighty-five Elizabethtowners applied to Philip and the Proprietors for new land patents between 1675 and 1678. Proprietors in turn agreed that rents could be met with "country pay" (particularly grains), but relented not one bit on the demand that they *must* be paid in some fashion.

QUAKERS FIND A HAVEN

Beneath the surface goodwill and harmony lay a tangle of financial and personal difficulties besetting Sir George Carteret and Lord Berkeley. Control of New Jersey must soon pass from their hands, to be divided in a manner that after three centuries still strongly influences New Jersey's thought and action. The troubles of Berkeley and Carteret, and particularly of Berkeley, had one good effect: they brought Quaker settlements to the Delaware River and attracted William Penn to America.

"Detected in the basest curruption" and deprived of office, unstable Lord Berkeley experienced serious monetary woes; on March 18, 1673, "for and in consideration of one thousand pounds" he sold his half of New Jersey to Major John Fenwick, a newly converted Quaker and former officer in Cromwell's army. The sale momentarily relieved Berkeley and his creditors, but it thoroughly confused the New Jersey situation, for Fenwick apparently acted as front man for another Quaker, Edward Byllynge.

Harassed and persecuted in England because of their shunning of church ritualism and by their refusal to swear oaths or to bear arms, the Society of Friends—or Quakers—fervently wished for an American haven. Liberal treatment accorded Quakers in Shrewsbury first brought New Jersey to the attention of the Friends, who recognized that New Jersey could be the center of Quaker settlements that someday might extend from the Hudson River to Chesapeake Bay.

William Penn came into the American scene for the first time in February, 1674, to arbitrate a nasty dispute between Byllynge and Fenwick over ownership of the land acquired from Berkeley. Penn, Gawen Lawrie, and Nicholas Lucas acted as trustees and divided West New Jersey into 100 sections. Penn's major contributions to Pennsylvania's history are correctly noted—but he began his work in New Jersey.

Quaker arbiters decided that Fenwick deserved as his share only one tenth of the land bought from Berkeley. Fenwick protested bitterly but Penn urged him to desist: "I entreat thee, fall closely to thy business . . . make the best of what thou hast; thy grandchildren be in the other world before the land thou hast allotted will be employed."

Fenwick heeded the advice, for he had political and financial ambitions. He guided the ship *Griffin* into a cove off Delaware Bay in July, 1675, to found Salem (from the Hebrew word *Sholem*, meaning "peace"). Fenwick bought a region comprising all of modern Cumberland and Salem counties from the Indians, including in the purchase price such un-Quakerlike valuables as 300 gallons of rum and a quantity of guns and powder. He laid out Salem town and planned villages at Cohanzick (Greenwich) and Finn's Point. A promoter in part, he wrote home that "if there be any terrestrial Canaan, 'tis surely here, where the land floweth with milk and honey."

Fenwick's rush to colonize irritated other Friends, who recognized that their holdings in New Jersey had to be more carefully defined by George Carteret. Eventually, on July 1, 1676, Carteret for his part and Penn, Byllynge, Lawrie, and Lucas for the Friends, signed the Quintipartite Deed (so called because of the five signers) and divided New Jersey into two provinces. Carteret found the unpretentious Quakers his match in worldly affairs: the dividing line, from Little Egg Harbor to the northwesternmost point of New Jersey, gave the Friends 4600 square miles in West New Jersey and Carteret 3000 square miles in East New Jersey.

POWER IN THE PEOPLE

Quaker colonization could now begin in earnest. To speed settlement, the Friends issued a remarkably liberal document, "The Concessions and Agreements of the Proprietors, Freeholders and Inhabitants of the Province of West New Jersey in America," in March, 1677. Designed to attract new settlers, "The Concessions" also offered the sincere hope that "there we lay the foundation for after ages that they may not be brought in bondage, but by their own consent, for we put the power in the people."

Penn and Byllynge probably authored "The Concessions and Agreements" jointly and they deliberately made the document easy to understand. These were not "liberties" printed in bold type with myriads of fine-print exceptions between the lines; the clear-cut "Concessions and Agreements" deserves a place among all great treatises guaranteeing individual freedoms. Within the document are many of the principles embodied in the Declaration of Independence ninety-nine years later.

"The Concessions and Agreements" established a system of annual secret balloting for election of 100 Assemblymen and ten commissioners of state. The proprietors had no veto power; the only limiting provision for local rule was that West New Jersey laws must not conflict with English law. Full liberty of speech was guaranteed in legislative debate and citizens could be "witnesses of the votes and inclinations" of their representatives.

"The Concessions" guaranteed trial by jury, equal tax assessments, swift punishment of perjurers, and freedom from illegal arrest or imprisonment for debt. Astonishingly, in an age when most preferred to regard Indians as savages or worse, disputes with the natives were to be settled by a jury of six *Indians* and six settlers. Above all, religious freedom was assured by the assertion that "no man, nor number of men on earth, have power or authority to rule over men's consciences in religious matters." The difference between that liberal Quaker philosophy and Newark's early brand of narrow religious "freedom" is evident.

Such terms found eager acceptance among English Friends. Late in August, 1677, the first Quakers to arrive under terms of "The Concessions" sailed up the Delaware. Long-time Swedish settlers aided the newcomers in negotiations with the Indians and guided them to a site the Quakers first called New Beverly, then Bridlington, and eventually

Burlington. The Burlington founders spent the first winter in wooden shacks or caves, but in the spring of 1678 they laid out a town curiously divided along High Street: Yorkshiremen would dwell north of High and Londoners would live south of it.

Mahlon Stacy, an arrival at Burlington in the early winter of 1678, went upriver the following spring to found a town (now Trenton) at "ye falls of ye de la Warr." No one dared venture north of the Delaware's "ye falls" until much later, but other settlements soon developed at Gloucester and Greenwich. By 1681 more than 1400 Quakers lived in West New Jersey. They built substantially; they were here to stay. The time for adventurers and fortune seekers had passed.

SAD DAYS FOR THE CARTERETS

Matters deteriorated in the eastern province. Sir Edmund Andros, successor to Robert Nicolls as governor of New York, coveted the allegiance and/or obedience of the 5000 people who lived in East New Jersey by 1680 but he discreetly kept hands off until Sir George Carteret died on January 13, 1680. Then he acted.

First Andros bluntly warned Philip Carteret not to govern "without legal authority" (meaning sanction by the New York governor). Then, on April 30, 1680, Andros sent soldiers across the Hudson River to drag the East New Jersey governor out of his Elizabethtown bed. The contemporary German traveler Jasper Danckaerts related the episode in detail:

> They entered the house, I know not how at midnight, seized him naked, dragged him through the window, struck and kicked him terribly, and even injured him internally. They threw him, all naked as he was, into a canoe—and carried him in that condition to New York, where they furnished him clothes and shoes and stockings, and then conducted him to the fort and put him immediately in prison.

Carteret's trial in May, 1680, electrified the provinces. Three times Andros sent out juries; three times the defiant juries returned, either unable or unwilling to find Philip guilty of riot and illegal government. The jury urged Carteret to return to New Jersey, but "not to assume any authority or jurisdiction there." English law, "The Concessions," obdurate juries, and all that sort of thing troubled the imperious Andros not at all, however. He simply ignored the courts and proceeded to take over local town governments in East New Jersey with far less "legal authority" than that he had warned Philip about assuming.

Philip, considerably weakened in health, returned to Elizabethtown to build a new brick mansion. There he brought a bride, the widow Elizabeth Smith Lawrence of Long Island, and her seven children by her first marriage, to swell considerably the Elizabethtown population of

700. All settled down in the governor's large house, set amid 2000 acres suitable for the wanderings of the governor's suddenly acquired brood. Philip found little solace among Jerseymen. Heated debate broke out in the Assembly in October, 1681. The Assembly vigorously complained that their rights were being eroded away and Philip took the unprecedented action of dissolving the legislative body. Philip died in December, 1682, at the age of forty-four, and the widow Carteret wrote his mother in England that the "barbarious and inhuman action of Sir Edmund Andros and his merciless soldiers . . . hath shortened his life many times."

ENTER THE MULTIPLE PROPRIETORS

The old rule weakened, and the influence of Berkeley and Carteret ended officially when George Carteret died and trustees of his estate offered East New Jersey at public auction. Twelve men, including William Penn and other Quaker associates in West New Jersey, successfully bid £3400 for the Carteret property and were granted East New Jersey on February 1, 1682. For a short time Quaker interest dominated both East New Jersey and West New Jersey.

The twelve new owners made little effort to foster a Quaker tone in East New Jersey. For one thing, Quaker philosophy would not permit interference with the religious beliefs of well-entrenched Baptists and Congregationalists. Equally, William Penn in 1682 abandoned his original plans for building a City of Brotherly Love near what is now Paulsboro in Gloucester County and instead built his Philadelphia on the higher west bank of the Delaware River. His principal interests shifted permanently there.

Control of East New Jersey soon spread into many hands. The original twelve buyers sold half interests to another twelve, several of them Scots, creating the Twenty-Four Proprietors of East New Jersey. Many of these, in turn, sold fractional shares to others and the proprietorship became an outright business enterprise. Recognizing the difficulty in administering informally their vast land holdings, the owners in August, 1684, organized the Board of Proprietors of the Eastern Division of New Jersey (which still functions, incidentally, as one of America's oldest continuously operated businesses).

The Proprietors located their East New Jersey capital at "sweet, wholesome and delightful" Ambo Point on the Raritan River and offered inducements for settlers to locate there. Real growth began in 1686 when the Earl of Perth permitted 200 oppressed Scots, most of them Presbyterians, to immigrate to Ambo Point. Gratefully the Scots called their village New Perth; older residents with considerable reluctance gave ground in the compromise name of Perth Amboy.

The new East New Jersey proprietors lost little time in exploiting their holdings. They began paying themselves dividends, the first permitting each holder of a full share the right to take up 10,000 acres, and by 1702 the Proprietors had voted themselves three such handsome dividends, amounting to a total of 17,500 acres apiece.

East New Jersey thus acquired large landholders; along the Millstone and Raritan rivers, in Monmouth County, and elsewhere estates of a thousand or more acres were common. In vivid contrast, earlier arrivals had huddled together (by choice) in small towns or occupied farms of 100 to 200 acres. All settlers, great and small, were expected to pay rents to their newly acquired landlords, and no nonsense—this was business now, not sentiment.

West New Jersey had little land difficulty; the Council of Proprietors of the Western Division of New Jersey, organized at Burlington in 1688 (and also still in existence), had liberal provision for purchase of real estate and farms of 300 and more acres were usual for settlers as well as Proprietors. West New Jersey's troubles lay not with land but with trying to find a stable government.

During its existence between 1676 and 1702, West New Jersey had several major shifts in governmental authority. Edward Byllynge, still in England, demanded—and received—recognition as governor in 1680, and sent Samuel Jenings as his deputy. When Byllynge died in 1687, his land holdings (and right of government) went to Dr. Daniel Coxe, a land manipulator and speculator in several colonies. Coxe, in turn, sold his shares and governing powers in 1692 to the West Jersey Society, a group of forty-eight businessmen and speculators living in or near London. They cared most about the possibilities of profit from their investment; the views of colonists didn't trouble them particularly. As members of the Established Church, they felt no reason to limit West New Jersey colonization to Quakers.

The potential for trouble was evident, but trouble could wait. There was too much else to be done first. Above all, more people had to be induced to come to the Jerseys.

PROMOTERS, WORK, AND GROWTH

The East New Jersey Proprietors hired George Scot, one of the earliest of public relations men, to set forth the merits of the province in 1685. Mr. Scot likened the climate to Naples, wrote glowingly of the fishing, the forests, the fertility of the fields, the quantity of the game. He wrote unblushingly that "from an apple-tree-seed in four years (without grafting) there sprang a tree that in the fourth year bore such a quantity of apples as yeelded a barrel of syder."

Scot found Sandy Hook Bay "not to be inferiour to any Harbour in America." He said the thick black soil bore "great burthems of corn."

Shrewd publicist though he was, Scot recognized that New Jersey's natural riches must be supplemented by a wealth of talented people. He wrote: "All Sorts of Tradesmen may make a brave Lively-hood there, such as Carpenters, Shipwrights, Rope-makers, Smith, Brick-makers, Taylors, Tanners, Cowpers, Mill-wright, Joyners, Shoe makers and such like." In truth, they could.

That emphasis on work—for even the "riche soile" called for labor—marked the full and final swing from the gold-seeking Dutch adventurers to the serious English colonization. Settlers from England, Scotland, Ireland, plus the Dutch and Swedes, sought their fortunes through their own labors or the work of indentured servants and slaves. An iron venture had been started in 1674 in Tinton Falls, leather workers were busy in Elizabethtown and Newark by 1680, gristmills and sawmills used water power on a score of streams before 1690. Small merchant ships sailed in and out of Newark, Elizabethtown, Perth Amboy, Burlington, and Salem, bound inward from Europe or outward for the West Indies. This was work, not adventure.

Both Jerseys grew slowly. Rough Indian trails around the northern edges of the Pine Barrens and south of the Watchung Hills were widened into crude roads as travel increased between the outlying regions and the two provincial capitals in Perth Amboy and Burlington. But the lay of the land and the dependence on water transportation generally kept settlers close by the rivers and creeks that emptied into the Delaware and Hudson rivers.

The forbidding hills north and west of Newark and Elizabethtown made early home builders stay close to the plains, even as they spread outward from original towns. Quaker missionary William Edmundsen wrote of his 1675 trip that started at "a landing" (later Inian's Ferry and now New Brunswick) on the "Rarington" River. Edmundsen went overland from there to the Delaware River, and on the way he did not encounter a single settler.

West Jersey colonists pushed eastward from the Delaware River, contrary to the general American pattern of westward movement. Still, the more than a million acres of pine forests in southern New Jersey formed a tremendous natural barrier between the Delaware River and the Atlantic Ocean. The deep, mysterious forests, underlain with a dirty white sand that bogged wagons down worse than mud, caused settlers to shun the region. Farmers called the region the Pine Barrens, not because the area was truly barren, but because they couldn't visualize it as yielding traditional farm crops.

Eastward on the ocean front, only an occasional squatter occupied coast lands before 1700, but he had to be a man who disliked people —or, just as likely, was no favorite of society himself. These squatters lived by fishing or beachcombing or by helping to round up cattle which roamed freely on the strand. There was one notable exception to the squatter tradition: the whalers at such places as Harvey Cedars (on Long Beach Island) and at Cape May.

Those who went a-whaling along the New Jersey shore came from Long Island or New England, including many *Mayflower* descendants (it has been claimed since by one writer that more descendants of *Mayflower* passengers now live in Cape May than at any place except Plymouth). Those original Cape May whalers built thirteen houses at Town Bank on a high bluff overlooking the Delaware Bay in about 1690, and sallied forth in small boats to battle whales weighing up to 250 tons. Whaling took courage, but a single whale beached, stripped, and turned into blubber and whale "oyle" meant $4000 in gold.

If they survived, whalers prospered. William Penn wrote of eleven Cape May whales "caught and worked onto oyle in one season" and said, "We justly hope for a considerable profit by a whalery, they being so numerous and the shore so suitable." Three whaling companies worked simultaneously at the Cape May point where Delaware Bay met the boundless ocean, leading one Gabriel Thomas to declare in 1698 that "prodigious, nay—vast—quantities" of "oyle and whalebone" were produced every year.

SOLID ROOTS OF REBELLION

Whaler or squatter, each lived in blissful ignorance of the political winds sweeping through East and West New Jersey. East New Jersey governors continued to quarrel incessantly with recalcitrant inhabitants who grew ever bolder as a second generation of Jerseymen came along. West New Jerseyans elected their own governor in 1684 and 1685 in open defiance of Proprietor Edward Byllynge, who had claimed the sole right to name the governor. Clearly the tiny seeds of dissatisfaction had begun to sprout into a solidly rooted rebellion.

Troubles between citizens and governors exploded into violence in the year 1700—a violence so widespread and so explosive that it earned the name "The Revolution." This Revolution assuredly wasn't aimed directly at the King, but it was a rebellion against *any* authority which interfered with rights as the New Jerseyans interpreted them. A new breed of independents was maturing in America.

Andrew Hamilton, off-and-on governor of both East and West Jersey since 1692, returned in 1700 after a stay in England to find himself in deep trouble. Anti-Proprietary anger was bubbling through most of the two provinces. Some 250 men signed a Grand Remonstrance to King William, repudiating Governor Hamilton and asking for a governor who, "as an Indifferent Judge may decide the Controversys Arising between the Proprietors and the Inhabitants of your Majesty's Province."

Such resort to lawful, if nonetheless rebellious, procedure failed to placate the more inflamed; mob rule took over in several areas. Samuel Carter led a throng into Essex County Court at Elizabethtown in March, 1700, and denied its authority. When an attempt was made to arrest Carter, it was met with "generall noise and hollowing with unseemly actions and insolent gesture."

At about the same time, a Monmouth County mob "beate the saide pretended sheriff to the shedding of blood on boath sides" during a successful foray on the jail to free a man named Richard Salter. A few days later Governor Hamilton came to investigate with forty or fifty armed men, only to be turned away by a force four times as large. At Newark, judges were "grosely abused, some of their clothes torn off their backs with many other abusefull words and actions Received from the Rabell of Elizabethe Towne."

Hamilton endeavored in March, 1701, to try Moses Butterworth, one of Captain Kidd's notorious pirates, at Middletown. Townspeople deliberately chose that same day for militia training. Court proceedings droned on against the noise of a "Drum beating Continually." It made such noise that the court could not examine the prisoner.

Suddenly more than 100 Middletowners and friends burst into the courtroom and "did traytorously seize ye Governor and ye Justices, the King's Attorney General and ye under Sheriff and ye Clerke of ye Court and kept them close prisoners under a guard from Tuesday ye 25 March until ye Saturday following." All were held pending recovery of a wounded rioter—with the clear implication that some official necks, maybe Hamilton's included, would stretch if the rioter died. The rioter recovered; it would have been an interesting test of intentions if he had succumbed.

Less impetuous West Jerseyans also rebelled, although trouble there was far less overt than in East Jersey. When Quaker proprietors gained control and voted a heavy tax for use in defending proprietary titles, some sixty to seventy angry persons swept down on Burlington in March, 1701, and in what was described as a "Tumultuary and Riotous manner" broke open the jails and temporarily drove the administration into hiding.

The time, clearly, had come for proprietary surrender of government. Quietly the Proprietors began to work out a capitulation among themselves, aware that real estate, not palace intrigue, paid best in the long run. When the Board of Trade in England recommended late in 1701 that the provinces of East New Jersey and West New Jersey be placed directly under royal rule, they willingly agreed—and in April 1702, yielded the reins to Queen Anne.

THE SOLID FOUNDATIONS

Blossoming independent spirit continuously highlighted the period from Dutch surrender in 1664 to Proprietary surrender in 1702, but in this time the solid foundations of New Jersey were laid.

Above all, the geographic, political, and economic division between East and West Jersey was intensified. The two areas took on definite "tone": West Jersey becoming closely identified with the philosophy of the mild Quakers, East Jersey with the more militant Presbyterians. West Jersey became an area of large farms and plantations, as the result of both land policies and fewer colonists, while East Jersey assumed a pattern of power concentrated in town governments jealous of their local prerogatives.

Division of governmental authority and responsibilities also began. Despite the powerful New England town spirit, East New Jersey took the lead in founding counties: Bergen, Essex, Middlesex, and Monmouth counties were set up as vaguely defined areas in 1675 (and redefined in 1681). Somerset then split from Middlesex in 1688. West New Jersey proceeded more slowly in establishing counties. Burlington and Salem counties were set off in 1681, followed by Gloucester in 1686 and Cape May in 1692. Thus nine of New Jersey's twenty-one counties were well established by 1692.

Correspondence to relatives in England from seventeenth-century settlers showed a definite inclination to like the colonial life of the Jerseys. Letters to England waxed so enthusiastic in the late seventeenth century that some of the folk at home must have written back in disbelief. One James Claypole of New Jersey took pains to answer such a correspondent indignantly: "As to thy judgement of the letters from West Jersey that they are to decoy people, that is known to be otherwise."

More directly, and in a manner familiar to latter-day writers of postcards, Mahlon Stacy, founder of Trenton, penned a simple phrase back to England:

"This is a most brave place; whatever envy or evil spies may speak of it, I wish you were all here."

5

Power of the Purse

Queen Anne accepted the surrender of the East New Jersey and West New Jersey Proprietors on April 15, 1702, with understandable haste, for as the seventeenth century waned, the Crown had decided to extend as soon as possible its control over all proprietary and charter colonies. New Jersey's capitulation and the joining of the Jerseys into one colony pleased the Queen, although William Penn protested that "the surrender was knavishly contrived to betray the people."

Lewis Morris, destined to become New Jersey's most dominant colonial personality, helped shape the surrender. The terms gave the Proprietors continued (albeit unofficial) political control of the united province through an appointed council, wherein Proprietor influence was powerful to the time of the Revolution. The Council tended to be aristocratic and with rare exceptions sided with the governor (who also tended to be aristocratic).

As for government "by the people," only those who owned more than 100 acres of land could vote and only those with holdings of 1000 or more acres of land could sit in the Assembly—the chamber of alleged popular government. Such property qualifications were not designed to encourage office holding among the rioters whose demands and turbulent behavior had provoked the "surrender."

Queen Anne agreed that the Assembly would meet alternately in Perth Amboy and Burlington, the capitals of old East and West New Jersey and the towns where the Proprietors maintained their influential land businesses as well. Power, therefore, continued with the privileged except for one thing: the Assembly retained the right to raise and distribute money. On that one tangible base New Jersey assemblies would shape a stubborn resistance to royal governors, for an obdurate and dictatorial governor usually could be made conciliatory under the threat to withhold his salary.

Uniting the Jerseys could not be accomplished simply by written agreement. New York and Philadelphia already exerted powerful influences on either side of the colony, but equally important, within the province itself a heterogeneous population had made New Jersey an early melting pot. Here by 1702 were the Dutch, Swedes, and Finns, first on the scene. Here were the English, Scots, and Irish who had come since 1664 to take advantage of the relatively good terms that were accorded new settlers. Here were sprinklings of Germans and French Hugenots.

Later in the eighteenth century someone (Benjamin Franklin is usually credited but it might have been James Madison) would deride New Jersey as "a barrel, tapped at both ends, with all the live beer running into New York and Philadelphia." He erred overmuch: New York and Philadelphia, for all their commercial and intellectual importance in colonial America, did not keep New Jersey from developing its own unique, if split, personality.

CORNBURY: WORST POSSIBLE GOVERNOR

Not all the live beer ran out, by any means. Lord Cornbury, the first governor of united New Jersey, discovered that soon enough. His Lordship was Queen Anne's cousin, but his other personal qualifications for office were slight. He was of lackluster mental ability, a noted bigot, a man of unsavory personal habits, and a spendthrift. Cornbury hoped his fiscal condition, at least, might be cured quickly in America.

After all, he would rule both New York and New Jersey. That dual appointment by Queen Anne disappointed Jerseymen, who had hoped for their own governor. West Jersey expressed particular worry; a shared governor assuredly would live in New York, a situation unlikely to enhance his knowledge of the peculiar needs of those who dwelled by the Delaware.

Lord Cornbury arrived in 1703. As expected, he promptly settled down in lively New York while New Jersey's 15,000 inhabitants awaited his pleasure. That average of fewer than two people per square mile might have misled even a wise governor into believing that he dealt with country bumpkins, but Cornbury found that little New Jersey had enough intrigue and dissension and possibilities to excite his greed.

East New Jersey Proprietors divided sharply into Scotch and English factions (England and Scotland were not united until 1707). West New Jersey Proprietors were split between Quakers and Anglican Church members. Further complicating provincial disunity were the Elizabethtown Associates, holders of land granted in 1664 and 1665 by Governor Nicolls. The Associates had fought for their rights before—and they would fight again.

Cornbury promptly chose sides, with his decision based mainly on prospects of quick financial return. He first supported an East-West alliance of Scotch Proprietors and Quakers, but when those two groups failed to assure him of a handsome advance salary, he turned hopefully to the English Proprietors and Anglicans to form the Cornbury Ring.

Recognizing that a rapid turnover of land holdings would insure the greatest profits in the shortest time, the Ring moved audaciously. It took over the offices of registrar and surveyor general in the East New Jersey Proprietors and then stymied Quaker authority in West New Jersey on the grounds that religious beliefs wouldn't permit Quakers to swear an oath of allegiance. The Scotch-Quaker faction was helpless, and Cornbury's supporters dumped more than a half million acres of New Jersey land on the market between 1706 and 1709.

THE ASSEMBLY CALLS A HALT

Cornbury's incessant quarrels with the Assembly and his sordid manipulations prompted voters to elect a rebellious Assembly in 1707. The new legislators wasted no time in writing a bill of complaints that detailed Cornbury's refusal to honor Quaker credentials in the Assembly, his acceptance of bribes, and his high-handed treatment of West New Jersey Proprietors.

Speaker Samuel Jenings defiantly read the list of grievances directly to Cornbury, who listened with a "countenance of authority and stubbornness." One witness called Jenings' behavior "So odious an insult, so Detestable a Pride as has never before been offer'd to the person of a Governor." Cornbury himself exclaimed that "Jenings had impudence enought to face the Devil!"

The Assembly's audacious behavior prompted one of Her Majesty's officials, Robert Quarry, surveyor general of customs, to write home in prophetic vein that the Assemblymen held such wild notions that they would not be satisfied "unless the Queen will allow them to send representatives to sit in the Parliament of Great Britain!"

The Assembly's written complaints went to England, and Queen Anne's patience with her dissolute and fortune-hunting cousin finally ran out in 1708. Officially she gave him leave to return to England. Privately, she was quoted as saying that "his near relations to her . . . should not protect him in oppressing Her Subjects."

Paradoxically, Cornbury's calloused philosophy of government proved vital to New Jersey freedoms, for Assemblymen came to realize the power they held in controlling the purse strings. By refusing to vote appropriations for matters dear to the heart of a governor—particularly his salary—the Assembly could win almost any point. Assemblymen boldly liberalized voting laws to give the franchise to anyone "worth fifty pounds current money of this Province in real and personal estate" (compared with the previous measure that restricted voting only to those with 100 or more acres of *land*). Underscore that: liberalization of voting privileges underlies all democratic advance.

ROBERT HUNTER: "IDEAL" GOVERNOR

Two inept successors served short terms after Cornbury before Governor Robert Hunter arrived in 1710. Hunter faced extreme difficulties, for the Ring still sold lands as it pleased and government had come nearly to a standstill because of strong disagreement between the Assembly and the Council.

Hunter struck vigorously in the spring of 1711 to end the deadlock between Assembly and Council, asking the English government to dismiss four New Jersey Councilors, despite their powerful connections in England. The governor allied himself with the Scotch Proprietors, and his stature was enhanced in 1713 when the four Council dismissals were approved in England. With Council control in his hands and with a cooperative Assembly to heed his bidding, Hunter sought to eliminate governmental ills.

Reforms came quickly. Quakers gained the right to affirm rather than to swear allegiance and thus could hold office and serve on juries. Lowered legal costs opened the courts to wider groups of people. Equally noteworthy, the Assembly in 1717 issued £4000 in bills of credit (paper currency), important because later New Jersey Assemblies would become outraged over English refusal to approve paper-money measures. Paper money, indeed, would become one of New Jersey's most inflammatory rallying points.

Donald L. Kemmerer, in *Path to Freedom*, called Robert Hunter "the most nearly ideal governor colonial New Jersey ever had: he was able, talented, eminently respected, and on the whole, popular. . . . Hunter found New Jersey wracked with political dissension and suffering from the lack of much long-needed legislation; he left it in the most peaceful condition it had known for decades."

Hunter talked of spending his declining years in New Jersey: at least he liked the colony well enough to build a house here. The colonists, in turn, liked him. When inhabitants of a large area—comprising all of modern Hunterdon, Morris, Sussex, and Warren counties, and part of Mercer—broke away from Burlington County in 1714 to form New Jersey's tenth county, they named their area Hunterdon to honor the popular governor.

THE GOVERNOR AND THE LOAN OFFICE

Hunter did not retire to his New Jersey home; he returned to England in 1719 "with a violent pain in my hipp" (probably sciatica). Governor William Burnet arrived in 1720 to inherit the good feeling. Cultured, studious, and practical, Burnet generally let the Assembly have its own way. He quarreled with them twice in his first two years, first seeking to raise the property-holding qualification of the Assembly (which was never done) and secondly asking a financial support bill for five years (he settled for two years). The governor reconciled himself to such opposition and thereafter maintained generally pleasant relations with the Assembly.

Burnet cooperated in the establishment of a New Jersey loan office in 1723, shrewdly planned to increase the amount of paper money in the colony and to limit the cycles of inflation and deflation that accompany such currency. New Jersey badly needed paper money; as an agricultural colony between America's two most prominent towns, the province found the commerce of New York and Philadelphia constantly draining away its supplies of money.

The loan-office bill set up a land bank operated by the colony, and it was a shining light among colonial financial schemes in America. The loan office issued £40,000 of paper money in small bills up to three pounds. The first £4000 went to wipe out state debts; the remainder was loaned out in amounts up to £100—secured by mortgages on the land or property of the borrower and payable in twelve years. Within two years the enterprise succeeded so well that the value of New Jersey money surpassed that of both New York and Pennsylvania.

When Governor Burnet was transferred to Massachusetts in 1728, demands for a New Jersey government distinct from that of New York were accelerated. The commercial, social, and government disadvantages of being an appendage of another colony were all too clear. Even the benign governments of Hunter and Burnet couldn't eclipse the fact that by sharing its governor with New York, New Jersey was always in second place.

Both Hunter and Burnet acutely sensed the stirrings of independent thought. Hunter had written home prophetically that "these colonies were infants sucking their mother's breast, but . . . would weane themselves when they came of age." Burnet's awareness of an independent New Jersey spirit came in 1721 when the Assembly protested his "intermeddling with the business of the House." The governor promptly dissolved the Assembly and warned that such perversity made it "evident you are not so much contending with me . . . as directly with His Majesty, whose instructions you have entirely disregarded."

New Jersey Yearns for Stature

Burnet's departure prompted both John Kinsey, prosperous and energetic West New Jersey Quaker, and Lewis Morris, the leading figure in New Jersey colonial history, to ask England for a separate New Jersey governor. Kinsey had no individual in mind, but Morris had: when he declared that such an executive would have to be a man "of very uncommon ability," he had a clear feeling that Lewis Morris could serve very well.

Governor William Cosby, who came in 1732, made the need for a separate New Jersey governor all too clear. In his maiden speech to the Assembly, he promised to spend half his time in New Jersey. Assemblymen should have known better, but Cosby's blandishments prompted the legislators to vote him a bonus of £200, which he took before hastening off permanently to New York. He met the New Jersey Assembly only once in the next four years and provincial government slowed to a near standstill. Morris hastened to England late in 1734 to protest, boarding a vessel under a convoy of armed boats from Shrewsbury, a wise precaution because Cosby had sent soldiers to head him off.

Morris made every possible political contact in England, but after a year he admitted that high officials were unwilling to risk their reputations for "any such trifle as a plantation governor, or all of them put together." His persistence nevertheless caused leading Englishmen to heed New Jersey demands. One of them remarked of Morris: "I have reason to believe from himself that if your Grace would please to recommend him to be governor of New Jersey it would make him easy."

Morris debated and pleaded unsuccessfully until word reached London that Governor Cosby died of tuberculosis in 1736. Morris promptly departed "that noisy, stinking, and very Expensive town, London" (a typically frank Morris summation), and his stay abroad seemingly gained him nothing, for in June of 1737 Lord Delaware was appointed as governor of New York and New Jersey, in perpetuation of the old system.

Lord Delaware never left England; he "resigned" the governorship to remain in England as an army colonel, proof of how lightly he prized the chance to rule two colonies. Perhaps England despaired or perhaps officials shuddered at thoughts of another visit from persistent, increasingly cantankerous Mr. Morris. In either case, a ship brought word in January, 1738, that New Jersey finally had gained a governor independent of New York. He was, of course, Lewis Morris.

THE SAD TERM OF LEWIS MORRIS

New Jerseyans received the news with "great satisfaction." Morris had served his province with distinction for nearly half a century, sometimes as an outspoken liberal. He had spoken forthrightly against tyrannical governors. He had shown in the past an ability to get on with people of all stations, and his friends numbered the most influential people in New Jersey and New York. The province finally had a native son in the chair, and everything pointed to a splendid regime.

Sadly, Governor Morris became disliked before his death; it's one thing to be battling against the governor, and decidedly another to be on the receiving end. As a wealthy Proprietor, Morris had never truly been democratic; he stood with "the people" when corruption in high places forced him to—he was, above all, scrupulously honest. When he became governor he sought to restore powers wrested away in two decades of stubborn Assembly battle.

Matters began well enough. Morris announced he would no longer meet with the Council during its debates, a concession designed to give the upper house more independence. It was not a popular concession, of course: the Council represented only high power. Since New Jerseyans had not been to the polls in eight years, Morris called an election. Hence, when the Assembly convened at Perth Amboy in the fall of 1738, optimism and good feeling held the day, but Morris lost no time before arguing with the Assembly.

Quickly it became apparent that the liberality and earnestness of a youthful Lewis Morris had become lost within the reactionary shell of an old Lewis Morris. The Governor complained that his salary was too small. A weaver sitting in the Assembly replied, "Let us keep the dogs poor and we'll make them do what we please." Morris would have applauded such an expression in his youth; now, as the "poor dog," he became enraged.

Morris and his Assemblies quarreled constantly over many things— over the Assembly's refusal to raise an adequate militia, over money bills, and particularly over the issuance of more paper money. The Assembly wanted more of the notes that had been so successful in the past, but Morris vetoed the measure. Taking his case to the people, Morris had broadsides and pamphlets distributed throughout the province, seeking to show that the Assembly sought powers not granted by the King.

Morris had much right on his side. He would have been negligent if he had failed to advocate an adequate militia and the demands for paper money came at a time when there was a surplus in the provincial treasury and bills enough in circulation. His argument that capable men should not accept public office at pauper's wages was undeniably sound.

Abuse followed abuse on both sides and came to a head in 1744 when the aged governor completely refused to consider *any* legislation. The Council and Assembly fell to fruitless bickering, and the only bill on which both could agree was "an act to encourage the destroying of crows, blackbirds, squirrels and woodpeckers." Governor Morris refused to sign even that.

A year later Morris convened the Assembly and reproached assemblymen for their obstinacy, declaring them to be a group of idiots. "Farmers and plowmen we confess ourselves to be," they answered, "but we resent the aspersion of idiots." Nevertheless, the Assembly took seriously his threat to veto all legislation unless he gained their support. They enacted laws to raise money for government and for militia, even as their dislike of the governor intensified.

A Changed New Jersey

Self-centered Governor Morris simply failed to keep pace with the changes within his colony. The limited New Jersey that he had known so well in 1700 was dramatically different by 1745.

Industry had come, on a modest but well-established scale. Both Newark and Elizabethtown were noted leather centers. Adventurers had found iron in northern hills, and before 1710 a forge fire had been lit at Hanover on the Whippany River. Within thirty years several forges and furnaces operated along the Rockaway River near what is now Dover, and new furnaces were blown in at both High Bridge and Oxford in 1742. Men knew, too, the potential of bog iron that lay mudlike in the river bottoms of Burlington and Atlantic counties, although development of southern New Jersey bog-iron empires would not reach full swing until the 1760s.

By Lewis Morris' time glassmaking had been started in the southern part of the province. Casper Wistar, Philadelphia button maker, imported four Rotterdam glass blowers to start a factory in Salem County in 1739–the first successful glassmaking venture in America. Wistarburg secrets slipped out; the town came to be called "the cradle of American glass blowing" after workers from the New Jersey plant spread out through southern New Jersey, to Pennsylvania, and on to wherever fine glass would be blown.

Fundamental in all colonial growth was improvement of transportation. New Jersey's enduring role as a dynamic transportation bridge between New York and Philadelphia, between North and South, had been cast by 1745.

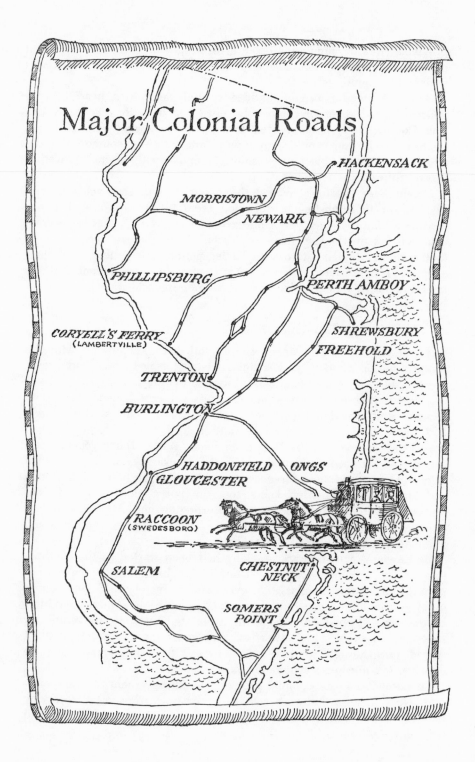

Major Colonial Roads

HACKENSACK

MORRISTOWN
NEWARK

PHILLIPSBURG
PERTH AMBOY

CORYELL'S FERRY
(LAMBERTVILLE)
SHREWSBURY
FREEHOLD

TRENTON

BURLINGTON

HADDONFIELD · ONGS
GLOUCESTER

RACCOON
(SWEDESBORO)

SALEM
CHESTNUT
NECK

SOMERS
POINT

Waterborne traffic expanded as the eighteenth century progressed. Creeks and rivers carried boats laden with Jersey fruits and vegetables to big town markets across the Delaware and Hudson rivers. Major harbors at Perth Amboy and Burlington—and lesser ports at Greenwich, Salem, Trenton, Newark, Elizabethtown and New Brunswick—stirred with the excitement of the wharves. Outward went Jersey wheat, flour, beef, bacon, and lumber products from the Pine Barrens. Inward came rum and sugar from the Indies, wines and olive oil from Spain, and manufactured goods from England.

New Jersey leaders also began to struggle with a never-ending need for new and better roads. The narrow cross-state trails of 1700 were widened before 1720 and improved roads had to be built and rebuilt to link the twin colonial capitals at Perth Amboy and Burlington. The race across New Jersey's slender waist had begun in earnest: in 1733, Solomon Smith and James Moon advertised that their two freight wagons would link Perth Amboy and Burlington "once every week or offt'er if that business presents." Competitors responded with similar boasts, often easier to make than to keep.

People hastened across New Jersey on the way to somewhere else or pushed outward to settle within the colony itself. Governor Morris certainly knew that his province attracted new settlers, for a 1745 census showed that New Jersey had 61,383 inhabitants, about equally split between the eastern and western sections. Forty years before, not more than 12,000 people had lived in the Jerseys.

New generations sought opportunity away from the few original towns clustered along the lower Delaware River or within the Passaic and Raritan river valleys. As these frontiersmen moved inland in the late years of the seventeenth century and beginning decades of the eighteenth, life that had been essentially geared to "town" or port living changed to an economy ever more dependent on farming. Those outward-pushing settlers founded or brought new vigor between 1710 and 1745 to such villages as Orange, Freehold, New Brunswick, Princeton, Trenton, Newton, Hackensack, Morristown, Dover, Mt. Holly, Bordentown, Westfield, Plainfield, and many others.

Growth in the hinterlands forced county realignments. People along the upper Delaware River wearied of the long trip to Burlington for county business and broke away in 1714 to found Hunterdon County with the seat of government at Trenton. Then Hunterdon residents in the Highlands chafed in turn at travel to Trenton. They left Hunterdon County in 1739 to form Morris, with the county seat at Morristown, naming both county and town for then popular Governor Lewis Morris.

Two additional areas were close to new county status. Dissidents to the south broke away from Salem County to form Cumberland in

1748, with the county seat at Bridge Town. Five years later residents in the northwest grew so disenchanted with the long trip to Morris-town for court sessions that they split off in an area comprising all of modern Sussex and Warren counties. They called their new county Sussex, with the seat at Log Gaol (now Johnsonburg). Those splits brought the total of counties to thirteen; no new counties would be formed until 1824.

Who Owns the Land?

New people always create new problems, and for Governor Morris they also aggravated the land question that had been stewing for eight decades. Who truly owned the land—the East and West New Jersey Proprietors, the Elizabethtown Associates, the Indians, or the people who worked it and improved it, squatters though they might be? Legally the Proprietors had right on their side, but the people who lived in the outward hills and plains had the power of possession.

There had to be a showdown. As early as 1735 a survey of land in Hunterdon County showed ninety-eight families occupying 13,000 acres of land without a shred of title. That survey unquestionably erred on the side of understatement, for other squatters drove off Proprietors' agents and threatened to kill them if they dared invade the area again. Exact surveys are difficult under such handicaps.

The East New Jersey Proprietors recognized that fighting dozens of individual squatters in the courts cost too much and solved nothing. Deciding to try sixty of the most substantial defendants among the Elizabethtown Associates at once, they filed a bill of particulars against them in chancery court in April, 1745. The chancellor trying the case was Governor Morris himself, a Proprietor and so patently on the side of the Proprietors that impartial justice would have been a miracle. When the Associates failed to answer the bill in chancery by August, the Proprietors began serving ejection notices.

Violence in the Province

Settlers reacted violently, particularly in the Horseneck, a swampy, forested land set in a sweeping bend of the Passaic River in western Essex County. Residents there based their land claims on a purchase from the Indians, although it is pertinent that the house in which the Indian deed allegedly was kept conveniently burned down during the dispute.

The Essex County sheriff arrested three Horseneck woodchoppers as squatters in September, 1745. Neighbors broke open the Newark jail and freed them. Four months later three ringleaders among the jail breakers were arrested, only to have a group "armed with cudgels" rescue them on the way to prison. The sheriff hurried to Newark, gathered thirty militiamen, and awaited certain trouble. It came that afternoon when 300 men strode through Newark to face the militia, warning that "if they were fired upon they would kill every man." The militia dispersed and within minutes the Horseneck crowd had released all prisoners in the Newark jail.

Outraged Proprietors sought new laws to stem the land rebellion, including a drastic statute to put troublemakers to death "without benefit of clergy." Led by some legislators outspokenly identified with the rioters, the Assembly stood firmly against action to quell the disturbances and thus encouraged further strife.

Governor Morris died on May 21, 1746, in the midst of the riots, but the influence of the seventy-five-year-old governor had ended long before. He had bogged down in fruitless dispute with the Assembly over everything, including his own salary—which the Assembly refused to pay him for his last two years in office, charging that he had performed no services of value. Ironically, Morris received the same treatment that he had helped generate against Lord Cornbury.

To Quell the Rioters

John Hamilton, Council president, became acting governor and promised to do "what's in my power, for the public good and honor and interest of the colony." He succeeded in getting the Assembly to appropriate £10,000 to help finance a British expedition against Canada, with the usual stipulation that the money be raised in paper credit. Significantly, the Assembly permitted the funds to be used only for supplies, fearing that additional troops might be turned against the squatters.

John Low of Essex County, an Assemblyman and a rioter, said: "Aye, perhaps you think I am a fool. Don't you think I see what one of the designs was, of raising these forces? Why, aye, I will tell you: when this Expedition is over, these very men will be used to quell the rioters!"

Spring of 1747 found unrest at its height. A mob broke open the Somerset County jail to free prisoners. Morris County rioters threatened to oust anyone with a Proprietary title. A Middlesex County crowd of about 150 men, armed with clubs, came into Perth Amboy in July to release John Bainbridge, Jr., awaiting trial for his part in the Somerset County disturbance. John Deare, Middlesex sheriff, wrote that the throng came into town led by "two fiddles playing." They knocked down the sheriff and gave him a "grievous wound," struck the mayor, "broke one of the Constable's head and beat several of the others" before breaking down jail doors to carry Bainbridge off "huzzaing."

The situation verged on anarchy when Harvard-educated Jonathan

Belcher arrived from Massachusetts in August, 1747, to succeed the late Lewis Morris. The new governor promised to suppress the rioters, and mentioned vaguely that he would personally lead troops against disturbers of the peace, but in October he spoke quietly to a delegation of dissenters in the belief that "soft words turn away wrath but the wringing of the nose brings forth blood."

James Alexander, a leading Proprietor, declared in 1748: "As the locusts in Hungary eat up every green thing before them, so have the rioters destroyed all timber on the lands on the East side of the Passaic River, between Newark and Elizabethtown." Belcher threatened to set up a military government with troops from New York, fearful that the New Jersey situation might win him disfavor in England.

Actually, his English superiors already had lost patience with Belcher. In July, 1749, there were threats to send over a new governor, backed by English troops, and some in London felt strongly that New Jersey and New York should be reunited. Belcher finally received "smart orders" late in 1751, telling him to appoint an impartial commission to study the causes of rebellion and ordering the Assembly to cooperate in helping to bring about "peace and tranquility."

The riots subsided. Ringleaders fled the province in fear of the King's wrath, Proprietors eased terms for their property, and some squatters even took to paying the repugnant rents. Most important, the onset of the French and Indian War made men conscious of the need to defend rather than to rebel. Belcher could turn to other problems, particularly the constant demands for a new loan office and more paper money. The pleasant loan-office income had finally run out, and New Jersey taxes had to be voted in 1752 for the first time in nearly three decades.

New Jersey Ignores a War

Forces far outside of New Jersey dominated the next decade, but throughout the French and Indian War, New Jersey leaders never abandoned their struggle for paper money. A British request in 1753 for 120 men and £500 for carrying on defense against the French in the Ohio Valley met complete rebuff; New Jersey Assemblymen pleaded that the province was too poor, particularly with the English ban on new paper money.

Adequately protected on either side by soldiers that Pennsylvania and New York sent to guard the frontiers, New Jersey could afford to use the same threats on the Crown that it had long used on it governors—unless it got its way in money matters, it could not lend help. Assemblymen bargained with the Crown through Belcher: Give us £70,000 in loan-office bills, they said, and we'll gladly support the war.

Temporarily frightened by ominous war news from the north in 1755,

New Jersey decided to raise 500 militia men for service under Colonel Peter Schuyler in upper New York. Then, after General Edward Braddock's disastrous defeat in Pennsylvania in July, 1755, marauding Indians brought the French and Indian War deep into Sussex County. Warring braves who swept down from New York in the fall of 1755 and the spring of 1756 to attack that county's people made the struggle no longer only the King's concern. It had become as well a war of the New Jersey frontier.

Belcher dispatched the provincial militia to Sussex, but Indians filtered through the county, frightening the legislature into appropriating funds for a system of stone blockhouses along the upper Delaware. Raids throughout the upper Delaware River Valley sent the area into panic, and in May, 1756, Indians murdered the Swartout family near Swartswood Lake.

The troops and blockhouses stopped the Indians. Negotiations were begun with the Indians. Once the Indian threat disappeared, New Jersey again became peevishly parsimonious. Even news that Colonel Peter Schuyler and half the New Jersey regiment had been captured at Oswego, New York, in 1757 failed to loosen the purse strings. New Jersey that year earned the doubtful distinction of being the only colony to refuse to contribute her quota of men or money to answer the King's requests. True, other colonies failed to live up to promises—and perhaps to promise, and then renege, was worse.

Paper Money and Support

Jerseymen did fight far beyond their own soil. Peter Schuyler was a native son and in the summer of 1757 most of the New Jersey regiment under Captain John Parker was captured on a waterborne scouting expedition on Lake George. Governor Belcher proposed dispatching large bodies of militia up the Hudson, but he collapsed and died in Princeton a month later while attending commencement at the College of New Jersey. John Reading succeeded him as acting governor, the Assembly pushed through two paper-money bills totaling £80,000, and thereafter supported the "King's war" with considerably better grace.

The New Jersey regiment was strengthened to 1000 men, each paid a twelve-pound bounty to avoid the necessity of drafting. Thanks to its newly won paper affluence, the Assembly generously outfitted the regiment handsomely in blue uniform coats faced with red, buckskin breeches and gray stockings. Each brightly dressed soldier among these Jersey Blues also received a scanty pay allowance and a monthly "dollar for drinks to His Majesty's health." With paper money in the till, New Jersey was not stingy.

A threat to house 600 English soldiers in private homes in Newark,

Perth Amboy, and Elizabethtown in late 1757 spurred quick Assembly action to build barracks. Generosity played no part—those troops were "ailing with scorbutick complaints" and prompted a rash of protesting petitions to the Assembly. Funds were voted to build barracks in Elizabethtown, New Brunswick, Perth Amboy, Burlington, and Trenton at a cost of £1400 each. Troops moved into Trenton barracks late in 1758, and all five were completed by 1759, at costs two to three times the original estimates. The Trenton barracks, fully restored, still stands, but all others are mere memories.

Francis Bernard, probably the best New Jersey governor since Robert Hunter, arrived from England in the spring of 1758 to succeed the late Governor Belcher. He found the colony badly frightened by renewed Indian sorties in Sussex County, brought on by the Assembly's characteristic but untimely piece of frugality in cutting funds for border guards. Bernard worked energetically and concluded a noteworthy peace treaty with the Indians at Easton in August, 1758. Three months later he helped establish the country's first Indian reservation at Brotherton (Indian Mills) in Burlington County.

Within seven months the frontier guards could be sent home from Sussex and a new township, Montague, was set up in "a country that a year ago no one would venture to live in." Thanks poured in on Governor Bernard for his aid to the frontier.

Thanks bought no necessities of life, however; Governor Bernard asked for a transfer out of New Jersey in 1759 unless his salary could be boosted—and paid directly by the Crown rather than doled out by a New Jersey Assembly which still used the power to withhold salaries as the meanest kind of weapon. Bernard declared that his struggles to care for a growing family forced him to ask a transfer. "Until Nature sets bounds on the number of my children, which is not done yet, I know not how to limit my wants or desires," he wrote as he left to become governor of Massachusetts.

ENGLAND TURNS FIRM: AN ERA ENDS

Nearly six decades of Assembly power, interspersed with an occasional strong governor or at least a governor capable of compromise, neared its end. Undistinguished Thomas Boone succeeded Bernard in 1760, and he in turn gave way to Josiah Hardy in 1761. Hardy served well for a year, then made a supreme mistake: he appointed a judge to serve "during good behavior" instead of "during the King's pleasure." True, judges had been appointed "during good behavior" in England since 1688, but the Crown decided that particular bit of English law was not valid in royal colonies.

Lewis Morris had appointed his son, Robert Hunter Morris, Chief

Justice of New Jersey "during good behavior" and had not been questioned. Governor Belcher had appointed a judge to the supreme court on similar terms without trouble. The chief difference now lay in the fact that King George III had come to the throne: a new philosophy of government pervaded Great Britain. The King heeded advice that England must govern its colonies with a stern hand.

There were many reasons. The French and Indian War had drained the treasury; England's national debt had doubled and expenses of government had tripled. Restlessness and stubbornness in all colonies, including such things as the New Jersey land riots and the New Jersey Assembly's brazen use of money bills to get its way, disturbed the Crown deeply. England believed, probably correctly, that the colonies could well afford to pay taxes to help support their government. The good old days of "no taxes" must come to an end.

One tragic victim of the new policy was William Franklin, thirty-three-year-old son of Benjamin Franklin. Young, respected, intelligent, and sympathetic to both American and British problems, William Franklin might well have become one of America's greatest men after he became governor of New Jersey in 1763. But by the time the younger Franklin arrived to take office, the tide of British influence in the New World had begun to ebb swiftly; it would be Franklin's tragic duty to oversee a shipwreck—not to herald the happy voyage of a respected ship of state piloted by King George.

6

Portrait of 100 Years

New Jersey neared its 100th birthday as an English colony when Governor William Franklin was about to assume office. Samuel Smith of Burlington, scion of a distinguished West New Jersey family, became the unofficial one-man celebrant of the centennial by publishing his monumental *History of the Colony of Nova Caesaria or New Jersey*. Although this first genuine record of the province did not appear until late in 1765, the timing and the preface unmistakably indicated that the 100th anniversary prompted the book.

Smith fretted some because New Jersey merited scant attention, but he also recognized a reason; in his preface, he wrote: "That a century should pass, and very little appear abroad of what the settlers here have been doing, is not so much to be wondered at, when their difficulties in procuring the conveniences of living are considered." Unfortunately, he wrote, the records of New Jersey "were as much secrets to most of the inhabitants, as they commonly are to strangers."

Smith recognized above all, that the East-West complex already had become firmly fixed on New Jersey. He noted: "As the province has very little foreign trade on bottoms of its own, the produce of all kinds for sale, goes chiefly to New York and Philadelphia; much of it is there purchased for markets abroad, but some consumed among themselves. The inhabitants as to dress and manners, form themselves much after the neighbouring provinces; the western, about as far as the tide flows up the Delaware, those of Pennsylvania; the remainder, those of New York."

The eighteenth-century historian saw his province to be in good shape: "Harmony reigns in a considerable degree, in all branches of the legislature; the publick business is consequently dispatched with ease, and at small expense." The thirteen counties were thriving (except Sussex, "the frontier county and but lately settled"). There weren't many strangers arriving from Europe, but "the natural increase must be far greater."

Jerseymen made their livings as best they could. Smith told of settlers along the upper Delaware who brought wheat down the hazardous river on rafts or flatboats, the latter often carrying as much as 500 to 600 bushels of grain. Perth Amboy had a port "as good as most on the continent," but shippers found "no great success." Burlington, the alternate capital, enjoyed considerably more trade, mainly because of local exchange with Philadelphia.

Essex County, home of Newark and Elizabeth, raised considerable amounts of farm products, "but their plantations are too high in value to be generally large." Bergen County, "opposite and adjacent to New York," had substantial opportunity for "advantageous intercourse with that market." The Raritan Valley in Somerset and Middlesex counties raised wheat in "large quantities; they send their flour down Raritan River, to New York." Salem, Gloucester, and Cumberland counties even that early knew the blessings of agriculture, and Hunterdon's lush soil supplied flour for New York and Philadelphia. Morris County, "for a lately settled county, is populous."

New Jersey Becomes "Typically American"

Smith stressed the strong Dutch influences lingering in Bergen, Somerset, and Middlesex counties. Bergen's inhabitants, "being the descendants of the low Dutch or Hollanders that originally settled therein under the Dutch title, preserve the religion of their ancestors, and worship after the manner of the reformed churches in the united provinces. . . . Their language, in general, bears the Dutch accent, nor have they forgot the customs of Holland."

Old traditions did linger, but broad social changes had swept—and were sweeping—across the land. More than anything else, New Jersey had become a genuine meeting ground, for people on the New York–Philadelphia pathway inevitably learned of every new thought, every new fad, every serious movement. True, the carriers of ideas passed through, but not so rapidly in those days as in this, and the people who live beside a pathway always are influenced by those who travel it.

Wheaton J. Lane, author of the classic study of the state's early transportation, *From Indian Trail to Iron Horse*, summed up the pathway role in this fashion:

> New Jersey enjoyed a greater amount of intercolonial travel than any other part of America. The result was a wider tolerance and a greater interest in affairs beyond the immediate locality. Travellers commented upon the good-natured liberality of the native Jerseyman. Gradually the Puritanism of the northern towns broke down and the general cultures of East and West New Jersey became more and more alike. In the colonial period as well as later, New Jersey was literally a melting pot in which fused a culture more typically American than that of New England or the South.

THE WEARISOME WAY OF TRAVEL

Fundamental in travel, of course, were the roads. New Jersey's colonial roads, because of the amount of traffic upon them, were perforce better than those of other provinces, but they are best described as wretched. By 1760 the routes still followed the leisurely trails of the Indians or meandered around the edges of large farms. When important property owners protested a road infringing on their property, surveyors obligingly ran the right of way around the edges of fields.

Road maintenance always bordered on chaos. A 1716 law authorized local overseers to "call out" inhabitants to keep roads in repair and anyone summoned who did not appear, shovel in hand—or send a substitute—had to pay a daily fine of four shillings, six pence. With modifications made in 1760, the practice of repairing roads "by labor" rather than "by taxes" persisted for another half century.

Peter Kalm, Swedish botanist who toured New Jersey and other colonies between 1748 and 1751, took a dim view of travel between Philadelphia and New York:

The roads are good or bad according to the difference of the ground. In a sandy soil the roads are dry and good; but in a clayey one they are bad. The people here are likewise very careless in mending them. If a rivulet be not very great, they do not make a bridge over it; and travellers may do as well as they can to get over. Therefore many people are in danger of being drowned in such places, where the water is risen by a heavy rain.

Mud made travel a nightmare in spring, and summer sun baked hard ruts into the roads. Stones or logs were dumped in low spots but generally the traveler made out as best he could; both overseers and "labor" cared little about convenience for itinerants. Veteran travelers preferred to cross New Jersey in the winter months, when hard-frozen surfaces permitted sleighs to glide smoothly and when ice afforded easy crossings of rivers.

Those desiring to move rapidly in and out of New Jersey (and there were many, even in the eighteenth century) recognized that poor roads were matched by vague ferry schedules. Winds and tides constantly slowed boats on the Delaware and Hudson rivers. Just as delaying were ferry operators. They usually also kept the tavern at the ferry stop and thus saw no reason to hurry passengers on their way.

For the first sixty years of the eighteenth century a trip across New Jersey required a ferry ride from Philadelphia to either Bordentown or Burlington, followed by a jolting stage wagon ride to the Amboys, and then another long and uncertain ferry trip to New York by way of the Arthur Kill. In 1764 a new road across the New Jersey meadows linked Elizabethtown and Paulus Hook (Jersey City) to provide an all-land route from Burlington County to a point opposite New York. That at least shortened time on the water.

HANNAH CALLENDAR ON THE ROAD

Rival stage lines boasted of quick service and smooth rides. However, the testimony of riders was closer to the truth than the blandishments of advertisements. Consider the experiences of Hannah Callendar, a young Quaker miss who crossed New Jersey in 1759 on the Burlington–Amboy stage. Hannah and a girl companion stayed the first night in Burlington. But let Miss Callendar continue:

> We rose 2d day morning at 4 o'clock, dressed ourselves by moonlight, breakfasted and set out in the stage wagon for Shaw's. Our more particular company comprised Richard Smith, Senior, and James James, some sailors shipwrecked in the *King of Prussia*, a humorous old Dutchman, and an officer of the Jersey Blues. One of the sailors by last night's debauch and early rising, became the jest of brother tars, saying it was a rough sea and made the passengers sick. . . .
>
> By seven o'clock we arrived at Crosswicks, where we breakfasted at Douglas's. Passed through Allentown. Took another passenger in, Dr. Noel. Dined in Cranberry at Prigmore's. Here we fell in company with other stages, those from Bordentown. Took the wagon that goes from here to Amboy Ferry. Diversity of objects and company filled our minds with abundance of ideas. Saw the wrecks of two stages occasioned by [intoxicated] drivers and passengers. Crossed the head of the famous South River, whose navigation benefits New York with wood.
>
> We arrived at Amboy Ferry by six o'clock, little fatigued considering the length of the journey—fifty miles. The house was full of people, being the place for both stages. Notwithstanding the drinking and roaring appeared strange to us, it did not keep us awake all night.
>
> At five o'clock the people began to stir about the house, which aroused us and we went and sat at the door. At nine o'clock we took our boat. Our humorous passengers, the sailors, had intelligence of a Man of War, the *Nightingale*, being in want of hands and pressing. One o'clock they went ashore at Amboy, and brought some ham and cold veal aboard and very civally offered us part! We then set out and went between the islands: the shores are prettily diversified with country seats and cultivated lands. We saw the post road to York. It is a very pretty sail and the porpoises tumbling along add to it. The sailors landed first on Staten Island. We hoped they would have stayed there, but they all came aboard again, rolling stones in for ammunition, declaring it should be warm work if the press-gang did take them. This raised Anna's and my fears, but the men were so comical that I told them I believed it took a great deal to break a sailor's heart. Very true miss (one replied) a merry life and a short one is their maxim.
>
> We landed on Whitehall stairs about six o'clock.

OUT OF THE ORDINARY

Important to Hannah, the gay sailors, the humorous Dutchman, and to all other travelers were the momentary friendships they formed—and fundamental to such good fellowship was the roadside tavern. Every village had its colorfully named tavern or inn: The Rose and Crown, Wheat Sheaf, and Unicorn in Elizabeth; the Half Way Home in Bergen, the Black Horse in Perth Amboy, the White Hart and Red Lion in New Brunswick, the Sign of the College in Princeton, the Sign of the Green Tree and the Royal Oak at Trenton, the American House in Haddonfield, the Death of the Fox in Woodbury, the Bull's Head in Bound Brook, and the Sign of the Seven Stars in Repaupo.

Taverns or inns (also called "houses" and "ordinaries") were an absolute necessity; a 1668 law ordered every New Jersey town to provide an ordinary for the relief and entertainment of strangers. Taverns sprang up everywhere and often served as much to keep the local populace amused and informed as to entertain those passing through. In pre-Revolutionary War days, and for long years after, the local ordinary represented the political, legal, and social center of a community, where major affairs took place, where revolution was fomented, and where news and gossip were exchanged. The ordinary was town hall, theater, newspaper office, lodge hall, and overnight stop, all under one roof.

Inevitably, as whenever or wherever spirits are on tap, excesses prompted action. A 1704 New Jersey law gave four hours in the stocks for drunkenness, and forbade anyone to "tipple and drink on the Lord's Day," a stricture considerably modified by the clause: "excepting for necessary refreshments." The 1739 legislature issued warnings that taverns were for "accommodating strangers, travelers and other persons . . . and not for the encouragement of gaming, tippling, drunkenness and other vices so much of late practiced at such places."

Townspeople looked up to the tavern keeper. He distributed mail, held sheriff's sales, often acted as judge in local trials, and served as host for community gatherings. His place was the center of possible excitement and intrigue. Visitors livened dull lives; a stranger in the tavern usually couldn't order a meal until he gave details of himself and his purposes. It wasn't a matter of discourtesy: it was a hunger for something new, for the biggest thing that could happen was a new face in town. If he happened to wear an eye patch or strange clothes, so much the better for setting tongues to wagging. Woe betide the shy.

Visitors and townspeople all gathered in a main assembly room in front of the fireplace. Here drinks were dispensed in variety (one 1758 list for a New Jersey inn included fifty beverages), food was served and guests raised voices in roaring song or heated argument. Sleeping rooms were above the taproom and guests slept two or more to a bed, first come, first served. When the innkeeper ran out of beds, latecomers slept on the public-room floor—after others retired or went home.

A TIME OF GREAT AWAKENING

Life had to be gay in the taverns, if anywhere. Colonial New Jerseyans found little warmth and gaiety in their daily doings. Life in the fields was hard and tedious. Homes were cold and drafty, even under the best conditions. Churches offered small cheer, either in the physical facilities or in the nature of the sermons. The times allowed for not much joy, particularly among the poorer classes (and the poorer classes included nearly everyone).

Church meant much to colonists at midpoint in the eighteenth century, for a time of religious explosion had shaken ministers and worshipers alike. The period has been called the Great Awakening, although it might better be called the Great Religious Revolution. Amid the feverish attention to religion and to revivals, a spirit of defiance of old ways could be detected.

Despite the traditional power of religion, church attendance definitely had waned in all of America by 1700. William Warren Sweet declared in his *Religion in Colonial America* that most early settlers came to America to better their economic conditions, not because of religious spirit. Sweet said that "church membership was an exceedingly selective matter."

The so-called Great Awakening, a stirring spirit of religious revivalism tinged with a bold defiance of established church order, stirred the New World to its foundations, and no name was more important than that of the Reverend Theodore J. Frelinghuysen of New Jersey's Raritan Valley, called by Sweet "the first outstanding revivalist" in the Middle Colonies. Mr. Frelinghuysen came from Germany in 1720 to serve four congregations in the Raritan Valley between present-day Somerville and New Brunswick. The young minister held a powerful belief that people ought to feel deeply about their religion. Church, he argued, ought to be far more than regular sitting in a pew.

Mr. Frelinghuysen found most of his Dutch Church members unwilling to accept new ideas; their principal aim was to preserve the Dutch Church as a symbol of their Dutch nationality. They cared not a bit for an emotion-stirring religion, but Domine Frelinghuysen continued to preach fervently in the face of strong warnings that his sermons ran counter to tradition. He urged a personal searching of the soul beyond mere church membership. Sweet commented:

> The well-to-do, the kind who generally hold the principal offices in churches, were scandalized; the poorer people and the younger generation were inclined to support their young and enthusiastic Domine.

Making no effort to hide his sentiments, Frelinghuysen printed on the back of his sleigh, in Dutch, this message:

> Niemends tong, nog niemends pen,
> Maakt my amders dankik ben;
> Spreek, quaad-spreekers, spreek vonder end,
> Niemands en word van u. geschend.

Translated, that said for all to see:

> No one's tongue, nor no one's pen,
> Makes me other than I am;
> Speak, evil-speakers, speak without end,
> No one heeds a word you pretend.

Frelinghuysen's impassioned ministry affected every Dutch Reformed church in the colonies, and echoes of his philosophy reverberated in other Protestant churches. Superiors pronounced Frelinghuysen's doctrines heretical but the young minister persisted in his fiery calls for an understandable faith. His preaching attracted large numbers of new people to the church, and eventually Domine Frelinghuysen's theology won support from most Dutch ministers in America.

PRESBYTERIANS JOIN IN PROTEST

Rebellion also shook the Presbyterian Church in the Middle Colonies, fomented by the evangelical teachings of Reverend Gilbert Tennent in Neshaminy, Pennsylvania. Tennent's foes derisively called Tennent's school the "Log College" (and it *was* a log building), but graduates influenced Presbyterians in all the colonies. The strength of the Log College crowd was impressive in New Jersey. There Gilbert Tennent's four minister sons centered their evangelical war between New Brunswick and Freehold.

Presbyterian ministers who had been trained in Scottish universities protested vigorously when the brash, young Log College generation formed new Presbyteries to permit the licensing and ordaining of men who held the new evangelical beliefs. The older ministers countered by insisting that all candidates for the Presbyterian ministry must hold diplomas from either New England or European colleges.

The Great Awakening reached its apex when the Reverend George Whitefield toured the colonies in the early 1740s. The most powerful evangelist of his time, and one of the greatest in all history, Whitefield preached often in New Jersey. He pursued a wearing itinerary, moving as rapidly as possible into such scattered New Jersey locations as Greenwich, Amwell, Gloucester, Salem, New Brunswick, Newark, and a variety of other towns and crossroads villages.

Tremendous crowds gathered to hear Whitefield. The *American*

Weekly Mercury for May 1, 1740, said that 7000 people gathered at New Brunswick. To judge better the enormity of that crowd, remember that there were only about 60,000 people in New Jersey. Based on present New Jersey population, a comparable throng would number 800,000 people. Whitefield himself wrote in his diary of that May Sunday at New Brunswick:

> Preached morning and evening to near 7 or 8,000 people: and God's Power was so much amongst us in the Afternoon sermon that had I proceeded, the Cries and Groans of the Congregation, I believe, would have drowned out my Voice. One woman was struck down, and a general cry went through the assembly. We collected both times 20 Pounds Sterling for my Orphans [in Georgia].

Two Colleges but Little Education

Out of the evangelical preachings came two major New Jersey colleges, both established to provide American-trained ministers. These were the College of New Jersey, founded in 1746 at Elizabethtown by followers of the Log College ministry, and Queens College, chartered at New Brunswick in 1766 as a direct outgrowth of the Reverend Theodore Frelinghuysen's urgent preachings to Dutch Church congregations in the Raritan Valley.

New Jersey had the distinction of being the only colony with two colleges founded before the Revolution. The College of New Jersey moved to Newark in 1747 and then built Nassau Hall in Princeton and transferred the college there in 1756. Of the first six College of New Jersey graduates in 1748, five became Presbyterian ministers; the sixth, lawyer Richard Stockton, was a New Jersey signer of the Declaration of Independence. The College of New Jersey has become Princeton University, of course, and Queen's College, after a long series of early trials, has become Rutgers, The State University.

Zeal for higher education centered on religious training, for other education in the middle of the eighteenth century was generally considered unnecessary. The colony had no public schools, although Quakers in West New Jersey made attempts to provide at least a rudimentary education for all children. Private academies for the small wealthy class provided fundamental training despite irregular schedules and poorly trained schoolmasters, who, often as not, were carefree wanderers stopping between journeys or between bouts with alcohol. The emphasis was on learning a trade. Except for young Quakers, girls seldom went to school, lest education hinder them in performing their duties as wives and mothers. The scarcity of letters by colonial women can be traced to this lack of education.

Near-illiteracy was the rule in most of New Jersey—and in most of the colonies, as far as that is concerned, for those were times of a simple agricultural economy. People worked hard, lived hard, and went to church when they could. Still, in the intellectual darkness of those days, shafts of light appeared. Several towns started public libraries; Burlington opened New Jersey's first public library in 1757; and by 1765, Samuel Smith noted that libraries of some sort also had been started in New Brunswick, Newark, Elizabethtown, Trenton, Mt. Holly, and Haddonfield.

SMALLPOX, IGNORANCE, AND HOPE

All people, rich or poor alike, necessarily faced their futures with fear and uncertainty, for their far from merry lives were also short. Smallpox epidemics swept the colony repeatedly; even inoculations for smallpox after 1745 failed to help much. Mothers and children died young; often either or both died in childbirth. Disease struck hard and often. Death constantly stalked the village streets.

By mid-eighteenth century, New Jersey had far more quacks than doctors, and even doctors fought disease with ignorance compounded with old wives' remedies. Some used as their guiding light *Salmon's Herbal,* a 1300-page book devoted to herbs and potions. Truly, not many used it, for it cost fifty pounds, English money. Much cheaper (and probably as effective) "cures" included bloodletting, vomiting, purging, and such niceties as "cupping a patient on the feet." If none of these things cured patients, they at least gave victims the feeling that they weren't being ignored.

Most doctors earnestly hoped to better their profession. Since many of them were ministers as well as physicians, there had to be a moral uneasiness about obviously worthless medicines and potions. During the French and Indian War, information-starved American doctors eagerly talked with learned physicians who came from England to treat wounded British soldiers. The growing need for knowledge led sixteen doctors to organize the first medical society in America, the New Jersey Medical Society, in July, 1766, in New Brunswick. The society leaned a bit to stuffiness: when Dr. William Burnet of Newark lectured on "The Use of the Lancet in Pleurisy" in the first year, he delivered his entire speech in Latin. But they swore to be "diligent, faithful, honest" and vowed that they "will not keep secret any nostrum or specific medicine of any kind." They agreed as well to "assist gratis the distressed poor."

ALL THE NEWS AND NO PRINTERS

Jerseymen who suffered from a lack of knowledge in all things, whether it was news of themselves or of new trends in scientific and medical thought, could partially blame Queen Anne. In 1702 she had decreed that no one in New Jersey could "keep a press for printing" and expressly warned that "great inconveniences may arise by the liberty of printing in our said province." New Jersey's first printer began work—with royal permission—in Burlington in 1723, when the temporary need arose to print provincial laws and paper money. The province didn't get a permanent printer until James Parker established a press at Woodbridge in 1751; seven years later he started New Jersey's first periodical, *The New American Magazine. The New American* lasted two years, but the last issue in March, 1760, contained the lament, often repeated in colonial days and later, that the magazine had failed because of a "deficiency in the number of subscribers."

News sifted through New Jersey by way of outside publications until the Revolution. The *Archives of the State of New Jersey*, published by the New Jersey Historical Society, show how out-of-state editors in New York, Philadelphia, and Boston regarded New Jersey. Initially, most of the news concerned shipping, for Perth Amboy, Burlington, Salem, and Cape May still hoped to rival Boston and New York as seaport towns. Piracy was mentioned at times and Indians were referred to in slighting terms. But, as William Nelson, editor of the *Archives*, said, understating the case slightly: ". . . the dusky natives had no newspaper to represent their point of view." Attention soon shifted mainly to runaway slaves and indentured servants; Editor Nelson had this to say about slave advertisements:

> The curious garbs worn by the runaways—relics of finery indicating often their former gentle condition, or the sterner stuff wherewith the common people were clad; the references to branding, showing the prevalence of that barbarous custom as a punishment for crime; the peculiar descriptions of some of the servants—the "Leering down Look," "proud hambling Gate," "walks Crimplin," "he is so prodigious a Lyar that if observed he may easily be discovered by it," "with a long Nose and a wild Look," "goes crooked and groans very much in his sleep," "speaks by clusters," "talks West Country," etc.—all throw a flood of light on the conditions of the toiling masses.

Property—or a Moral Concern?

Negro slavery was common in New Jersey in the colonial period, despite increasing Quaker opposition. New Jersey in 1737 had 3981 slaves in a population of 47,402—one slave for every twelve people. Bergen County's Dutch farmers particularly used Negro labor, although slaves were common elsewhere. Nearly every house in Perth Amboy "swarmed with black slaves" in 1758, for example; and when President Samuel Finley of the College of New Jersey died in 1766, his estate included "two negro women, a negro man and three negro children," all offered for sale.

Most slaves were considered well treated, by the eighteenth-century standards of their masters, for slaves were an economic asset. Among Dutch farmers, slaves were "generally treated as members of the family, living under the same roof . . . even sitting down at the same table." When a slave misbehaved—with standards of behavior being entirely a judgment or a whim of the owner—vicious treatment was his lot. Burning at the stake was often the punishment; at Perth Amboy a Negro charged with murder was burned alive in 1729, and in 1738 another slave charged with murder was burned at the stake at Ricky Hill. Swarms of spectators, for all the religious fervor that might have stirred them on Sundays, attended the burnings in carnival spirit and applauded the agonies of the condemned.

A few voices began to be heard on such blatant evils. In all America, no antislavery voice was more persistent than that of the Reverend John Woolman of Mt. Holly. When twenty-three years old in 1743, Woolman firmly told an employer who asked him to sign a bill of sale for a slave: "I believe slave-keeping to be a practice inconsistent with the Christian religion."

Woolman journeyed far, through New England and the South as well as through New Jersey, and everything that he saw strengthened his conviction that slavery must be abolished. In 1754 he published "Some Considerations in the Keeping of Negroes," in which he contended the slave holding violated all precepts of the Bible. Largely as a result of that, the Philadelphia Yearly Meeting moved to "induce Friends who held slaves to set them at liberty." Woolman was not given to voicing convictions only among those who agreed with him. He paid personal visits to slaveholders to tell of his opinions, and on rare occasions he won them to his view. When he died of smallpox in England in 1773, the first seeds of abolition had begun to sprout, although Quakers long were the only major religious group to find slavery inconsistent with their principles.

Not All People Went West

If New Jersey had paused to observe its centenary in 1764, provincial fathers would have been hard pressed to inform the widespread populace. Despite the absence of a newspaper, the miserable communications and the poor transportation, the province was attracting new residents: not everyone on the high road was going elsewhere. Samuel Smith unofficially counted some 100,000 people living within New Jersey in 1765, as nearly as he could guess, a rise of about 40,000 in twenty years.

By 1764, some sixty towns and villages were called by name, and another thirty-five or more straggling hamlets were known by the name of the tavern or the prominent citizen in their midst. Settlers lived in far-off Wallpack, beyond the Kittatinny Mountains; and squatters were scattered along the barren seacoast. Ironworkers and glassmakers struggled for success in the forests. To the north, long and trying negotiations with New York to establish a common border were nearing an end; in 1769 the provinces of New York and New Jersey established the present boundary line, well south of the line that New Jersey claimed—thus relieving, or perhaps robbing New Jersey of thousands of acres of territory. Stability had come, to the border.

Most eighteenth-century travelers who saw New Jersey liked what they saw. Peter Kalm, the visiting Swedish botanist, was surprised by the fine farms and by the thick population in the central part of the province. He offered a good reason for that expanding population:

> It does not seem difficult to find out why the people multiply here more than in Europe. As soon as a person is old enough, he may marry in these provinces, without any fear of poverty; for there is such a tract of good ground yet uncultivated, that a new-married man can, without difficulty, get a spot of ground, where he may sufficiently subsist with his wife and children. The taxes are very low, and he need not be under any concern of their account. The liberties he enjoys are so great that he considers himself as a prince in his possessions.

Kalm marveled at the richness of the earth. At one point he commented on New Jersey corn, "usually eight feet high, more or less." Elsewhere in the province he was amazed at peaches, which were rare in Sweden, where "hardly any people besides the rich can eat them." Here, "every countryman had an orchard full of peach trees which were covered with such quantities of fruit that we could scarcely walk in the orchard without treading upon the peaches that had fallen off."

HANDSOME WOMEN AND GOOD SPIRITS

Kalm's views of the good things of life were echoed. Andrew Burnaby, a young graduate of Queen's College in Cambridge, England, passed through New Jersey in July, 1759, and committed enthusiastic praise to his diary. Princeton he admired for its "handsome school and college for the education of dissenters." New Brunswick charmed him much; "at this place and Philadelphia were the handsomest women that I saw in America." The Raritan Valley near New Brunswick was "exceedingly rich and beautiful, and the banks of the river covered with gentlemen's houses." Newark, "built in an irregular scattered manner, after the fashion of some of our villages in England," won his approval and he especially liked the church, "erected in the Gothic taste with a spire, the first I had seen in America." (That probably was Trinity Church, although he did not name it.) He found an eighteen-mile trip to see the

Passaic Falls rewarding; they were "very extraordinary, different from any I had hitherto met in America."

Perhaps most important, Burnaby found Jerseymen tolerant and eager to please: "The New Jersey men as to character are like most country gentlemen; good-natured, hospitable, and of a more liberal turn than their neighbors, the Pennsylvanians. They live altogether upon their estates, and are literally gentlemen farmers."

Naturally, Mr. Brunaby suffered from the fault that nearly always betides a traveler: he saw only the best. There was still widespread poverty amid the plenty; not all people were gentlemen farmers by any means, nor did all of them eat peaches. Beauty soon faded in the coarse, ravaging marks of smallpox or in repeated childbirths. Most people still lived in meager, drafty homes, with dirt floors and no heat except for fireplaces. They struggled against ignorance of all kinds, in religion, reading, sickness, and agricultural practices. They were beset with a variety of prejudices and masses of misinformation.

That, after all, *was* America in colonial days. However, a mood of indulgence pervaded the state as the 1760s moved along, for political battles over nearly a century had established certain basic rights and privileges for most people. The financial condition of the province was good. All of this high feeling, then, would benefit Governor William Franklin, about to become New Jersey's last—and probably the best—royal governor.

7

Slow Strides to Independence

Perth Amboy came briskly alive on the morning of February 25, 1763, for on that day eagerly awaited Governor William Franklin and his young bride were coming to town. Early in the morning, the Middlesex Troop of Horse jogged off along the road to New Brunswick, where the governor and his lady had spent the night before. Snow lay on the land and ice clogged the rivers, but Perth Amboy exuded a warmth of spirit; when the Franklins arrived, "a numerous concourse of people" waited to hear him take the oath.

New Jersey liked what it had heard about this new young governor. The fact that his father was Benjamin Franklin gave him a good start, but by 1763 the thirty-three-year-old Philadelphia-born and Philadelphia-educated William Franklin could stand on his own achievements as a lawyer.

Tall, handsome, and athletic, the new governor also had the wit to speak briefly. When Perth Amboy's city fathers welcomed him on February 25, Franklin responded by saying, in full:

"I thank you for you kind congratulations. The esteem which you so gratefully and justly express for my predecessor is no less agreeable to me. And wherever I may reside, which is as yet uncertain, I shall be glad of every opportunity of showing my regard for the City of Perth Amboy."

Thus, brightly, began the thirteen years that Governor Franklin would spend in New Jersey. He felt strong loyalty to England and recognized that most American colonists shared that. Yet he understood the temperament and yearnings of an emerging America. More than any other colonial governor, Franklin combined patience, wisdom, and tact to keep his subjects within reach of the King and Parliament.

BRITAIN TURNS FIRM

Despite his personal charm and ability, Franklin soon faced difficulties. New Jersey and her sister colonies had begun to flounder by the fall of 1763 in the deepening depression brought on by the French and Indian War. England's plight was worse than that of her colonies, however; her national debt had doubled and annual expenses had tripled because of the war. She desperately needed more income.

George Grenville, head of King George's ministry, decided that the American colonies must share the burdens of their mother country. He announced in October, 1763, that no colonization could take place beyond the Allegheny Mountains, an order that only someone completely ignorant of the vastness of America could think possible of enforcement. To back his edict, Grenville proposed quartering 10,000 soldiers in America—a show of strength intended to subdue the Indians, impress the newly conquered Canadians, and keep restless Americans within bounds.

To pay for the troops, Parliament passed the Sugar Act in 1764. At first glance it seemed somewhat magnanimous, for it cut the duty on molasses in half and reduced other items. The generosity cloaked the strength of the law: for the first time, it would be *strictly enforced*. Friendly colonial courts, always lenient to a bit of smuggling, would no longer try violators; instead they would be judged by British admiralty courts.

More seriously, Great Britain prohibited all trade between American colonies and the French West Indies, a principal market for New Jersey products. Unlike the South, which could exchange tobacco or rice for British goods, the Middle Atlantic and New England colonies depended heavily on West Indies molasses and money to keep a balance in the three-cornered trade among the Indies, the northern colonies, and England.

PAPER MONEY AND STAMPS

By forbidding the issuance of more paper money, Parliament in 1764 also struck directly at New Jersey and all other colonies which had long depended on printing new paper currency to correct economic woes. New Jersey, whose provincial debt of nearly £300,000 topped that of all colonies, teetered on the edge of fiscal ruin. Without new paper money (and perhaps with it) New Jersey faced deflation and widespread depression.

Hard times hit farmer and city dweller alike; New York and Philadelphia papers carried advertisements of New Jersey farms for sale and debtors seeking relief. In the midst of this, Parliament announced that effective November 1, 1765, colonists must pay stamp taxes on legal documents, printed matter, licenses, playing cards, and even university degrees.

Cortland Skinner of Perth Amboy (who would become an active Tory when war broke out and was therefore no burning radical) reflected a conservative view in October, 1765:

"Everything here is in the greatest confusion, and the first of November is dreaded."

The Stamp Act placed Jerseymen in double jeopardy. Tax levies of any kind were bad enough, but more dangerous to New Jersey liberty was the stipulation that moneys realized from stamps sales would be used to pay governmental and military expenses—including the governor's salary. For years the New Jersey Assembly had kept recalcitrant governors in line, as described, by threatening to stop their earnings. The Stamp Act levies would rob the legislators of that major bargaining strength.

JERSEYMEN REFUSE TO BE STAMPED

Governor Franklin appointed William Coxe of Burlington as Stamp Officer but when Coxe sought to rent a house for his office, he was refused, unless he would insure the house "from being pulled down or burned."

James Parker, the Woodbridge printer, fanned the spreading anti-stamp fire by publishing a short-lived *Constitutional Courant* on September 21, 1765. The *Courant,* called "the most remarkable of the inflammatory papers" aimed at the Stamp Act, proved to be a one-day wonder. Parker took the paper to New York for sale on the streets, and although the *Courant* declared itself to be "No Wise Repugnant to Loyalty," outraged agents of the King suppressed the publication because of its outspoken denunciations of Parliament.

Donald L. Kemmerer points out in his *Path to Freedom* that England "carelessly selected the tenderest portions of the American goose's anatomy from which to pluck, for the stamp tax was felt most by lawyers and the thirty-odd newspapers—two of the most vocal groups of the community."

New Jersey had no newspaper, but as September faded, the colony's lawyers met in Perth Amboy to debate the Stamp Act. They refused to disobey it; such action went against their legal grain. They simply resolved not to conduct any business requiring stamps, preferring that their private interest be a secondary matter. That legal resistance and loss of income, unspectacular though they have come to seem in contrast with the impassioned speeches and flaming torches of Massachusetts and Virginia, took fortitude. Such passive opposition set a pattern soon followed by legal minds in most of the colonies.

STAMP ACT CONGRESS

Out of Massachusetts came much more radical action, the kind most cited in history. The New Englanders asked all colonies to send delegates to a protesting Stamp Act Congress in New York on October 7. New Jersey Assembly Speaker Robert Ogden hesitated, believing that colonial protests might carry more weight if not forwarded too quickly. Such dalliance aroused Richard Stockton of Princeton. He asserted that if New Jersey failed to attend, "We shall not only look like a speckled bird among our sister colonies, but shall say implicitly that we think it no oppression." Twelve members of the Assembly finally met with Ogden at Sproul's Tavern in Perth Amboy with authority to choose three delegates.

Ogden, Hendrick Fisher of Somerset County, and Joseph Borden of Burlington attended the Congress. Ogden was only one of two delegates (the other being from Massachusetts) who disapproved the Congress's "declaration of the rights and grievances of the colonists" and the writing of protesting petitions to King George. Ogden preferred protests forwarded by individual colonial Assemblies and he faced a wrath that forced him to resign his Assembly seat because of the dissatisfaction of his Essex County constituents.

Written protests to offend the King were one thing, but New York merchants found a more effective way to fight. They suspended imports of all English manufactures in October, knowing that British merchants would bring pressures on Parliament stronger than any American group. Philadelphia and Boston merchants adopted similar nonimportation restrictions, but New Jersey merchants did not need to take united action, since most of New Jersey's commerce was via New York or Philadelphia.

WOE TO STAMP HANDLERS

No stamps were in New Jersey by the November 1 deadline, and when Governor Franklin's Council asked William Coxe, the Stamp Officer, the reason, Coxe frankly said that bringing in the stamps "would occasion disorders and bloodshed." Besides, added the realistic Coxe, "I should be injured both in person and estate." Franklin's advisers suggested leaving the stamps aboard the ship *Sardoine*, which had brought them to America.

The Sons of Liberty, a loosely organized but growing band of radical rebels, visited Mr. Coxe in December, 1765, and warned him that if he had anything to do with stamps, they would treat him "in such a way and manner, as perhaps will be disagreeable both to yourself and to us."

Elizabethtowners in February, 1766, erected a gallows and affixed a rope which they swore would exactly fit the neck of the first stamp distributor in New Jersey. Crowds in Middlesex, Hunterdon, Sussex, and Monmouth counties cheered Sons of Liberty speakers who vowed British subjects could be taxed "only by their own representatives."

Meanwhile, the lawyers of New Jersey who had in September so nobly announced their fast of "no stamps, no work" began to feel the emptiness of their pocketbooks. They met in February, 1766, and decided that if the Stamp Act had not been repealed by April 1, they would be back in business, without stamps in defiance of the Crown. Some lawyers in Elizabethtown and in the courthouses of Cumberland and Sussex counties resumed work immediately, risking fines by not affixing the stamps to legal documents.

"The Most Firm Loyalty"

England backed down, her economy badly crippled by the nonimportation agreements, and word of the Stamp Act repeal reached New Jersey on April 3, 1766. Six weeks later "an elegant entertainment" in Burlington celebrated the repeal amid bonfires and "other demonstrations of joy." Significantly Governor Franklin joined principal inhabitants in toasts to the King, the Queen, the Parliament, and a variety of other British worthies. Similarly, the Sons of Liberty in Woodbridge combined a celebration of King George's birthday early in June with a public observance of the Stamp Act repeal—"and the most firm loyalty seemed to glow in every breast."

Frustrated on stamps, England next announced the Townshend Acts drawn in May, 1767, by Chancellor of the Exchequer Charles Townshend. He imposed import duties on glass, paper, red and white lead, and tea, with duties to be collected in colonial ports. Collections would help maintain governors and judges in America, since Townshend correctly deduced that royal officials dependent on colonial legislatures for salaries often bent judgments to fit expediency.

Indignant Jerseymen joined other provinces in nonimportation agreements and petitions to the King. Boycott once more proved more effective than protest. Again England capitulated, removing the tax on everything but tea, keeping that as a symbol of England's *right* to tax colonists. Tea became socially unacceptable, and much later it would bubble into violence in a series of "tea parties."

Ironically, repeal of the Townshend Acts was announced in England on March 5, 1770, the very day that British soldiers killed five persons among a mob gathered on the Boston Common. News of the repeal did not reach America until May, but neither the Boston Massacre nor the repeal stirred New Jersey residents much. They were far more antagonized by New York profiteers who had stocked up on scarce British goods and were selling them at high profits. In protest, the graduates at the 1770 commencement of the College of New Jersey wore homespun suits rather than pay the high prices demanded in New York. Woodbridge extremists announced tar and feathers would be applied to violators of Non-Importation Agreements, the supply being lodged under the "Liberty Oak" near "Execution Dock."

Time for Harmony

The hard-working Franklin gained reasonable harmony for a time. He managed to get the Assembly to provide money for British soldiers quartered in the colony's five barracks and talked the Assembly into permitting him to dispense the barracks funds—the first time since Governor Cornbury's days, sixty years before, that a New Jersey governor was directly authorized to spend the people's money. Franklin delighted the frugal Assembly by turning back a surplus of £105.

Money problems plagued Franklin constantly. The governor sided with the Assembly in the belief that the colony should have the right to issue legal-tender paper money but England rebuffed his request. New Jersey's Assembly reacted bitterly. Though members voted to pay Franklin's salary, they resolved not to supply the King's troops. The governor changed the Assembly's mind only after strenuous effort.

Thievery in the State Treasury

While all about them the New World smoldered on the edge of war, New Jersey politicians took time out to wrangle for nearly three years over a robbery that had comic-opera overtones except for a deep principle involved. The trouble began on July 21, 1768, when thieves broke into the Perth Amboy home of Stephen Skinner, treasurer of East Jersey, and made off with the provincial funds.

Skinner stoutly denied blame for the loss of the £7814 in an iron chest, but investigation revealed that he had carelessly left the key in his desk. Franklin's inquiries failed to resolve anything, perhaps because the colony's attorney-general and Speaker of the Assembly was Cortland Skinner, Stephen's brother. Nagging doubts about the crime endured; money-conscious Jerseymen showed far more interest in the missing funds than in rebellion.

Two years passed amid a rising chorus of protest against Stephen Skinner. Franklin declared that he saw no evidence of wrongdoing, and he accused the Assembly of desiring Skinner's removal so that they could appoint a new treasurer and thus rob the governor of his power. The quarrel continued, although Franklin reported in November, 1773, that the arrest of a gang of counterfeiters near Morristown apparently solved the robbery.

Two dozen petitions, bearing two thousand signatures, demanded Skinner's removal in February, 1774. Fortunately for Governor Franklin, the treasurer resigned, a resignation coincidentally taking place immediately after the Assembly caustically warned Franklin that it would not touch any appropriation bills unless he removed the discredited treasurer. Franklin saved face, but the Assembly had forced Franklin to submit to its will. It was in keeping with the spirit of the times.

TIME FOR BIGGER THINGS

Franklin continued trying to serve both King and Jerseyman, but when he won no applause from either, he grew increasingly bitter. Opportunities for advancement in British governmental service disappeared for William when angry King George reacted to Benjamin Franklin's anti-British declarations by removing the elder Franklin as head of the Post Office in America in December, 1773. Benjamin candidly wrote his son that the action meant no more promotions; retire and be "well settled on your farm," the father advised the governor.

William ignored the advice. Restlessness and rebellion worsened, and Governor Franklin took sides against his father when patriots disguised as Indians poured aboard the ship *Dartmouth* in Boston Harbor in December of 1773 to dump unwelcome British cargoes of tea. As the British moved harshly after the Boston Tea Party, closing the port of Boston in June, 1774, and placing it under martial law, William defended the action in a letter to Benjamin. Father and son stood on opposite edges of a widening chasm; within a year they would no longer be on speaking or writing terms.

The governor's position on colonial affairs now stood counter to most of his constituents' views. When Virginians reacted to the closing of Boston port in June, 1774, by calling for a congress of delegates to meet annually in consideration of mutual colonial concerns, Franklin refused to call the Assembly into session to appoint such delegates. The governor slammed the door shut, but immediately found it burst open by an angry populace taking matters into its own hands.

Residents of Lower Freehold in Monmouth County adopted a resolution on June 6 calling Boston's cause "the cause of all." Five days later Essex County residents strongly supported their Monmouth neighbors and soon after, in order, Bergen, Morris, Hunterdon, Middlesex, and Sussex counties fell in line. Their local meetings, which evolved from the Virginia plan of "committees of correspondence" to keep one another informed on matters pertaining to "liberties and privileges of the King's subjects," were truly government of the people—of an indignant people.

FIRST PROVINCIAL CONGRESS

Indignation turned into action. Seventy-two delegates from local correspondence committees assembled in New Brunswick on July 21, 1774, without permission from governor, King, or Parliament. The delegates first carefully swore allegiance to the King and renounced claims to independence, but they also pointedly called Parliament's tax laws unconstitutional and oppressive. Stephen Crane of Essex County was named Speaker. The delegates selected James Kinsey, John DeHart, Stephen Crane, William Livingston, and Richard Smith (brother of historian Samuel Smith) to represent them at the Continental Congress scheduled to convene in Philadelphia on September 5. Fittingly, three of the five delegates (Livingston, DeHart, and Crane) came from Essex County, where the rebellious spirit of the New England town meeting had long been manifest.

The First Continental Congress at Philadelphia divided into moderate and radical camps, the latter led by New Englanders. The delegates were still cautious, appealing to the King while setting forth their claims to all rights due Englishmen, including the right to be represented if they were to be taxed. The first Continental Congress said nothing of independence, but the mood for complete severance grew everywhere, inflamed in New Jersey by intemperate statements such as the one uttered in Essex County in the early winter of 1774 by Chief Justice Frederick Smyth.

"People are guarding against imaginary tyranny, three thousand miles distant," Judge Smyth told a grand jury, in smug assumption that England knew best.

Outraged, an Essex juror replied to the judge in the New York *Journal:*

> We cannot persuade ourselves that the fleet now blocking up the Port of Boston, consisting of ships built of real English oak and solid iron, and armed with cannon and ponderous metal . . . nor the army lodging in the town of Boston, and the fortifications thrown about it are all creatures of the imagination. These, Sir, are but a few of the numerous grievances under which America now groans. These are some of the effects of that deliberate plan of tyranny concerted at "three thousand miles distant" and which, to your Honour appears only like a baseless fabric of vision.

Governor Franklin grew increasingly uneasy. On December 6, 1774, he wrote Lord Dartmouth, secretary for the colonies, that "many sensible and moderate men" worried in fear that England might feel "the Congress has left her no other alternative than either to consent to what must appear humiliating in the eyes of all Europe, or to compel obedience to her laws by military force."

PARTY IN GREENWICH

That stern warning was on the high seas when Jerseymen in the flourishing Cumberland County port town of Greenwich gathered for a tea party of their own. Greenwich's tea came ashore on December 12, 1774, when the master of the brig *Greyhound* decided not to risk his cargo to the infuriated patriots of Philadelphia. He took it instead into Greenwich and stored it in Dan Bowen's cellar. Cumberland County heard that an indignation meeting on December 23 would "consider" the tea, but more than twenty "Indians" materialized on the night of December 22, took the tea from Bowen's cellar, and burned the hated cargo in the street.

Next day the Reverend Philip Vickers Fithian wrote, apparently with tongue in cheek because he since has been identified as a "burner": "Some rave, some curse, and condemn. Some try to reason; many are glad that the tea is destroyed, but almost all disapprove the manner of destruction."

Seven of the arsonists were tried in April, 1775, but none was concerned about punishment. Sheriff Jonathan Elmer, brother of one of those on trial, summoned a sympathetic jury whose foreman was Daniel Elmer, Jonathan's nephew. Their verdict of innocence surprised no one; Cumberland County was in no mood to punish tea burners.

PEACE, OR ANARCHY?

Governor Franklin disregarded the darkening clouds. He convened the Assembly on January 13, 1775, and warned that approving such actions as the New Brunswick conference the previous July would be a long step toward dissolving the form of government he felt New Jersey was privileged to enjoy. He painted a picture of peace and happiness under England and contrasted that with the "Anarchy, Misery and all the Horrors of Civil War." He urged them to compile a list of grievances, promising that the list would reach the King's eyes.

Fearful lest this soothing talk to the New Jersey Assembly might cause members to disapprove of the resolutions drawn by the Continental Congress in Philadelphia, Livingston, DeHart, and Elias Boudinot hastened to Perth Amboy to urge quick Assembly confirmation of the resolutions. Assemblymen stiffened after hearing the trio, turned their back on Franklin, and adopted the resolutions unanimously on a second ballot. They reappointed the five delegates to the Continental Congress.

That business done, the Assembly drew up its list of grievances, which Franklin refused to forward. So the Assembly itself forwarded them to King George.

Despite the coolness between governor and Assembly, few in New Jersey talked about outright independence in early 1775. Leaders in other colonies were more vehement. Patrick Henry of the Virginia House of Burgesses, declared passionately in March, 1775, that "the next gale that sweeps from the north will bring to our ears the clash of resounding arms! Our brethren are already in the field!" He was only slightly premature, for on April 19, 1775, minutemen at Lexington and Concord battled British regulars on the roads west of Boston. The time for talk had ended; as the "gale" roared over New Jersey it swayed a populace now eager for fray.

The eagerness later would become a confused Tory-Patriot pattern within New Jersey—a pattern drawn and redrawn according to which side seemed likely to triumph—but in April of 1775 patriotic spirit filled the Jersey air. After a fast-riding dispatch rider brought news of Lexington and Concord, Newark leaders resolved unanimously on April 24 that they were "willing at this alarming crisis to risk their lives and fortunes in support of American liberty." Everywhere militia companies took "uncommon pains to perfect themselves in Military Discipline." One company marched by the Governor's Mansion in Perth Amboy in May with "Colours, Drum and Fife."

FRANKLIN'S LAST STAND

If he heard the fifing and drumming of a war already underway, Franklin didn't admit it. He tried in May to get his Assembly to accept Lord North's Resolution of Conciliation, which said, in effect, that if a colony would provide funds for its own government and defense—*to be spent by Parliament*—it would be relieved of duties and taxes except for the regulation of commerce.

Franklin spoke magnificently for the Conciliation, but the Assembly repudiated him. It told him bluntly that "we cannot suppose you to entertain a suspicion that the present house has the least design to desert the common cause, in which all America appears to be both deeply interested and firmly united." The governor's last big plea had been made. His days were numbered.

Governing power in the state, nearly completely out of Franklin's grasp, now also left the hands of the Assembly. The Provincial Congress moved boldly into action to supersede the Assembly, holding its second session in Trenton in May, 1775, with nine New Jersey Assemblymen among the eighty-seven delegates. The Congress organized as determinedly as if the whole body of English law stood behind it. Members reconvened in August, announced a regular system of elections (the first regular elections since the nearly forgotten days of the Proprietors), and enacted a series of harsh military laws.

REGIMENTATION FOR "LIBERTY"

The August laws passed by the Provincial Congress ordered all effective men between sixteen and fifty to enlist and bear arms or else be fined four shillings monthly. Those who ignored the order would be reported to the Committee of Safety, "to be dealt with as they shall direct." Ten battalions of minutemen were ordered organized, but the Provincial Congress, showing the same reluctance about financial support for soldiers that their Assembly counterparts always had displayed, refused to raise £30,000 in taxes to pay the militia. In acts verging on martial law, the Congress also ordered tax collectors to seize and sell goods and chattel of anyone who had not paid the taxes levied in May.

Kemmerer declared in his *Path to Freedom:* "Altogether the regimentation was greater than Parliament ever dreamed of, and may explain in part why it was soon said that Toryism was increasing in New Jersey."

General George Washington, newly selected commander-in-chief of the revolutionists, passed through New Jersey late in June on the way to beleaguered Boston. He rode into Trenton on June 24, where a hard-riding courier brought news of Bunker Hill. The next day a committee of the Provincial Congress welcomed him in Newark and accompanied him across the meadows to Hoboken as he proceeded to the seat of war.

Franklin worked desperately all summer to alert moderate Jerseymen to dangers as he saw them. He met the Assembly for the last time in November, 1775, and after urging the delegates to be cautious in their dealings with England, Franklin poignantly asked the delegates whether he should remain in New Jersey or take refuge. "It is high time," the governor said, "that every man should know what he has to expect."

THE ASSEMBLY WAVERS

Faced with that stark awareness of what war must bring, the Assembly wavered. It assured Franklin that the people of New Jersey meant him no harm. An Assembly prepared a petition to King George, "humbly beseeching him to use his interposition to prevent the effusion of blood; and to express the great desire that this House hath to a restoration of peace and harmony with the Parent State, on constitutional principles." The New Jersey delegates to the Continental Congress were instructed to seek an early reconciliation with England.

Thoroughly alarmed over the possibility that New Jersey might sue for a separate peace with the Crown, the Continental Congress hastily sent John Jay, George Wythe, and John Dickinson to Burlington to dissuade the Assembly. The visitors harrangued the House for about an hour on the subject and persuaded members to drop their design. Tacitly, at least, New Jersey's Assemblymen agreed when John Dickinson told them that England must not be permitted to look upon American organization as "a rope of sand." The New Jersey Assembly did nothing bold—assuredly there was no Patrick Henry in its midst—but by tabling its petition to the King it once more marched to the beat of the American drum, a bit to the rear and uncertain as to step, but in line nevertheless.

Franklin had a recurring nightmare: he wrote Lord Dartmouth in September, 1775, his concern lest he be "seized upon and led like a bear to some place of confinement in New England." The fear came closer on January 8, 1776, when violent knocking on the door awakened Franklin and so alarmed the ailing Mrs. Franklin, that the governor was "not without apprehension of her dying with the fright." Outside, a band of soldiers waited while Colonel William Winds asked Franklin if he would pledge not to flee. The governor agreed, was given parole, and stayed on in Perth Amboy.

The tide for independence, strong everywhere, rolled over New Jersey as the undeclared war spread in 1776. Sharply divided loyalties appeared, and many Jerseymen stoutly, if quietly, continued to profess loyalty to England. Yet when the New Jersey Provincial Congress met at New Brunswick on January 31, 1776, ties with the mother country already stretched close to the breaking point.

Thomas Paine's *Common Sense*, published that January, enjoyed wide circulation. Jerseymen read the understandable, fiery words of the radical pamphleteer:

> 'Tis not the affair of a city, a county, a province or a kingdom, but of a continent. . . . Now is the seed-time of continental union, faith, and honor. . . . Time hath found us. Time hath found us! O, ye that love mankind, stand forth. . . . Ye that dare oppose not only tyranny but the tyrant, stand forth!

Governor Franklin read Paine's pamphlet with exasperation, of course, but he wrote that it would have the "one good effect . . . of opening the eyes of many people of sense and property, who before would not believe that there were any persons of consequence, either in or out of the Congress, who harboured such intentions." He meant, naturally, that Tories must now speak up.

New Jersey's Provincial Congress devoted its time mainly to military matters between January 31 and March, 1776. Colonel William Maxwell's West Jersey battalion was sent to Quebec to aid General Benedict Arnold, and the Provincial Congress supplied a third battalion to bolster American arms. Such attention to military preparedness had elements of normal New Jersey financial instability; when a battalion of New Jersey militia was ordered to New York, the order had to be withdrawn because the bare New Jersey treasury couldn't buy arms to equip the soldiers.

Recognizing the imminence of an open declaration of war, the Continental Congress recommended on May 10 that colonies "adopt such governments as should, in the opinion of the representatives of the people, best conduce to the happiness and safety of their constituents in particular and America in general." State constitutions followed in the wake of that declaration.

New Jersey voters (those with fifty pounds in real or personal properties) went to the polls on May 28 and chose a new Provincial Congress strongly in favor of independence. Governor Franklin, blandly ignoring such evident will of his people, infuriated the insurgents by summoning the Assembly to meet on June 20. He clung to hopes that he could induce the moderate Assembly to continue friendly relations with Great Britain.

Franklin had gone too far. When the Provincial Congress convened in Burlington on June 10 it declared the governor to be "in direct contempt" of the Continental Congress. Colonel Nathaniel Heard of Middlesex was ordered to approach Franklin, "with all the delicacy and tenderness which the nature of the business can possibly admit," and offer him parole at Princeton, Bordentown, or his own farm at Rancocas. When Franklin refused all of these, Colonel Heard arrested the governor on June 17 and brought him to Burlington under guard.

Franklin vented his rage in a letter to the Assembly, calling his captors "desperate gamesters" and "pretended patriots bent on an Independent Republican Tyranny." He adamantly refused to answer questions of New Jersey's Provincial Congress. The Continental Congress sent Franklin to Connecticut, to be watched by Governor Jonathan Trumbull, the only colonial governor known for strong anti-King sentiment. Franklin was exchanged in November, 1778, for a revolutionist held by the British. He returned to New York to become an active head of the Loyalists and then went to England in 1782 to live out his years.

On June 22, the Provincial Congress named five delegates to the Continental Congress, including fiery John Witherspoon, president of the College of New Jersey, and a bold advocate of liberty. The other delegates were Richard Stockton, Abraham Clark, John Hart, and Francis Hopkinson. The five were empowered to join with other delegates at Philadelphia "in the most vigorous measures for supporting the just rights and liberties of America." And, if necessary, they were instructed to join "in declaring the United Colonies independent of Great Britain." The five would become New Jersey's signers of the Declaration of Independence.

CONSTITUTION WITH CAUTION

As a final stride to independence, the Provincial Congress hastily prepared and adopted the first New Jersey constitution. The document could scarcely be called a masterpiece of either deliberation or of powerful protest. Jacob Green of Morris County and his committee began deliberations on the constitution on June 24; eight days later it was ready for adoption.

Even the signing of the first state constitution on July 2, showed the overpowering reluctance that had ever been the role of Jerseymen in this march to independence. Thirty members of the Provincial Congress abstained, and of the thirty-five who had the courage to express an opinion, nine voted against the document—meaning that only twenty-six out of sixty actually voted *for* the document. The adopters agreed on a cautious closing: "If a reconciliation between Great Britain and these colonies should take place and the latter be taken again under the protection and government of the Crown of Great Britain; this charter shall be null and void." But other colonies weren't exactly passionately eager to adopt constitutions; New Jersey was the third province to adopt its own document, preceded only by New Hampshire and South Carolina.

The New Jersey constitution sought to eliminate irritants of long years' standing. It guaranteed regular elections on the second Tuesday of each October, with voters choosing three Assemblymen and one Councilor for each of the thirteen counties, thus adopting a bicameral legislature of upper and lower houses. Assemblymen were given sweeping powers, including the right to initiate all money bills—which the Council, or upper house, absolutely could not alter.

As for the governor, framers of New Jersey's first constitution made certain that he would be at the mercy of the Assembly, just as royal governors had been. First, the Council and Assembly elected him annually (with the Assembly providing three out of four votes). Worse, the governor continued to face the galling prospect of depending on the Assembly for his income; again, no more powerful or humiliating weapon could be devised than forcing the chief executive to beg for his salary.

So, when thirteen colonies joined to declare their independence on July 4, 1776, New Jersey stood shakily among those who saw themselves as "endowed by their Creator with certain inalienable rights." This point had been reached in New Jersey, not through the fire of a Patrick Henry or the acid of a Sam Adams, but rather through a deliberate, agonizing debate that probably typified the genuine feelings of most people in all thirteen colonies.

8

Revolution's Crossroads

New Jersey's first constitution provided only that "some fit person within the colony" be chosen as governor, and when legislators convened in Nassau Hall at Princeton on August 30, 1776, to choose a chief excutive, two names came quickly to mind: Richard Stockton of Princeton and William Livingston of Elizabethtown.

Stockton seemed an ideal choice. Scion of a notable New Jersey family, he was a distinguished young lawyer, had signed the Declaration of Independence, and was fervently liberal. Livingston, on the other hand, had spent the first forty-nine years of his life as a citizen and lawyer of New York, moving his family to Elizabethtown in 1772. Some doubted his initial fervor for independence, but when war became inevitable, Livingston wrote: "We have passed the Rubicon. We cannot recede nor should I wish we could." He quickly aided the cause through inspired, sarcastic writings aimed at the British.

Legislators split evenly for Stockton and Livingston on the first ballot taken on August 30. Then the Livingston backers began a strong behind-the-scenes campaign. John Stevens, chairman of the election, met secretly with Stockton the next morning, apparently to dissuade him from pursuing the governorship. Later in the day the legislators chose William Livingston as the wartime governor and therefore the first governor of the *State* of New Jersey (as the province had renamed itself on July 18, 1776). Livingston was re-elected annually thereafter until his death in 1790.

MASTER OF A SPLIT STATE

The governor faced a state divided against itself. True, patriots of the stature of Livingston and Stockton were joined by others of top rank: Francis Hopkinson of Bordentown, lawyer and brilliant writer; William

Alexander (or Lord Stirling), wealthy landholder of Somerset County; John Witherspoon, president of the College of New Jersey; and a large number of young lawyers and intellectuals. Clergy of the Presbyterian and Dutch Reformed churches stood firmly for independence.

However, for nearly every top-ranked revolutionist, New Jersey also had a Tory dissenter of stature. Ex-Governor William Franklin led the list, of course, but many others were like-minded. Attorney General Cortland Skinner and Chief Justice Frederick Smyth remained loyal to King George. Leading officers of the East New Jersey Board of Proprietors favored the government which had given them so much power and wealth. Many older lawyers, doctors, and leading merchants opposed the war. Anglican ministers in Perth Amboy and Burlington assailed the split with the mother country.

Nor could the state count on aid from the substantial Quaker settlements in the western and southern parts of the state. The Quakers were opposed to war under any circumstances, but many of the Quakers also owned large plantations and might have had to wrestle doubly with their conservative consciences if they had been forced to declare.

Within the rank-and-file, there were many vigorous patriots; Essex County in particular seethed with a genuine dedication to the war. The New Jersey militia under such leaders as Philomen Dickinson and Jonathan Dayton would perform with distinction, and many New Jersey regulars would stay stubbornly with the fight throughout the long Revolution. Lord Stirling of Somerset and William Maxwell of Warren County were New Jersey officers who went on to serve their country nobly.

Nevertheless, New Jersey had strong pockets of Tory sentiment among ordinary citizens. Monmouth County was a noted center of British sympathy. Bergen County's Dutch farmers were, at best, neutral. Even strongly democratic Essex County had its share of Tories, and Sussex County contributed the state's most famous Tory (except for Governor Franklin). He was James Moody, whose narrative of his exploits and sufferings as a Loyalist is a minor Revolutionary War classic.

Moody told his story in a pamphlet published in England after the war. Describing himself as a patriot who wanted only to defend his rights as an Englishman, Moody felt "rebellion is the foulest of all crimes." After Sussex neighbors shot at him in March, 1777, he led eighty-three neighbors into the camp of the British.

Moody claimed that he personally recruited 500 Jerseymen to follow him later in 1777, probably an inflated figure. He led an audacious raid on Tinton Falls in Monmouth County in June, 1778 and spied on the Morristown encampment at Morristown in the winter of 1779–80. He led a daring dash into the Morris County hills in May, 1780, to capture "some person of note" (probably Governor Livingston, who was then living in Morris County).

The most famous Moody exploit was a raid on the Sussex County jail in Newton to release a prisoner. He later hid "as a partridge in the mountains," was captured and released after torture. Ironically, his captor was General Benedict Arnold—whose own dallying with the British probably saved Moody's skin. Moody spent his last days as an exile in Nova Scotia.

ENEMY AT THE DOORSTEP

Many Jerseymen remained outwardly neutral, refusing to tip their hands, and that reluctance must get sympathetic understanding. After all, patriotism often shines more brightly when the enemy is on another doorstep. When enemy soldiers march across the terrain, the long-time neutral is likely to suffer least. Wisdom dictated that New Jersey would become a state of warring tides, for whoever held the state also controlled, or neutralized, both New York and Philadelphia, the chief towns in America.

Early in July the war became a reality for New Jersey. A British fleet of more than 100 ships dropped anchor off Sandy Hook, bringing General William Howe's mighty army from Halifax. A few days later the troops marched ashore on Staten Island and the spectacle of thousands of mighty Redcoats drilling, with only the Arthur Kill between them and New Jersey, created panic. Then Admiral Richard Howe brought his great fleet in to block the harbor: the conquest of the revolutionists appeared imminent. Wavering spirits began preparing for a switch in allegiance.

Washington organized a "Flying Camp" near Perth Amboy, ordering Brigadier General Hugh Mercer to have 3300 troops ready to speed wherever they might be needed. Mercer could count 1200 New Jersey militiamen on hand early in July, but by July 20 most of the New Jersey troops had been temporarily excused to harvest the hay in their sun-baked fields.

If Howe had swung westward from Staten Island into New Jersey for his first strike, victory probably would have been easy, for Mercer's camp was never more than a token force, undermanned, poorly armed, and ill supplied. Morale was low and thievery was high at the Flying Camp. Soldiers pillaged the countryside, until Abraham Clark of Elizabethtown could write in October: "We have not had the enemy among us, but Staten Island hath not suffered from the British troops scarcely the tenth part of the damage this town hath from the Militia."

Howe defeated Long Island's defenders in late August and moved relentlessly toward full conquest of Manhattan Island. The strong American position in the fort at Paulus Hook (Jersey City) was outflanked and had to be abandoned on September 23. British troops immediately occupied the empty works. The crisis neared; as October turned into November, New Jersey braced for inevitable invasion.

Washington knew that the American rebellion was foundering. As he led the fading flower of Continental military strength into Bergen County in the middle of November, the general surveyed his fewer than 5000 "much broken and dispirited" soldiers and wrote: "I am worried almost to death with the retrograde motion of things." Eastward, in contrast, Lord Cornwallis rested with thousands of well-equipped British regulars.

The moment had come for England to end the war. British troops smashed into Fort Washington on Manhattan Island on November 16 for a victory that, by the end, had cost America 2600 men. Four days later, in one of the infrequent shows of British daring and imagination, Cornwallis led his men along a steep, little-used path up the rocky, rugged Palisades overlooking the Hudson River in Bergen County. His daring action forced General Nathanael Greene's garrison to abandon Fort Lee. Greene's force of between 2000 and 3000 men left behind stores of badly needed tents, cannon, and supplies.

Washington recognized that he must leave the muddy campground by the Hackensack River or face certain engulfment. Southwestward he must go, not because victory beckoned that way, but because he must somehow keep his evaporating army between the advancing British and Philadelphia. Retreat might buy him time. Buglers sounded the call to march, and the ragged army straggled wearily across the Hackensack River at Acquackanonk Bridge on November 21. As they marched, late-fall rains beat against them, and the cold northeast winds augured an early winter.

PURSUIT ACROSS NEW JERSEY

Lord Cornwallis followed, but never rapidly enough. His troops entered the north side of Newark as the Americans left the south side, but then the brisk pursuit slowed on orders from General Howe. The British watched the American army cross the wide Raritan River near New Brunswick, dawdled while the Continentals moved through Princeton and tarried as Washington neared a dead end on the banks of the Delaware River. One exasperated Tory wrote that the British command calculated "with greatest accuracy the exact time necessary for the enemy to escape."

Thomas Paine, the former Englishman whose brilliant passages had helped stimulate revolt, now worked only to keep fading hope alive. He limped along on the journey across New Jersey and scribbled at every stop. His words, written under extreme duress, became "The Crisis," whose stirring paragraphs begin: "These are the times that try men's

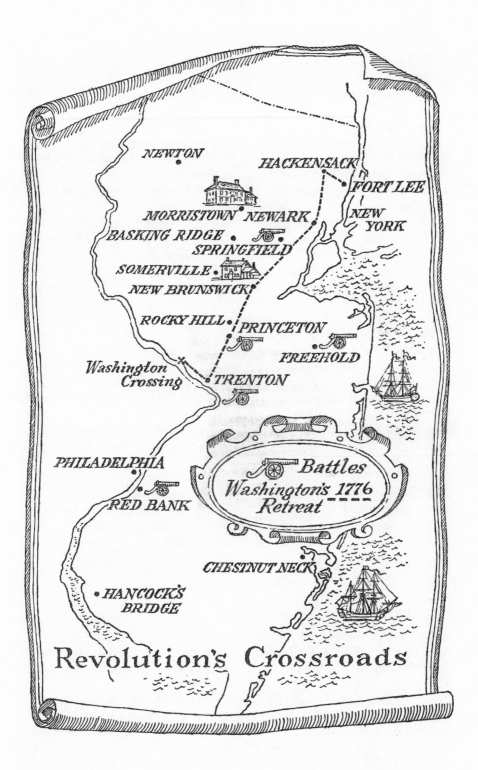

NEWTON

HACKENSACK

FORT LEE

MORRISTOWN NEWARK

NEW YORK

BASKING RIDGE

SPRINGFIELD

SOMERVILLE

NEW BRUNSWICK

ROCKY HILL

PRINCETON

FREEHOLD

Washington Crossing

TRENTON

PHILADELPHIA

RED BANK

Battles
Washington's 1776
Retreat

CHESTNUT NECK

HANCOCK'S BRIDGE

Revolution's Crossroads

souls. The summer soldier and the sunshine patriot will, in this crisis, shrink from the service of the country. . . ."

Paine's cry sounded all too true in New Jersey. Local militiamen saw no reason to rush from their homes to join this nearly lost cause; their own villages might soon be attacked. On the last day of November a brigade of Jerseymen and a brigade of Marylanders left the ranks when their enlistments expired. Home they went to flaming fireside at a time when the fading spark of revolution needed them most. General Greene, for his part, declared that Jerseymen acted "scurvily," ignoring the fact that New Englanders and Southerners also left—and with far less impelling reason. If the main army collapsed, those Jerseymen had homes to defend against an invader.

Foes sneeringly labeled Washington a master of "defeat and retreat," but his carefully calculated flight across New Jersey gave him precious time. Before his ragged army reached the Delaware on December 7, the general ordered confiscation of every boat for miles up and down the river, foiling quick pursuit. That shrewd action kept the British a river's width away from the Americans.

The strange timidity of the British on the pursuit across New Jersey will ever be cause for conjecture. Some argue that General Howe felt the American spirit would wither away in the approaching winter; the wretched army must weary of starvation and freezing. Undoubtedly he felt as well that Tories would flock to his cause—and hundreds of Jerseymen *did* rush to sign oaths of allegiance to King George, including many once-vocal "revolutionists" who hoped their former deeds and words might be forgotten or forgiven.

Howe and Cornwallis stationed Hessians at Burlington, Bordentown, and Trenton, moving the main British army back to New Brunswick and Perth Amboy, with an outpost at Princeton. The generals looked forward to a fine winter. Amiable, fun-loving William Howe returned to New York's pleasures, and Lord Cornwallis booked passage to England, casually agreeing to return in the spring, "if there is another campaign, which we doubt."

RECALCITRANT GENERAL LEE

Fully across the Delaware by December 8, Washington needed all the help that he could get, whether it be British complacency or loyalty from his staff, and he grew daily more puzzled by the strange actions of Major General Charles Lee, the ex-British officer who had volunteered his services to America in 1775. Orders to Lee to bring his large force of 3000 men forward from White Plains to join Washington had been ignored since November 21, and on December 9, Lee insolently wrote that he intended "to reconquer (if I may so express myself) the Jerseys."

Time has made it evident that Lee never intended to join Washington, whose abilities he openly criticized. When Lee paused on December 13 at the Widow White's in Basking Ridge, he penned a letter attacking "a certain great man" as "damnably deficient." Lee meant Washington and made no effort to conceal his thoughts.

Lee got the chance to display his own damnable deficiencies. British Dragoons closed in on the general on the morning of December 13 as he enjoyed a late breakfast at Mrs. White's. The Dragoons hurried Lee out of the widow's home, clad only in dressing gown and night shirt, and carried him overland to New Brunswick in attire fit more for boudoir than battlefield.

The British boasted that they had captured "the only rebel general we had to fear." That opinion diminished despite Lee's offer to give Howe a quick means of overwhelming the Americans. Later they gladly exchanged the troublesome, egocentric general. Actually, in December, 1776, the loss of Lee aided Washington, for it temporarily rid the army of an insolent subordinate and it enabled General John Sullivan to march Lee's men from Basking Ridge to join the main army across the Delaware.

Chaos and fear gripped New Jersey as December's days sped by. The state legislature fled, from Princeton to Trenton to Burlington—and then dissolved completely. Marauding bands of Tories, Hessians, and British roamed the state to wreak vengeance on neighbors. A group sallied into Hopewell seeking John Hart, one of New Jersey's signers of the Declaration of Independence. Hart and his children escaped to seek safety in a cave in the Sourland Mountains, but the invaders killed his wife and ruined his fine home. British troops made Richard Stockton, another signer, flee Morven, the ancestral home of the Stocktons at Princeton. Governor Livingston became an itinerant with a price on his head.

Hessian and British troops plundered the prosperous countryside between Newark and Trenton. Ignoring Howe's severely worded but never-enforced orders forbidding looting, the plunderers failed to distinguish between Tories and patriots. A man named Nutman, "a remarkable Tory" of Newark, met the British with "huzzas of joy," and his conquering heroes returned the cordiality by stripping him to his toes. Such actions helped stiffen opposition, even among those who once had been unfriendly to revolution.

Quietly and without organization, a counterattack began. Angered and disillusioned Jerseymen struck back with a form of guerrilla warfare and every bush, every copse, every tree became a possible harbinger of sudden death for the British and Hessians. The dread of an unseen foe striking from darkness made royal forces uneasy as they foraged through the Middlesex countryside. Hessians in Trenton complained "We have not slept one night in peace since we came to this place." By December

18, British troops were forbidden to move anywhere outside of New Brunswick without armed escort.

The colonies needed something far more telling than bush warfare, however, to sustain the struggle through the winter. Reports on December 22 showed only 4707 American soldiers fit for duty at the Pennsylvania encampment, a drop of more than 1000 men in two weeks. Washington reported many of his men were "entirely naked and most so thinly clad as to be unfit for service." Even that sad rabble might disappear when their enlistments ended with the new year. After December 31, the "Grand Army" seemed likely to shrink to 1400 men, less wholesale desertions. And why should anyone stay?

CHRISTMAS STRIKE

Washington recognized that a lightning stroke must be chanced, and he chose Christmas as the most likely time for Trenton's Hessians to be off guard. Amid as much secrecy as possible, plans were made for the holiday attack. Late in the afternoon of Christmas Day, John Glover and his detachment of Marblehead boatsmen began ferrying 2400 Americans across the ice-clogged Delaware River to McConkey's ferry house in New Jersey, eight miles north of Trenton. The plan called for two other American forces to cross simultaneously, one led by General James Ewing against Trenton Ferry; the other, led by Colonel John Cadwallader, to cross at Bristol for an attack toward Mt. Holly. Neither Ewing nor Cadwallader was successful; Washington and his men were alone.

For his part, Colonel Johann Gottlieb Rall, Hessian commander in Trenton, scoffed at repeated warnings of an imminent American push. He declared: "Let them come. We want no trenches. We will go at them with bayonets." He inspected his outposts at twilight after a wandering group of Americans fired on a Hessian outpost. Satisfied that this was the threatened "attack," Rall went for a hearty supper and an all-night card game.

A "storm of wind, hail, rain and snow" dangerously delayed the crossing and put it hours behind schedule, but at 4 A.M. two American columns began the march on Trenton. Four hours later, their arrival partially hidden by driving sleet, advance units pushed past amazed Hessian pickets on the outskirts of town, slammed into Trenton, and attacked the dazed Hessians. Colonel Rall awakened to the sound of gunfire and bravely sought to rally his troops, but fell mortally wounded in the sharp, fierce battle in the streets of Trenton. Within two hours the town was Washington's in one of history's most incredible military victories.

Recognizing that Trenton could not be held against certain counterattack, the victors rounded up Hessian prisoners—more than 900 officers and men—and marched northward back along the icy roads and re-crossed the Delaware to Pennsylvania. Behind in Trenton lay 106 Hessians killed or wounded, including the stricken Rall. Astoundingly, the colonial troops suffered only four wounded, including Lieutenant James Monroe, later the fifth President of the United States.

The Trenton debacle appalled the British command, try as it might to shift all blame to the conveniently dead Rall. Lord Cornwallis canceled his trip home, took his bags off the ship, and hastened back toward Princeton. British bonfires lit the road from Princeton to Trenton and soldiers drilled in a show of power. Despite that all-too-obvious enemy strength, Washington did precisely what the British felt he could not do: he recrossed the Delaware on December 30, and dug in along Assunpink Creek on the south side of Trenton. Cornwallis moved his main army down from Princeton on January 2, reaching Trenton in the early evening. Prudently, he decided to wait for morning before annihilating Washington.

Across the Assunpink on the American side, bright bonfires and loud noises of men throwing up earthworks satisfied Cornwallis that "the old fox" feared the approaching dawn. While Cornwallis slept, Washington withdrew his 5000 men and hastened toward Princeton on roads turned hard by a sudden cold snap. Rags wrapped around wheel rims smothered the sounds of cannon being moved and soldiers marched silently to keep from alerting British outposts.

Advance troops under Brigadier General Hugh Mercer reached Stony Brook, about two miles from Princeton, at sunrise. Suddenly a British force on the way to aid Cornwallis rode out of the dawn and slashed into the formation. Mercer fell mortally wounded, his troops retreated wildly, and a stunning upset victory seemed within the grasp of the small British detachment. At this point Washington rode up with the main army, exposing himself to blistering enemy fire as he regrouped his bewildered men and repulsed the attack. The field was not lost, but the element of surprise exploded in the wild sounds of battle.

Cornwallis heard the distant firing and forced his army along the road to Princeton, "in a most infernal sweat—running, puffing and blowing, and swearing at being so outwitted." The British general reached Princeton at noon, but again the "fox" was gone, with another smashing victory to his credit. The contented sleep of Cornwallis at the Assunpink had cost the British about 400 in killed, wounded, and captured at Princeton, against about forty killed or wounded for the victorious Americans. Twice, in less than ten days, the mighty royal army had been outwitted, outgeneraled, and outfought. The fires of rebellion, banked in December, flamed in January.

Washington turned northward to Morristown after the Battle of Princeton, another complete surprise for the British, who surmised that surely the Americans would head for New Brunswick, where the military treasury was stored. When Cornwallis found Washington had again escaped and headed for the Morris County hills, he continued his growing reputation as a poor prophet by assuring his superiors that the American commander "cannot subsist long where he is."

FORTRESS IN THE HILLS

Morristown was a military stronghold. The several ranges of the Watchung Mountains to the south and east were easy to defend, and, as an inner defense, the Great Swamp south of Morristown was nearly impenetrable. More, the hills to the north were filled with active forges to feed an iron-hungry army. As a bonus, enthusiasm was high in Morristown for the rebellion.

No American town could know unalloyed joy in 1777. The army continued to melt away through expired terms, and those who stayed had too little of everything—food, clothing, and shelter. They also faced an epidemic of smallpox, most dreaded of eighteenth-century sicknesses. Washington took dramatic action in February. He ordered everyone, soldiers and civilians alike, to be inoculated by army physicians with a mild form of the pox as the only known means of checking the epidemic. Early in March the general could write that the unique mass inoculation was "attended with amazing success."

As spring nudged winter aside on the Somerset and Middlesex plains beneath the Watchung hills, night raids and roadside killings by American regulars and guerrillas brought unceasing terror to the British. Washington moved the main body of his army from Morristown to an open camp on the southern edge of the Watchung Mountains in May, 1777, the better to annoy General Howe, fresh from a splendid social season in New York and now in New Brunswick to resume the war.

Howe made a massive feint westward on June 13, hoping to draw American forces out of the mountains and into open battle on the flat land. He threw up redoubts near Middlebush and Somerset Court House but Washington refused to budge. Night after night snipers cut down the British, until his Lordship wearied of such phantom warfare. He pulled back on June 19 and at month's end took his army to Staten Island. Three weeks later he loaded his army on ships and sailed south on the Atlantic, through Chesapeake Bay and on the long way to Philadelphia.

WAR ON THE DELAWARE

Another pleasant winter neared for General Howe, marred only by the annoying fact that American defenses on the Delaware River banks and in the river kept supplies from reaching Philadelphia. River barriers included two forts on the New Jersey side, at Billingsport and Red Bank (Fort Mercer) and Fort Mifflin on Mud Island in the Delaware near Philadelphia. The river bristled as well with *chevaux de frise*, ingenious devices made of heavy timber, armed with stout iron spears facing downstream. Rows of those sharp spears, sunk just below the surface, created a formidable hazard for wooden-bottomed ships.

Billingsport fell on October 3, making Red Bank the last American-held mainland position on the Delaware. Four hundred men of the 1st and 2nd Rhode Island Regiments followed Colonels Christopher Greene and Israel Angell into Fort Mercer on October 7 to strengthen the fort against certain British assault. Greene altered the outer defenses, moving his main fire power in from the outer rim, although leaving the exterior appearance the same as a ruse.

The expected attack came. Hessian Colonel Curt von Donop and some 1200 Hessians reached Fort Mercer shortly after noon on October 22. Von Donop placed siege guns outside the fort and called on Greene to surrender in the name of King George.

"We'll see King George damned first," shouted Greene in answer. "We want no quarter!"

Von Donop responded by driving his Hessians through the unmanned outer posts, but tricky inner defenses impeded the attackers and exposed them to merciless crossfire. More than 150 Hessians (some sources say 500) fell dead or wounded in forty minutes of fighting. Colonel von Donop was mortally wounded. He died several days later, reportedly saying with his last breath:

"I die the victim of my ambition, and of the avarice of my sovereign."

During the battle the sixty-four-gun British ship *Augusta* opened fire on Fort Mercer. One of the *Augusta*'s stray cannonballs ripped through a nearby house into a room where serene Quakeress Mrs. Anne Cooper Whitall sat spinning. Mrs. Whitall picked up her spinning wheel and angrily stalked off to the cellar. After the battle, as she bound up Hessian wounds, she scolded them for coming to America to butcher helpless colonists. Next day the *Augusta* ran aground and American ships set her afire. More than 100 British seamen died in a ripping explosion caused when flames reached powder stored below decks.

The debacle at Fort Mercer created deep concern in Philadelphia, since the news of General John Burgoyne's surrender of 5000 crack British troops at Saratoga on October 14 already had staggered the British and Tories in the city. Howe foresaw the possibility of a bleak winter without victory, without rich food, and perhaps, in severe emergency, even an absence of his much-pursued feminine comfort.

Howe's fears did not become reality. Fort Mifflin on Mud Island surrendered on November 16 after incessant bombardment, leaving Fort Mercer untenable. Four days later Colonel Greene moved his Rhode

Islanders out of the fort and blew it to bits and the British could concentrate again on the pleasures of city life. Howe's foes settled down to endure a harrowing winter at Valley Forge, a time brightened only by news that France had agreed on February 6, 1778, to pledge full military support to the United States. But in the depths of despair, General Baron von Steuben began drilling the ragtag civilian soldiers into a hard-bitten army.

ATTENTION TO SOUTH JERSEY

While the main armies waited for the spring thaw, the war went on in New Jersey. Roving bands of Loyalists and British troops rounded up South Jersey livestock for Howe's minions. South Jersey beef received American attention, too; General "Mad Anthony" Wayne paraded 300 cattle out of Salem County and north to Valley Forge late in February.

British Major John Simcoe decided in March that he must "chastise the rascals" of Salem County. His 300 Hessians, Tories, and assorted well-wishers silently surrounded Judge William Hancock's House at Hancock's Bridge on March 21. Inside, thirty men slept. Some of Simcoe's followers personally knew all of those asleep in the house, but the invaders massacred friend and stranger alike.

Howe's spectacular lack of success in Philadelphia brought Sir Henry Clinton as a replacement in May, with orders to evacuate Philadelphia and head for New York lest a French fleet bottle him up in the Delaware River. Clinton completed transfer of troops to the New Jersey side on June 18 and set his ponderous wagon train moving diagonally across the state. Could this march go unchallenged?

Washington decided to follow, to pose at least a threat and just possibly to strike a telling blow at Clinton's flank. His forces broke camp at Valley Forge and crossed the Delaware at Coryell's Ferry (Lambertville) on June 22. General Philomen Dickinson, commander of the New Jersey militia, was ordered to impede the long British columns by firing at the flanks and by tearing up bridges. Dickinson's men performed with notable success, but the British forces moved sluggishly across state, despite the harassment.

GENERAL LEE AT MONMOUTH

The American army moved over the Sourland Mountains to Hopewell, where a council of war met to decide on definite action against the British columns. Charles Lee, back from British prison through an exchange after his December, 1776, arrest at Basking Ridge, was "passionately opposed" to an attack, fearing that British regulars would annihilate the Americans. Anthony Wayne, asked by Washington for an opinion, snapped "Fight, Sir!" and Nathanael Greene and the Marquis de Lafayette agreed heartily. Washington sent Lafayette forward to put pressure on the British, but unstable Charles Lee once more came to the fore, demanding that he be given command of the advance units as the senior officer. Washington acceded, reluctantly giving in to military protocol.

The two armies edged toward an inevitable battle in the deadly heat of Sunday, June 28, on the plains west of Freehold in Monmouth County. Washington instructed Lee to attack at dawn, "acquainting him at the same time that I was marching to support him."

Onlookers found Lee to be "irresolute and confused" on the battlefield. He waited until nearly eight o'clock, long after the surprise that would have been his at sunrise, before sending his troops forward. Without warning, Lee amazed his troops and subordinate commanders (not to mention the British) by ordering a withdrawal before the armies had been fairly engaged, leaving some of his units in precarious positions far to the front. Washington reached the scene as Lee's ill-timed retreat took on semblances of a rout.

One colorful account has it that Washington "swore 'til the leaves shook on the trees." Lee himself declared that Washington uttered some "very singular expressions." There is certainty that the general roundly censured the uncertain commander. Even Lee's most ardent admirers have never been able to praise his actions at Monmouth. He was, at the very least, confused and frightened—and, at the very worst, might have been treasonous, although that has never been proved.

Washington sent Lee to the rear, rallied the disorganized troops, and forced them forward into battle under the scorching sun. That long, wild Sunday proved that Continental soldiers could stand up to a highly disciplined British army on an open battlefield (something which many military observers, particularly Lee, had not thought possible). On the other hand, Lee's strange morning behavior placed such a burden on late-starting American troops that the British could not be driven from the field. Clinton led his troops over the Navesink hills that night and successfully ferried them to New York.

The Battle of Monmouth brought severe casualties to both sides. British losses reached nearly 400 in killed and wounded; American casualties were 226 dead or injured. Hundreds of other men fell victim to the brutal June sun, helping to create an American legend named Molly Pitcher. Molly (really Mrs. Mary Ludwig Hays) had followed her cannoneer husband John to battle, and during the steaming battle carried a pitcher of water to thirsty soldiers, thereby earning the nickname. When husband John fell wounded, Molly stepped up to replace him at his cannon.

Charles Lee came to full comeuppence after the battle. Court-martialed on charges of "misbehaviour before the enemy," Lee hurt his defense by sneering contemptuously at Washington's "tinsel dignity." The court found him guilty and suspended him from any command for twelve months. Lee's days as a military troublemaker at last were over, but his name lives on as one of the most controversial figures in military history. No one ever will know what he had in mind at Monmouth—and he has fervent defenders even now.

PRIVATEERS HIT THE CROWN

The war in New Jersey took a more devious turn when Clinton transferred his seat of operations to Southern states. Privateers based in southern New Jersey carried the war to British shipping, sailing out of Barnegat Bay and Little Egg Harbor to hunt down merchant vessels off the coast. Their captured cargoes brought prosperity to Toms River and Tuckerton and a small privateer boom town arose at the forks of the Mullica River. By midsummer of 1778 no British merchant ship was safe off the Jersey coast without armed escort.

The Crown's officers decided in October to subdue these "nests of pirates" and chose Chestnut Neck on Great Bay (near modern Atlantic City) as the spot to teach a lesson. Some 800 British troops overwhelmed the Chestnut Neck defenders on October 6, 1778, and proceeded up the Mullica River toward the several ironworks within the pinelands. Hastily recruited woodlands volunteers tore into the Redcoats next day and sent them streaming back to Chestnut Neck.

Such matters delighted local dwellers and perhaps even deluded them about the course of the war, but the Revolution dragged on. New Jersey's strategic placement between New York and Philadelphia once more lured Washington back into the state for winter quarters as the winter of 1778–79 neared. This time the troops encamped at Middlebrook (near Bound Brook) while the general lived in the newly built Wallace House at Somerville.

INTERLUDE IN NEW JERSEY

That winter, fairly mild and with little threat of British attack, gave Washington at least two memorable evenings. He enjoyed "an elegant dinner" and fireworks at a party given on February 18 by General Henry Knox to celebrate the first anniversary of the French alliance. Then, at a "pretty little frisk" at General Nathanael Greene's headquarters in the middle of March, the general was observed to have danced with Mrs. Greene "upwards of three hours without once sitting down," in a rare (and probably more traditional than true) show of endurance.

Threats of an enemy attack on West Point pulled the Americans out of Middlebrook on June 3, 1779, for a forced march to the Hudson but the attack never came. That summer the revolutionists gained prestige when Virginia's "Light Horse Harry" Lee (no relation to Charles) successfully assaulted the British fort at Paulus Hook on August 19. Lee captured 119 British under the very muzzles of the big British guns in New York.

But Washington learned that not all was serene in Jersey. His teacher was daring Colonel John Simcoe, who had engineered the massacre at Hancock's Bridge in March, 1778.

Simcoe led his Queens Rangers out of New Brunswick on October 27, 1779, and pounded through the Millstone River valley in a dash that many historians have labeled the most daring single exploit of the war. He and his Rangers covered fifty-five miles in a single night. They coolly drew supplies from an American quartermaster, burned the courthouse at Millstone, and struck terror through the valley. Pursuers captured Simcoe near Middlebush but most of the raiders made their way safely back to New Brunswick.

Winter drew near; Washington decided to stay in New Jersey again— for the third time in four winters, and for the second time in Morristown. Valley Forge is the symbol of supreme American courage, but the second winter in Morristown brought this comment from the late Douglas Southall Freeman, the distinguished biographer of Washington: "The winter of 1779–80 at Morristown and Jockey Hollow was a period of far worse suffering than the corresponding months of 1777–78 at Valley Forge."

DREADFUL DAYS IN MORRISTOWN

Snow swirled about Washington as he reached Morristown on December 1, a sign of things to come, for the winter of 1779–80 was the worst of the eighteenth century. Four snows fell in November, seven in December, six in January, four in February, six in March and one in April—twenty-eight in total. A blizzard early in January left snow four feet deep on the level, and many soldiers lay dead in their collapsed tents, "buried like sheep in the snow."

Nearly 12,000 troops endured that winter in and near Morristown, eventually getting quarters in rude huts in town or at nearby Jockey Hollow. The intensely cold temperatures and heavy snow were accompanied by a woeful lack of supplies. A regimental clothier in the Pennsylvania Line reported some troops "as naked as Lazarus," and an officer in Stark's Brigade wrote there was "many a good lad with nothing to cover him from his hips to his toes save his blanket." Washington called the situation of the army "with respect to supplies beyond description."

General and Mrs. Washington stayed in the Ford Mansion, the home of the late Colonel Jacob Ford, Jr. Mrs. Ford and her four young children lived in two rooms; the Washingtons and as many as fifteen to seventeen staff officers occupied the rest of the stately white mansion. Mrs. Washington arrived December 28, and town ladies who called for a social visit found her in "a speckled homespun apron and knitting a stocking." She kindly suggested to the visiting matrons that "American ladies should be patterns of industry to their countrywomen."

"I do declare," recalled one of the visitors, "I never felt so ashamed and rebuked in my life."

That winter the town also knew the agony of the court-martial of General Benedict Arnold, the crippled hero of Saratoga and other engagements and a man second only to Washington in esteem. Despite Arnold's indignant denials that he had favored Tories in Philadelphia the previous summer, the court found him guilty. Washington issued as mild a scolding as possible but the badly stung Arnold refused to accept the verdict. There is evidence that Arnold's indignity was sham; he probably had already begun the negotiations with the British that led to his defecting the following September.

Despite the air of depression, the winter did offer some reasons for brightness. Lafayette, returning from a voyage to France, reported in May, 1780, that a French fleet was on the way to America. Young Colonel Alexander Hamilton passed the winter successfully wooing Miss Betsy Schuyler, who lived with her uncle down the street from Washington's headquarters. Then, when Don Juan de Miralles, a visiting Spanish nobleman, died of pneumonia in April, Morristown was treated to its most brilliant funeral. A guard had to be placed at the grave to prevent plundering, covered as everything was with gold and silver ornamentation.

Life in the new world seemed better in the spring, for news came that even the British public was opposing the war, both for its cost and for its futility. Heightened French aid was on the way to make American victory more certain. The tide definitely had turned. However, Washington wrote on June 6, 1780: "One year rolls over another, and without some change, we are hastening to our ruin."

BATTLES FOR SPRINGFIELD

That same day, Hessian General Knyphausen crossed to New Jersey from Staten Island with a force of some 6000 Hessians, British, and Tories. Fear gripped northern New Jersey, for Clinton had just captured Charleston, South Carolina, thus lessening pressure on British in the southern campaign. Many saw Knyphausen's attack as an assault on Morristown to capture military supplies, others felt it was a prelude to a march toward West Point, the guardian of the open Hudson River waterway to the interior.

Knyphausen advanced through Elizabethtown on June 7 and headed west toward the Short Hills gap in the Watchung Mountains on the road leading to Morristown. Colonel Elias Dayton and his 3rd New Jersey Militia contested the advance, turning stone fences, trees, and houses into a series of temporary fortresses in a show of militia strength that surprised and angered the invaders. General William Maxwell's New Jersey Brigade joined Dayton at Connecticut Farms (now Union) and held up Knyphausen's push for three hours.

After Dayton and Maxwell withdrew from Connecticut Farms, the invaders burned most of the houses and barns in the village. One of Knyphausen's men fired through a window and killed Mrs. James Caldwell, wife of the Reverend Caldwell, as she crouched in a corner protecting her infant. That senseless killing brought forth heightened local fury; militiamen pursued the fleeing enemy nearly all the way to Elizabethtown.

Seventeen days later, on June 23, Knyphausen returned, this time with more than 5000 men. General Greene had about 2500 Continental regulars to oppose him but before the day was far along, General Philomen Dickinson had rallied more than 5000 New Jersey militia. Master strategist Greene delayed and frustrated the invaders, and at Springfield Reverend James Caldwell, whose wife had been murdered sixteen days before, passed out Watt's Hymnals for use as wadding in American cannon. His shout "Give them Watts, boys!" has echoed down through the years.

Once more the British torches proved more dastardly than their rifles; all but five buildings in Springfield were destroyed by enemy-set fires. Their mission accomplished, the invaders raced eastward to Staten Island through a ceaseless musket fire. This time Knyphausen lost between 400 and 500 men in a major assault—and repulse—that gets only scant attention in American history.

Washington showed reluctance to leave New Jersey, aware that Clinton—now back from the South—might strike again toward Morristown or might hit West Point. Wary of a foray up the Hudson Valley, Washington established headquarters in the Theunis Dey mansion in Preakness from July 1 to July 29 and again from October 9 to October 27 before going into winter encampment at New Windsor, New York. Outward, his army spread on a line from Morristown to West Point.

MUTINY IN JANUARY

Poorly equipped, seldom paid, irked by the slight attention accorded soldiers by Congress, the American army grew mutinous in that fifth winter of the war. Late on the afternoon of January 1, 1781, the normally stable Pennsylvania Line turned on its officers at Morristown and set off for Philadelphia to demand better treatment from Congress. General

"Mad Anthony" Wayne pleaded with the mutineers to stop, then followed them to Princeton and Trenton, where a series of meetings with members of Congress satisfied the revolters that matters would be better if they returned to Morristown.

Morristown's mutiny produced one of the Revolution's most fetching tales. Miss Tempe Wick, teen-aged daughter of Farmer Wick of Jockey Hollow, met some of the Pennsylvania mutineers as she rode her horse on a road near her home. The Pennsylvanians stopped her and demanded her horse. When one of them grasped the bridle, Tempe slashed him with her whip and galloped off. She reached home, and legend says that while the Pennsylvania mutineers vainly searched the barns and thickets, she hid with the beloved horse in her bedroom.

The spirit of mutiny reached Pompton by January 20, when about 300 New Jersey troops left their huts near that town and ambled overland to brigade headquarters at Chatham to seek better treatment. They went peaceably, declaring "a great affection for their officers," and returned to Pompton quietly (upon promises of a hearing on their complaints).

Washington moved harshly to stem this mutinous spirit, for its spread would ruin the army. Three among the Pompton men were selected by lot to be executed, with twelve of the other mutineers chosen to execute the three who must die. Two of the three men were shot by fellow mutineers, turned executioners. The third was spared. Mutiny ended, checked by prompt and stern retaliation.

Washington's full command journeyed across New Jersey only once more, this time late in August, 1781, on the way south to the eventual showdown with the British at Yorktown. This march had an air of both urgency and new excitement, for the American forces needed to reach Yorktown while the French fleet held the sea lanes off Virginia. The excitement was anticipation, stirred by the beautifully disciplined, handsomely uniformed French force that marched across New Jersey on the way from encampment at Dobbs Ferry, New York, to Virginia. Yorktown's long siege ended in Cornwallis' surrender on October 19, 1781, and for all but mopping-up activity, the long war had ended as well.

New Jersey had one more savage episode, the hanging of Captain Joshua Huddy at Gravelly Point in Monmouth County, before the bitterness ended. Huddy commanded a little company of twenty-three men holding a blockhouse at Toms River during a minor engagement in March. The blockhouse fell and Huddy was captured by a group of Loyalists. The American captain expected soldier's treatment but instead was hanged in an execution that men on both sides saw as murder rather than military necessity.

Continental leaders matched brutality with brutality. They decided to execute an innocent British captain to avenge Huddy. Twenty-year-old Captain Charles Asgill, Jr. was chosen by lot for the hanging. Asgill, son of a wealthy baronet, stayed in Chatham while he awaited the noose. An avalanche of protest on both sides of the Atlantic, particularly from France—and from both sides in the fray—halted the execution. Young Asgill was released in November on orders from Congress, much to the relief of all concerned.

Last-minute savagery seems of no consequence when a war has ceased—and this war was over. America was free; now it could set about the task of making a nation arise from a scattering of dreams.

9

Founding a Nation

Congress proclaimed war's end on April 14, 1783, nearly eight years to the day after the first shots of rebellion had cracked over the greens of Concord and Lexington. More than one former colony welcomed the news with mingled solemnity and joy; New Jersey church bells rang out from Newton to Salem while ministers called congregations together in thanksgiving. Then, soldiers and civilians alike lifted glasses of "Jersey lightning" in heartfelt toasts to an independent nation.

Neither prayers nor toasts could hide the fact that although the thirteen states were independent they certainly were not united. The question that the world rightfully asked was simply this: Could Southern planters and New England merchants, with their conflicting interests, pull together for the common weal—including the common weal of tiny states such as New Jersey?

Many doubted it. One Jerseyman, William Peartree Smith, summed up the general despair in April, 1783, in a letter to Elias Boudinot, the Elizabethtown squire then serving in Philadelphia as President of the Continental Congress: "I don't know whether it would not have been best for us all had he [George Washington] lain hold of the helm; for I am confoundedly afraid that the Stupid Crew will sink the ship, when escaped the storms and got safely into port."

Persistently disavowing those who would give him unlimited powers in their spirit of adulation, Washington sent a circular letter to governors in June. He urged Americans to unite in seizing "a fairer opportunity for political happiness than any other nation has ever been blessed with." He asked each governor to decide whether "the revolution must ultimately be considered a blessing or a curse—not to the present age alone, for with our fate will the destiny of unborn millions be involved."

WHERE WAR HAD PASSED

New Jersey's Governor William Livingston received Washington's letter amid vivid proof of war's cruelty, for few if any states had suffered more from the direct impact of the Revolution. Soldiers marching and counter-marching across the state from 1776 to 1781 had lain waste to fields, had terrorized the population, and had set the torch to homes, churches, and barns. Beside nearly every road between Trenton and New Brunswick could be seen the weed-covered ruins of buildings ravaged during the occupation days of 1776.

A 1782 survey by the legislature showed more than 2000 instances of British and Hessian depredations in Bergen, Essex, Middlesex, Somerset, and Burlington counties—with nearly one-third of the cases in Middlesex County alone. Sadly, since battle is a composite of the passions of men, the survey also revealed hundreds of properties where American soldiers had wreaked havoc, particularly in Bergen and Morris counties.

Still, the barns and the churches could be rebuilt. Much more distressing was the gulf that inevitably had opened between those who had become revolutionists and those who had remained loyal to Great Britain. Sentiment against Tories ran high in New Jersey, for during the war an estimated 5000 citizens of the state remained loyal to King George. The majority of those Loyalists had fled to New York; now they wanted to return, forgiven, to resettle their lands.

War's end underscored the naturally fierce feeling against Tories. Many bitterly opposed their return, and when toasts were said in celebration of peace, denunciations of Tories mingled with toasts to freedom. Some Tories who dared to return were insulted, abused, and coated with tar and feathers, particularly in Middlesex and Monmouth counties—both of which had known the unrelenting pressure of Tory raiders during the war. When a group of leading merchants in 1784 proposed forgiveness for Tories, except those who had been guilty of "licentious cruelty" during the Revolution, few of the Loyalists reached out to grasp the olive branch, recognizing that it might suddenly be replaced by a hickory club. Bands of them soon migrated to Nova Scotia, where New Jersey traditions are still found in many towns.

FLIGHT TO PRINCETON

Postwar troubles sharpened during the spring of 1783, and as a result, Princeton suddenly became the capital of the infant nation.

Congress, struggling in Philadelphia with problems of war debts, demobilization, and chaotic finances, heard ugly grumblings from soldiers still in uniform. Eighty men in the 3rd Pennsylvania Regiment mutinied at Lancaster, Pennsylvania, on June 19 and marched on Philadelphia to demand—by force, if necessary—their back pay and some definite idea of when they would be released.

When soldiers fixed bayonets and surrounded the hall where the law-makers sat, President (of the Congress) Elias Boudinot hastily adjourned Congress on June 24. Two days later the body reassembled at Nassau Hall in Princeton. Boudinot undoubtedly chose Princeton for personal reasons as well as hope for safety: he was a native of Princeton and his widowed sister, Mrs. Annis Boudinot Stockton (wife of the late Richard Stockton), lived in the handsome Princeton mansion called Morven (now the official New Jersey governor's mansion).

Proud little Princeton sought vainly to entertain the visiting dignitaries. The village had only sixty to eighty homes, and, although townspeople offered their best, Congress found the place too small and too provincial. Still, Johann David Schoepf, the German natural scientist who passed through while Congress was in session, wrote that there could be "no finer, airier and pleasanter place for the seat of the Jersey Muses."

Summoned by Congress to receive the official thanks of the nation, Washington left his Newburgh headquarters on August 12 and headed southward for Princeton. The village was so crowded that General and Mrs. Washington stayed at Rocky Hill, three miles east of Princeton, in a twenty-room house on the late Judge John Berrian's handsome farm.

Late in the morning of Tuesday, August 26, Washington mounted his small roan gelding and trotted off for his meeting with Congress. The village swarmed with crowds eager to catch a glimpse of America's great-est hero. Distinguished personages rubbed elbows with plain farmers; townspeople stood shoulder to shoulder with black-gowned collegians.

Thirteen cannon boomed a salute as Washington entered Princeton from the east and made his way slowly to Nassau Hall, where Congress awaited him. No one applauded and no one rose as Washington entered, the silent reception symbolizing the subordination of military authority to civil. President Boudinot, seated, read the glowing message of thanks and Washington replied formally. The general turned and walked quietly out of Nassau Hall as Congress voted to adjourn. Washington imme-diately returned and the adjourned Congressmen cheered as lustily as had the crowds in the streets.

BACK TO BUSINESS

It was not all emotional ceremony in Princeton, although things were pleasanter in the New Jersey interlude than either before or after. Con-gress gathered in Nassau Hall on November 1 to receive enthusiastically official word that a final peace had been signed with England at Versailles. That afternoon Peter John Van Berckel of the Netherlands, the first foreign minister to be received by the now formally free United States, spoke to Congress and welcomed the new nation into "the ranks of sovereign and independent powers."

Days grew short both for Congress in Princeton and for Washington at Rocky Hill. Congress adjourned on November 4, setting Annapolis as its next point of convention. Washington appeared on the balcony of his Rocky Hill headquarters and read an affectionate farewell message to his select personal bodyguard. A week later he departed to make the long voyage home to Mount Vernon and what he thought would be his long-awaited retirement to the life of a farmer.

Clearly, however, the thirteen colonies of the new United States drifted aimlessly under the Articles of Confederation. States stood independent and supreme; the national government, at best, was advisory —with no power to tax, no power to regulate either foreign or interstate commerce, and no strength to enforce its own laws.

All states were plagued with economic depression and money woes. The last cannon had scarcely sounded before England began flooding New York and Philadelphia marketplaces with wares far below prices that were asked for comparable American-made goods. "What is to become of our money?" asked "A Plain Farmer" in the *New Jersey Gazette* on July, 1782. He answered himself:

> It is gone; and I will tell you where. It is gone to New York to buy goods, and goods of those kinds which are not only useless, but ruinous to any people and particularly to a plain frugal people. Powder and ball, musquets and bayonets cannot conquer us, but we are to be subdued with British geegaws. We can deal with an open enemy; but now, like worms, they are eating through the bottom of the vessel, and we go down without seeing our destruction.

Things were bad enough without such competition. Lessened postwar demands crushed most New Jersey industry. Iron establishments collapsed; most of the nearly 100 furnaces and forges put out their fires and Southern New Jersey glassworks were stilled. Typifying the problems of American producers were the seven Stanger brothers who opened a glassworks at Glassboro in 1775 with high hopes and found themselves in debtors prison by 1780. Their glass was as good as ever, but their credit had been ruined by the worthlessness of the Continental currency.

Like most states, New Jersey tried paper money as a panacea. The legislature issued nearly £200,000 in paper currency between 1783 and 1786, but most New York and Philadelphia merchants refused to accept the New Jersey money as legal tender, preferring their own notes. Soon the psychology of inferior worth spread even within the state, and values of New Jersey money plummeted.

Each state had the right to set its own tariffs, and when New Jersey's two big neighbors increased their duties to keep out British goods, the net result for Jerseymen who shopped in New York or Philadelphia was increased costs. Hopefully, the New Jersey legislature proclaimed in 1784 that for twenty-five years all goods could be imported into Perth Amboy and Burlington without duty, but foreign shippers failed to take advantage of the generosity.

NEW JERSEY STAGGERS CONGRESS

The bitterness against powerful neighbors boiled over early in 1786 in an eruption that served to expose both New Jersey's trade difficulties and the appalling weakness of a confederation of states. The two chief deficiencies of the Articles of Confederation—the inability of Congress to levy taxes and the lack of power to regulate trade—stood starkly revealed.

Congress had called in September, 1785, for $3,000,000 to be shared by thirteen states according to their supposed ability to pay. The need was evident, for internal problems beset Congress, and even more compelling was an undeclared war that the Barbary pirates of Tripoli were waging on American shipping in Mediterranean waters. In asking for the $3,000,000, Congress stressed that weapons must be found to combat the piracy, lest United States trade be crippled forever.

New Jersey's share was $166,716, fair enough in proportion to the state's size. However, at the same time, New York stiffened duties against all imports, treating New Jersey cabbages and pork the same as Madeira wines. New Jersey had been handed the last straw. On February 20, 1786, the legislature adopted a resolution refusing to pay one cent until the state's grievances were met. The resolution declared that the national government was "weak and unjust," that New Jersey had been "ill used" by New York for years, that New Jersey had been made to bear "more than her share of expenses."

The refusal stunned Congress, not only because the money was needed, but also because the obduracy of the small state struck at the very heart of the confederacy. If the nation had to beg funds from one of its smallest units—and that state could refuse to pay—how could the United States ever assume its place as a world power?

TARNISHED COAT OF CONFEDERACY

Congress sent a three-man committee to Trenton to plead with the legislature for New Jersey to pay its quota. Charles Pinckney of South Carolina stood figuratively with the nation's hat in hand. He admitted that the state had a grievance against New York, but he presented a picture of national troubles, of Indians on the rampage west of the Alleghanies, and of pirates loose on the seas. He underscored the tarnish that would coat the confederation if New Jersey persisted.

The legislature listened respectfully and on March 17 rescinded its resolution not to pay. Then, like most sister states, New Jersey merely neglected to forward the money. In effect, one was as bad as the other, but at least the honor of Congress was salvaged and at no expense to New Jersey taxpayers.

Continuing wrangles between states led Virginia to propose a conference at Annapolis in September, 1786, "to take into consideration the trade and commerce of the United States." New Jersey joined eagerly with Virginia, Delaware, Pennsylvania, and New York, but New England sent no representatives and the South stood aloof except for Virginia. Significantly, the New Jersey delegation carried instructions to consider not only commerce but "other important matters."

The Annapolis conclave recognized that no action could be taken by only five states. Delegates proposed a session in Philadelphia the following May to consider means to "render the Constitution of the Federal government adequate to the exigencies of the Union." The first uncertain step toward a strong government had been taken; Virginia appointed delegates on November 9. Fifteen days later New Jersey became the second state to endorse the Constitutional Convention.

VIRGINIA VERSUS NEW JERSEY

Governor Livingston led a six-man delegation to Philadelphia late in May, 1787, and they arrived to find debate already begun on the carefully conceived Virginia Plan. Reduced to fundamentals, Virginia proposed a strong federal government, with power vested in a national legislature of two houses, one chosen by the people and the other by the state legislatures. There would be one national executive and a national judiciary. Representation would be based on shares of money paid by states to the national quota or on the number of free inhabitants within each state.

Virginia's plan stirred New Jersey's William Paterson to angry words on June 10. He declared (and true enough) that the Philadelphia convention had not been called to shape a new government, but rather to "alter or amend" the Articles of Confederation. Arguing that small states would be "more enslaved" than ever under the Virginia plan, Paterson concluded harshly: "Neither my state nor myself will ever submit to despotism or tyranny."

Paterson brought in New Jersey's counterproposals on June 15. Essentially, New Jersey called for one house of Congress, with each state having equal representation regardless of size; a group of chief executives rather than a single leader and limited federal control over state activities.

Alexander Hamilton reacted to Paterson's proposal with instant, acidulous disapproval. He called the New Jersey Plan "the old Articles of Confederation with new patches . . . pork still, with new sauce." Hamilton was not far wrong, but the New Jersey recommendations provided a genuine basis for compromise, for small states at least could rally to that solid point of dignity. Eventually the convention agreed on two legislative bodies, in which the large, populous states would rule the House of Representatives (as in the Virginia Plan) and small states would be equally represented in the Senate (as in the New Jersey Plan).

Four of the New Jersey delegation (Livingston, Brearley, Paterson, and Jonathan Dayton) signed the new Constitution on September 17 and went home to work for adoption. Delaware ratified first, followed by Pennsylvania and then New Jersey. Delegates who considered the Constitution on December 19 at Francis Witt's Blazing Star Tavern in Trenton unanimously endorsed the document. Next day, public announcement at Trenton's courthouse attracted lusty cheers. A light infantry company fired thirteen rounds for thirteen states—with additional rounds for Delaware and Pennsylvania.

DEMOCRACY IN SHABBY DRESS

Democracy being the unpredictable thing that it is, New Jersey put on a shabby demonstration when it selected its first four representatives to Congress in 1789. The slanderous, dishonest campaign is described in detail in Richard P. McCormick's *Experiment in Independence,* and the proceedings show that election chicanery is not a twentieth-century phenomenon.

Faced for the first time with an opportunity to choose representatives state-wide, New Jerseyans adhered to their old East Jersey versus West Jersey patterns. The main "East Jersey" candidates were Abraham Clark and Jonathan Dayton. The "West Jersey" or "Junto" ticket actually included two East Jerseyans, Elias Boudinot and James Schureman, and two West Jerseyans, Thomas Sinnickson and Lambert Cadwallader.

Voting began on February 11 amid storms of vituperation in all areas. Seven counties, all north of Trenton, closed their polls on or before February 23. Essex County and all of West Jersey kept polls open as late as April 23 in an election fraught with scheming and irregularity. James Madison's comment that voting had been conducted in "very singular manner" was gentle understatement.

The New Jersey Council, charged with determining the winners, waited only for full West Jersey returns and blandly certified Schureman, Cadwallader, Boudinot, and Sinnickson as victorious on March 18 although Essex County votes still weren't totaled. Final but too-late returns from Essex showed Clark and Dayton would easily have been second and third to Schureman in total votes (Sinnickson received only 124 votes in Essex and Cadwallader a mere seventeen).

Governor Livingston certified the Council-approved results but suggested that final determination be in the hands of those "to whom it appertains," meaning Congress. The House of Representatives, to no one's surprise, approved the full "Junto slate" in September. Clark and Dayton had ample revenge a year later. Both won, and Dayton went on to become Speaker of the House in 1794.

DEFENDER OF THE MOTHERS

Politicking stopped temporarily in April, 1789, when George Washington passed through on the way to New York to be sworn in as first President of the United States.

"An admiring concourse" greeted him on April 21 as he entered Trenton. The General passed under a flower-festooned archway, visibly touched by the message on the arch: THE DEFENDER OF THE MOTHERS WILL BE THE PROTECTOR OF THE DAUGHTERS. White-robed little girls and thirteen young women (each representing a state) strewed flowers in Washington's path as they sang an ode written especially for the occasion, by Major Richard Howell (later Governor Howell):

> "Welcome, mighty Chief! once more
> Welcome to this grateful shore!
> Now no mercenary foe
> Aims again the fatal blow—
> Aims at thee the fatal blow."

Washington thanked Trenton's "Matrons and young ladies" who received him "in so novel and grateful a manner at the Triumphal Arch." He moved on to stay overnight in Princeton and at Woodbridge. Along the way, "farmers assembled at crossroads, gentry bowed dignified welcome from the porches of wayside inns, and soldiers who had fought their nation's battles saluted and cheered." Elias Boudinot entertained the President in Elizabethtown, before Washington boarded an "elegantly adorned" boat which carried him past wildly cheering crowds to New York, where he was inaugurated on April 30.

Pleasantly in the minds of many as their hero journeyed to New York lingered the wishful thinking that Trenton might still become the nation's capital.

Back in 1783, when Congress had passed halcyon days at Nassau Hall,

talk of selecting a "permanent residence" had begun. New Jersey legislators offered "any district to the extent of 20 miles square" and granted
£ 30,000 in specie for the purchase of lands and erection of buildings.
Elbridge Gerry of Massachusetts (who later earned undying remembrance in the word "gerrymandering" as a term for splitting areas for
political advantage) moved in October, 1783, that the capital be located
either "on the banks of the Delaware near Trenton or of the Potomac
near George Town."

Southerners loudly protested a Trenton capital, declaring that their
interests would be subjected to the commercialism of New England.
Congress compromised: meetings would alternate for the time being
between Trenton and Annapolis. Francis Hopkinson of Bordentown, tart
satirist, called this a "miraculous pendulum."

Congress came to Trenton in November, 1784, grateful for the £ 300
the New Jersey legislature appropriated to refurbish Jacob Bergen's
French Arms as a meeting place. Members rapidly became annoyed at
the lack of good accommodations, occasioned because the state legislature had convened in town at the same time and had taken most of the
best beds. The restless Congress left the day before Christmas.

Congress quietly abandoned both Trenton and Annapolis in January,
1785. Slowly but inevitably the wheels ground against Trenton's hopes
for national honor. Alexander Hamilton and Thomas Jefferson used the
capital-city location as a pawn in a political deal. Hamilton guaranteed
Northern votes to place the capital on the Potomac in return for Jefferson's support for Hamilton's scheme to have the federal government
assume state debts.

Although Congress failed to appreciate the merits of the site at "the
falls of the Delaware," the state legislature liked Trenton and on November 25, 1790, chose it as the permanent seat of state government despite
opposition from New Brunswick and Woodbury. The state bought three
and three-quarters acres of land (an area comprising the present state
capitol) in 1791 and began work on the statehouse built with roughcast
bluish stone.

"THE HELM IS NO MORE"

The Trenton capitol came too late for Governor William Livingston to
enjoy it, for he died on July 25, 1790, after serving as New Jersey's first
governor under the constitution of 1776—and the always re-elected chief
executive. Reverend Dr. Alexander Macwhorter of Newark, the leading
Presbyterian minister in the state, said in the funeral oration:

"It is not a single family that this day mourns. It is not a single society, town or county, but our whole feels the stroke, and our bereaved

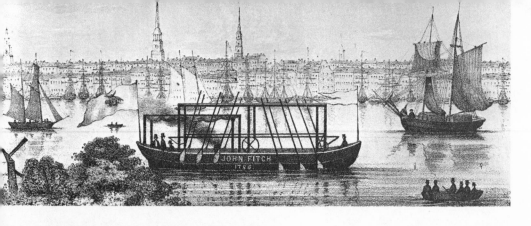

When transportation and industry transformed America in the early nineteenth century, New Jersey was in the forefront. Artists began to give on-the-spot impressions in paintings and sketches. John W. Barber and Henry Howe, itinerent New Englanders, best captured the period with numerous engravings in their *Historical Collections of the State of New Jersey*, first published in 1844 and revised in 1853 and 1868. Quaint, and sometimes crude, the Barber and Howe sketches show New Jersey riding railroads and rapidly filling the sky with smoke.

John Fitch's steamboat, first in America, ran in New Jersey waters in 1786, and a tiny locomotive puffed into Rahway in the mid-1830s. A third travel dimension was the Morris Canal between Jersey City and Phillipsburg. The canal "climbed" a hill west of Newark on this inclined plane.

Charm pervaded Bordentown and Burlington, two Delaware River port towns, before transportation was in full swing. A watercolor, ABOVE, of about 1835 shows stagecoach traffic converging on a Bordentown steamboat, and a lithograph, BELOW, of the same period shows Burlington.

Memories of Indians persisted in the names of Hoboken, ABOVE, still wooded and pastoral in pre-Civil War days, and Lake Hopatcong, BELOW, as it looked after Morris Canal waters raised its level.

Barber and Howe traveled far for their woodcut views—to Cape May Island, past the Presbyterian church at Bloomfield, down the bucolic road leading to Crosswicks, ABOVE, *and over the stone bridge into dignified old Elizabethtown,* OPPOSITE.

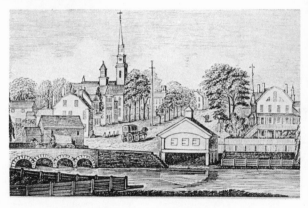

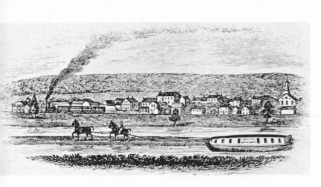

ABOVE, *canalboat and railroad train at Bound Brook;* OPPOSITE, *the church spires of Toms River;* BELOW, *the beginnings of commerce at Camden and the busy look of New Brunswick —all these were fit subjects for Barber and Howe.*

Recording the view, then transferring it to woodcut, Barber and Howe saved for posterity such images as the mighty wooden span across the Delaware at Trenton, the train that meandered by the churches of Madison, the smoking chimneys of Dover, ABOVE, *and the growing splendor of Vineland,* OPPOSITE.

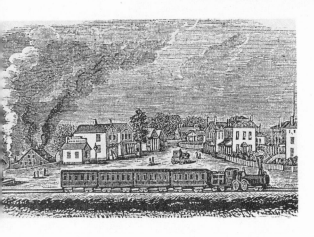

ndustry, prosperity, soot. Barber and Howe faithfully *aught these in the view from the bridge at Millville, the* *cene of Bridgeton with schooners in the foreground, and* *he central part of Bricksburg,* ABOVE. *Not all people wel-* *omed such change; a broadside of the 1840s,* OPPOSITE, *varned Jerseymen of the dangers of a railroad monopoly.*

Paterson, pleased with its railroad locomotive shops and its ironworks, still gloried in the beauty of its eighty-foot falls in the 1850s.

Iron's invasion of once-picturesque Trenton, on the other hand, dominated everything, including the State House, by 1860.

state is most sensibly affected. The head, the guide, the director, and he who held the helm of our government is no more."

Dr. Macwhorter's eulogy was not overstated. The loss of William Livingston was severe; as a brilliant writer, a keen legal mind, a vigorous governor, and a solid factor at the Constitutional Convention, he had helped New Jersey through its difficult toddling years. Livingston would be missed, but there were others to take up the burden.

The legislature chose William Paterson of Raritan (Somerville) to succeed Livingston. An early advocate of independence, Paterson had served well in the Constitutional Convention as the warm champion of States' rights. He had said in Philadelphia that "New Jersey would not have sent delegates to any assembly that would destroy the equalities and rights of the state."

Paterson promptly supported the Constitution and was chosen as one of New Jersey's first two United States Senators (the other being Jonathan Elmer of Cumberland County). He soon became a leading Federalist, urging support for strong national government.

When Paterson stepped up to the United States Supreme Court in 1793, he was succeeded as governor by another advocate of strong federal power, William Howell of Trenton. Although settled and staid by 1793, Howell always would bear a revolutionary stamp, for he had been one of the young firebrands who had burned British tea in Greenwich in December, 1774.

The Federalists rode high, in New Jersey and elsewhere, in the decade after the adoption of the Constitution. Chief national spokesman of the Federalist cause was Alexander Hamilton, Washington's brilliant, caustic young Secretary of the Treasury. Hamilton's career touched New Jersey intimately on at least three occasions during the period of Federalist supremacy.

A SOCIETY FOR MANUFACTURES

For one thing, Hamilton had New Jersey in mind when he proposed in 1791 that America begin its own system of manufactures if it was to compete successfully with other nations. Hamilton flew in the face of American tradition. Benjamin Franklin once had said that manufactures were not desirable except to use the "idle time of children," and John Adams had declared in 1780 that "America will not make manufactures enough for her own consumption these thousand years."

Hamilton first advanced his manufacturing proposals in a detailed report to Congress, suggesting that the industrial town might be in New York, Pennsylvania, or New Jersey—although there is evidence that he favored a location at the seventy-foot falls of the Passaic River. The New Jersey legislature approved the Society for Establishing Useful

Manufactures in November, 1791. The sponsors named their town Paterson, a move not calculated to annoy Governor William Paterson.

Paterson started as America's first planned industrial city in 1792, at a time when only fifty people lived within earshot of the thundering falls. The society built a cotton mill (powered by a bull on a treadmill) and population leaped to more than 500 in 1796. The mill failed in 1797 and Paterson's population plummeted to fewer than fifty people. The planned industrial city would succeed—but the time was not ripe.

CITY ON THE WEST BANK

Hamilton's second New Jersey vision involved the sandy hills and open marshlands at Paulus Hook, directly across from New York City. Paulus Hook offered little reason for hope; in 1800 the only buildings were a ferry house, a few outbuildings and a shanty where a sign proclaimed "Oygh-stars for sale Hear." Fewer than ten people lived in the dunes; Paulus Hook existed solely as the western terminus for an uncertain ferry.

In the face of that negative evidence, Hamilton told friends that someday a city must arise at Paulus Hook, reasoning that throughout history most great cities had arisen on the west bank of broad rivers. New York City lawyer friends (Anthony Dey, Richard Varick, and Jacob Radcliffe) leased the land in 1804 for 6000 "Spanish milled dollars" annually. Hamilton drew the charter for those "Associates of New Jersey."

The Associates divided their land into 1000 lots, advertised their holdings, and gave land to church associations—not the best land, for when the Catholics tried to build, one wall collapsed in the marshy soil, and the Methodists had to construct a high plank walk to reach their church. The project appeared to be a dismal failure; it would be reincorporated in 1820 with a new name—Jersey City—before Hamilton's predictions came true.

Many reasons have been advanced for the early failure of Hamilton's dream city: too rigid control by the Associates, miserable ferry service, and New York City's insistence that it controlled all land up the low water mark on the New Jersey side of the Hudson River. All were factors, but perhaps greatest reason of all was a dismal affair at Weehawken on July 11, 1804.

Hamilton visited Weehawken early in the morning of July 11, climbed a bluff to a small grassy plain, and there met his long-time political enemy, Aaron Burr, Jr. He had come to answer Burr's challenge to a duel.

The rendezvous had been in the making for years. Newark-born Aaron Burr had been graduated from the College of New Jersey, served brilliantly in the Revolution, and gained distinction as a lawyer. At every turn, however, he seemed to face Hamilton—in the courts, in politics, in public life. Hamilton had schemed to keep him from being named President in 1801; after thirty-five ballots Burr and Thomas Jefferson remained deadlocked in the House of Representatives. On the thirty-sixth ballot Hamilton's undercover maneuvering paid off: Jefferson was named President and Burr Vice-President.

Then, in 1804, Burr sought election as governor of New York, only to be frustrated again by Hamilton's behind-the-scenes opposition. Burr heard reports that Hamilton had slandered him and issued the challenge for the duel at Weehawken. Burr's bullet tore into his foe's body, and hours later Hamilton died in New York—to the ruination of Burr's career, to the unquestionable loss to the nation, and to the woe of the Associates of New Jersey at Paulus Hook.

Weehawken's dueling ground provided melancholy punctuation for the chapter of declining Federalist power within New Jersey. The trend had been well underway, of course, with the election of Thomas Jefferson and his ideas that the power of a nation must rest within the hands of "the people" rather than in an aristocracy. In 1801, Joseph Bloomfield was elected the state's first anti-Federalist governor, a post he held until 1812. Only once more would the Federalists regain leadership, and that would come when state and nation faced another war with Great Britain.

"PEACE" IN 1812

New Jersey Federalists rode a "peace" platform to victory in the fall of 1812, not difficult to do, since New Jersey had none of the War Hawks so common in other states. The Federalists pulled together a variety of antiwar elements—the sincerely pacificist Quakers of West Jersey and the considerably less altruistic industrialists and merchants of East Jersey who felt war with England must bring commercial disaster. Holding these diverse elements together was a general apathy that refused to face the fact that soon British guns might be booming off the Jersey coast, for the war already had begun. Voters backed peace in 1812 so overwhelmingly that Federalists controlled both houses of the legislature and swept Aaron Ogden into the governor's seat.

Quickly the victory-flushed Federalists moved to consolidate their position, but they overreached themselves. First they gerrymandered the state to insure that four of six New Jersey representatives in the United States Congress would be Federalist. Then, in what would prove to be a political disaster, the Federalist-controlled Assembly scathingly denounced the war as "inexpedient, ill-timed and most dangerously impolitic." All the gains won in the Revolution might disappear in this newest conflict, the Federalist Assembly argued. It went so far as to suggest that military despotism in France was more dangerous than England's dominance of the seas.

Governor Ogden called the attention of his Federalist Legislature to the state's unpreparedness and in January, 1813, urged stepped-up training of the militia. More than 6000 New Jersey men were called into action, some of them serving out of state—but the militia refused to serve out of New Jersey (in common with militia in most other states). Despite legislative promises to sustain the struggle where necessary and the demonstrated sincerity of Ogden's efforts, Federalist office-holders suffered severely in the October, 1813, elections; power returned to the anti-Federalists, who named William S. Pennington as governor. Peace was not so dear as it had seemed in 1812, certainly not peace at any price.

New Jersey might have faced serious problems in the War of 1812 had England pursued the conflict with vigor. The long, exposed, and little-defended coastline beckoned to an aggressive enemy. As in the Revolution, the richest United States commercial prizes were New York and Philadelphia; these should have made Great Britain see the wisdom of harassing shipping in the Delaware and Hudson rivers.

England did establish an effective blockade off the Jersey coast late in 1813, but except for minor skirmishes between British ships and a variety of blockade runners or Jersey privateers, the war scarcely affected the state. There were alarms in Cumberland and Cape May counties involving British incursions ashore to seek cattle near the Maurice River or fresh water at Cape May Point, but these were minor. War was far away, in Canada or in the burning of Washington.

New Jersey's chief memory of the War of 1812 came from the first-rate hero it gave the nation: Captain James Lawrence. "Captain Jim" was born October 1, 1781, in a substantial brick house in Burlington, son of the mayor of the little port town. He tutored in astronomy and navigation in Burlington, left there in 1798 to become a midshipman aboard the twenty-four-gun U.S.S. Ganges, and distinguished himself for gallantry against the Tripoli pirates.

The young Burlington skipper's succession of early victories in the War of 1812 earned him command of the fifty-gun frigate Chesapeake in 1813. Lawrence accepted a challenge from the fifty-two-gun British ship Shannon on June 1, 1813. The ships clashed in fierce broadside combat. The Shannon's guns killed sixty-one and wounded eighty-five of the Chesapeake's crew of 371. The Shannon suffered thirty-three killed and fifty wounded.

Midway in the battle a bullet tore through Lawrence's body. As they

carried him below, Captain Lawrence delivered the phrase still known
to every schoolboy:

"Don't give up the ship!"

They did give up the *Chesapeake* soon after, and Captain Jim died
four days later in Halifax, Nova Scotia. War moved away, and as
peace settled the time had come to acknowledge a fact of life: New
Jersey simply was in the doldrums.

WESTWARD THE WAY

The Census of 1820 told a rather pointed story. True, population had
risen from 184,000 in 1790 to 277,500 in 1820—a modest increase of
nearly 95,000—but nothing compared with growth in other states. New
York State was up more than a million people in the same thirty
years, Pennsylvania up 600,000, while North and South Carolina both
had doubled populations between 1790 and 1820. More startling were
happenings in Ohio, Kentucky, and Tennessee. Ohio, not even a state in
1790, had 581,000 residents in 1820; Kentucky, with 73,000 persons in
1790, totaled 564,000 in 1820; and Tennessee rose from a mere 35,000
to 422,000 in the 1790 to 1820 period.

Westward the way beckoned. Families streamed out of New Jersey
to join New England Yankees seeking greener lands beyond the Allegheny Mountains. Major roads west were across New Jersey to
Easton, Pennsylvania. By 1815 wagon trains with as many as fifty
families each passed westward. Families went in every conceivable
way, dragging their goods in handcarts—and in one case, wheeling their
five children in a wheelbarrow.

Soil depletion in Cumberland and Salem counties between 1800 and
1820 forced farmers westward. One Salem County family headed by
Zadock Street founded Salem, Ohio, in 1803, and by 1820 had wandered
on to establish both Salem, Indiana, and Salem, Iowa. Street's descendants went all the way to the coast, to found another Salem in far-off
Oregon.

Families from Essex County and neighboring counties packed belongings and moved westward to seek new starts in Ohio, Kentucky, Indiana, and Illinois. Ohio's early history is intimately bound to those New
Jersey emigrants, and both Cincinnati and Dayton, Ohio, had Jerseymen
among the founders. Just to show how far westward lay the way for
men of the state, Colonel Zebulon M. Pike of Mercer County explored
the Colorado peak which bears his name and James Marshall of Lambertville discovered California's gold in 1848.

Thomas Gordon, who published his still-used *Gazeteer of the State
of New Jersey* in 1834, summed up the immigrations:

The state has been an *officina gentium,* a hive of nations, constantly sending out swarms, whose labours have contributed largely to build up the two greatest marts of the Union, and to subdue and fertilize the western wilds. Instead, therefore, of being distinguished for the growth of numbers within her borders, she is remarkable for the paucity of their increase.

While other states grew, New Jersey stagnated: that's what Gordon meant. She sat firmly astride the great corridor linking New York and Philadelphia but she dozed while travelers cursed the mud and ruts in New Jersey roads as they rolled elsewhere. But for those who listened, off in the distance sounded the whistles that would completely transform both the United States and the bogged-down state of New Jersey. The mellow tone of steam could be heard in steamboats and railroads and in factory whistles. New Jersey would follow that siren call to growth.

10

Towpath and Iron Horse

"Thy inhabitants, O State, are respectable—thy senators are wise—thy militia is formidable—and thy daughters are fair; but some of thy ways are bad. Whoever travels the road from Stony-Brook steep, to Rocky Hill, in a wheel carriage does it at the hazard of his life."

So "A Traveler" expressed himself to the people of New Jersey in the *New Jersey Journal* in October 2, 1793. "Thy public ways call loudly for amendment," he declared. Casting about for a villain, the "Traveler" concluded:

"If the surgeons of Princeton object to having the roads mended for fear travelers will have no bones broken, they ought to get their bones broken!"

New Jersey, like all America, had bogged down beside its muddy trails as the eighteenth century turned into the nineteenth. There were roads aplenty to link towns and crossroads; they wandered outward like spokes from hubs at Paulus Hook, from Newark, from Morristown, from New Brunswick, from Trenton, from Burlington, from Salem, and from Cooper's Creek. Significantly, by 1800 neither Cooper's Creek nor Paulus Hook had achieved identity beyond their ferry landings; their places in history as Camden and Jersey City, respectively, lay ahead—and radical new means of transportation would change both from ferry stops to big cities.

Roads were miserable. The colonial system of overseers periodically called out property owners to fix strips of road adjacent to their land, as they had since colonial times. Revisions of the long-standing practice were made in 1794, but changes were aimed to protect property owners rather than travelers. Quite naturally, therefore, roads were wretched. Henry Wansey, an English traveler, could have been thinking of any road when in 1796 he found the road between New Brunswick and Trenton "full of loose stones and deep holes, in going over which we were so violently shook, that when we got down, many of us could scarcely stand."

Complicating the hazards of travel were the two broad rivers on either side of the state and the numerous streams between. Stagecoaches forded shallow streams when possible or waited for small ferries. The fact that many ferrymen also owned taverns, as always coupled with the truism that travelers stranded in taprooms spend money, made service erratic—despite a 1779 law forbidding ferrymen to "deny or unnecessarily delay the speedy carrying over of any passenger."

Everyone except ferry owners, therefore, thankfully hailed word of extensive toll-bridge construction in the 1790s. There would be charges, but travelers wouldn't be subject to the whims of wind, weather, and bartenders in ferrymen's clothing.

Wooden spans were completed across both the Passaic and Hackensack rivers in 1795 to improve travel between Newark and Paulus Hook. Combining stock sales and funds from a lottery, builders erected a 492-foot-long bridge over the Passaic and a 980-foot-long span over the Hackensack. A causeway of logs was laid in the "trembling" marshland between the bridges. Thin layers of sand and gravel covered the logs, but scarcely in the grand manner; travelers still complained that constant jolting on the causeway made for painful sacroiliacs.

Southward at New Brunswick, a new 990-foot bridge crossed the wide Raritan River on thirteen stone pillars. The opening in 1795, coinciding with the availability of the Passaic and Hackensack bridges, at least made the way between New York and Philadelphia three ferry trips shorter.

Impressive though those three North Jersey spans seemed, American engineers hailed the Trenton bridge over the Delaware as the masterpiece of the day. The New Jersey legislature authorized the span in 1798, declaring that "a good and permanent bridge across the river Delaware . . . would greatly facilitate travel between this and Southern States." Pennsylvania had to enact similar authorization, and did so in 1799, but five more years elapsed before construction began in May, 1804.

"Elaborate exercises" opened the Trenton bridge to traffic on January 30, 1806. The structure stretched 1008 feet from end to end, its five massive wooden arches resting on four tall stone pillars. Builders meant that bridge to stay—and it did. Five other Delaware River bridges washed away in a freshet in 1841, but the Trenton span stood firm. In the 1840s, railroad tracks were laid on the wooden floor and the bridge defied the elements for another thirty-five years before it was replaced in 1876.

By 1806, a traveler could proceed on land or over bridges from Philadelphia to Paulus Hook. He could also use the same facilities to reach Hoboken. John Stevens hired a paid lobbyist to convince the

Legislature of the wisdom of building a new road from the Hackensack bridge to Hoboken, warning that a "choice of ferries" must be available. The fact that one of the two "choices" happened to be John Stevens' Hoboken ferry was not coincidental. The legislature approved the road.

PAY-AS-YOU-GO

Clearly, however, something far more drastic than toll bridges had to be conceived to meet the overwhelming travel demands of a pulsating, eager young nation. People on the move cried out for service; American goods had to be moved.

First America tried toll roads, on the theory that strangers who used the roads ought to help pay for them. Surprisingly for a corridor state unsurpassed in volume of through traffic, New Jersey lagged far behind the rest of the country in such pay-as-you-go travel. New England alone had forty-eight toll roads and New York had chartered thirteen before New Jersey caught the fever in 1801. Once smitten, Jerseymen ran the malady into epidemic proportions.

Eventually the state legislature chartered fifty-one turnpikes in the period between 1801 and 1829, nearly all of them north of a line between Burlington and Perth Amboy. Only about half of those roads were built, but about 550 miles of more-or-less improved toll roadways reached through much of North Jersey before the turnpike rash subsided. Toll roads proved to be too little and too late but they gave New Jersey the reasonably firm basis for its highway network of the future.

New Jersey's first toll road charter was awarded in 1801 to build the Morris Turnpike in three sections—first, Elizabethtown to Morristown, by way of Springfield; second, Morristown to Stanhope via Succasunna, and third, Stanhope to Newton and Milford, Pennsylvania. Five years later, in 1806, sponsors of the Washington Turnpike received approval to construct a toll road from Morristown to Hackettstown through Mendham and Schooley's Mountain to Phillipsburg. The New Jersey Turnpike was chartered the same year to go from New Brunswick to Phillipsburg, by way of Somerville, Whitehouse, and Clinton. Several turnpikes were built to join Paulus Hook, Newark, New Brunswick, and Trenton. All of these are still basic roadways, albeit much changed.

Toll roads seemed, in prospect, like gold mines on wheels, for legislation gave charter holders every tool to extract wealth. Turnpike speculators could take over existing roads and rebuild them. They could condemn property for their right-of-way. They could put their "pike" or barrier on the new roads and charge tolls, averaging about one cent per mile per horse (one half cent for horse and rider). Unfortunately or fortunately (depending on whether one was a stockholder or a traveler) people could use turnpikes without toll on the way to or from either worship or work. They could also "shun the pike" and take back roads if they preferred free passage to convenience or speed.

YANKEES, SHEEP, AND CONESTOGAS

Heavy traffic swarmed over some of the toll roads. In season, hundreds of wagons loaded with farm produce passed daily over the New Jersey Turnpike on the way to ships at New Brunswick. The Morris, Washington, Union, and New Jersey turnpikes provided popular routes west for New England Yankees rolling out to Pennsylvania and on to the Appalachian Valley. Drovers from the northwest country herded sheep and cattle and pigs past the toll pikes on the way to Newark and Jersey City markets. Huge, brightly painted Conestoga wagons used the roads, with wagon and team of six horses often stretching an impressive sixty feet from front nose to tailgate. "Flying" stagecoaches raced over the macadamized toll roads, but still managed always to stretch a New York–Philadelphia trip out to more than a day, regardless of roadbeds or bridges.

Turnpike charters called for solid roadbeds, topped with crushed stone, but charters and practice were not the same. Thomas Gordon noted in his 1834 *Gazetteer of the State of New Jersey* that "we do not recollect to have seen, in any direction, five continuous miles of roads paved with stone." Gordon noted that many nontoll roads proved superior to the turnpikes, particularly in "the slate and sandstone regions where the hard rock approaches the surface."

The War of 1812 cast all roads into wretched perspective. Booming demands for farm supplies and manufactured goods made freight haulers powerful; the federal government alone spent $2,000,000 on freightage in New Jersey, where 4000 wagons and 20,000 horses and oxen tried to meet military demands. This prosperity completely ruined the highways, turnpikes, and free roads alike. Wagon trains turned the New Brunswick–Trenton roads into "hopeless ruts and quagmires." On rainy days drivers often refused to take loads, but in dry spells or when winter froze the surface they fought one another with whips and drove their teams across the state in spirited and profitable competition.

Colonel John Stevens of Hoboken watched with knowing eye as the transportation system disintegrated during the War of 1812. A lesser man might have said, "I told you so," for Stevens had vigorously warned as early as 1811 that prompt steps must be taken to improve transportation lest America sink in the mud of its roads.

The solution, Stevens argued, lay in steam, on land, and on water. He appeared before the New Jersey legislature in 1811 to seek a charter for a railroad on which steam engines would run. Legislators eyed him with incredulity, even pity, before refusing. Soon after, the Erie Canal Commission rejected his plan for a railroad between Albany and Lake Erie. A year later, *before there was a railroad anywhere in the world,* Stevens took his case to the public in a remarkable pamphlet, "Documents Tending to Prove the Superior Advantages of Railway and Steam Carriages Over Canal Navigation." He wrote, in part:

> I can see nothing to hinder a steam-engine from moving with a velocity of 100 miles per hour. In practice it may not be advisable to exceed 20 to 30 miles per hour, but I should not be surprised at seeing carriages propelled at 40 or 50.

The date, bear in mind, was 1812. Stevens said a railroad, would make all states "one family intimately connected." He saw increased revenues for all states, savings for farmers in marketing costs, and an ability to transport armies in twenty-four hours "a greater distance than would take weeks or months to march." Such thinking brought the sixty-two-year-old Stevens only ridicule. Newspaper editors lampooned his ideas; one wrote that "if the contraption doesn't blow up, it will terrify livestock to death." Archibald Douglas Turnbull, Stevens' careful biographer, wrote that men who gathered to discuss the Stevens' work exclaimed:

"Heard John Stevens latest? He's making a damned fool of himself over steam wagons!"

Anyone who thought John Stevens a fool had forgotten the colonel's earlier days. By 1812 his knowledge and use of steam as a propelling force should have been beyond dispute. Already he was a power in the steamboat wars that flared in New York Harbor—and the steamboat portion of John Stevens' life had to be fought out before he could devote full attention to railroads.

POOR JOHN LEADS THE WAY

Twenty-five years before, as others laughed when John Fitch launched America's first steamboat on the Delaware, Stevens saw the potential. "Poor John," as Fitch has been aptly called, had secured in 1786 a fourteen-year charter from the New Jersey legislature for exclusive steamboat rights on the Delaware in 1786. One of John Fitch's boats made regular runs between Philadelphia and Trenton in 1790, but despite nearly 3000 miles of accident-free travel the ledger showed only red ink.

John Stevens found John Fitch neither amusing nor queer. Stevens secured a patent on an improved steam engine and boiler and built a steamboat at the Soho works in Second River (Belleville) in 1798. Six years later he made the first steamboat to use twin propellers. Stevens launched his early masterpiece, the *Phoenix,* in 1808. One hundred feet long, sixteen feet in beam, the ship achieved better than five and a half miles per hour.

Unfortunately, Robert Fulton of New York already had sailed his *Clermont* up the Hudson to Albany the year before. That feat secured a monopoly on New York waters for Fulton and his backer, Robert Livingston. The Fulton-Livingston monopoly kept Stevens from using the *Phoenix* in the Hoboken–New York ferry run, so with characteristic daring the colonel in June, 1809, ordered the vessel to sea and around Cape May to Philadelphia. The doughty *Phoenix* made it and John Stevens had another "first": the first steam-powered vessel to cruise on ocean waters.

Stevens fell before the Fulton-Livingston stranglehold on the Hudson. His ferry boat *Juliana* carried as many as 1500 passengers daily between Hoboken and New York, but in 1813 the monopoly-defying *Juliana* had to flee through Long Island Sound to Connecticut with six of Fulton's slow boats vainly trying to catch her. Stevens bowed to the monopoly; he carried Hoboken–New York passengers thereafter on a "teamboat"–its paddle wheels driven by teams of horses which walked in circles on the boat deck to revolve the drive shaft.

DOWNFALL OF MONOPOLY

Exciting days took over the New York waterfront. Monopoly power was blatant, and all interstate traffic stalled as the battle waxed hot. The full story can't be told here, but a detailed analysis of the brawling, vital years can be found in Wheaton J. Lane's *From Indian Trail to Iron Horse*, a precise account of all transportation in New Jersey up to the Civil War.

Monopoly power finally was broken by an Elizabeth entrepreneur named Thomas Gibbons and his aggressive captain, Cornelius Vanderbilt (who later achieved both fame and fortune in railroading). Vanderbilt supplied the cunning and belligerency in the battle. Month after month the daring young captain plied monopoly waters, his steamboat *Bellona* boldly carrying on its flag the message: "New Jersey Must Be Free!" His exploits enthralled the New York waterfront; the wily Vanderbilt used every ruse to escape arrest and to embarrass anyone in his way.

Vanderbilt's daring was only a side show; the main struggle had to be fought in the courts. Eventually the dispute reached the U. S. Supreme Court, where Chief Justice John Marshall declared in 1824 that the monopoly could not rule interstate waters. Marshall's biographer, A. J. Beveridge, said this decision "has done more to knit the American people into an indivisible nation than any other one force in our history, excepting only war."

Only Congress could regulate interstate commerce, Marshall ruled. The monopoly had been defeated, thanks to a fighting Jersey pair and Chief Justice Marshall. New York became a free port; all steamboat transportation, freed from state monopolies, surged rapidly ahead everywhere.

OFF ON A SIDING

John Stevens had long before turned his full attention from steamboats to railroads. First he walked across the state in 1814, making the nation's first railroad survey—from Lower Landing (near New Brunswick) to Cranbury and thence (as he noted in his journal) to Trenton by way of "the Devil's Brook, the Hide's Town Road, and so to Princeton, up to Rowland's Tavern and the Ten Mile Stone; past the Quaker Wood by Jacob Haw's stable." In Trenton at the end of his hike, the colonel noted that he paused at the Steamboat Hotel and treated himself to a well-earned whiskey and cider.

Stevens' survey encouraged the New Jersey legislature to grant him America's first railroad charter in 1815. Few really believed in railroading; Stevens couldn't get capitalists to back his line. Ten years later Stevens built America's first railroad locomotive and ran his "Steam Waggon" over 630 feet of circular track near Stevens Villa in Hoboken, hoping to rouse interest. The Waggon achieved speeds of twelve miles per hour and easily climbed a thirty-inch slope Stevens built into one side of the track to prove that his steaming monster could run uphill.

Public acceptance grew cautiously, but by 1825 another transportation system excited legislators and bankers more. This time the hope lay in canals, already popular in nearby states. New Jersey canal enthusiasts built two of the waterways—the Morris Canal over the high hills of North Jersey and the Delaware and Raritan Canal across the state's flat and narrow waist. Pennsylvania's anthracite coal fields promised dividends to those who invested in canals. John Stevens' railroad was off on another siding.

George P. Macculloch, Morristown engineer, literally went fishing to find the Morris Canal. As he sat idly in a boat on Lake Hopatcong in 1822, his eyes ranged outward to the surrounding Highlands. He began to evolve a plan: Why not raise the level of Lake Hopatcong, move the water westward down the Musconetcong River valley to reach Pennsylvania coal and eastward down the Rockaway River valley to give iron works in Morris County a new life?

Macculloch's plan stirred enthusiasm among ironmasters in the Morris County hills. Good sense should have been a deterrent—Lake Hopatcong lay 914 feet above sea level—but Macculloch pushed ahead. Morris Canal stock rates in 1825 brought "multitudes" into Jersey City to over-subscribe the $1,000,000 stock issue seven times. Unfortunately, however, many of the first subscribers failed to back their promises with cash.

Work began October 15, 1825, with a ground-breaking celebration at Lake Hopatcong. Within a year 1100 workmen shoveled their way through the high hills, and in 1827 work began on a dam to raise Hopatcong's level five feet. The first boats passed from Phillipsburg to Newark in November, 1831, just before winter cast the full chill doubt on the canal by icing over the waterway.

Morris Canal never fulfilled the get-rich-quick hopes of its builders, but the hill-climbing waterway was one of the nineteenth century's engineering wonders. The canal rose 914 feet from Newark Bay to Lake Hopatcong, then eased down 760 feet to the Delaware River at Phillipsburg—a total rise and fall of 1674 feet in ninety miles! Canalboats "climbed" the hills on "cradles" drawn up inclined planes by water power.

The splendor of the engineering dream could not overcome misman-agement, faulty construction, and railroad competition; even before ex-tension to Jersey City in 1836 the route was doomed.

Widening of the Morris Canal in the 1840s helped some, and then an industrial boom before and during the Civil War made dividends possible. Such prosperity simply misled stockholders; the Lehigh Valley Railroad leased the canal for ninety-nine years in 1871 and completed the downfall of the waterway. Ironically, the Hudson River frontage in Jersey City proved the only truly valuable portion of the canal after 1871. Nevertheless, George Macculloch's canal gave the North Jersey hills an economic boost that persisted for decades.

CANAL ON THE LEVEL

Far more successful was the forty-three-mile-long Delaware & Raritan Canal, finally chartered in 1830 after its backers had sought legislative approval for twenty-six years. Built to eliminate the then long ocean voyage between New York and Philadelphia, the D.&R. ran on nearly level ground, requiring only fourteen locks between Bordentown, Trenton, and New Brunswick. The first commercial cargoes that passed through in May, 1834, included lumber and stone headed south for the new state penitentiary at Trenton and anthracite coal headed north for New York City's furnaces.

Few changes had to be made during the Delaware & Raritan's long history. It was wide enough (seventy-five feet) and deep enough (nine feet) to be useful until the early 1920s. Great quantities of coal passed through during most of the nineteenth century, outnumbering all other cargoes ten to one. Steam tugs operated on the Delaware & Raritan by

1850, making the through trip in twenty hours. In contrast, a cross-state trip on the Morris Canal required five days.

Tonnage on the Delaware & Raritan exceeded that of the Erie Canal in some years, and in the 1860s and early 1870s the waterway often showed annual profits exceeding $1,000,000. Still, railroad competition doomed the canal; the Pennsylvania Railroad leased the utility in 1871 (the same year that the Lehigh Valley acquired the Morris Canal). The Pennsylvania methodically throttled the canal, but the waterway died hard: it still carried more than one million tons of freight annually in the early 1890s.

The demise of New Jersey's two canals should not have been a surprise; the Delaware & Raritan knew the searing breath of the railroads from its chartering on February 4, 1830. That same day the state legislature, in a show of impartiality mixed with indecision, chartered both the canal and the Camden & Amboy Railroad to compete for traffic across the waist of New Jersey. As an omen, the railroad stock sold out in ten minutes; it took a full year to dispose of D.&R. paper.

Back on the Track

Although the Camden & Amboy Railroad grew directly from John Stevens' pioneering, the aging Hoboken inventor wasn't even represented on the board of directors. His sons, Robert L. and Edwin A., took care of the directing, but John tossed a gala party to mark granting of the charter. He was eighty-two years old in 1830, and John Stevens' spirits at the party were "as sparkling and abundant as the champagne."

John Stevens correctly is called the father of American railroading, but Robert Stevens nurtured his father's railroad to vigorous growth. Robert invented the T-rail, the "hook-headed" spike to fasten the rails to ties, and the "iron tongue" (or "fish plate") to join rails—all three still standard on modern railroads. The first of Stevens' T-rails, rolled in Wales under Robert's personal direction, came out "twisted and crooked as snakes," but Stevens perfected a means of straightening them while they were still red-hot.

Robert Stevens went to England to get George Stephenson to build a ten-ton locomotive. The engine arrived months later at Bordentown, where a twenty-three-year-old Yankee handy man named Isaac Dripps put the *John Bull* together, improving as he went along. Dripps used a whiskey barrel on a flatcar for water supply, and a Bordentown shoemaker made a leather hose to carry the water to the *John Bull's* boilers.

The *John Bull* made its first run in Mile Hollow at Bordentown on November 12, 1831. Legislators, stockholders, friends—and a host of skeptics—filed by long tables laden with hot oyster soup and other delicacies before being invited for a ride at thirty miles per hour. During the day the beauteous Madame Caroline Murat of Bordentown, niece by marriage of Napoleon Bonaparte, boldly rode the train as if to prove that even in 1831 a pretty girl was an asset on a train's maiden day.

Commercial service began in January, 1833, with horses drawing the carriages. The *John Bull's* first trip in September, 1833, was somewhat marred by an accident when the engine collided with a wandering hog on the return trip from South Amboy. The hog lost its head, the *Bull* plunged into a ditch, and a passenger "in his fright turned a summerset out of the window."

Two months later, two illustrious riders escaped death in another derailment. John Quincy Adams was not injured in the wreck but Cornelius Vanderbilt, hero of the early steamboat monopoly wars, suffered a crushed chest. Vanderbilt recovered and eventually became one of the most powerful of nineteenth-century railroad barons.

The public responded nobly despite the frequent accidents. The seven-hour trip from New York to Philadelphia, including steam ferry service, appealed to travelers who remembered vividly when a twenty-four-hour passage across New Jersey was considered fast. Traffic from the start was brisk, although at first the C.&A. by-passed New Brunswick, Princeton, and Trenton in favor of such villages as Jamesburg and Hightstown. That was rectified in 1839 in a straight-line route from Trenton to New Brunswick.

Spectacular successes on the Camden & Amboy encouraged other railroad enthusiasts. Paterson capitalists, aware of the winter limitations of an ice-locked Morris Canal, applied for a charter in 1828, only to be frustrated by the canal lobbyists. The need was too obvious to be ignored and backers of the Paterson & Hudson River Railroad secured the state's second railroad charter on January 21, 1831. A toast to the canal interests concluded the charter celebration a month later when Mr. T. B. Crane proposed:

"The enemies of the railroad—may they be rode on a chestnut rail, sharp edge up!"

William Gibbs McNeill and George Washington Whistler jointly planned the route of the new Paterson & Hudson River Railroad. That partnership had another angle: McNeill's sister married Whistler, and their artist son, James Abbott McNeill Whistler, later commemorated the marriage in his famed portrait of "Mother."

The P.&H.R. pushed eastward, conquering bogland and rivers alike. The road's two wide spans over the Passaic and the Hackensack rivers were the first railroad drawbridges ever built. As the Paterson builders slowly laid tracks toward Jersey City, the New Jersey Railroad Company, composed mainly of Newarkers, also sought to reach eastward to Jersey City—and southwestward to New Brunswick.

The New Jersey Railroad Company received its charter on March 7, 1832, despite vigorous opposition of both Morris Canal and Camden & Amboy stockholders. The Newarkers gained their charter by agreeing to build only as far as New Brunswick, to link with the C.&A. Railroad.

Newark and Paterson builders both conquered the marshes, although each railroad allowed a full year for embankments to settle before they dared run a locomotive over the soggy ground. By 1835, Newarkers raced daringly across the meadows at thirty-five miles per hour. Patersonians took life more calmly: the trip to Jersey City required an hour—provided the lightweight cars didn't jump the track, and provided the passengers and crew didn't agree to pause in the Meadows to hunt snapping turtles. When the two railroads jointly dug a deep cut through Bergen Hill in 1838, locomotives could chug to Jersey City in comparative ease.

Westward to the Hills

Before the 1830s expired, two more railroads were in existence, both with eyes on coal fields to the west. The Elizabethtown & Somerville gained a charter only four days after the Paterson & Hudson River in 1831, but five years elapsed before its first horse-drawn train journeyed the few blocks from the Elizabethport ferry docks to Broad Street, Elizabethtown.

The deliberate pace of the Elizabethtown & Somerville gave the Morris & Essex Railroad a chance to catch up despite its wait until January 29, 1835, for a franchise. The Morris & Essex challenged the Orange Mountains, the first railroad in New Jersey that elected to climb hills. M.&E. backers chose their right-of-way largely on the willingness of people to donate land and/or to buy stock. The railroad was open to Morristown on January 1, 1838, and promptly provided early morning eastbound and late-evening westbound trains for businessmen who hoped to work in New York and live in New Jersey. The highly durable commuter was about to be born despite a ride of three hours each way.

Down on the flat plain beneath the Watchungs, the Elizabethtown & Somerville reached the latter town on January 1, 1842, nearly eleven years after chartering. Embarrassments along the way included the doleful day in 1839 when a carriage and team of horses raced the railroad's little "Eagle" engine from Elizabethtown to Westfield. The horses won easily, by ten full minutes. Eventual arrival at Somerville called for what the poverty-stricken railroad considered a handsome fete: lemonade and cake in the village inn.

The slow-starting Elizabethtown & Somerville defeated the Morris & Essex in the tortoise-and-hare race through the mountains to the Pennsylvania coal fields beyond. John Taylor Johnston, who became a vigorous twenty-eight-year-old president in 1848, provided the spur. He changed the railroad's name to the Central Railroad of New Jersey (Jersey Central) in 1849, and early in July, 1852, "eight splendid cars, drawn by the gigantic locomotive *Pennsylvania* and accompanied by Dodsworth's band," reached Phillipsburg and the link with the coal field.

The competing Morris & Essex steamed into Dover in 1848, only to pause overlong to proclaim itself "as substantial as the iron mountains." The line was built to Hackettstown in 1854, and a completion spike driven at Phillipsburg in 1865 proclaimed that the M.&E. had won its thirty years' war with the Highlands.

The Jersey Central and the Morris & Essex both grew sleek on an anthracite diet. They made stockholders happy (until the Jersey Central went into receivership in 1877) but they also transformed and strengthened the areas through which they ran. The M.&E. and Jersey Central each studded their rights-of-way with little jewels of towns where New York-bound commuters would hold dominance for nearly a full century.

FARMS, IRON, AND VACATIONERS

Southern New Jersey didn't get its network of railroads until the 1850s and 1860s. Monied men preferred to invest in railroads reaching the sure riches of anthracite or in railroads exploiting the lucrative Philadelphia–New York passenger trade. They found scant appeal in the potential of the flourishing farmlands along the lower Delaware River or the bog-iron empires and glassworks of the Pine Barrens. That hordes of people might someday have enough leisure and spare cash to ride through them, to vacation by the seaside, seemed a ridiculous notion in the 1840s.

Tracks did get to Woodbury in 1856, to Millville and Glassboro in 1860, and all the way to Cape May in 1866, but the greatest of South Jersey railroads proved to be the Camden & Atlantic, organized in 1852. The Camden & Atlantic had little to recommend it: backers hoped to serve a few bog-iron furnaces and glassworks along the way or possibly pick up carloads of fruit and vegetables.

The Camden & Atlantic eventually owed its success not to iron, glass, or vegetables but rather to Dr. Jonathan Pitney's insistence that someday Absecon would be "the El Dorado" of the East Coast. Dr. Pitney and other railroad backers grandiosely put a name, Atlantic City, on a railroad map in 1850. That "city" of sand dunes and green flies had as assets twenty-one eligible voters and Dr. Pitney's faith that it had unlimited "healthfulness."

The first Camden–Atlantic City train carried 600 dignitaries and the press to an opening party in the still-unfinished United States Hotel at Atlantic City on July 1, 1854. Visitors were most pleased that the train would get them quickly back to Philadelphia. Despite its forlorn beginnings, Atlantic City grew. Railroad officials speculated in ocean-front land valued at $17.50 per acre—hoping it might someday be worth "as high as $500." Their fondest dreams were far eclipsed; by the 1890s, railroads had made Atlantic City the nation's prime summer resort.

Railroads pushed westward through all America—up hills and down valleys and across deserts. Wherever they went, they held the promise of bringing the natural wealth of the West to the resource-hungry East. When that wealth came to the East the chances were good that New York or Philadelphia would be the major ports of call. The state between had to benefit. Beside the tracks, New Jersey hamlets grew into villages, villages became towns, and towns burgeoned into cities. Pounding factories, many making products unknown or not needed a century before, depended upon railroads to bring in raw materials and to send out products made in New Jersey. A whole generation had arisen by 1850 that could scarcely remember the mud-slowed traffic of 1830.

New Jersey could never be the same; railroads completely transformed the state, for better or for worse. Village ways, so peaceful in the mud of 1830, began to disappear beneath the smoke and cinders and clacking wheels.

11

Invasion of Skills

Holding back the rising tide of industry after railroads and canals crossed New Jersey would have been nearly as difficult as stemming the ocean's waves. Everywhere that steel rails reached to serve industry, more factories blossomed. Wherever the canal towpaths reached, the sounds and sights of people at work became commonplace. Transportation brought New Jersey face to face with its destiny: industrialization.

Thanks to the transportation revolution, New Jersey became completely transformed in the three decades between 1830 and 1860. Jersey City and Camden grew from nondescript ferry landings to important industrial cities. Newark and Paterson gained national recognition for manufacturing prowess by the 1850s. Other towns—Elizabeth, New Brunswick, Hoboken, Trenton, Dover, Boonton, Millville, Bridgeton, and Glassboro, to mention only a few—became part of the manufacturing boom.

Fortunately New Jersey had on hand the skillful Thomas Gordon to note how things were in the earliest days of the transformation. His 1834 *Gazetteer of the State of New Jersey* depicted the state at the very time that it awaited its destiny. Gordon tended to be optimistic, but he was a good reporter.

". . . the state is, in the aggregate, agricultural," Gordon wrote. "Such is the character of all the counties, except Essex, part of Bergen, and part of Morris. The glass and iron manufactures of Burlington, Gloucester and Cumberland are not sufficient to exempt them from this classification." (Remember that in 1834 Paterson and Elizabeth were still in Essex County; Hoboken and Jersey City still in Bergen County.)

Things remained "old-fashioned" in Gordon's time. Water turned the wheels in gristmills (857 of them), sawmills (655 total), and fulling mills (more than seventy). Cider distilleries (388 in the state) earned Gordon's nod for the strength of their product, "notwithstanding the influence of Temperance Societies upon distilling." Twenty-eight iron furnaces and 108 "forge fires" dominated the fairly simple economy, and twenty-nine paper mills used the clear water of New Jersey streams to make vitally needed paper.

Elsewhere, Gordon found that "the fabric of shoes, boots and harness gives employment and wealth to many individuals in Newark, Bloomfield, Rahway, Burlington." He noted that the last three of those leather towns, plus Plainfield, also made hats and clothing for the Southern market. Somehow he overlooked Orange, where others reported that some thirty-two hatters of the 1830s made so much headgear that "all the running streams of the region were discolored with hat dyes."

Coaches, cabinetware, and chairs formed "large articles of export from Newark and Rahway." Gordon pointed out that "for some years past Trenton has not been in a very thriving state." Jersey City dozed by the Hudson River mud flats, despite "an extensive pottery" and a flint-glass factory paying "$750 the week wages" to about eighty hands. Camden, with only thirty-five houses, was largely "employed in tillage" and proud of the wide wood lots where "inhabitants of the great city" (Philadelphia) found "shade and recreation in the hot season."

Gordon guessed that swelling industrial vigor would follow the canals and railroads. He predicted that "at no distant day" New Jersey, "instead of pouring forth her population to fertilize, enrich and bless other lands, will give to her sons full employment, and the means of wealth within her own limits."

Gordon's descriptions of industry must be judged within the framework of his time. For one thing, there was no genuine city in New Jersey: Newark, with a population of 10,953, led all towns in the 1830 census—and no other town boasted more than 4000 residents. But then, New York in 1830 had only 242,278 inhabitants and Philadelphia claimed 80,462.

Francis Bazley Lee gave this description of New Jersey industry of the 1830s in his *New Jersey As a Colony and As a State* (published in 1902):

> Except in rare instances the manufactories were insignificant. . . . Few establishments contained more than a score of employees. No legislation regulating the number of hours constituting a day's work, sanitation, stated payment of wages, or the responsibility of the master as to the use of dangerous machinery had yet been enacted in New Jersey. The men and the superintendent or overseer met upon even ground. The chief owners often worked at machines.
>
> It has been truthfully said that there was no hard and fast line

drawn between country and city life. With no congestion of population
there were no wage workers, as in England, upon the verge of pauperism,
nor were there vast and constantly increasing fortunes accumulated by
successful manufacturers. Men of mental nobility turned from the farm
to the shop and back again to the fields, or went from one trade to
another with varying degrees of success.

Women were practically unknown in any factory or mill, being kept
out of such work by the powerful influence of custom, by distressingly
low wages, and by their lack of capacity necessary to change from
domestic relations to those of the shop.

Industry in prerailroad and precanal days tended to be closely allied to the needs of immediate neighbors, excepting such specialties
as iron manufacture, glassmaking, and shipbuilding. A firm might be
dignified by the name "company," but by today's standards the average
industrialist was little more than a smithy or a carriage maker. Entrepreneurs found no difficulty in going into business, for little capital
was needed. Going out of business was just as easy; business came
and went.

The nearness of natural resources restricted manufacture. Iron, clay
products, glass, leather, paper, textiles—the leading commodities in the
early 1830s—all could be made from materials found close at hand.
Lumbering and shipbuilding were major industries, for timber stood
tall and thick in the forests, except near iron forges and furnaces.
There the voracious appetites of the furnaces ate through thousands
of wooded acres surrounding each manufactory.

New Jersey already had a small reservoir of badly needed skills,
mainly brought from elsewhere. Founders of Paterson had allotted
$50,000 of their limited capital to import skilled mechanics from En-
gland and Scotland in the 1790s. When Robert Fulton began making
steamboat engines at Jersey City, shortly before 1810, British-born and
British-trained Charles Stoudinger supervised the work. England
frowned on the exodus of its trained men, but they left anyway for
the lure of American opportunity.

John Clark, one of those imported from England, leased part of the
failing Paterson Cotton mill to establish the state's first bona-fide machine shop in 1795. Clark made excellent machines, but his greatest
contribution to New Jersey industry was in turning out skilled mechanics. Nearly every Paterson industrial enterprise of note during the
first half of the nineteenth century depended on men trained directly
by Clark or by one of Clark's protégés.

A few farsighted employers developed their own pools of trained
hands. Moses Combs of Newark, who rode a prosperous crest after
he imaginatively shipped two hundred pairs of sealskin shoes to
Georgia in 1790, needed skilled leather workers. He made them, too

—setting up a school of apprentices, possibly the first such school in the United States. Many of Combs's men became celebrated Newark leathermakers in their own right before the Civil War.

The supply of skilled hands grew. More workers came from England and Scotland. More employers followed the lead of Paterson's Clark and Newark's Combs. Yet New Jersey's greatest good luck lay in attracting Yankee mechanics away from the factories of New England.

Paterson's Society for Establishing Useful Manufactures (generally called the S.U.M.) turned to New England in 1793, inducing Peter Colt to resign as treasurer of the State of Connecticut to manage the struggling city by the Passaic Falls. Colt succeeded Major Pierre L'Enfant, the French planner who had drawn a scheme for a grand city of Paterson that couldn't possibly be fitted to either the rocky terrain of Paterson or the barren purses of the village's capitalists. L'Enfant eight years later laid out the city of Washington, D.C. He was not a failure; he simply thought too big for the Paterson of his day.

Peter Colt and his New England relatives dominated Paterson for sixty years. Whoever controlled the S.U.M. controlled Paterson, and by 1816 the Colts owned 1991 of the society's 2620 shares. Peter's son Roswell became "governor" of the S.U.M. in 1814, and kept a tight grip on Paterson's industrial life until his death in 1856. Another of Peter's sons, John, in 1822 became the first man ever to substitute cotton for linen in sailcloth. The U. S. Navy bought John's cotton sailcloth and soon Paterson-made sails "spread their snowy wings on every corner of the globe." John Colt thus firmly encouraged a textile complex that would be basic in Paterson for 125 years. John's brother Christopher made the first silk in Paterson, and a sister, Sarah, organized Paterson's first Sunday school.

Those powerful and respected Colts have been nearly forgotten. The Colt name lives on, not because of the Colts who succeeded in Paterson, but because of Sam Colt, a dismal failure beside the Great Falls.

Something of a fast-talking drifter in his youth, Sam Colt invented his repeating revolver in the early 1830s and started an elaborate four-story Gun Mill in 1835 to produce hundreds of repeating rifles and pistols. He decorated many of the weapons with gold or silver inlay and sent them off to "princes, governments and distinguished men the world over." General Thomas S. Jesup successfully used Colt rifles against Florida's Seminole Indians in the spring of 1838 and praised them enthusiastically. Everyone liked the fast-shooting weapons; they simply weren't buying. Sam's Gun Mill fell under a sheriff's sale in 1842 and Colt left Paterson, broke and dispirited.

Sam and his creditors sold even his patents and manufacturing rights, but Colt bought the rights back on the eve of the Mexican War for fifty dollars (the man who owned them tried to sell weapons to Mexico and became, technically at least, an "alien"). War proved the value of the Colt weapons. Sam Colt prospered, but not in Paterson. He relocated in Hartford, Connecticut, and there won fame and fortune.

Sam Colt's return to New England was only just, in view of what that area had contributed to New Jersey. The point was never better proved than when sad-faced, brilliant Seth Boyden left his Massachusetts farm in 1815 and brought to Newark a device he had perfected for slitting a leather hide into several thin layers. The slitter increased the value of each hide, but Boyden gave it away and opened a small harness shop on Broad Street. He promptly began to accumulate a small fortune for himself and his young bride.

Boyden manifested a peculiar indifference to money, however. He gave up successful harness manufacture to develop a new method of silver-plating buckles, and he forgot silver-plated buckles to make America's first patent leather in 1819. That done, he turned his back on leather to find the secret of malleable iron. This nation depended completely on England for the easily worked iron, but on July 4, 1826 —the fiftieth anniversary of the Declaration of Independence—Seth Boyden announced in Newark that he knew the secret. America had gained another freedom from England.

Wealth beckoned again, but in 1835 Boyden sold his malleable iron works and made several excellent locomotives (including three for the Morris & Essex Railroad and one for a Cuban Line). Newark's restless inventor then ranged, successfully but unprofitably, through much of pre-Civil War research: telescopes, daguerreotypes, simple electrical devices, work on Morse's telegraph. He trekked off in 1849 to California to seek a fortune that he easily could have found in Newark from his silver buckles, patent leather, malleable iron, or locomotives. He did not find a fortune in California, either.

Boyden let others have the gold; after his return to New Jersey he worked on a hair dye, then spent his declining years developing improved varieties of strawberries (and gave away the plants to Hilton neighbors). Rightly called "The Uncommercial Inventor," Boyden died at eighty-two, soon after telling a friend that he had enough ideas "to last two more lifetimes."

Seth Boyden typified an age of quick rise and sudden failure, a time of rapidly changing industrial emphasis. Boyden's success with iron helped prove one thing: it was an age of iron, a time for using the metal as never before.

The Morris Canal revived iron towns in the Morris County hills. Grass growing in the streets of Dover, Rockaway, and Boonton disappeared, and the clang of forge hammers once again filled the air. Canals and railroads added an iron core of strength to Newark, Pat-

erson, Jersey City, Hoboken, and Trenton. Old ways had to give
ground. America's first hot blast furnace was introduced at Oxford
in 1834, thus raising production by 40 per cent. Seven years later the
first successful anthracite furnace outside of Pennsylvania was blown
in at Stanhope.

Within most success stories based on change, there can always be
found the story of failure elsewhere. While canals, railroads, and anthracite coal meant prosperity in the northern hills, they also sounded
the death knell for charcoal-burning iron furnaces in southern New
Jersey. Pineland bog-iron empires collapsed in the face of brisk competition; the last southern New Jersey furnace put out its fire in 1854.

Railroads were little short of magical to iron men. They carried New
Jersey iron products everywhere—and they also became the best customers. Trenton and Paterson showed what the combination of iron
and railroads meant to New Jersey.

Trenton's industrial rise began in 1845, when Peter Cooper and
Abram S. Hewitt opened their Trenton Iron Company to fill a Camden & Amboy Railroad order for $180,000's worth of rails. Within
three years Cooper & Hewitt owned mines at Andover and Ringwood and had built the nation's largest blast furnaces at Phillipsburg.
They poured out such massive amounts of iron from their fifty-eight
furnaces and six rolling mills that the Trenton Iron Company became
the nation's foremost iron establishment only five years after its founding.

Cooper and Hewitt became the first Americans to try the noted
Bessemer steel process, using it at Phillipsburg in 1856 (it failed because of low-grade ores, but no other company in this country even
tested the process until after the Civil War). Trenton Iron Company
also made the nation's first structural iron beams (I-beams) in 1854—
for such varied buildings as Princeton's rebuilt Nassau Hall, the new
Harper & Brothers' building in New York, and more than 100 federal
buildings, including the Capitol at Washington and Fort Sumter in
Charleston Harbor.

Trenton Iron Company's success enticed others to the booming city.
Makers of anvils and iron grillwork settled in several shops, but the
biggest catch was John Roebling, who moved his wire-rope factory
from western Pennsylvania to Trenton capital in 1859. Roebling had
attracted national attention in 1854 when his cables suspended a railroad bridge over Niagara Falls. Orders poured in to the Trenton plant;
Roebling and sons through the decades completed such spans as the
Brooklyn, George Washington, and Golden Gate bridges.

Paterson's iron-wise mechanics also leaned on the railroad to find a
challenge worthy of their skills: the locomotive. Once again a Connecticut Yankee led the way.

Connecticut-born Thomas Rogers joined the New England-to-New Jersey migration in 1812. He became the "best hand in town" and retired in 1831 at age thirty-nine with a fortune of $40,000. The next year Morris Ketchum and Joseph Grosvenor, "men of capital but no mechanical ability," lured Rogers out of retirement to make the iron bridges on which the Paterson & Hudson River Railroad crossed the Hackensack and Passaic rivers.

Despite the demonstrated skills of its home-town mechanics, the Paterson & Hudson River Railroad turned to England for its first locomotive. The engine arrived in crates; Rogers put it together and openly declared that he could do much better. He could—and he did.

Rogers' first Paterson-built engine, the "Sandusky," impressed viewers and hearers by introducing the lonesome wail of the steam whistle to railroading in the fall of 1837. He sold The Mad River & Lake Erie Railroad the whistling demon for its projected line in Ohio, and in 1838 the Ohio legislature decreed that all Ohio railroads must lay their rails to conform with the Sandusky's width between wheels (four feet, ten inches).

Orders for Paterson locomotives poured in to Rogers. He built five the first year and by 1850 could complete two locomotives every week. Some of Rogers' workers broke away to set up fierce rivalry within the city. Paterson had three great locomotive builders before 1860, and only Philadelphia could challenge Paterson's claim to national locomotive supremacy. Three major builders completed $1,565,000's worth of railroad engines in 1860, placing Paterson just a bit ahead of Philadelphia. Paterson locomotives literally raced around the world; the city's factories made more than 12,000 engines before orders dwindled away in the late nineteenth century.

Iron gave the major strength, but less durable commodities added to New Jersey's burgeoning industrial vigor. Diversity, hallmark of the New Jersey economy, showed from the start. Here would be made beer and bottles, bricks and terra cotta, paper and silk, overshoes and soap.

Brewing, for example, was already a major Newark industry by the 1850s. Surprisingly, since Germans who flowed into Newark during the 1840s created the demand for beer, a Scotsman led all brewers. Peter Ballantine founded his Newark brewery in 1840 and within seven years built larger quarters. Peter's three sons joined their father in 1857, and the firm took the name it still holds: P. Ballantine & Sons. Soon other brewers joined Ballantine in Newark, including Joseph Hensler, Gottfried Kreuger, and Christian Feigenspan.

Brewers bought bottles, thus aiding the state's glassmakers to a true golden age between 1840 and 1860, when nearly one-third of the nation's glassworks operated in the Garden State. These were mainly in

Salem, Gloucester, and Cumberland counties—except for P. C. Dummer's firm in Jersey City. Dummer's 1827 patent for molded glass marked the start of that important part of the industry.

Southern New Jersey towns sprang up on glass foundations. Makers turned out jars, bottles, decanters, jugs, pickle jars, patent-medicine containers, window glass, hollow ware, and plate glass. Plant owners prospered, usually in wanton disregard of their workers, who lived under near-feudal conditions approaching serfdom. After 1850 many glassworks began a shift westward to take advantage of readily available coal or natural gas—although enough stayed in New Jersey to keep the industry briskly alive.

Good sand meant good glass. Just as naturally rich clay beds in the Hackensack and Raritan river valleys gave rise to brickmakers.

American cities took on an increasingly red hue in the 1850s, when brick buildings replaced old wooden structures (usually because disastrous fires swept through entire blocks of city buildings). The first of New Jersey's major brickmakers was James R. Sayre. Sayre opened his kiln in 1850 at Wood's Landing, named for James Wood's small brickyard. Soon the schooners and barges took so many of Sayre's bricks from the landing that the village changed its name to Sayreville.

Elsewhere, ceramics makers went far beyond bricks. Flemington gained a reputation for fine pottery. Woodbridge became firmly set on clay when Michiel Lefoulon, a Frenchman, opened the Salamander Works in 1825. Lefoulon varied his output from bricks to pottery to make Salamander the state's largest clay handler before 1870. Alfred Hall, a Cleveland brickmaker, made America's first terra cotta at Perth Amboy in 1849. Within a decade, Hall's firm was called "The Kindergarten for Terra Cotta Makers."

Middlesex ceramics firms flourished easily; clay lay nearly at their feet. Not so Trenton and Jersey City, both of which earned reputations despite having to bring in clay—by rail or canal to Trenton, by windjammers from Hackensack River pits to Jersey City.

Jersey City's clay fame, while fleeting, left a double mark. There in 1829 David Henderson made America's first molded pottery but more important, Henderson's sent forth skilled workers who influenced pottery making elsewhere. Two of his workers, James Bennett and William Bloor, migrated to East Liverpool, Ohio, to establish prominent potteries. Ironically, that formed the basis for the eventual shift in pottery leadership from New Jersey to Ohio.

East Liverpool reciprocated in 1852 when two of her own, William Taylor and Henry Speeler, came east to Trenton to make yellow ware and Rockingham ware (clay objects fired with a lead or alkaline glaze). Trenton already had a modest clay background, but after Taylor became the first man ever to fire a glass kiln with anthracite coal, Trenton was on the way to ceramics leadership.

In addition to iron in the Highlands, glass sand in the southern New Jersey flatland, and clay in the mid-section, New Jersey also had another vast resource: good, clear water—vital to the more than fifty paper mills operating in the 1840s and 1850s.

The state might even have ruled America's paper trade. Charles Kinsey of Paterson patented in 1807 a machine for making paper in one continuous roll, the first such major breakthrough this side of the Atlantic (although such machines had been perfected in France four years earlier). Kinsey's ingenuity failed to impress his partners in the Kinsey, Crane & Fairchild cotton mill. Cotton was their business, they warned Kinsey. They kept spinning—and failed like all other Paterson cotton makers in the Panic of 1816.

Papermakers clustered in and near Paterson, Whippany, Millburn, and Trenton when the Census of 1850 showed New Jersey to be the fifth-ranking state in paper production. New York and Philadelphia newspapers turned to New Jersey mills to meet demands estimated at 12,000 tons annually in 1856. The New York *Herald* bought everything that McCall & Lewis could produce in their Trenton plant. The Condit paper mill in Millburn made "some of the largest sheets used by the press of New York," while the Eden Mill in Whippany processed eight to ten tons weekly for *Frank Leslie's Illustrated Newspaper*.

Recognizably, any area grows industrially only as it grasps new things. Thus, when silk and rubber both emerged as important commodities: in the two decades before the Civil War, New Jersey welcomed them and became the richer.

Silk edged into the industrial scene in the late 1830s when Christopher Colt established Paterson's first silk mill in 1838. He failed two years later, but the failure proved Paterson's gain. John Ryle, highly experienced English millman, took over the Colt silk enterprise in 1840. Ryle was twenty-two years old, but already boasted seventeen years of silk experience (he had gone to work in an English factory at age five!).

Ryle succeeded admirably, stepping upward from a memorable day in 1840 when he cornered half of America's available raw-silk supply —and he would have cornered it all if an early-rising Philadelphian hadn't bought the other half of the one bale on the New York docks. That single bale represented the only known raw-silk supply in the country at the time.

John C. ("Yankee") Benson came down from New England in 1851 to become Ryle's first silk competitor in the city, and many others soon followed the call of silk in Paterson. Ryle led them all: he turned out the first skein of sewing silk in America, became the first man ever to wind silk on a spool, and made America's first silk flag. He hired 500 employees by 1856 (a time when a payroll of twenty was still a cause for comment). His fortune mounted to such heights that he could drop a half million dollars in the Panic of 1857 and not be close to losing his silk shirt.

Silk brought a sense of luxury, but on New Jersey's muddy roads and foot paths a pair of rubber overshoes could be infinitely more satisfying. Hopes for producing a good type of rubber interested men in many states, but the difficulties seemed insurmountable. When Horace Day opened the state's first rubber factory at New Brunswick in 1839, his rubber-coated carriage tops had an "intolerable" smell and his rubber shoes turned "hard as bricks" in winter. Since an eager public bought, Day shrugged his shoulders, held his nose, and kept making his crude products.

Day's troubles had only begun. First his bright young aide, Christopher Meyer, grew weary of arguing with his boss over the poor quality and left in 1844 to start a plant in nearby Milltown. Meyer made 1000 pairs of shoes weekly by 1846, and during the Mexican War sold rubber pontoons to the army. Meyer's defection hurt enough, but the big blow came in 1852 when Charles Goodyear sued Day for violation of his vulcanizing patent.

The Goodyear-Day trial became a nineteenth-century classic in both the rubber industry and in legal circles. Daniel Webster represented Goodyear in the trial at Trenton, and seldom has a case been so stacked against a defendant. The city of Trenton welcomed Webster wildly. The judge and jury showed open deference to the great Senator. Only Day seemed surprised when he lost, to Goodyear legally and to Daniel Webster emotionally.

Meyer made legal peace with Goodyear and assumed rubber leadership in New Jersey until 1856. Charles V. Mead arrived in Trenton that year to check for Goodyear the report that a small Trenton rubber plant had violated his employer's patent. Mead closed the plant, then promptly reopened it himself, apparently infringing on Goodyear's claims in the same fashion as the unfortunate original owner. Regardless of that, Mead succeeded: he founded five distinct rubber plants in the city before his death in 1880 and made Trenton the state's prime rubber center.

Dramatic changes had begun. The small entrepreneur was still able to come and go, but industries employing fifty or more men were also becoming more common. Variety had come as well. Paterson placed strong reliance in its locomotives and silk, but its machine makers and ironworks gave added strength. Trenton had paper, rubber, and ceramics to buttress its iron. New Brunswick found that wallpaper making and rubber production mixed well with clay industries. On opposite ends of the state, Jersey City and Camden encouraged widely varying industries to seek locations by their railroad terminals and shipping docks.

Two of Jersey City's newcomers proved durable. Joseph Dixon perfected a graphite crucible which made possible the production in Jersey City of this country's first high-grade steel in 1848. Dixon later made lead pencils and stove polish as a happy and lucrative adjunct to excellent crucible business. William Colgate offered a contrast when he moved his soap plant from New York to Jersey City in 1847. Many called it "Colgate's Folly"—although that snap judgment didn't prevent their traveling many miles to see as much as 45,000 pounds of soap bubbling at one time in a single vat. The Folly stayed on, its payroll soon mounting into hundreds of people.

When it came to proving the value of industrial diversity, Newark topped all New Jersey rivals by 1860. Newark had the Morris Canal, good railroad connections and a wide bay for shipping. It also had a Yankee tradition of individual enterprise (and plenty of Yankees and others to make the tradition go).

Newark's emergence as a city of industrial variety began early. Dr. Jabez G. Goble, "an eminent and public-spirited citizen," took a careful look in 1836, when Newark officially became a city. Dr. Goble pridefully declared no city of "similar extent and population" exceeded Newark in the "number, variety and beauty of workmanship" in manufactures. He then documented an impressive variety: leather, hats, carriages, clothing, saddles, coach axles, coach lace, bowie knives, malleable iron, patent leather, silver plating, jewelry, cutlery, buggy railings, statuary, lathes, mechanics' tools, looking glasses, bellows, and so on through several more pages.

Newark welcomed men with ideas. Just as it had welcomed Peter Ballantine, the Scot, and Seth Boyden, the Yankee, it also welcomed two young foreigners who stopped by in 1848.

Jacob Wiss, on his way from Switzerland to Texas with two St. Bernard dogs, tarried in Newark in 1848 to make cutlery (using his dogs on a treadmill to supply power). His reputation for fine scissors mounted; he never left the city by the Passaic. Edward Balbach, who arrived from Germany the same year, let others seek gold in California; he found his on the floors of Newark's jewelry houses. Opening a small refining plant in 1851 to handle jewelry floor sweepings—the only such place in the United States—Balbach drew trade from cities throughout North America. By 1875 Balbach handled more gold and silver than the U. S. Mint ($2,820,000 for Balbach against $2,125,000 for the Mint).

Certainly Newark and Paterson, above all others, typified the spirit of growing New Jersey industry, but Newark and Paterson also discovered the harsh fact that where industry thrives in boom times the populace suffers most the sting of depression. The panics of 1837 and 1857 hit all industrial cities in the state, but Newark and Paterson, as the most industrialized, felt them most severely in 1837. By 1857, hard times also struck cruelly in Jersey City, Trenton, Camden, and Hoboken.

Newark newspapers detailed the suffering in 1857. One told of a young man arrested for stealing meat from a butcher stall. He "begged piteously" for his family, so the butcher and policeman accompanied him to his house.

> There they found his wife and two children, who had no food since Friday morning, and who were now bitterly crying. The young mechanic had been without labor for several weeks, and, without credit, he was too proud to beg. The butcher promptly placed the meat upon the table.

On November 18, 1857, a mass meeting in Newark's Military Park drew 2000 unemployed workers, who appointed a committee "to wait on the city authorities and ask them to give work to the unemployed." Similarly, in Trenton at about the same time, workers assembled in mass declared: "We ask not alms, but work, that our wives and children may not starve."

Something had happened in America's cities. Three decades before, when "the spindle rusted in the socket and the wheel rotted in the pit" (as L. R. Trumbull described the depression of 1816 in his *Industrial History of Paterson*), America was not dependent on industrialized towns. Men stepped easily from the farm to factory bench and back again. Even in 1837, New Jersey remained sufficiently rural to make suffering less sharp; the farm was still there to fall back on.

By 1857, however, a solid, city-bound working class had grown up. The first trickles of immigration added nonfarm workers to city rolls. Factories demanded more skills. People became tied to their city benches and huddled together in city flats, far from the rows of vegetables which could sustain them even when mill doors were closed. Depression struck bitterly in the ranks of workers—and often undercapitalized owners went down with their employees. So, as the clouds of Civil War began to gather on the horizon, New Jersey knew both the wonders and the woes of industry.

Emphasis on an emerging industry can be misleading. Actually, in 1860, New Jersey was still essentially rural. Industry lined the railroads and the canals—thin lines of urbanization on a narrow vector from Camden to Trenton and then to New Brunswick, Elizabeth, Newark, and Jersey City; factories were important along parts of the Morris Canal from Dover to Paterson. (To a very modest extent, there was some trace of industry beside the railroads that ran out to Plainfield and over the hills to Morristown.) Thomas Gordon undoubtedly would have expressed proper amazement if he had written about New Jersey in 1860. Population had more than doubled between his time of 1830 and the critical year of 1860—from 320,779 to 672,035. Yet only Essex, Burlington, and Hudson, in that order, had county populations exceeding 40,000. Most of southern New Jersey was very sparsely populated, the sandy shores were deserted, and the hills of Hunterdon, Sussex, and Warren were open to roaming cattle and sheep.

Considerably more telling than population counts was New Jersey's national industrial rank. In 1810 the state stood seventh; in 1860 it ranked sixth—but in 1810 there were only seventeen states. The sixth place in 1860 was among thirty-three states. That made the rise far more dramatic.

Industry had come to stay, to influence men's lives and men's opinions. Farming was still *the* way of life—but in 1860 New Jersey had 56,000 factory workers. Some 11,000 of the hands sewed apparel, about 8000 worked in iron, another 8000 made textiles, and about 6500 turned out leather goods. Newer industries trailed far behind. Apparel, iron, textiles, and leather; industry retained strong overtones of colonial days. Changes were more in degree than in kind.

The industrialist made himself heard in political circles. Factory owners in Newark and Trenton vigorously sought for a lessening of the tension developing between North and South; substantial Southern markets for clothing, shoes, and carriages made factory owners think twice before approving a war over anything so incidental (to them) as slavery.

County lines had changed, too, because of industrial growth. Politicians heeded the pounding of hammers and the whir of shuttles; between 1837 and 1857 they created seven new counties. Four of the new counties, Passaic (1837), Mercer (1838), Hudson (1840), and Camden (1844) were distinctly industrial areas chafing to be free from rural bounds. Atlantic (1837) and Ocean (1850) were created to keep the state political boat from being rocked by too many industrialists. The last new county, Union, was carved from industrial Essex in 1857 in a reverse split, with rural Union finally winning the freedom from Newark dominance that it had long craved.

This concern for or against industrialism reached throughout the state. It reached out into taverns and secret societies and into homes, where people discussed the assets and the liabilities of industry and such un- loved by-products as immigrants and depression and social problems. New Jersey needed time to wrestle with its conscience before the Civil War brought it joltingly to maturity.

12

Search for a Conscience

Intellectual discontent stirred throughout New Jersey in the three decades before the Civil War, both disturbing the public conscience and distressing those who wished that the good old colonial days had never ended. People searched constantly for something different or better—for better education, for government closer to the people, for more humane ways of dealing with the unfortunate, for some acceptable solution to the ethical and economic problems of slavery.

Old ways and old times came to be doubted. Churches faced dissent from within and from without. Workingmen knew the intermingled blessings and agonies of increased work opportunities offset by periods of cruel depression. Great numbers of immigrants arrived from Europe, eager to find the opportunities of America. Discontent was in the air, and every part of the nation felt the same stirrings, the same doubts, the same hopes. America was in the throes of serious social change.

Perhaps this heady awareness of the potential of democracy had begun in the wide open lands west of the Alleghenies, where men who carved out their own destinies felt little identification with the rigidities of colonial days. Perhaps it grew from the solid intellectual traditions that were flowering in New England amid searching inspection and testing of all thought. Certainly President Andrew Jackson gave this "new America" voice and encouragement with his stress on the importance of the "common man," for Jackson reflected the excitement and vigor of his times.

The whole world seemed turned upside down. Railroads and canals sped news and ideas quickly. Increasing numbers and qualities of newspapers permitted an exchange of philosophies and information. Increased numbers of factory jobs, with an emerging concentration of people in Eastern industrial cities, focused attention on social ills and the need for improved educational opportunities.

ON THE EDGE OF CHANGE

One measurement of the changes about to take place in the second quarter of the nineteenth century can be found in picturing Jerseymen as they were in 1826, when all America exulted on the fiftieth anniversary of the Declaration of Independence.

The 1820s remained a time when family prestige and influence still completely dominated social, political, and economic life. The gulf between classes was nearly as inflexible as the caste system of feudal times. At the top of the social and economic ladder stood the clergy and lawyers, along with large landholders and the landed country gentry. Next came the farmers, the storekeepers, and the artisans, followed by apprentices and day laborers. At the bottom, despised, were slaves and half-breed Indians. Historian Francis Bazley Lee once wrote of the period:

> There were no sudden changes of fortune, and patramonies were usually as slowly dissipated as they were accumulated. In such static conditions any alteration was an evolution rather than a revolution.

Times had to change. Mechanics could come into town, as Seth Boyden did in Newark and Thomas Rogers did in Paterson, and with the sheer genius of their minds and the skill of their hands they could develop new ways to make fortunes. Boyden's work with patent leather and malleable iron revolutionized industry in Newark; Rogers' ability to make railroad locomotives made millionaries out of Paterson mechanics. Such men had no need to rely on family backgrounds or fortunes.

THE NOT-SO-GOOD DAYS

But if the 1820s were simple days, they were not necessarily "good," in the sense of puritanical restraint. Nearly every political campaign knew slander and vituperation, topped by flagrant chicanery at the polls. Alcohol flowed freely on all occasions—at political rallies, at weddings, at christenings, at barn raisings, and at funerals. Drunkenness, disorder, and gambling became the hallmarks of amusement centers, to the extent that Philadelphians complained in 1821 of Sunday morning bells that summoned the young to embark for Camden, "where they may engage in every sort of mischief and dissipation."

Young men everywhere loved speed, of course, and they recklessly raced their wagons and sleighs down village streets and over turnpikes. Village and country fairs advertised horse-racing tracks, solemnly advertised to be for the "improvement of the breed." Both Jersey City and Camden welcomed visitors to tracks where breeding always ran a distant second to bookmaking. Those two tracks were closed in 1845 after townspeople wearied of blatant excesses.

Cruelty and violence excited a populace whose only amusements usually ranged from husking bees to wakes. The vicious sport of bull-baiting attracted throngs to Jersey City and Paterson. The sight of a bull being torn to pieces by dogs could fill the 3000-seat ampitheater built by Jersey City entrepreneurs in 1825; capacity crowds ("mostly from New York," according to one historian) gathered every Friday to watch "the sport afforded by bulls, bears, buffaloes and dogs fighting." Paterson bull-baiters, incensed when police tried to break up their sport in June, 1836, turned both the bull and the dogs loose on the law enforcers.

FESTIVITY ON THE GREEN

Closer to the public taste, and much more available, were public hangings in the courthouse towns. The executions supposedly warned potential murderers away from their evil passions, but spectators who flocked to the hangings saw them as festive occasions rather than as moral lessons. A hanging in Mt. Holly was a case in point:

> The day of the hanging was made a holiday—a festive occasion—by 10,000 people who came to the sport from all the countryside and even from neighboring states. Along the road were tents and booths in which liquor was sold and in which gamblers plied their tricks. Around the gallows were several companies of militia drawn up in a hollow square. At the appointed time the murderer arrived in a carriage, escorted by a troop of cavalry and accompanied by six ministers of as many sects, and sat down on the raised platform while one of the ministers read his confession to the gaping crowd.

Down to his doom plunged the murderer as thousands cheered, but in the wake of that Mt. Holly execution the people of the evolving nation felt powerful twinges of conscience. A storm of protest after that debacle had momentous consequences, and it prompted the Pennsylvania legislature to enact an 1834 law confining execution to jail yards. New Jersey and New York both enacted similar laws in 1835.

Two or three decades before, the Mt. Holly affair undoubtedly would have aroused some local disapproval, but those few who protested a hanging in a local square in 1800 or 1810 had no influence beyond the sounds of their own voices. The protesters were isolated in 1800; by 1833 they were closer together in time and spirit—and the difference lay in improved communication, particularly in the world of newspapers. New Jersey had but six weekly newspapers in 1800, all of them poorly edited and all ever on the brink of failure. In contrast, there were about twenty-five papers in the state by 1830, and the Newark *Daily Advertiser* appeared in March, 1832, as the state's first daily paper.

WHERE IDEAS MIGHT MEET

Editors struggled constantly to stay alive in the face of rising public costs and their own editorial incapabilities. In 1830, the day of the great newspaper was far in the future but publication was at least reasonably regular. Whatever the quality of the news gatherings, public opinion now had a major forum; varying shades of opinion and indignation and enthusiasm gradually began to be available. Newspapers came quickly: New Jersey had forty papers by 1840 (four of them dailies) and the number had jumped to fifteen dailies and seventy-five other periodicals by 1860. The rise of a public conscience and the spirit of reform were closely allied to the growth and the improved quality of newspapers.

Editors of the early nineteenth century seldom led the way in shaping public opinion, but even by opposing those who would change the world, editors provided a place for airing ideas. Newspapers also mirrored the changing world, more often in the advertisements rather than in the news columns. The rash of advertisements for railroad service in the 1830s and 1840s, for example, told of improved transportation. The advertisements offering accommodations at Long Branch, Cape May, and The Squan (Manasquan) bespoke the increasing interest in summer vacations along the shore and increasing numbers of people with the leisure to rest. Merchants cautiously advertised their wares in the 1830s and after 1840 even began to suggest modest gift-giving at Christmastime.

Possibilities of bringing New Jersey into line with nineteenth-century philosophies intrigued all thinking people, and nothing proved more worthy of the reformers than the New Jersey constitution of 1776. Only five days had gone into framing that document and only forty-eight hours had elapsed between introduction and adoption. The adoption could scarcely be called an overwhelming vote of confidence: of the sixty-five members of the Provincial Congress which adopted the constitution, thirty members refused to vote either for or against.

TIME TO STAND PAT

Many conservatives doubted the wisdom of tinkering with an old and honored constitution, arguing that revision might lead to greater evils. South Carolina, Maryland, Georgia, Vermont, Massachusetts, and Pennsylvania all had radically revised their original constitutions by 1800, but that in no way changed the minds of those dedicated to preserving the original New Jersey laws.

Proponents of change struck vigorously at the weaknesses of the 1776 parchment. The governor's powers were too broad, he could not be impeached even for misconduct, and his election by the legislature rather than directly by the people robbed the public of a direct choice. On the other hand, the governor had no appointive or pardoning power and his veto could be overridden by a simple majority of the legislature. Worst of all, the governor had to be re-elected every year, a mighty club to put in the hands of the legislature.

The constitution had other weaknesses. The governor was also the chancellor and presiding justice when the upper house of the legislature acted as the highest court. There was no machinery to amend the constitution: a major flaw. Legislators, as well as the governor, had to be re-elected each year, following the theory of John Adams that "where annual elections end, tyranny begins."

The Broad Seal War

Tyranny's failure might be insured by annual trips to the polls but the system did not bring good government to New Jersey. Nothing proved this more than the state-wide Congressional elections of 1838, an event with repercussions into the very halls of Congress and an occurrence of so little dignity that it earned the mocking name of the Broad Seal War.

Voters went to the polls on the ninth and tenth of October, 1838, to choose between Democratic and Whig tickets for the six seats in the House of Representatives (at that time all Congressmen were chosen state wide rather than by districts). First returns showed clear Democratic majorities for five seats. But when all returns were in only Joseph F. Randolph, a Whig, was elected beyond any possibility of dispute. Whig county clerks in Cumberland and Middlesex counties had far more to do with the outcome than the voters. The Whig clerk in Cumberland County simply suppressed the Millville Township returns and so manipulated the Deerfield Township returns as to set "the seal and silence of death upon the public will." Millville and Deerfield had both favored the Democrats over the Whigs. The Middlesex clerk blandly neglected to include *any* return of the heavy Democratic victory in South Amboy. Public confidence was not strengthened by knowledge that the Cumberland and Middlesex clerks had both held up their returns until they knew the extent of Democratic successes elsewhere.

Governor William Pennington and his all-Whig Council gathered on October 24 to certify election results. Ignoring the storms of protest that swept over them, the governor and his Council announced that to their "official knowledge" no voting had taken place in either Millville or South Amboy. If there had been an election, they argued, why hadn't the clerks turned in the results? With Millville and South Amboy safely out of the way, all six Whigs had squeaked through to victory. Governor Pennington affixed the Broad Seal (or Great Seal) of the State of New Jersey to the "official" returns and sent the six Whigs to Washington with his blessing.

Such tongue-in-cheek certification might have been ignored in other times, but in Washington the House of Representatives was so closely split between Whigs and Democrats that a single vote could make the difference in organization and choice of the Speaker. Bitter dispute rocked the House over the New Jersey candidates, and ten days elapsed before intervention by ex-President John Quincy Adams (serving out his years as a Congressman). Adams stepped into the Broad Seal War and worked out a conciliation whereby Democrats organized the House before New Jersey's five disputed Whigs took their seats. Eventually the House certified Whig John Randolph as an official member—but replaced Pennington's "Congressmen" with the five Democrats who apparently had won in the first place.

TIME FOR A CHANGE

Certainly the moral standards of New Jersey politicians couldn't be blamed entirely on the state constitution of 1776, but the Broad Seal War proved to be the last major test that the old parchment could take. Governor Pennington urged constitutional revision in his 1840 annual message. Three years later Democratic Governor Daniel Haines of Sussex County also endorsed constitutional change. The conservative opposition had been broken: Whigs and Democrats agreed and rural and industrial counties alike stood staunchly together in asking for a new set of laws.

Sixty delegates gathered in Trenton for the opening of the Constitutional Convention on May 14, 1844. Remarkable harmony prevailed because the delegates were essentially men of character and stature and representative of the best in both political parties. They moved in dignity and they debated in comparative leisure; more than six weeks elapsed before the convention completed its work on June 28. Enthusiastic tripartisan support led to a 20,276 to 3526 victory when the public voted on the new constitution on August 13. The small turnout of less than 24,000 citizens spoke eloquently of the limited suffrage permitted by the 1776 laws.

More than anything else, the new laws of the state secured the masses' right to vote, excepting only such as paupers, idiots, the insane, criminals, Negroes, and women. Any white male U.S. citizen over twenty-one years of age could cast a ballot, provided he had lived in New Jersey for one year and was a resident of any given county for five months. The old, restrictive property qualifications no longer prevailed; a man did not have to be well off to vote. Democracy of an advanced sort, for the times, had come to New Jersey.

The constitution of 1844 also explicitly spelled out the division of government into definite executive, judicial, and legislative branches, although the governor's appointive powers also gave him considerable influence in the judiciary. The governor's term was extended from one year to three but he could not succeed himself. And, for the first time, he would be elected directly by the people rather than by the legislators.

Unquestionably the constitution had strengths; its Bill of Rights guaranteed a broad list of freedoms, particularly the philosophy that "all political power is inherent in the people." Other freedoms, many of them fundamental in the U. S. Constitution as well, ranged through freedom of religion, press, and speech and the reasonable assurance of justice in the courts. Provision was made for a limited system of free education. It was not a full Bill of Rights, for Negroes were not meant to be included, but it was a giant step ahead.

Weakness threaded the document, too, although it would take passing years to reveal the flaws completely. The governor lacked power despite the extension of his term; his veto still could be overridden by a simple majority of the legislature—an assured means of hamstringing his power. Further, the process of amending the constitution of 1844 involved difficult and lengthy procedure, including a provision that "no amendment or amendments shall be submitted to the people by the Legislature oftener than once in five years."

The new constitution proved that the will of the people could be heard in New Jersey. A new spirit of change and reform gained strength, manifested in everything from socialistic communities to determined efforts to improve the lot of the underprivileged and the ill-used people of America.

To Eliminate Social Evil

One social notion that did not strike the fancies of most people was the growth of "ideal" communities, wherein (if the founders could be believed at all) the social evils of the world might be eliminated. Such socialistic dreams excited many areas of the country in the 1840s. Those were the years of Brook Farm, Oneida Community, New Harmony, and many such Utopias in other parts of the nation. Ralph Waldo

Emerson wrote to Thomas Carlyle in the autumn of 1840: "We are all a little wild here with numberless projects of social reform. Not a reading man but has a draft of a new community in his waistcoat pocket."

Charles Fourier, the French economist whose philosophy underlay most of the American dream colonies, believed that men and women could live together, sharing their resources in a communal society and yet enjoying such benefits of capitalism as interest on investments, a share of profits, and wages for their labor. He argued that the rich should keep their wealth, but he insisted that rich and poor could live together to the everlasting benefit of each.

Fourier's chief American advocate was Albert Brisbane, father of noted newspaper editor Arthur Brisbane. The elder Brisbane advocated a series of communities called Phalanxes (from the Greek military formation). Each Phalanx would be self-supporting, growing its own food, making its own clothes, and manufacturing all other needs. Residents would live in huge hotellike structures called phalansteries.

The most notable of all enterprises in the Fourier movement was Brook Farm near Boston, founded in 1842 and perpetuated in history because of the many literary lights who joined the colony. Brook Farm is always cited by social historians, but the North American Phalanx near Red Bank was far more successful; Brook Farm lasted six years, while the Phalanx enjoyed twelve flourishing years.

RISE OF THE PHALANX

Ten families from Albany, New York, founded the North American Phalanx in 1843 after buying 643 Monmouth County acres for $14,000. The Albany people invested $8000 of their own money and sold stock to make up the balance. They built a three-story phalanstery—with bachelors on the third floor, families on the second floor, and the community dining area on the first floor. By 1847, the population was about ninety, including scientists, writers, doctors, lawyers, artisans, laborers, and farmers.

At first all went well. People worked happily in the fields or shared the work in their big house. A resident might dig potatoes in the morning, teach French in the afternoon, and wash dishes after the evening meal. Night after night the Phalanxers gathered in the grand salon to discuss politics and economics and to plan the machine shops and mills that were built to expand the community's economic base.

Women had equality in all things, including the duty to labor in the fields, and such unconventionality troubled non-Phalanx neighbors. Red Bank ladies expressed shock when Phalanx women appeared on the streets wearing bloomers, a sort of Turkish trouser covered by a skirt.

The Phalanxers sought no strife; quickly they took to wearing skirts when they visited Red Bank.

The Phalanx thrived as its products gained ready acceptance in the outside world, but by 1853 disagreements had invaded the Utopia. Some residents fretted over their small pay (nine cents per hour) and some expressed concern because the colony lacked religious discipline (each person was permitted full religious liberty). Many yearned for independence and risk rather than communal life and security. Fire swept through the flour mill, sawmill, machine shop, and smithy in 1854. The Phalanx disbanded soon after; the farm was broken up and sold. As proof that the project was fiscally sound, every nonresident stockholder received 100 per cent on his investment, while resident stockholders were paid 60 per cent.

Utopian thought did not cease in New Jersey. Several who had grown disenchanted with the North American Phalanx founded the Raritan Bay Union in 1853 on the Eagleswood estate near Perth Amboy. The Union closely followed the Phalanx pattern, but Marcus Spring, the founder, wanted the Raritan Bay Union to "hold an intermediate position between the North American Phalanx and ordinary society."

Some forty families joined Spring at Eagleswood, and, despite vows not to emulate the Phalanx near Red Bank, their first move was erection of a brownstone community house patterned on the phalanstery of the North American Phalanx. The Raritan Bay Unionites worked together in community fashion, declaring that "every man will be paid for what he does and no man will be paid for nothing."

Notable figures joined the Eagleswood venture, including Theodore D. Weld of Belleville, the celebrated Grimke sisters, who had fought vigorously for abolition of slavery in their native South Carolina, and James G. Birney, well-known abolitionist who had campaigned for President of the United States on the Liberty Party ticket. Elizabeth Peabody, who later founded the first American kindergarten at Boston, taught at Eagleswood.

The Perth Amboy venture attracted such literary figures as Henry David Thoreau and Ralph Waldo Emerson to observe and to lecture. In 1859, Mrs. Marcus Spring, wife of the founder, provoked violent censure by bringing two of John Brown's executed raiders to Eagleswood for burial despite an angry mob that planned to meet the boat at Perth Amboy and throw the caskets overboard. Mrs. Spring calmly arranged to land the bodies at Rahway, and conducted a secret burial at Eagleswood.

But idealism couldn't make Eagleswood succeed either. The Raritan Bay Union disbanded in about 1859, although the school lived on. The phalanstery became a military school, then a hotel, and later part of a tile factory. The bodies of the two John Brown followers were removed in 1899 to North Elba, New York, for burial near John Brown. Nothing remained of Spring's utopia.

No Time to Mourn

The passing of communal ventures prompted little mourning. Too many other needs agitated the minds of reformers who were concerned much more with the plight of debtors, prisoners, and the mentally ill.

Humane treatment of prisoners had been long in coming. When the first state prison opened at Trenton in 1799, its aim was reflected in an inscription above the main entrance: "Labor, Silence, Penitence . . . That Those Who Are Feared for Their Crimes May Learn to Fear the Laws and be Useful. Hic Labor, Hoc Opus." Emphasis was on punishment: everyone worked at hard labor, meals consisted of "corn meal mush and molasses for breakfast and the same for supper; at dinner, soup or salt herring and bread." Water was the only beverage.

Local jails ranged from wretched to poor. Murderers, debtors, the insane, and the poor, without regard to age, sex, or the nature of their crimes, were herded together in dank quarters which were usually little better than "dungeons in the basement of the court house." Burlington County won a measure of praise in about 1810 when it erected its Debtors Jail and Workhouse, largely because Robert Mills, the distinguished Philadelphia architect who designed the structure, also prepared a sociological brief to accompany his plans. He urged that "infants in crime" not be associated with "veterans in wickedness" and he suggested the bathing and fumigation of all new prisoners, and periodically of all prisoners. He framed a prison motto: "Justice Which While It Punishes, Would Endeavor to Reform the Offender."

Such a motto failed to appeal in an era when men, women, and children often were sent to jail simply for being poor and unloved or without someone to say they were not a public charge. It took New Jersey until March 9, 1842, to abolish imprisonment for debt, not a spectacular performance but not much worse than other states, for Maine had become the first state to move against the practice in 1835.

Increasing concern began to be shown for the lawbreaker. The New Jersey legislature appointed a commission to study the dank, foul state prison in 1829; it took only a few visits to the stone structure to convince the commission that the prison was little more than a "hatching ground for new crimes."

The commission minced no words in its report. The prison was "without form or unity in design" so that the "prisoners are removed as far as possible from the institution or control of the officers." Small wonder that the prison fostered "gambling, fighting, and other mischief without detection." The prisoners and their keepers engaged in smuggling goods in and out of the prison. Witnesses told of severe riots within the walls and of discharged prisoners coming over the wall of the prison to rob the institution or to release prisoners.

The legislature hired John Haviland, pioneer prison architect, to design a new prison. Haviland built a prison that was a model for light and fresh air—and therefore a considerable stride forward. Basically he followed the concept that prisoners could best be reformed by keeping them in individual cells for eating, sleeping, working, exercising, and receiving "moral instruction." If a prisoner had to be moved, a hood was placed over his head to shield his identity and to prevent communication with fellow inmates.

Solitude was supposed to create a state of remorse and reformation, but the Haviland system (except for the light and fresh air) was quickly discredited. Two years after the prison was opened in 1836, a legislative committee reported "few known changes for the better among the inmates." Then, in 1840, the prison physician, Dr. James B. Coleman, wrote that the effect of solitude on the prisoner was "a diminished force of his organs generally . . . the mind suffers . . . and when absolute derangement does not take place, its powers are considerably weakened." Dr. Coleman's report made little difference; the state could not afford another prison—and in practice, so many prisoners were incarcerated that solitary confinement quickly became forgotten in the need to share cells.

IF MINDS STRAYED

When public policy provided that everyone likely to become a public charge, whether for crime, debt, or senility, must be put behind bars, a suffering group suffered more. Caught in that impartially tight net had to be the insane, the odd, the eccentric, the mentally disturbed. These might have been the most violated prisoners of all, for they had neither stolen nor gone into debt; they were simply out of touch with reality.

An 1839 legislative commission studied an appeal by Dr. Lyndon A. Smith of Newark, president of the Medical Society of New Jersey, that means be found to aid the mentally ill. The commission found 338 lunatics and 358 idiots in New Jersey, many confined to poorhouses or jails, such as a twenty-eight-year-old woman who had been in chains in the Gloucester County jail since she was sixteen years old. Stressing the fact that insanity could be cured in some cases—as had been proved by Dr. Philippe Pinel of France sixty years before—the commission urged that an asylum be built in New Jersey. The conservative legislature tabled the report.

Dreadful conditions persisted, and when misery persisted anywhere, it came to the attention of Dorothea Dix, the earnest young Massachusetts reformer whose tart revelations of the treatment of the insane in Massachusetts and Rhode Island already had shamed much of New England's prideful into grudging change. Miss Dix arrived in New Jersey in 1843, bringing a keen eye for sordid detail and a tenacity in dealing with obdurate legislators.

Dorothea Dix personally visited nearly every jail and almshouse in the state, discovering brutality and neglect that sickened her. She found the blind, the aged, and the poor housed with criminals. She saw the insane treated as wild beasts, fastened in cells because their keepers feared them as they might fear a vicious panther.

No section of the state escaped either the attention or the wrath of Miss Dix. Salem County had a jail without beds, for the law did not demand such a luxury. She found one Salem man, imprisoned for insanity for thirty years, who had been out of his quarters "but ten times in more than nineteen years." Salem keepers beat insane inmates with blocks of wood, and Miss Dix found a former county judge "chained for safety." Cumberland and Cape May offered equally miserable treatment, and in Gloucester County a pauper inmate was "keeper" of the insane. Burlington County kept its insane in "dreary confined cells, pervaded with foul air." Monmouth had two small cells, complete with chains and a straw bed.

County after county fell under Miss Dix's scorn. She singled out Middlesex for a demented man chained "in a sort of a box," next to a cold, damp cell where a madman stood naked except for a laced straitjacket. Essex County let her see men, women, and children thrown together in what Miss Dix called "the primary school and the normal school for the state prison." She found accommodations in Passaic County "loathsome," and she wrote of Morris County accommodations that were "dark, damp, unfurnished, unwarmed and unventilated."

Miss Dix presented her stinging rebuke to the New Jersey conscience in January, 1844, dropping it into the laps of the New Jersey Legislature and asking for $150,000 for a state asylum. The Senate heard her report in embarrassment but the first action on the report was a resolution to vote $1000 "to carry Miss Dix across the Delaware, and get her out of the state."

Miss Dix received that news with fury, and promptly began a one-woman lobby, meeting with legislators individually. She triumphed, and in April, 1844, went with legislators to look at a hundred rolling acres in Ewing Township north of Trenton that had been picked for the hospital. Work began two years later on the sandstone building. The first inmates moved into the nation's most modern mental health hospital in 1848. Miss Dix called the Trenton asylum "my first child" and in her late years she came back to live in an apartment in the building until her death in 1887.

SHALL EDUCATION BE FREE?

Since the plight of the insane and the criminal caused such concern, it might be expected that New Jerseyans would move to make free education an actuality. They did, but with agonizing slowness.

Even through the 1820s the New Jersey system of education remained much as it had been in colonial days, when education beyond family training was deemed essentially a church obligation. Church schools became academies, and by 1830 most major towns in the state had such schools to train children of the well-to-do. Gordon's *Gazetteer* of 1834 listed more than forty private academies, scattered throughout New Jersey. At the lower end of the economic scale, children also received some learning, since state law made it mandatory to provide rudimentary education to "minor slaves, apprentices and pauper children." Between the penniless and the wealthy lay the great bulk of struggling New Jersey families; legislators simply ignored the academic needs of children in this class.

Continued agitation for broader educational opportunity led to creation in 1816 of a state fund of $16,000 "for the support of free schools." Private and church-supported schools, a formidable opposition composed of the power elite, fought the fund, but all too evident needs forced legislators to transcend the opposition. State funds were allocated to counties on the basis of state taxes paid by counties; counties, in turn, gave funds to their towns in proportion to county taxes paid. Since wealthy areas paid the most taxes, they received the most money back. That helped sorely distressed cities such as Newark, but the poor rural areas remained as backward as ever.

Professor John Maclean of the College of New Jersey spoke vigorously in 1828 for a "common school" system, supported by a combination of state aid, local taxes, and a small tuition charge. That same year a public meeting of "the friends of education" in Trenton reported that 12,000 New Jersey children between the ages of five and fifteen were not receiving schooling of any kind. Those who were in school had schoolmasters who were "amenable to no tribunal, and subject to no inspections or supervision." The group strongly favored establishment of a system of public schools.

The legislature heeded the urgent plea and in 1829 passed the first comprehensive school law in New Jersey. It provided for common schools to be established and supervised by local townships with state funds to be matched by local moneys. The act called for educational censuses and records, a decided gain because it provided an awareness of the task to be done. However, legislators in 1830 and 1831 watered down the law, even to the extent of letting private and parochial schools share in the pitifully small sums available.

COMMON SCHOOL SYSTEM

Pressure for good public education could not be turned aside. Governor William Pennington in his message of January, 1838, recognized that "public sentiment and public interests alike demand a thorough revision of our common school system." Later that month a distinguished group of New Jersey leaders—including both church officials and heads of private academies—formulated an "address to the people," which urged, in part:

> Tax yourselves for the support of common schools and you will never be in danger of taxation from a foreign power. You will need less taxation for the support of pauperism and the punishment of crime. Look to your schoolhouses. See that they are convenient of access, that they are comfortable; that they are neat and tasteful. Look to the teachers. See that they are taught themselves and apt to teach—men that fear God and love their country. See that they are well accommodated, well treated and well remunerated.

The legislature responded by increasing annual school aid to $30,000 and eliminating grants to private schools. The picture had begun to brighten. Newark established free public schools in 1836, and two years later the city opened a high school (now Barringer High School), the first in the state. However, most New Jersey school districts continued to charge tuition until 1871, when free schools finally came into being, although Newark, Jersey City, and Paterson all had eliminated charges by 1846. Newark, as befitted the state's largest city, tried to extend education. In 1858 it had a Negro school (very progressive for the time) and a school where vagrant and destitute children were "taught such studies as seems expedient."

Bright spots obscured the picture, unfortunately. In 1839, only 89 of 139 schools even bothered to submit reports, and of those reporting, statistics showed fewer than half of children between five and sixteen in schools. School buildings were wretched. Dr. T. F. King, a medical doctor, who became the first State Superintendent of Schools in 1846, had this to say about the buildings in his 1848 report:

A merciful man, being merciful to his beast, would not winter his horses in places appropriated at present for district schoolhouses.

Let him travel over our state, in what direction he will, and if he sees a building, some sixteen feet by twenty, with the clapboards off in some places, in others hanging by a single nail, the roof open, the door with one hinge and that a leather one, the windows wanting glass, but abounding in old hats, caps and cloaks, or copy books, he may with tolerable certainty set it down for a country schoolhouse.

INDUCEMENTS TO A THIEF

More bluntly, Thomas C. Rogers, a superintendent of Waterford schools in Camden County, declared that the state penitentiary "presents more inducements for a horse thief to seek his subsistence and comfort in its rooms than any common school or academy, founded and supported by the state, offers to an aspiring youth a thirst for knowledge."

The quality of teaching was miserable. Generally teachers knew little more than their pupils and often school districts hired teachers without background, culture, or anything save "moral character" (and many a candidate had precious little of that). A Monmouth County educator in 1850 protested: "We have to depend on the cullings of New England for teachers rather than educating our own sons and daughters." One telling reason was the low salary scale; the highest-paid educator in the state in 1850 was Isaiah Peckham, principal of Newark's high school—who was paid $1027.28, exactly, per year.

Slowly the situation improved. Teachers themselves, earnestly seeking self-improvement, began to gather together for mutual understanding and enlightenment. County teacher associations came before 1850, and in 1853 about fifty teachers from eight counties met in New Brunswick to organize the State Teachers Association (forerunner of today's New Jersey Education Association).

Governor Rodman Price, called "the father of New Jersey's normal school" (at Trenton), declared in 1854: "I regret to say that our educational system is inferior to that of many of the states." Ignoring those who declared his support of public education would ruin him politically, Price in 1855 pressed through the legislature a bill establishing a state normal school ("normal," by the way, from the French école normale, in which teachers were trained for the lower grades).

The legislature voted a grudging $10,000 for the school and offered to place it anywhere—as long as some community furnished "suitable location and buildings without expense to the state." New Brunswick, Beverly, Orange, Princeton, Pennington, and other towns made inadequate bids for the school; the legislature in 1855 accepted Trenton's offer of free land and $14,000 for buildings.

Concurrently, forward-looking principals in Newark and Paterson opened Saturday teacher-training courses in their towns in April, 1855, bolstering attendance by deducting a day's pay for every day's absence from classes. Trenton's state-supported normal school began classes in a rented hall on October 1, 1855, three weeks before textbooks arrived and nearly eight weeks before the entrance examination was given on Thanksgiving Day. The examination asked such questions as "What is the shape of the Earth?" and "Where is the Territory of Nebraska?"

The question about Nebraska had more than passing importance at that, because in 1855 New Jersey, and all the nation, had to be concerned with questions far beyond state borders. The question most nagging at the public and private conscience—slavery—was nearing a showdown. Teachers, and those whom they taught, soon would know intimately of Nebraska and Kansas and Georgia and Virginia and points south and west. Boys just entering New Jersey school doors in 1855 would in their lifetimes come to know United States geography all too well, for war between North and South was coming closer with each passing year.

Keep Him in Place

Eventually all had to reach some decision on slavery, but in 1850 the average New Jerseyan ignored the Negro—so long as he "kept his place" (and that place was one of poverty, illiteracy, and degradation). Quakers were the chief exception; their church had long given wide interpretation to the theory that "all men are created equal." Such opposition to slavery as there was in New Jersey centered mainly in areas where Quakers were strongly represented.

The years had brought some slow legal action. New Jersey forbade the importation of slaves into the state in 1786 and two years later adopted an act making it illegal to move a slave out of the state without his consent after he had lived here for twelve months. That 1788 act also ordained that all slaves should be judged and punished on the same basis as all other human beings, although that lofty practice was seldom followed—and it suggested that all slaves be taught to read.

Antislavery forces on February 18, 1804, pushed through the New Jersey legislature an "Act for the Gradual Abolition of Slavery." The act stressed the "Gradual" more than the "Abolition," since females born of slaves remained bound servants for twenty-one years and males held that status until age twenty-five. Then all would be free.

The 1846 act abolished slavery by making all slaves apprentices, giving them such rights as consent to a sale of themselves. Children born of apprentices were free—but bound out for service by the local overseer of the poor after reaching six years of age. Historians play

When Civil War tore America apart, New Jersey found itself in the middle—a passageway for escaping slaves and a state where sympathies at first lay equally divided between North and South. The conflict brought its heroes and its tragedies, and in its wake New Jersey was unmistakably industrial and urban. Seaside resorts sprang up to cater to growing wealth and leisure time. Artists wandered by to sketch the beauty that remained in the hills. But it was a time of intrigue, of invention, of industry, and of immigration; all these were part of transformed New Jersey.

William Still, Burlington County native, was a bulwark in the national Underground Railroad movement.

Many Southern slaves on the Underground were helped to freedom by crossing on ferryboats plying between Philadelphia and Camden.

17

Judson Kilpatrick, Sussex County's wild-riding general, and Philip Kearny, pictured as he might have met his death at Chantilly, Virginia, were the state's greatest Civil War heroes.

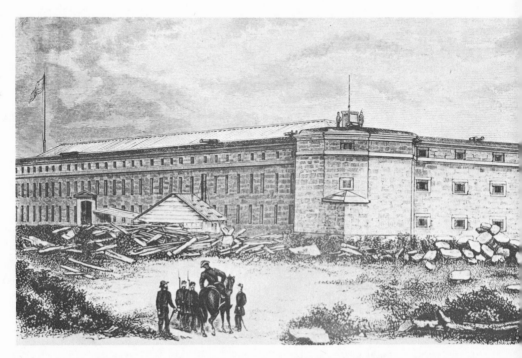

But far from the battlefields, Southern prisoners died by the hundreds in the flooded, disease-ridden prison camp at Fort Delaware off Salem County.

Newark emerged from the Civil War as the state's foremost center of industry and finance, and the waters of the Passaic River teemed with traffic.

Rutgers College, founded in 1766, grew on its New Brunswick hillside to eminence in both liberal arts and agricultural science--and in time came to be the state university.

Leslie's Weekly of 1872 paid much attention to Long Branch, ABOVE, *serene and supreme atop its ocean-front bluff; but many who preferred peace and quiet frequented Cape May,* BELOW, *boastful after the Civil War that it led all resorts.*

ABOVE, *the 1872 book* Picturesque America *included this romantic view of Eagle Rock in Essex County.* BELOW, *at the same time, Granville Perkins portrayed the magnificence of Delaware Water Gap in the rugged wilds of northwestern New Jersey.*

Inventiveness was encouraged in the "idea factory" that Thomas A. Edison established at Menlo Park in 1876. Here part of his inventive crew lolls on the steps of the building in which Edison perfected the incandescent lamp in 1879.

It was also at Menlo Park that Edison invented the phonograph, whose facility in transmitting sound soon had all the world listening.

Immigrants who awaited their futures in front of New York's Castle Garden learned of the opportunities in New Jersey for those with strong backs and good minds. Thousands of them worked on the streets, in the factories, in the brickyards, and on the farms. By 1910, Perth Amboy and Passaic ranked among the top three cities in percentage of foreign-born.

Paterson applauded each time one of its giant locomotives was hauled through town past the city hall to a railroad siding, but the industry had begun to die by 1900.

At the Clark thread factory in Newark, women and children labored for small wages in the 1890s.

with words when they boast that in 1860 New Jersey had 25,318 "free blacks" and only eighteen slaves. That stretches semantics to the utmost; the usual difference between freedom and slavery was slight.

But while some bent words to ease their consciences, and the majority completely ignored the question of slavery, a few in New Jersey operated quietly and courageously to aid the Negro.

On the Underground

That aid persisted along the lower Delaware River and it moved mysteriously across New Jersey, spiriting runaway slaves through the state on the underground railroad. The underground railroad had no tracks and no timetables, but it followed definite routes, had precise "stations" and daring "conductors." Routing of the "bundles" followed the exigencies of any given emergency. When fugitive-slave agents lurked about the Raritan River ferry landings, the way led inward and circuitously around New Brunswick to Jersey City. When Jersey City teemed with slave seekers, the "railroad" rolled its escaping slaves toward New England through the hills of Morris and Passaic counties.

Some sources say 40,000 escaping slaves crossed New Jersey on the underground, but that is probably much too high a total. Unquestionably, however, thousands of frightened Negro runaways first sensed hope when they saw blue and yellow signal lights set by sympathizers on Salem and Cumberland shores. Following the lights across the Delaware, the fugitives found the way to Quaker helpers and others who set them on the road to liberty.

Both slaves and their conductors breathed more freely when a shipment left New Jersey. This state, alone among all Northern states, supported enforcers of the Fugitive Slave Act and offered no opposition when slaves were seized here.

The 1850s moved swiftly along. All social conscience began to solidify on the one question: How should the Negro be treated? Men would argue the merits and disadvantages of slavery, usually convinced it was a matter of property, not human beings. For a time it seemed that the question might be resolved by talk, and men tried that. Then it became clear that North and South were speeding on a collision course. The two must meet in violence. When they did, there could be no such thing as neutrality, no such thing as saying, "It's not my concern."

13

Northernmost of the Border States

New Jersey's role in the Civil War astonishes anyone who believes that the state's geographical placement among Northern states automatically made it a solid bastion of Union support. Nothing could be further from the truth; throughout the war, powerful opposition surged within the state—against Abraham Lincoln, against Abolitionists, and against armed "interference" in "Southern affairs."

Politicians always had moved slowly to aid slaves within the state; only California and New Jersey among the free-soil states permitted full enforcement of the Fugitive Slave Law within their borders. Lincoln twice failed to win popular support, although he did take four of seven electoral votes in 1860. Legislative leaders often spoke bluntly—and sometimes passionately—for the Southern cause, or at least for peace on essentially Southern terms. New Jersey, in truth, might well be called the northernmost of the Border States.

Despite such rabid pro-Southern sentiment, the state did its share and more. It met every request for troops with as much speed as other Union states (and, indeed, sent thousands more soldiers than requisitions called for). It had its great heroes and its dedicated soldiers. It gave 6300 lives to the Union's cause. However, the memorable story was the power of the antiwar forces.

PRO-SOUTHERN TINGE

Many factors combined to give New Jersey its decidedly pro-Southern tinge. At first it was essentially a matter of the economy, since several industrial areas depended heavily on their Southern sales. Newark, as the prime illustration, sent more than two-thirds of its shoes, clothing, leather goods, and carriages to markets below the Mason-Dixon Line. Trenton merchants traded actively in the South.

There also were traditional and social bases for pleasant feelings toward the South: most of the regular summer visitors to Cape May hotels came from Richmond and Baltimore, and between one-third and one-half of students at the College of New Jersey in Princeton had always come from Southern states, mainly Virginia. There were historic reasons: New Jersey's powerful championing of States' rights at the Constitutional Convention in 1787 led many state leaders to argue that the plight of the Negro slave was solely the business of Southern states, to be worked out in their own way and in their own time.

Bitter political currents seethed within the state. Democratic power centered in Essex and in Bergen counties; when war impended, sentiment in those regions became as much stubbornly anti-Republican as antiwar, but the effect was the same. These areas abounded in Copperheads. (Copperheads were antiwar Democrats who wore in their lapels Indian heads cut from copper pennies and whose enemies likened them to "snakes ready to strike without warning.") The nearness of New York City's powerful Copperhead leaders made Democratic Bergen an especially fertile breeding ground for bitter antiwar feelings.

Even the state's first Republicans were wary of risking open quarrel with Southern sympathizers. They ran simply as Opposition candidates (opposition to Democrats) and they found room under their broad banner for such varied company as former Whigs, Abolitionists, advocates of firmer tariffs, and such miscellany as the Native Americans or Know-Nothings, who based their political philosophy on hatred of foreigners and Catholics. These "Americans" believed that the influx of Germans and Irish Catholics would ruin America—but when anyone questioned them about their secret credo, they stoutly declared that they knew nothing (hence, "Know-Nothings").

No Help for a Native Son

Republicans in New Jersey were strong enough in 1856 to gain the vice-presidential nomination for William L. Dayton on the first national Republican ticket headed by John C. Frémont of California. One of those he defeated for the vice-presidential nod was Abraham Lincoln. Born in Basking Ridge, Dayton had won a fine reputation as a lawyer in Freehold and Trenton. But even with a favorite son on the ticket, New Jersey backed Democrat James Buchanan for President by a smashing majority.

The traditional independence of New Jersey voters mainfested itself in that same year. Despite giving Buchanan an 18,000-vote margin over Frémont, the state elected William A. Newell as its first Republican (or Opposition) governor to break a Democratic stranglehold on the statehouse. Three years later, the Opposition solidified its position by electing Charles S. Olden, retired Princeton farmer and merchant, as governor, although his margin in the 1859 election was a scant 1600 votes in a total vote of 105,000.

Another New Jersey Republican won national attention in February, 1860, when William Pennington of Newark was chosen Speaker of the House of Representatives after weeks of sullen bickering between Congressmen of the North and the South.

Pennington had been elected in 1858 by the First New Jersey Congressional District, centered on Essex County. Scion of a distinguished family, Pennington had been governor of the state from 1837 to 1843, the central figure in the Broad Seal War of 1838 that had stalled business in the House of Representatives for ten days while Congress debated whether to seat a disputed New Jersey Congressional delegation.

Having won in his first bid for national office, little-known Republican Pennington expected nothing when Congress convened on December 5, 1859, to choose its Speaker—a duty normally as controversial as a June breeze. That choice threatened to tear the government apart in 1859, for the thirty-sixth Congress felt acutely the increasingly wide gap between North and South. Republicans at first stuck doggedly behind John Sherman of Ohio, a moderate but dedicated antislavery man. Democrats, badly split, offered various names in the vain hope of rallying support.

Government ground to a halt. The Senate met each day and adjourned immediately. President Buchanan delayed his annual message for twenty-two days. Fifty-three days dragged by before Sherman suddenly withdrew on January 26 and nominated Pennington. Republicans and independents promptly united behind the mild, middle-of-the-road Jerseyman, and on February 1 packed galleries cheered Pennington's election. Only Congressman Hickman of Pennsylvania failed to join in the applause; his voice could be heard shouting indignantly, "We've elected a Black Republican! We've elected a Black Republican!"

"IMPARTIALITY AND JUSTICE"

Hickman erred. While Pennington did not approve of slavery, neither would he act to abolish it. Horace Greeley had sneeringly included the Jersey lawyer among those he labeled "old Whigs varnished over with Republicanism." Thus, in his acceptance speech, Pennington could promise "impartiality and justice for all." And he could say in genuine hope:

"I feel I have a natural heart, embracing all parts of our blessed Union."

Pennington served with dignity, if not distinction, while the nation veered toward war after Abraham Lincoln's nomination in 1860 as Republican candidate for President. Abraham Lincoln's nomination cast the division in state politics into sharp perspective. His uncertain New Jersey backers continued to call themselves the Opposition Party and Democrats took the state. Lincoln lost the popular vote by a fairly close margin, 62,800 to 58,000, and he gained four electoral votes only because the Democrats hurt themselves by placing three distinct Presidential slates on the ballot. Stephen A. Douglas won New Jersey's other three electoral votes. Lincoln's strength lay mainly in southern New Jersey, as shown by the ten counties that he carried—Passaic, Morris, Mercer, Ocean, Burlington, Salem, Gloucester, Atlantic, Cumberland, and Cape May.

Democrats scored heavily in the industrial counties of Hudson and Essex. The rabidly anti-Lincoln Newark *Journal* warned its readers: "If Lincoln is elected, many of our journeymen will be compelled to face the rigors of winter and meet the terrible answer everywhere: No WORK! No WORK!" Plainly the editor felt that without Southern markets, Newark industry would collapse.

Newark's anti-Republican vote also ousted Speaker of the House Pennington, the state's only truly national figure at the time. Pennington took his defeat calmly, but the Newark *Mercury,* as violently pro-Republican as the *Journal* was anti-Republican, blamed his defeat on "the band of mercenary and unprincipled men engaged in Southern trade." The *Mercury* editor said they had followed "the wishes of their Southern masters."

Lincoln's election brought war clouds ever lower, and as they darkened, strident Democratic voices supported the Southern cause. Editor Edward N. Fuller of the Newark *Journal* led the way. On December 22, three days after South Carolina seceded, a Fuller editorial titled "SOUTHERN CAUSE OUR CAUSE" thanked Carolinians for saving America from "a worse calamity than disunion—abolitionism!" Fuller asked sympathy for "the brave spirits of the South" and reiterated his constant theme that New Jersey would serve itself best by siding with the seceding states.

Other leading Democrats played variations on the Fuller theme, some urging compromise, others taking a far more conciliatory tone toward the South.

Commodore Robert F. Stockton, one of a long line in the noted Princeton family and a distinguished naval hero, told a Constitutional Union convention at Trenton in December that New Jersey should "supplicate to the North to yield." The Newark *Journal* quoted Stockton as saying, in effect, that Negroes "weren't worth fighting for." Soon after,

Judge David Naar of Trenton warned that without the South "New York will be no more than a fishing village and New Jersey but little better." Ex-Governor Rodman Price spoke out strongly for the seceding states. As late as April 9, 1861—three days before the attack on Fort Sumter—many state newspapers were carrying his astonishing statement: "I say emphatically that New Jersey should go with the South for every wise, prudential and patriotic reason."

In his Annual Message of January, 1861, Governor Olden showed deep concern at the deteriorating national situation, but counseled moderation. He suggested that a Peace Conference might be a way for all states to iron out their differences. "The troubles connected with slavery," Olden said, "have in great measure been brought on by a few persons of extreme views both in the North and South." Olden's mood bespoke compromise, but the conservative governor clearly spelled out for the South his resolve that New Jersey would defend the Union should that become necessary. A respected contemporary wrote that if Olden had not been elected governor in 1859 "there can be but very little doubt that New Jersey would have been forced to cast her lot with the South."

PEACE BASED ON SLAVERY

A month later, Governor Olden led a nine-man delegation to the Peace Conference called in Washington to support the plan proposed by Senator John J. Crittenden of Kentucky. Crittenden would save the Union by extending the southern Missouri border line to the Pacific as the northern limit of slavery—and would also guarantee noninterference with slavery. The New Jersey delegation seemed a sincere effort to represent many views, but both Robert F. Stockton and Rodman M. Price, whose sympathies for the South were well known, were members. Matters had progressed too far for the Peace Conference to succeed; it disbanded in disagreement. War was near.

Aware that the state between the Hudson and Delaware rivers had rejected him in November and was teetering on the edge of outright Southern support in January, President Lincoln deliberately included doubtful New Jersey in the long itinerary that he followed in February, 1861, from Springfield, Illinois, to his inauguration in Washington, D.C.

New Jersey went wild over the gaunt, sad-faced man whom other states had chosen to be President. Lincoln crossed from New York to Jersey City on February 21 to find 25,000 noisily enthusiastic persons packed into, around, and atop the railroad depot. He went by train to Newark, where the city gave him a reception that Lincoln himself said exceeded anything he had seen since leaving Springfield. As the President proceeded slowly through the immense Newark throng, an eyewitness wrote:

Men, women and children were temporarily insane. The ladies from their perches scattered flowers and threw kisses; the hoarse throats of men roared cheer after cheer; all the city was in the streets and the streets could not have known themselves, so wild was the delight.

Elizabeth, Rahway, and New Brunswick hailed the President with booming cannon and applauding crowds. Princeton students gave his slowly moving train a skyrocket cheer. Trenton streets were filled with thousands hoping for a glimpse of Lincoln as he paused in town to make brief appearances before both houses of the Democratic-controlled legislature. The President there expressed the hope that "this Union, the Constitution and the liberties of the people shall be perpetuated."

Solemnly he said, "The man does not live who is more devoted to peace than I am. None who would do more to preserve it. But it may be necessary to put the foot down firmly." The audience broke into a long, loud cheer before Lincoln continued. He asked, "And if I do my duty and do right, you will sustain me, will you not?" The legislators shouted, "Yes, yes! We will!"

His duty to New Jersey done—and on the record he really didn't owe the state very much—Lincoln moved toward the destiny neither he nor his country could avoid.

FERVOR AFTER SUMTER

Southern guns pounded Fort Sumter in Charleston Harbor on April 12. Built-up tensions exploded in a war fervor that enveloped New Jersey now that the open split had come. Lincoln called for 3120 men from the state on April 17, and within less than a week 10,000 men and boys had volunteered. Hundreds more hastened to New York or Philadelphia to enlist for fear that the South might quit before New Jersey got into action.

"Peace" men were still around, a few of them as vocal as ever, but generally they were scorned or ignored. Every city, town, village, and crossroads hamlet from Sussex to Cape May succumbed to the military fever. Governor Olden told a special session of the legislature that the issue was the Union's existence—"and the place indicated for its determination is the field of battle." The governor borrowed $451,000 from private banks, then induced the legislature to authorize a state loan of $2,000,000 to wage the war.

Flags flew everywhere, including divided Princeton, where nearly half the student body promptly returned home to fight for the Confederacy. Flemington raised $5000 for the soldiers in a single night. Railroad magnate John I. Blair offered twenty dollars to the family of every Warren County volunteer. Businessmen of Jersey City outfitted the 2nd Regiment and Newark temporarily buried its Southern sympathies in a great outdoor rally. Cumberland County began recruiting its famed Cumberland Greys. Cape May joyfully learned that its telegraph line to Trenton, out for many months, would be rebuilt as an emergency link with the exposed coast.

Governor Olden chose thirty-eight-year-old Theodore Runyon, a Newark lawyer to command the state's four militia regiments. The Newarker was surely an impartial choice: as a Democratic delegate to the Electoral College, he had voted for Douglas. Runyon pulled together troops which descended on Trenton in every variety of uniform known to the New Jersey militia (and in some varieties not known to militia anywhere). The gathering troops brought little with them but gaudy uniforms and enthusiasm. The state, in turn, had little to give these men eager to serve their ninety-day enlistments.

John Y. Foster detailed the dismal story of those first war days in his book *New Jersey and the Rebellion* (1867). He called the militia "a system of shreds and patches" and termed the supply of arms "altogether unfit for active service." The military bureau? "As ignorant, practically, as the people themselves of the realities and business of war." The lack of preparedness wasn't anyone's fault; it simply had been a long time between wars.

New Jersey's weapons were stored in the sodden, gloomy State Arsenal, built originally in 1798 as a state prison. Many laughed openly when Governor Olden detailed Trenton's Company A to guard the "weapons"—two cannon captured at Yorktown in 1781, a cannon taken at the Battle of Trenton in 1776, and about 11,000 flintlock muskets so ancient and rusted that they scarcely would have made good clubs, much less shooting irons. Worse, the state did not have so much as one round of ammunition on hand, although some of the local "uniformed companies" brought their own to Trenton.

Blissfully ignorant of their deficiencies, all of New Jersey's 3000 officers and men were off to war by May 3, sailing down the Delaware aboard fourteen "propellors" (hastily converted steam ferryboats). Simultaneously, a Captain Charles Smith frantically searched New York City before he found 36,000 rounds of ball cartridges and matching percussion caps in a private dealer's hands. Smith bought the entire supply for the state's powderless army. He smuggled the precious hoard out of the city, raced it across New Jersey on a special train, and helped distribute the ammunition while the New Jersey flotilla steamed across Chesapeake Bay.

FIRST IN WASHINGTON

Despite the delays, the disappointments, and the deficiencies, all four New Jersey regiments marched through the streets of Washington on May 6. The Jerseymen could pridefully note that they were the first fully organized, fully equipped brigade to reach Washington.

Union generals put the Jersey regiments to work erecting fortifications around the capital. The Jerseymen grumbled; they wanted to move South before the Rebels quit—few thought that the "Johnny Rebs" would last. Every official estimate predicted a short war. When Governor Olden asked permission in April to send more New Jersey troops, Secretary of War Cameron refused, ordering that if more than enough men had been recruited in New Jersey, "reduce the number by discharge." During the spring orgy of flag raisings throughout the state, Congressman John T. Nixon of New Jersey's Fifth District made a reassuring, if naïve, statement at a Bridgeton ceremony:

"This rebellion could easily be put down by a few women with broomsticks!"

Less than three months later, Congressman Nixon rode out to Bull Run, Virginia, to join a gay crowd anticipating the crushing of the Confederacy in one battle. Forward on July 21 marched the loosely disciplined, brightly uniformed Union army, some 5000 men stronger than the 30,000 equally loosely disciplined and brightly uniformed Confederates waiting for them. Nixon was displeased that New Jersey troops were given the job of protecting the rear, but before day's end he was glad to have those troops between him and the front.

By nightfall the Union army had fled in panic from Bull Run, heading back toward the Jersey troops who stood with bayonets drawn, blocking roads and fields in an effort to slow the wild surge to the rear. The disorganized Northern army couldn't realize that the Southerners were in no condition to pursue. Later, newspaper correspondents asked why the fresh New Jersey troops had been held back—with the clear inference that Jerseymen preferred their rear-guard position. The truth was that they had simply followed orders that chaotic day.

END OF A DREAM

Bull Run's shocking setback ended the fiction of a brief holidaylike struggle, and it provoked controversy throughout the North. On the one hand, there were those who urged that manpower requirements be stepped up to meet the threat of a long war. On the other, increasingly bold Copperheads and Peace Democrats demanded that the

North seek a truce. New Jersey found itself caught tightly in the grip of both forces.

Men went off to war all summer, including five regiments recruited as a result of a curiously casual telegram that President Lincoln sent Governor Olden three days after Bull Run. The dispatch said the Union would accept five more New Jersey regiments "if tendered in reasonable time." Olden took the request seriously; by October 4 the state had eight full regiments—two brigades—in and near Washington.

About this time, New Jersey found a general, the much-rebuffed Philip Kearny, to lead its lackadaisical (and sometimes rebellious) troops. Refused a commission by both the federal government and his home state of New York, largely because of jealousy at both levels, Kearny accepted a New Jersey brigadier generalship four days after the Bull Run debacle. Kearny had fought the Indians in California, had shone in the Mexican War (where he lost his left arm), and had won fame and decorations with French troops in Algeria and Italy. He was as distinguished a soldier as the North could claim.

Kearny transformed the First New Jersey Brigade from a careless rabble, whose members weren't about to give up civilian "rights" merely because they wore a uniform, into a tightly disciplined and tough fighting force. His men respected him; many even idolized the "One-Armed Devil." Eventually they would redeem his boast: "I can make my men follow me to hell!"

Up Rise the Copperheads

But that would come later. With the South unable to follow up its Bull Run triumph and the North thoroughly frightened by its loss, the war settled into a stalemate. The antiwar elements in New Jersey boldly resumed the opposition that had simmered after the Fort Sumter cannonading. Nine days after the Battle of Bull Run, an "immense and enthusiastic" Bergen County peace meeting was held at Schraalenbergh (now the towns of Bergenfield and Dumont). In many other sections of the state, all the way south to Cumberland County, similar peace meetings were held, but Bergen led the way.

Bergen's recalcitrance has been attributed to the fact that its large proportion of Dutch farmers opposed war in any form, particularly a war likely to upset their economic security. The county then was firmly Democratic, thus stood philosophically against "Lincoln's War." The proximity to New York City, where a strong Copperhead movement flourished, was the more likely reason why Bergen became a ready testing ground for antiwar sentiment.

New Jersey's Copperheads found their leader in September, 1861. To be precise, the federal government created a leader for them when

Secretary of War Cameron ordered the arrest of Colonel James W. Wall of Burlington, a noted Peace Democrat. A United States marshal secretly took Wall to prison at Fort Lafayette in New York on September 11. The government offered no reason for the arrest and advanced no explanation when Wall was released on September 24 after he took an oath of allegiance to the United States. The Burlington colonel had been a frequent contributor to antiwar newspapers (particularly the New York *Daily News* and the Newark *Journal*) but his activities were no different from those of scores of other writers, in New Jersey and elsewhere.

Indignation at the treatment of Wall reverberated throughout the state. Copperheads fumed, and even loyal war supporters were upset at the flagrant violation of civil liberties. Wall returned home on September 27 to a torchlight parade and hero's welcome in Burlington. The incident was a significant factor in heavy Democratic successes at the polls in both November, 1861, and November, 1862. The latter election carried Democrat Joel Parker into the governor's chair. Parker had fully supported the war effort, to the extent that he had served as a major general at the outbreak of the conflict.

Parker defeated popular Dr. Marcus L. Ward of Newark, widely loved for his attempts to aid Union soldiers and their families. Personal liberties, as endangered by arrests such as Wall's, became an issue. There was also growing resentment of President Lincoln's forthcoming Emancipation Proclamation. Lincoln had given notice in September that he would issue the proclamation on January 1, 1863. When he did, the deed was not popular in New Jersey.

Copperhead power reached its peak in March of 1863 when the Democratic legislature elected Wall to fulfill an unexpired term in the U. S. Senate (somewhat to his dismay; he had hoped to be named later to a full term). State Senator Daniel Holsman of Bergen County headed the Copperhead group in the Senate, and the strongest voice in the Assembly was Bergen County's Thomas Dunn English, an antiwar pleader (who is best recalled for his romantic ballad "Ben Bolt").

Wall, Holsman, English, Editor Fuller of Newark, and Judge Naar of Trenton were heard often, but the chief Copperhead partisan was C. Chauncey Burr, an itinerent opportunist. Burr had been a clergyman, writer, wife deserter, theatrical press agent, and bigamist before coming to New Jersey. Here he became a prolific, virulent advocate of "peace." Burr spoke vehemently at a Trenton meeting called on March 4, 1863, to protest the Conscription Act. Burr's exact remarks are forgotten, but not this statement made by Judge Naar the same day:

"We are cutting each other's throats for the sake of a few worthless Negroes."

THE LISTS GROW LONG

By March, 1863, New Jersey people had begun to grow weary of the Copperheads as the lists of dead and wounded grew appalling longer. When darkness ended fighting at Gaines's Mill, Virginia, on June 27, 1862, the 4th Jersey Regiment had been surrounded; 55 had been killed, 127 wounded, and 500 taken prisoner. That same day at Gaines's Mill, only 965 of the 2800 men in the 1st Jersey Brigade reported fit for duty at midnight. Those dispatches did not make pleasant reading back home. Although a few saw the casualty lists as cause for pleading with the South for peace, the roll of the dead also stood as a compelling, if agonizing, reason for pressing the fight.

Sixteen New Jersey regiments of three-year volunteers already were under arms by July, 1862, but a month later the War Department called on the state to furnish another 10,470 men for nine months' service. New Jersey worked earnestly to meet the quota. Bridgeton claimed a record by enrolling 110 men in two days. In nearby Downe Township in Cumberland County, Company G of the 24th Regiment enlisted five sons of Mrs. Martha Cobb of Downe Township. Eleven full regiments of these "nine monthers" were in Washington by October 10, 1862.

Within forty days these newest warriors knew the horrors of war. One of the five Cobb brothers died of typhoid fever at Chain Bridge, Virginia, on November 14, and two of his brothers were wounded on the late November assaults near Fredericksburg. The 24th Regiment of short termers lost 160 men outside Fredericksburg. The 26th Regiment, "the Flower of Essex County," boasted that it "learned to drill on the battlefield." That emergency drilling was not effective: 123 men of the 26th fell dead or wounded in the siege of Fredericksburg.

ONE LAST PUSH FOR PEACE

With more than 30,000 New Jerseyans in arms as the war turned into 1863, the Copperhead leadership in the legislature made one last big antiwar drive in mid-March. A three-way split, involving Republicans, War Democrats and Peace Democrats, gave the peace supporters a voting edge.

Spurred by Bergen's delegations, both houses passed peace resolutions, opposing emancipation of slaves and urging the federal government to appoint a commissioner to meet with the South to stop hostilities. The war, the resolution said, "was unnecessary in its origin, fraught with horror and suffering in its continuance." While the resolution found favor with a majority in the soft seats of the legislature, troops in the field reacted angrily.

Two New Jersey regiments encamped near the Rappahannock River in Virginia took action. The 11th sent a written resolution to the legislature, saying "even the introduction of the so-called Peace Resolution was wicked, weak and cowardly." It continued, "secret enemies who at home foment disaffection" were every bit as much "traitors as the foe in arms." The 24th Regiment, "assembled in the hollow square," heard Lieutenant William E. Potter declare:

"It is a matter of regret and shame that as we endure the perils and sufferings of war . . . these traitors at home should be striving to outstrip each other in their haste to throw themselves at the feet of the slave power."

THE ABSORBING QUESTION

The Copperhead movement had reached its zenith. Although Democrats would control the state's politics for the rest of the war, they would be essentially War Democrats. To Democratic Governor Parker the "absorbing question" was "how are we to end the war and at the same time preserve the Union?" and he fully carried out the federal government's commands.

June of 1863 brought the conflict into the North's back yard. The move northward had begun two months before when General Robert E. Lee outmaneuvered and outgunned the ponderous Army of the Potomac along the Rappahannock River. On one day alone, April 30, the 1st Jersey Brigade lost sixty-five men killed and 359 wounded in a futile crossing of that river. Five weeks later, on June 5, the 26th Regiment joined the 5th Vermont in a daring surge across the river to silence a Confederate battery—and the desperate action cost a 26th Regiment soldier's life for every one of the fifteen minutes that it required.

The June 5 heroics by the 26th Regiment proved that the men who had enlisted for nine months the previous September could count the days, even if some of them wouldn't fight. As the 26th launched its attack, many in the regiment "fell behind, not through cowardice or inability to keep up, but deliberately because they thought there was no obligation on their part to fight after the 3rd of June." They were legally right, but some of the petals of the Flower of Essex County withered beside the Rappahannock. It made little difference to folks at home. Fighters and slackers alike received "a grand demonstration of welcome" when they reached home a few days later.

All eleven of the nine-month regiments came home in June, although never before had the Union so needed men. Lee had broken far past the banks of the Rappahannock, crossed Maryland, and moved on to Pennsylvania.

Governor Parker called for volunteer militia to go to Pennsylvania's aid, but the response could scarcely be called overwhelming in view of the fact that thousands of just-released trained soldiers were enjoying the ease of home. One Camden Company of volunteers "unaccountably disbanded" when ordered to Harrisburg. A Somerset County mass meeting demanded that the militia be kept home for self-defense, since "we have no confidence in the wisdom and ability of the Administration to protect the lives and property of the people of New Jersey." Despite such opposition several New Jersey militia companies did volunteer to go to Harrisburg, although none saw active duty.

Gettysburg's three-day battle stopped the Confederate army, a turning point from which began the slow southward movement that must one day reach Richmond. Jerseymen who fought at Gettysburg were veteran troops—the men introduced to war on the Virginia Peninsula, hardened along the Rappahannock, and inured to the mud and marching and killing through the long Virginia campaigns. These were men resolved to go all the way.

Manpower came hard after Gettysburg. Lincoln's draft call in July, 1863, touched off riots in New York City on July 13. That same day lesser riots occurred in several New Jersey towns, particularly Newark, where a mob tore down the front door of the prowar Newark *Mercury* and stoned the home of Provost Marshal Miller.

New Jersey staved off the draft in 1863 when Governor Parker asked President Lincoln to let the state meet its quota of 8783 men by enlistments. Lincoln replied that he would defer conscripting in New Jersey, "if the day is not too remote" when troops would march South. Parker promised full enlistments within ninety days "at the furthest"; Lincoln compromised at thirty days. By October 25, the state had mustered 4998 men, well short of its quota—but far better than any other state had done by drafting. Lincoln agreed it would be unfair to order a draft in New Jersey that year.

New Jersey's Draftees

An enduring fiction, much repeated, is that New Jersey never resorted to conscription in the Civil War, despite clear records to the contrary. U. S. Secretary of War reports for 1864 and 1865 showed 6981 men obtained from the March 14, 1864, draft call. (This is a most deceptive figure, because only 380 of these actually served personally. The rest bought their way out or hired substitutes.) Between November 1, 1864, and November 15, 1865, the Secretary reported that New Jersey had supplied 3614 "drafted men and substitutes."

The draft was an issue in the 1864 elections, but a major contributing factor in President Lincoln's failure to win New Jersey again was that his opponent, former Major General George B. McClellan, lived in West Orange. "Little Mac" had been relieved of command of the Army of the Potomac and ordered to report to Trenton "for further orders" which never came.

McClellan accepted the Democratic nomination to oppose Lincoln in 1864 despite a strong plank in the platform declaring the war a failure. McClellan earnestly sought to dissociate himself from that clause but could not. He carried New Jersey by 7000 votes, winning all seven electoral votes, but only two other states joined in support of the little general.

New Jersey secured its manpower, one way or another, to the extent that by war's end the state had sent more than 80,000 men to service—slightly more than the requested quotas of 78,248. (Again the figures are deceptive; they include re-enlistments, bounty jumpers, and deserters along with those dedicated to their service and the Union cause.) The state did its share, down to the veterans regiments organized in 1863 and 1864 and the 100-day regiments put together in 1864.

Consider the regiment of Veterans Volunteers organized in the summer of 1863 as the 33rd Regiment by George W. Mindil, a two-year veteran and colonel at the age of twenty. Mindil had led the 27th Regiment (nine-month men) and put the 33rd together in Essex, Passaic, Hudson, and Morris counties, aided immeasurably by generous bounties to enlistees. Nearly 85 per cent of those in the regiment had seen prior service and the unit left Newark September 8, 1863, resplendent in gaudy new Zouave uniforms.

Flamboyant Colonel Mindil and his Zouaves knew glory and horror. They fought in the siege of Chattanooga, helped storm Atlanta, marched with Sherman to the sea. Mindil stayed out front all the way, and when he led his regiment back home in August, 1865, he was a major general—a month before his twenty-second birthday! The 33rd fought in eight major battles, boasted that it had walked 1700 miles, and in the campaign from Chattanooga to Atlanta lost 300 out of 500 men in dead and wounded.

Contrastingly, New Jersey's 37th Regiment also served in its fashion. Recruited in May, 1864, at a time when manpower was at the bottom-of-the-barrel stage, the 37th had the weak and the maimed in its ranks along with the old and the very young. They served their 100 days amid the hoots and taunts of the "regulars." Once, in Virginia, some Vermonters looked at the youthful, unshaven faces of boys in the 37th and asked, "Who are you?" When a youngster answered, "The 37th New Jersey," one of the Vermonters exclaimed, "Oh, we thought it was some schoolhouse broke loose!" The 37th saw no battles, but eighteen of its men died from accidents or disease, and they were just as dead as those with the medals.

Just as dead, too, were the hundreds of Confederate soldiers who perished every month at Fort Delaware, the dreaded Northern prison on Pea Patch Island in the Delaware River just off the Salem County shore. Regular Union troops had been moved to the island early in the war to stave off expected Southern attacks, but when the Confederacy made no move to launch a seaborne assault up the Delaware, the forbidding granite fort was converted into a prison.

The first prisoners of war (about 250 of Stonewall Jackson's men) arrived after the battle of Kernstown in 1862 to begin filling up wooden barracks built to house 2000 men. One year later 8000 Southerners were crowded onto the damp island, and the worst was yet to come. Every Confederate prisoner captured at Gettysburg was taken to Pea Patch Island, from General James J. Archer to the last private. Some 12,500 captives swarmed in misery over the 178-acre island in August, 1863.

Salem County residents quickly learned that prison brutality and neglect were by no means confined to the dreaded Libby and Andersonville prisons maintained by the South. Confederates succumbed to disease, malnutrition, and carelessness at Fort Delaware in the North. In all, more than 2700 died in the prison. Salem County Quakers felt the deaths only slightly less strongly than the South—for more than 2400 of the dead were rowed ashore for burial at Finn's Point, near where New Sweden had built Fort Elfsborg more than two centuries before.

WILDERNESS, ATLANTA AND PEACE

The fighting and the killing increased in savagery in the last months of 1864 and the first months of 1865 when Grant drove through The Wilderness in Virginia and on to Richmond and Appomattox. Simultaneously, Sherman rammed through Atlanta on his way to the sea. Eleven days in the searing test of The Wilderness cost New Jersey the lives of 155 men and left another 671 with disabling wounds. In one deadly charge, the 15th New Jersey sent 270 men against two lines of rebel works and only 101 came back unscathed.

Northern victory came with the attack by Grant and his men. On April 2, a soldier of the 8th New Jersey wrote home after his unit had charged atop a picket post outside Petersburg: "We saw *THE END* shining luminously through the battle-smoke." When it did cease at Appomattox on April 9, an officer of the 2nd Jersey Brigade described the reaction:

"Officers and men were perfectly wild. There were greetings and congratulations and cheering; shoes and hats flew high in the air;

speeches were called for loudly and made, but could not be heard, the boys cheering at every sentence."

But for 218 officers and 6082 enlisted men, among others, the end had come long before. These were New Jersey's dead; those blasted to eternity or dead from wounds or disease. These were the lifeless heroes of Gaines's Mill and Gettysburg and The Wilderness and Atlanta. These were the men whose bodies John H. Lyon had sought on a state-financed tour of Maryland's battlefields in 1864. He found the dead—"in S. Puffenberger's field by outhouse" near Sharpsburg, in "Jacob H. Grover's orchard" near Antietam, in a shallow grave beneath "a large cherry tree" at Crampton's Gap, and in the Frederick Cemetery, where thirty-one were buried in more traditional graves.

OUT OF THE RANKS

Six thousand, three hundred dead and some 88,000 in uniform is no way to show who fought, any more than a skeleton tells how a man looked in life. Brilliant individual soldiers emerged from the New Jersey ranks. Among those who stood out:

Phil Kearny, the "One-Armed Devil" of a cavalryman who forged the 1st Jersey Brigade into a deadly fighting machine, who fought valiantly in the ill-fated Peninsular Campaign, and who died in a thunderstorm at Chantilly on September 1, 1862. Highly respected by both North and South, Kearny surely would have headed the Army of the Potomac had he lived.

Judson Kilpatrick, the Sussex County farm boy who earned a mixed reputation for his cavalry tactics. His men called him "Kill Cavalry," and many of his superiors doubted his intelligence, but when Sherman needed a man to lead the way to the sea, he chose General Kilpatrick. "He's one hell of a damned fool," Sherman admitted, but he was the man for the job.

Willie Magee, the Newark drummer boy, who enlisted in 1863 at age thirteen. Two years later he lay down his drumsticks and picked up a gun and led the 174th Ohio Regiment on a savagely successful assault against a Confederate battery near Murfreesboro, Tennessee. That won him the Congressional Medal of Honor at age fifteen.

John P. Beech, undersized Trenton potter who enlisted in 1861, served three years and twenty-two days as an ordinary private before getting his corporal's stripes, and then served through to war's end. Along the way he won a Medal of Honor for bravery at Spotsylvania's "Bloody Angle."

Charles F. Hopkins, Boonton corporal who won a Medal of Honor at Gaines's Mill, Virginia, and forever bore the marks of long imprisonment in the Southern prison hole at Andersonville. Hopkins escaped from Andersonville, found he couldn't get away, so returned among a new crop of prisoners and safely re-entered the prison.

Gersham Mott of Burlington, who enlisted as a lieutenant colonel in 1861 at the age of thirty-nine, received an average of one promotion and one wound a year (the last wound on April 3, 1865) and finished with the rank of major general and four wounds.

Henry W. Sawyer, Cape May captain who was captured in the brutal cavalry battle at Brandy Station, Virginia, on June 9, 1863, and sent to Libby Prison. On July 6, the Confederate government ordered him and Captain John Flynn of Indiana to be hanged in retaliation for two Confederate captains executed by the North. Direct intervention by the White House—plus an order that General Lee's son, "Roony" Lee, must be executed if Sawyer died—saved the Cape May captain.

DIVIDED NEW JERSEY

Those who lived came home to a still-divided state. They found many unaware of what the fighting had been about, including the state legislature, whose foot-dragging on emancipation continued on well into the Reconstruction period. The legislature acted much of the time as if the abolition of slavery had little to do with the so-called War between the States.

Governor Parker used his annual message of 1865 to question the Thirteenth Amendment abolishing slavery. Restoration of the Union should be the sole consideration of peace, he said, deploring the insistence that slavery must be ended as a prerequisite for the return of the seceded states. Emancipation, he thought, should be gradual, a matter for Southern states to solve by themselves.

The Democratic-controlled legislature agreed; it refused to ratify the Thirteenth Amendment in February, 1865. Failure to ratify hurt the Democrats in the November elections that year. The people in effect endorsed the amendment by electing as governor Republican Marcus L. Ward, "the soldier's friend" (so named because of his numerous wartime activities in behalf of soldiers and their families). Ward carried into office a Republican Senate and Assembly, and in January, 1866, the legislature approved the Thirteenth Amendment.

Since three-fourths of the states had ratified the Amendment and already had made it part of the Constitution on December 18, 1865, the legislature felt compelled to adopt this resolution of apology for its recalcitrant predecessors:

"New Jersey is gloriously redeemed in her political and moral history from the disgraceful stigma of being in sympathy, through her legislators, with the 'sum of all villainies.'"

Governor Ward also pushed through ratification of the Fourteenth Amendment (protecting the privileges of all citizens and refusing office to those engaged in a rebellion against the country). The Republican legislature approved it handily, but within a year the same Republican lawmakers refused to amend the state constitution to strike the word "white" from the section on suffrage.

Vigorous campaigning in 1867 revolved around the question of Negro voting. The populace left no doubt concerning its sentiments: it overwhelmingly supported Democrats who opposed the Negro vote. Heady with power, the Democrats gathered in March and rescinded New Jersey's ratification of the Fourteenth Amendment. Congress received the rescinding resolution, refused to honor it, and returned the document "to the gentlemen who presented it, for the reason that the same is disrespectful to the House and scandalous in character."

Democrats solidified their state-wide strength in 1868—and in the process gave Horatio Seymour a comfortable margin over Ulysses S. Grant in the Presidential race. Grant was elected President easily, but New Jersey continued to move counter to majority opinion in the North. Democratic strength persisted; in February, 1870, the legislature voted solidly against the Fifteenth Amendment (protecting the rights of all citizens to vote regardless of "race, color or previous condition of servitude"). Finally, in November, 1870, the legislature came back into Republican hands and this time both houses voted approval of the Fifteenth Amendment.

In time the state complied fully with the national law by eliminating the word "white" as a voting qualification in 1875. Thus, for New Jersey, the full fruits of Northern victory came more than a decade after Lee's surrender at Appomattox. The state's politicians had opposed the war in 1860, had permitted Copperheads to control the state in 1863, had persistently voted against granting Negro privileges in the Thirteenth, Fourteenth and Fifteenth Amendments. But, no matter how far out New Jersey had been, by 1875 it was in time with Northern thought. As a New York editor put it, New Jersey was "back in the Union."

14

The Backbone Turns Iron

Home came the heroes, older and infinitely wiser. They paraded through their cheering villages and towns, bearded men hardened in battles far away in distance and already fading in time. Some limped on wooden legs; some tried clumsily to grow accustomed to empty sleeves; and many still nursed the festers and sores of prison life. They recognized that both they and their New Jersey atmosphere had changed forever.

When they had gone away, rural life had completely dominated the state, excepting only Newark, Jersey City, and Paterson. None of those was very large: Newark in 1860 had only 72,000 inhabitants, Jersey City claimed 29,000 residents, and Paterson 19,500. Industry, suspicious of steam, depended mainly on waterwheels and raw manpower. Life had been placid and old-fashioned on the edge of Civil War chaos.

But wartime demands jolted New Jersey manufacturers out of their provincialism. The Union needed weapons and the accouterments of war. Factories spewed forth shoes, boots, rubber blankets, locomotives, uniforms, cavalry trappings, gun carriages, rifles, saddle blankets, brass buttons, and tents. Hewes & Phillips of Newark early in the war converted 50,000 muskets from flintlock to percussion and later made the *Monitor*'s turret rings in the then remarkable time of twenty-one days. Rogers Locomotive Works in Paterson delivered nineteen locomotives in three months, compared with the ten months that had been thought necessary. Trenton's iron foundries were busy night and day; the Trenton Arms Company made 3000 rifles in 1863 and 1864 at $16.50 each, while its neighbor, Emerson & Silver, filled an 1863 order for 1000 cavalry sabers, 300 artillery sabers, and 200 noncommissioned swords. There was work to be done—and it was done.

Industry found its muscles in war everywhere in the North, but it gained a full awareness that New Jersey was as good a place as any in all the land in which to make and deliver whatever the nation needed. New Jersey had been growing toward this challenge, and on this industrial maturing New Jersey would grow.

Returning soldiers found factories producing furiously "in a state gone wild over wealth getting and prosperity in general." Everywhere "a rosy and careless outlook" filled the atmosphere as industry satisfied the cravings for the ostentatious and the frivolous that follow any war. A few huge fortunes stood in sharp contrast to the intense poverty that already had descended on city slums where immigrant families huddled together to await the call of factory owners. Never before, in America, had the difference between top and bottom been so great.

There was a restlessness, but not the kind that caused the great social changes of the 1840s and 1850s. This post-Civil War restlessness was born of selfishness and the desire to let loose after the denials and sufferings of war. Reverend Dr. Abraham Messler of the Church of the Raritan in Somerville, who every five years gave a sermon surveying his church and its people, sensed the spirit of his day in his thirty-fifth-anniversary sermon in 1867. His words might have been delivered anywhere, after any war, in fact.

"War debauches the public mind so rapidly, and demoralizes the public heart so extensively," Dr. Messler lamented. "It occupies the public attention so entirely and debases and destroys so many things that are holy. It is worse than the pestilence, for it sweeps so many young men into bloody graves and corrupts so fatally those who live and return." The minister worried particularly about "youthful impiety" and about young men "adopting practices among themselves that are rapidly depraving them."

He might have directed that sermon at the New Jersey legislature, then trapped in the depths of cynicism and corruption in what has been called, more politely than necessary, "an era of personal politics." The willingness of the state's lawmakers to follow the dictates of a powerful railroad monopoly brought them nation-wide attention and disparagement.

STATE OF CAMDEN & AMBOY

New Jersey's destiny naturally was shaped along the iron backbone of the railroads between Philadelphia and New York, for by 1880 close to 75 per cent of the state's population lived in the eight railroad-oriented counties between Camden and Jersey City.

The struggle for this industrialized corridor began quietly in 1830, when the state legislature gave the Camden & Amboy Railroad a charter forbidding any competing railroad "within three miles of the commencement or termination of this road." By 1839 the Camden & Amboy gained a desperately needed outlet on the Hudson River, using tracks of the New Jersey Rail Road from New Brunswick, through Newark to Jersey City. Now there could be no holding the railroad overlords.

Probably the monopoly made sense in the 1830s, when a few capitalists dared risk their money in such ventures, but the passing years saw the power become obnoxious. The railroad operators—or the "Earls of Bordentown" and the "Marquises of Hoboken," as their opponents dubbed them—protected their precious rights with flattery, open bribery, and threats when necessary. State legislators were encouraged to stop at "Apartment 10 in Snowden Hotel at Trenton," the line's headquarters —"where no one connected with the legislature need go to bed sober for want of champagne or with an empty stomach for want of food."

William Sackett's gossipy, entertaining, and revealing personal reminiscences, *Modern Battles of Trenton*, give a witty but shocking picture of the series of puppet legislatures and unprincipled politicians who danced when the "Earls" and the "Marquises" played their tune. The faces of the puppets changed often but the fiddler remained the same. Camden & Amboy owners picked (and usually elected) their own candidates for the State Senate and Assembly. They reached high to decide who would represent New Jersey in Washington as United States Senators, and they reached low to cajole or frighten local mayors and councilmen interested in keeping even their rural seats. Sackett says bluntly of the Camden & Amboy:

> So absolute was its control of all departments of the State government that the state itself came to be known derisively among the people of other states as the "State of Camden and Amboy." There never was a more complete master anywhere of the destinies of a state than was this master monopoly of the affairs of New Jersey.

At the opening of the Civil War, the Camden & Amboy line between New Brunswick and Trenton was still a single track, on the most intensely traveled stretch of land on the continent. After considerable nudging, the railroad diverted some wartime profits for double tracking the road to take care of the huge volumes of freight and soldiers crossing the state. Protests against exorbitant fares and freight rates charged on government movements of troops and supplies prompted Congress to urge a competitor in 1864. The monopoly's Washington lobbyists and elected friends set up such a howl about States' rights that Congress backed off.

Playing a skillful game, the monopoly permitted the New Jersey legislature to grant the Jersey Central Railroad a charter for a bridge across Newark Bay in 1862. The Jersey Central could thus reach the coveted Hudson River waterfront—but the bridge also gave the Camden & Amboy an alternate route to tidewater should the New Jersey Railroad,

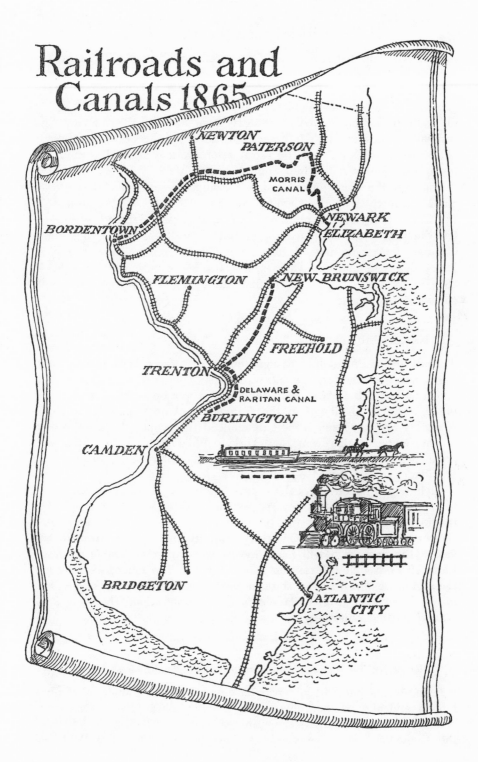

Railroads and Canals 1865

NEWTON

PATERSON

MORRIS CANAL

BORDENTOWN

NEWARK
ELIZABETH

FLEMINGTON

NEW BRUNSWICK

FREEHOLD

TRENTON

DELAWARE & RARITAN CANAL

BURLINGTON

CAMDEN

BRIDGETON

ATLANTIC CITY

the C.&A.'s link between New Brunswick and Jersey City, ever get independent notions.

Conquering Jersey City's South Cove proved a challenge, but the Jersey Central officers ingeniously imported New York City garbage to fill in the glistening mud flats 1000 feet out into the river. Jersey City residents protested as their homes, "invaded by the odor, were made almost uninhabitable," but the reclamation work continued without interruption. Trains rolled into South Cove in 1866.

That left the New Jersey Railroad Company with no choice but to affiliate directly with the Camden & Amboy if it wished to survive. If the C.&A. ever severed relations, the New Jersey Railroad would be left dangling with no place to go but New Brunswick. Quickly the Camden & Amboy pressed its advantage; it brought both the New Jersey Railroad and the Delaware & Raritan Canal into the fold in 1867 to form the United N. J. Railroad & Canal Company, with full control of the corridor.

ENTER PHILADELPHIA "FOREIGNERS"

A syndicate of Philadelphians agitated in 1870 for a franchise to build a new line from the Jersey Central's tracks at Bound Brook to a railroad which had been built from Philadelphia to a spot opposite Trenton. That posed a direct challenge to the Camden & Amboy and its minions. Assembly Speaker Leon Abbett denounced the proposed franchise as a scheme to race trains from New York to Philadelphia in less than two hours "without stopping at a single one of the intervening Jersey towns or villages." That would never do.

Such sanctimonious appeal to state pride was the major weapon in the arsenal of the United New Jersey Railroad & Canal Company. That provincialism evaporated on June 30, 1871, when the Pennsylvania Railroad leased all United Company property and rights-of-way for 999 years (the year 2870 will mark the expiration; Pennsylvania Railroad trains still cross New Jersey on leased tracks). The monopoly thus lost the argument that it served state interests; its directors now included as many "foreigners" from Philadelphia as the opposition. The New York *Herald* gloated editorially:

> The halo of New Jersey's glory has left her. Her Ichabod hath departed. The Camden and Amboy Road, the pride of the state and the ruler of her Legislatures, has been ceded to Pennsylvania.

Pennsylvania Railroad lobbyists took up where the Camden & Amboy left off and aligned themselves with the Republican Party. One party was as pliable as another; the Camden & Amboy had always favored the Democrats—and vice versa—but by the time the 1870 deal was completed, Republicans controlled the legislature. The Pennsylvania fought a delaying action, but by the winter of 1873 the legislature finally faced up to the fact that a law must come enabling any railroad to build a line anywhere.

Fervent scenes of rejoicing filled the State House in March, 1873, when the general railroad law passed both houses. Sackett says the state hailed the law "as a new earnest of prosperity and went wild with joy." Brass bands played in the streets of Trenton and "jubilee meetings were held in every town and village." The general railroad law signified more than a railroad triumph; it was symbolic evidence that the special legislation so characteristic of the New Jersey legislature might soon be curbed.

RAILROADS BRING PROSPERITY

Quietly, in the midst of the excitement over the passage of the law, the National Railway Company filed notice of its intention to build the long-anticipated line from Bound Brook to Trenton. The tracks were laid slowly from both ends and the initial trains rolled over the flatlands in 1876 to give the Pennsylvania Railroad some real competition. The new routes provided a run from Jersey City to Philadelphia and Washington via Bound Brook.

Railroads expanded rapidly after the general railroad law. Trackage in the state jumped nearly 50 per cent between 1870 and 1880, increasing from 1125 miles in 1870 to 1684 miles in 1880. State Geologist George H. Cook declared in 1876 that there was "a line of railway within five or six miles of almost every dwelling." Much of it was double track, some even three and four track. In Cook's words, New Jerseyans could easily visit New York or Philadelphia, "transact business there and return to their homes on the same day."

The state flourished beside that iron network. Commuters rode out to their mansions in the hills of Morris, to their homes along the plains of Union and began eying estate locations between the Oranges and Far Hills. Philadelphia tycoons looked for homesites on the lines radiating eastward from Camden. Rails stretched out to bring in raw materials and take away products of the glassworks of Cumberland, Salem, and Gloucester. New lines encouraged sharply rising production in the iron mines of Morris and Sussex. Atlantic City grew apace, with its three railroad links to Philadelphia, while tracks to the North Shore added a new string of quiet resort towns to go with the glistening bauble that was Long Branch—most notably Ocean Grove in 1869 and Asbury Park in 1870.

The railroads made industry hum. This was (and is) a state with only modest natural resources—some iron, some clay, some glass sand,

and that is about all. Transportation made the difference between a rural sleep and an industrial bustle.

Factories sprang up everywhere along the sidings as firms transferred from other states to be near the excellent markets of New York and Philadelphia. Steam power freed industry from its long dependence on water power; factories could locate anywhere, as long as a nearby railroad could bring in coal to run the steam engine and raw materials to feed the machines.

Some of the new companies were very big, such as the thread factory that George and William Clark opened in East Newark in 1865 to make the spools of thread they labeled O.N.T. ("Our New Thread"). The Clarks twice expanded, until by 1881 they were employing 2000 persons and using 3500 horsepower of steam, noteworthy for the time. Increased use of thread came from increased use of sewing machines. In 1873 Isaac M. Singer consolidated his several scattered sewing machine factories into one tremendous $3,000,000 plant in Elizabethport. Singer hired 3000 workers, an incredible work force for the 1870s.

Industry reflected varied tastes. Atlantic County had its wine makers in Egg Harbor City; Newark its bubbling breweries amid a myriad of other factories; Jersey City its sugar factories and stockyards, where in 1880 more than a million and a half cattle were slaughtered. Spurring the gigantic Jersey City beef business was New York's growing numbers of Jews, who required kosher meat. Slaughtering in Chicago made it impossible to get meat east in time to satisfy rabbinical laws.

Downstate, old Burlington town saw industry grow beside the railroad tracks that ran down the center of the colonial town's fine main street. Twenty-six makers of shoes settled in Burlington shortly after the Civil War. In 1867, John H. Birch built a three-story brick building to make carriages and other vehicles that would gain a world-wide reputation. Oddly enough, Birch jinrikshas also supplied the transportation needs of China. Downriver, Camden was home to Joseph Wharton's new nickel works, fine furniture makers, and the Esterbrook pen-point factory, plus a new little tomato cannery that Joseph Campbell hoped might catch on after he began packing tomatoes in 1869.

Trenton had its ironworks, the solid beginnings of a ceramics industry, and a notable rubber production. New Brunswick thrived on rubber and wallpaper, while surrounding Middlesex County towns annually made millions of bricks and other clay products. Hackensack and Little Ferry laid claim to making more bricks than practically any other location, and Paterson led the nation in silk, while continuing to send hundreds of giant locomotives chugging across America. Passaic had the stirrings of a textile business, including the East's foremost linen and linen-thread works.

South Jersey glassworks by the early 1860s were making some $1,500,000's worth of window glass and $2,000,000 in hollow ware every year—with thriving plants in Bridgeton, Salem, Glassboro, Millville, and Vineland. The Quinton Glass Works on Alloways Creek in Salem County annually turned out three million square feet of the finest French plate glass in the United States.

Iron made huge blasting furnaces and rolling mills glow in Dover, Wharton, Rockaway, Stanhope, Paterson, Trenton, Bridgeton, and Phillipsburg, while the iron mines of Morris and Sussex counties neared peak production (hitting a record 932,762 tons in 1882). In Warren County, the town of Washington dazzled the world with its fine organs and pianos, and Riegelsville's new paper mills won favor. Meanwhile, residents on the Morris County slopes near Kenvil each day waited anxiously to see whether the dynamite plant built in 1871 would stay or go out of business at the careless flick of a match. It stayed, and a decade later its success encouraged the United States Army to establish Picatinny Arsenal north of Dover.

NEWARK SHOWS ITS MIGHT

No city in the state could challenge Newark's claim to pre-eminence. Newark made just about everything—corsets, clothing, shoes, harnesses, carriages, machines, jewelry, malt products, paint, trunks, carpetbags, varnish, chemicals, hats, and hundreds of other necessities and luxuries. "Ye town on ye Passaick," much as it doted on its church spires and colonial greens, faced a future filled with belching smokestacks.

Newark showed its might in 1872 in an "industrial Exhibition" that won enthusiastic praise. Joseph Atkinson, Newark historian, called the Exhibition "the most remarkable, probably, in the world's history of the mechanical arts." Even given Atkinson's burst of local pride, the show must have been exceptional.

Nearly 1000 Newark manufacturers presented their wares when the Exhibition opened on August 30. Visitors, potential buyers, and critics flocked to the show, and Horace Greeley and Ulysses S. Grant, rival candidates for the Presidency, stopped by on the likelihood there would be more hands to shake there than anywhere for miles around. Mr. Greeley confessed that he had not been in Newark for more than forty years and expressed astonishment that in the interim the city had grown from 12,000 residents to ten times that number. Greeley had stayed away too long; New Jersey—which had voted against Grant in 1868—went heavily for the General in 1872.

William Henry Odenheimer, Episcopal Bishop of New Jersey, was moved by the Exhibition to pay lavish tribute. He called it an "element of perfection" where "the brazen padlocks glittered like gold; the huge shears were ornamented as if for simple beauty; the carriages and harness seemed as though they might have been made for a perpetual showcase."

A year later Newark, the state, and the nation lay paralyzed in the grip of the Panic of 1873, a depression that fell heavily on cities tied to steam engines and lathes. Joseph Atkinson recorded the effects of the crash: "Here in Newark, as well as elsewhere, strong, sturdy, stalwart and honest but hungry workingmen gathered in public places and revived the cry of 1857—'We ask not alms, but work!'" Historian Francis B. Lee found the effect in New Jersey "disastrous." He told of railroads, manufacturers, and farmers crippled. Municipalities, "which long had engaged in expensive and often useless improvements, were either bankrupt or were closely approaching that position."

Elizabeth declared itself bankrupt; even the handsome residences on Quality Hill were "abandoned to hostelers or to caretakers." Rahway staggered into insolvency, unable to cope with the financial burden of a new water works and other improvements. Jersey City teetered on the brink of ruin, and the wonder is that the city did not collapse. It surely wasn't for the lack of politicians willing to empty the city treasury.

Jersey City fended off bankruptcy simply because it grew faster than its home-town leaders and its state-wide enemies could ravage it. Railroads continued to expand, and as the backbone of iron grew stronger, the chief beneficiary of the ever-expanding web had to be Hudson County. Across the Hudson River lay a sophisticated and well-heeled populace, waiting to buy whatever rolled into Jersey City and Hoboken. The driving of the gold spike to take the Union Pacific Railroad to the coast in 1869 is acclaimed, but the driving of prosaic iron spikes in Hudson freight yards every day meant far more to the American economy of the time. The waterfront was worth fighting for; city and state leaders both set out to control it, with the winner certain to be enriched.

WATERFRONT, RIGHTS, AND SCHOOLS

The potential of land beyond tidewater level came into full realization when the Jersey Central Railroad built its garbage-ballasted freight yard out into the river in the 1860s. The Central's president, John Taylor Johnston, organized the New York Dock & Improvement Company and in 1864 blandly asked the legislature for a free grant of all the water frontage from Caven Point to South Cove. Fourteen State Senators considered Johnston's proposition reasonable, but on the night before the vote, three New Jerseyans offered to pay $1,000,000 for the land the railroad wanted for nothing. They pointedly directed advertisements in three Trenton newspapers at those Senators willing to give away valuable rights.

The offer came from a group interested both in protecting the state's riparian rights (title to land under tidewaters) and in keeping all moneys from sales of riparian property "forever sacred to the maintenance of her schools." Naturally the fourteen Senators backed off from Johnston's offer, recognizing that they could not give an outsider land that New Jersey men would pay a million dollars to secure.

The Central paid handsomely for its waterfront, and seven years later, in 1871, a bill authorizing the State Riparian Commission to sell or lease lands under tidewater appeared in the legislature. Governor Theodore F. Randolph urged passage, hoping to secure funds for general state purposes, particularly for a proposed new asylum at Morris Plains.

Randolph's crusade for the sales of riparian rights (and undesignated funds from their sale) was halted at the last minute by what Sackett calls educational zealots. They argued that an "implied contract" existed from 1864 to divert riparian moneys to the public school fund. What's more, they said, probably with considerable justice, a large increase in public funds would "only incite public jobbery and extravagence" if no "useful channel" could be established.

Assemblyman Nathaniel Niles of Morris County introduced in 1871 a bill appropriating the money from riparian sales to support public schools "perpetually." Advocates of Niles's measure shrewdly advised rural counties that their youth could be educated without expense to anyone (except, of course, Hudson County). Governor Randolph indignantly vetoed the bill, still hoping for undesignated funds, but both houses passed it over his veto.

Funds at last had become available to make free education a reality. The 1871 legislature adopted an act forbidding tuition charges in the schools and compelling all townships to have a nine-month school term. Amid the corruption, there still ran a solid support for advanced social and educational ideals.

"TALK OF THE NATION"

High purpose fell sadly by the wayside in other deeds of the Republican-dominated legislature of 1871. Eager to retain their power by any means, the Republicans recast the state's voting districts in a gerrymander that Sackett says was so manifestly unfair that it became the talk of the nation. The votes of thousands of people were rendered worthless for more than twenty years; while Democrats could roll up state-wide leads of 15,000 to 20,000 votes and elect all governors from 1873 to 1896, Republicans stayed firmly in power in the legislature.

Hudson County took a particular beating in the shabby realignment.

Legislators sliced the county into seven pieces—six tiny Republican regions and one huge piece confining nearly all the Democratic votes into a Jersey City region so ridiculously shaped that it was called "The Horseshoe." Thus the Grand Old Party insured itself of six seats and effectively disenfranchised nearly all Democrats in Hudson.

Having brought Hudson County to its knees, the legislature boldly moved in on the Jersey City Horseshoe. The Republicans adopted an act permitting the legislature to "manage" Jersey City with state-appointed commissions. The Democrats had themselves to blame: when they controlled the legislature in 1870, they had shown the way by adopting a bill to appoint a state-controlled police commission for Newark. The Democratic whip of 1870 became the Republican club of 1871.

The Republican "ring" appointed to supervise Jersey City lived high. It squandered money, enriched relatives, increased the public debt, and pushed up the tax rate. Even Republican newspapers voiced vigorous protest, but politicians refused to heed either warnings or protests. However, when ring-appointed City Treasurer Alexander Hamilton (no relation to President Washington's Secretary of the Treasury) skipped to Mexico with the city's funds, cries of shame rang through the nation.

Finally, in 1873 Governor Joel Parker called for changes in the state constitution to prevent the kind of special legislation that was cruelly choking Jersey City. The governor said bluntly:

"The general public laws passed at the last session are contained in about 100 pages of the printed volume of Sessional Laws, while the special and private laws occupy over 1250 pages of the same book!"

A bipartisan legislative commission disregarded some suggested amendments whose aims would return in later years to haunt subsequent legislatures. As a major example, there were strong feelings in 1873 that State Senators ought to be elected by senatorial districts of equal population to prevent small county domination of state affairs. That disregarded suggestion would come into full and painful review in the 1960s. Other disregarded suggestions included the extension of Assembly terms to two years and of Senate terms to four years (both extensions were finally adopted in the constitution of 1947) and the extension of terms of Supreme Court Justices to twenty-one years or life (also made law in 1947).

Voters in November, 1875, gave overwhelming approval to several amendments.

For one thing, the legislature could not regulate internal affairs of municipalities and no exclusive privileges or immunity could be given any public or private corporation.

No public moneys, local or state, could be donated to any "society, association or corporation." This struck directly at announced plans of Catholic leaders for a reform school (or Catholic Protectory) to be built with state funds but administered only by the church.

Voting privileges were eased, particularly by striking out the word "white" in the state constitution's Bill of Rights and by providing means for eligible voters "in actual military service" to vote absentee ballots.

Education was a beneficiary of the amendments. One put the full weight of public approval behind the demands for improved school conditions by directing the lawmakers to maintain an efficient public school system for all children between the ages of five and eighteen.

Jersey City promptly appealed for relief from the state-appointed commissions which governed the city. The Republican majority in the 1876 legislature ruled that the city's petition for freedom could not be accepted. The reason: since Jersey City was the only city in the state whose affairs were administered by a legislative commission, it would be illegal to pass special legislation in the city's favor! Jersey City went into the courts and in 1876 won the right to govern itself (or misgovern itself, if it so chose) like every other city in the state.

Jersey City particularly rejoiced, but since the effects of the Panic of 1873 were lessening, good feeling prevailed everywhere. New Jersey lightheartedly joined the other thirty-seven states in the Philadelphia Centennial Exposition of 1876 at Philadelphia.

On Jersey Day at the Centennial, staged August 24, Ex-Attorney General Abraham Browning of Camden gave the main address, permitting himself a touch of levity by telling his 30,000 listeners: "Our neighbors used to think, and many still do, that a cautious toad, which feeds upon vapor, would wisely have its life insured against death by starvation before venturing across those Jersey Deserts. But these jests have become pointless—mere pleasantries. We plead 'guilty' to them, as we do to the charges of growing peaches and pretty girls."

Having pleaded "guilty," Browning could back his boasts with solid facts. New Jersey, fourth smallest among all the thirty-eight states in 1876, was fifth from the top in manufacturing. It stood eighth among states with capital invested in manufacturing—a total of $79,606,719, a scant half million behind Missouri. But agriculture was not dead. "Admirably adapted to the growing of fruits and vegetables," Browning said, "New Jersey is fast becoming a fruit and vegetable garden for New York and Philadelphia."

Browning revived the oft-quoted declaration that "New Jersey resembled a beer barrel, tapped at both ends, with all the live beer running into Philadelphia and New York." Mr. Browning attributed that to Benjamin Franklin and admitted that the foremost young men

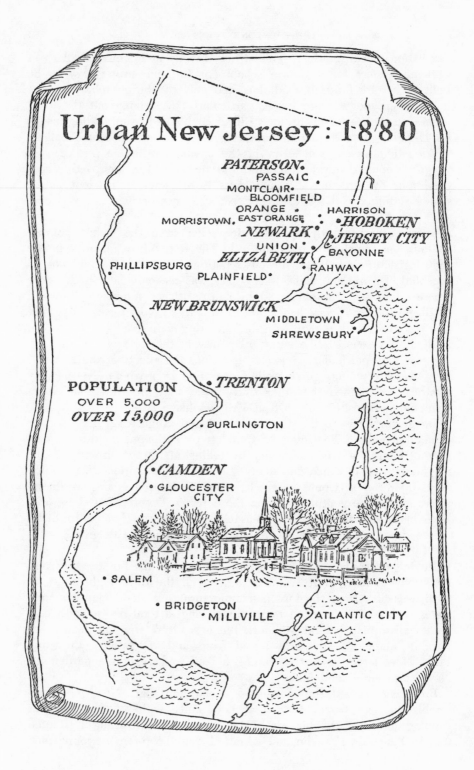

Urban New Jersey : 1880

PATERSON.
PASSAIC .
MONTCLAIR .
BLOOMFIELD
ORANGE .   HARRISON .
MORRISTOWN . EAST ORANGE   . HOBOKEN
NEWARK   . JERSEY CITY
UNION .   BAYONNE
ELIZABETH   . BAYONNE
PHILLIPSBURG . . RAHWAY
PLAINFIELD .

NEW BRUNSWICK
MIDDLETOWN .
SHREWSBURY .

POPULATION
OVER 5,000
OVER 15,000
. TRENTON

. BURLINGTON

. CAMDEN
. GLOUCESTER
CITY

. SALEM

. BRIDGETON
. MILLVILLE   . ATLANTIC CITY

of Franklin's time had crossed the borders, headed out of New Jersey, East and West.

"The reverse is true now," Mr. Browning exclaimed. "They [New York and Philadelphia] are paying us back, with usury. The overflow is from the cities, into the state. Their wealth and refinement are fast building rival cities on our shores; and ornamenting our hills and valleys with palatial residences and sloping lawns. And our whole sea coast, from Sandy Hook to Cape May, is becoming brilliant, with hotels and cottages, for summer resort."

Browning was right. The barrel *was* drawing people in, from many lands, even from New York and Philadelphia. The population had jumped dramatically from 773,500 in 1865 to 1,020,584 in 1875. That first million, achieved in two centuries, had been the hardest to reach; now people would come by the hundreds of thousands for decades.

New Jersey now was officially labeled "urban" by the United States Census Bureau, since 54 per cent of its population lived in towns or cities in 1880. Newark led with 136,508 people, closely followed by Jersey City's 120,722. Census figures badly misrepresented the true picture. Only nine towns and cities out of 270 municipalities had populations exceeding 10,000! Fourteen of the twenty-one still had no towns of even 10,000.

Beyond the city limits stretched the wide-open spaces, vistas broken only by villages or by bustling country towns whose importance as local centers of commerce often belied their small populations. These were towns where the blacksmith shop, the wheelwright, and the dry-goods store catered to country people. One didn't have to travel more than ten minutes out of Newark, Paterson, Camden, or Trenton to find well-tilled farmlands. Railroads did not reach all towns; mail and passengers still rolled in many areas on stage coaches.

New Jersey was "urban," officially, but its economy seemed far more linked to agriculture than industry. It was, as Mr. Browning forecast, a fruit and vegetable garden for New York and Philadelphia. The man of the soil was very, very much alive and important in what would continue to be the Garden State.

15

Revolution at the Crossroads

New Jersey farmers might have been forgiven in the winter of 1875 had they simply leaned back in their rockers and contemplated their good fortune. Nowhere else in all the land were markets so handy or pockets so filled with money to buy: cities were growing and resort towns were sprouting by the sea. The farmers responded so nobly that even in 1875 New Jersey stood first among all states in farm income per acre. It was a pretty picture to dream about on winter nights.

But agriculture was at the crossroads. Demands for land within the state had driven prices upward until in 1875 they stood at an average of eighty-seven dollars per acre, four times the national average. Impoverished soil was played out in many areas. Industry's magical rise beside the railroad track had lured away many farmers' sons, who did not want to be played out prematurely by the drudgery that befell the man of the soil.

Competition for labor was disturbing, but any farmer worth his acreage recognized that new opportunity beckoned in the very industries that took away his ambitious young sons. When a factory sprang up in the hinterlands, its workers could mean dollars to the farmer prepared to serve them with fruits and vegetables or milk and eggs. The times called desperately for science; an 1876 report warned that "the loose, slipshod policy so often practiced in ordinary farming" had become as obsolete in 1876 as a flint musket from the Battle of Trenton.

Two centuries before, colonists had called the Jerseys "The Garden of the World," a term first used in an atlas published in Scotland in 1684. Apple trees grew in abundance, the ground responded readily to the shovel and the hoe, and wide-open spaces on the hills and in marshlands near the coast permitted colonists to loose their cattle and hogs upon the countryside. It was a wonderful land to use, and a tempting area to misuse.

Early New Jersey farmers had grown apathetic about their natural riches. They would clear an area, crop it continuously until little nutrient remained in the soil, then abandon it. Happy, and prospering in their ignorance, they took all, gave nothing back. Peter Kalm, the esteemed Swedish botanist who traveled extensively in southern Jersey in 1748 and 1749, expressed his horror at men who farmed with the same agricultural methods as the Indians.

Nothing startled the Swedish visitor more than the lack of tenderness shown the queenly peach. In his homeland, "hardly any people besides the rich can eat them." Here, "you could hardly walk in the orchard without treading upon the peaches that had fallen off."

"Nay," wrote Kalm in indignation, "this fine fruit was frequently given to the swine!"

Inevitably waste caught up with the farmer. Sussex and Warren counties, the one-time "bread basket of the colonies," grew less productive. Southern farmlands that had so well supplied Revolutionary War foragers were played out. Many farmers in Salem and Cumberland counties heard the "Call of Kentucky" and move away in numbers between 1810 and 1820, engulfed by the twin disasters of depleted soil and the "cold summer" of 1816, when frost often touched the fields in July and August.

MARL TO THE RESCUE

Help came to the despairing farmer from a strange source. It was marl, a blue-green clay rich in potash, found in beds in a wide arc sweeping westward around the Pine Barrens of southern New Jersey. The spreading of marl on Salem County cornfields boasted yields nearly 400 per cent in the 1830s. An 1840 study said marl had enriched Monmouth fields by a half million dollars and had sent Salem land values soaring tenfold.

Concurrently, the sweetening effects of lime also gradually impressed the farmers. By 1850, fields in Somerset, Hunterdon, Warren, and Sussex counties showed remarkable results from lime, although some farmers burned their soils through overuse. Crudely, and often blindly, scientific farming had begun.

The farmer himself was undergoing gradual change. Although sorely handicapped by limited education, he read what he could on farming, but all too often he had no written material on hand other than an almanac or his weekly newspaper. He banded together with other farmers in loosely knit local societies, formed to exchange knowledge, promote county fairs, and promote racing.

He speculated in all kinds of agricultural crazes, eager for a big-cash crop that would make farming more profitable. Between 1810 and

1820 many were overcome with a mania for Merino sheep, an exceptionally woolly breed that intrigued all farmers in the nation. Attention centered on the Haddonfield farm of James Caldwell, first president of the Merino Society of the Middle States. Mr. Caldwell bought his sheep early, in 1806, and he sold early, in 1815, and was well out of trouble when the rush to buy Merinos ended in about 1820, leaving hundreds of Jerseymen holding a woolly bag.

Although the Merino fad quickened the farmer's pulse, *Morus multicaulis* made him positively feverish in the 1830s.

Morus multicaulis is the scientific name for the mulberry tree on which silkworms feed. The silkworm craze began on the premise that silkworms would eat mulberry leaves on trees planted on otherwise unproductive land. Happy worms would spin silk-laden cocoons, which, in theory, the fledgling silk industry would buy. This revenue would help farmers grow more cocoons.

Eight silk companies were incorporated in New Jersey between 1836 and 1838 to handle the anticipated huge volume of cocoons. More than 200,000 mulberry trees were planted in fields and along streets of villages and towns. Thousands of cuttings from these were planted in fields to make thousands more trees.

The craze increased in intensity when the 1838 legislature granted a state subsidy of fifteen cents a pound for cocoons. In Burlington a physician was found guilty of stealing another doctor's mulberry trees, and sent to prison for three years. The Burlington *Gazette* in 1839 dignified the madness by adding a subtitle to its masthead: *New Jersey Silk and Agricultural Register*. The Hunterdon *Democrat*, on the other hand, condemned the state bounty as "a tax for the benefit of the silk stocking gentry."

Too much planting and too little knowledge put an end to the get-rich-quick scheme. The fever subsided by 1840 in failure after failure. "Cocooneries" closed their doors, mulberry trees were chopped down, and about all that remained was a Mulberry Street in nearly every town. By 1846 even the Burlington *Gazette* gave up the silken ghost: it dropped the word *Silk* from its title.

For the farmer, *Morus multicaulis* represented less a greediness than an effort to rise above a life of drudgery. Farmers sought learning— but unfortunately, most favorite sources of information simply perpetuated old ignorance. The farmer needed new avenues of education.

Three men arrived on the scene to lift agriculture out of the deep furrow that had come to look suspiciously like a rut: James J. Mapes, William F. Phelps, and George H. Cook.

James J. Mapes, professor of chemistry and natural philosophy at the National Academy of Design in New York City, left the classroom in 1847 to buy a run-down thirty-acre farm on the southern outskirts of Newark. The miserable farm pleased him: "We selected it as suited to our proposed experiments, from the fact that all admitted the soil to be such as could not remunerate the farmer for its tillage."

The professor put in underdrains, plowed deeply to turn subsoil to the surface, and added manure and lime. The soil responded. Visitors flocked from all the East to see Mapes's demonstrations of farm tools and machines, flourishing grape vines, splendid pear trees, corn yielding 110 bushels to the acre, and potatoes giving 250 bushels per acre.

Mapes opened a school in 1851 for "Instruction in Scientific Agriculture" and trained disciples to spread his teachings. He went on the road himself, rolling over the hills of Sussex and laboring through the sandy roads of Cumberland to preach his basic message that the soil must be respected and encouraged. Mapes noted "a spirit of improvement" in Newton, encouraged a Freehold audience "anxious to avail themselves of the current improvements," and noted with satisfaction that the Warren County Agricultural Society was organized in 1850 after his second series of lectures.

Experimentation, demonstration, education, and spreading of information; these were the tools of James J. Mapes. These also were the fundamental aim of the College of Agriculture founded at Rutgers University in 1864. Mapes preceded the college by nearly two decades, but his feats have been nearly forgotten, except perhaps for his achievements in commercial fertilizer. He is remembered, when he is remembered at all, as the father of Mrs. Mary Mapes Dodge, author of the children's classic *Hans Brinker, or The Silver Skates.*

TEACHERS IN THE FIELDS

William F. Phelps, first principal of the State Normal School at Trenton, began in 1860 what agricultural historian Carl Raymond Woodward has called "the most important effort to teach agriculture in New Jersey prior to the establishment of the State Agricultural College."

Phelps felt that the best way to improve agriculture was to reach farmers through the local schools, where trained teachers could prepare young farmers for tomorrow and keep their fathers up-to-date. He believed that elaborate scientific knowledge wasn't necessary, but pleaded for dissemination of practical information that would help farmers "double the value of their labor."

When Congress passed the Morrill Land-Grant Act in July, 1862, providing federal money for training in agriculture and mechanics, Phelps sought the funds allocated New Jersey. In his view, a large agricultural college was impractical and unnecessary, for few of its graduates would become teachers and its program would not reach the masses, "except as a very indirect, complicated and expensive process of popularizing agricultural knowledge." He proposed that funds go to his Trenton school to train teachers "scattered through every part of the state," who would "mingle with the farmers" and carry knowledge to the very fields.

But the legislature voted the Morrill money to Rutgers, rejecting not only Phelps but also the equally eager College of New Jersey at Princeton. (It is interesting to conjecture how Princeton University's future might have changed had the agricultural money gone there.) The legislature chose wisely, in large measure because the Rutgers faculty included Dr. George Hammell Cook, professor of chemistry and natural sciences.

Cook left an old farm in Morris County to become New Jersey's foremost nineteenth-century agricultural voice. Educated as a geologist at Rensselaer Polytechnic Institute in Troy, New York, Cook accepted a teaching job at Rutgers in 1853 at the age of thirty-five. He brought an incredible capacity for work; colleagues remembered his average day beginning before dawn and ending after midnight. Nothing less could keep him up-to-date to his own satisfaction.

Cook could be remembered for his work as a geologist alone. He carried out mapping and geological surveys for the state, along with his college duties, and became State Geologist in 1864. One of his contributions was a detailed geological study of the greensand marl deposits, carefully related to farm interests and problems.

Eloquent voices spoke in behalf of Rutgers when the Morrill money became available, but the demonstrated efficiency of Professor Cook weighed more heavily in the college's favor than all the eloquence of Rutgers academicians. Farmers respected him, a particularly pertinent point, since "book farming" stood low in their esteem. Most agreed with one Mr. Cassidy of Newton who wrote in the *New Jersey Farmer* in 1859:

> Put them (those professors of agriculture) in the place of the majority of our farmers, with everything to be paid for from the produce of the farm, and they would not be able to live.

Dr. Cook was a shining exception. Week after week, year after year, he had driven his wagon over country roads to talk with farmers, joke with their wives, encourage their children, and exchange information and inspiration. When Rutgers was granted funds for the College of Agriculture (called Scientific School in 1864), the allocation was largely a personal tribute to George Hammell Cook.

THE STILL-IGNORED FARMER

The new school emphasized science and engineering and offered precious few agricultural courses. Stung by criticism from the farmers, Rutgers President William H. Campbell defended the practice in 1869: "The Trustees have considered it no part of their duty to turn the agricultural department into a school of manual labor. . . . Persons who desire to become skilled in the actual operations of farming, must do so by engaging in the daily routine of a farmer's work."

Young men with hands hardened by the plow evidently took him at his word. Only four students of all those enrolled in the first fifteen years wrote senior theses directly related to agriculture, and only 11 per cent of students in the first fifteen classes took their knowledge to farms.

Dr. Cook stepped into the breach, beginning a series of county lectures in 1866 and continuing until 1873, taking his vast knowledge and pleasant manner to county after county. He brought back to Rutgers copious notes on both good and bad farm practices. He was the long arm of farm knowledge, the original "extension agent" who carried forth answers and brought back questions.

The college bought an impoverished ninety-eight-acre farm, distinguished, Dr. Cook wrote, only by its need for improvement and its position near a railroad which enabled visitors to come for demonstrations in scientific agriculture. Many came to grumble over the "endless dollars" being spent at the farm, but Dr. Cook was at the location one afternoon each week to instruct and to soothe those who fretted over costs. By 1874 he could prove that the college's once worthless farm was becoming productive.

Rutgers asked the legislature for $3000 in 1876 to found an agricultural experiment station, then a radically new idea. Dr. Cook wrote that the lawmakers "fairly laughed at the idea." By the time the legislature voted $5000 for the station at Rutgers five years later, four other states had borrowed Dr. Cook's idea and had approved funds.

Dr. Cook was chosen as director of the experiment station. He immediately requested the state to cut his pay as State Geologist by $1000—his salary as director—although he continued in both jobs. Dr. Cook's contributions to New Jersey were monumental; Dr. John M. Thomas, president of Rutgers, was to say in 1925: "The services of George H. Cook have alone been worth more to the state of New Jersey than all the appropriations Rutgers has ever received from both state and federal governments."

"ENOUGH OF BLARNEY"

Help from Rutgers was not enough. Farmers were dissatisfied, even openly angry as they became aware that spreading prosperity seemed to pass them by. One means of expressing themselves was in the National Grange, founded in 1867 and a sweeping force when the first State Grange was organized in 1872. New Jersey farmers eagerly responded to the call for "a new Declaration of Independence" by Dudley W. Adams, second Master of the National Grange:

> We have heard enough, ten times enough [wrote the realistic Adams] about the "hardened hand of honest toil," the supreme glory of "the sweating brow," and how magnificent is the suit of coarse homespun which covers a form bent with overwork.
>
> I tell you, my brother-workers of the soil, there is something worth living for besides hard work. We have heard enough of this professional blarney. Toil in itself is not necessarily glorious. To toil like slaves, raise fat steers, cultivate broad acres, pile up treasures of bonds and land and herds, and at the same time bow and starve the god-like form, harden the hands, dwarf the immortal mind, and alienate the children from the homestead, is a damning disgrace to any man and should stamp him as worse than a brute.
>
> It is no wonder, then, that the farmers' sons, to get rid of the terrible monotony of farm-labor as now organized, find peddling tin kettles an acceptable substitute, or turning somersets in a third-class circus a fortunate escape. The reason why our country youths are so impatient of farm-labor is not that they are less virtuous than formerly, but that they are wiser; and the railroad has opened a thousand fields for their ambitious daring undreamed of as possibilities in the olden time.

Adams warned that not even the Granges, with their reading rooms, "their processions and picnics and the decoration of the Grange halls in company with the ladies of the order," would keep young men on the farm—"unless something can be done to render the labor less monotonous and disagreeable."

The Master of the National Grange left no doubt that the traditionally idyllic poetry concerning farm life had been written without consulting the man who owned a farm, much less the hired hand.

MILK, HENS, AND CHANGE

There were problems aplenty, over and above keeping young men on the farm. Railroads had hurt farmers at first, luring growers of wheat and raisers of beef from the West Jersey hills and far beyond the

Mississippi. Railroads opened markets for New Jersey products as far away as Boston and Washington, but the steel tracks also brought products from far away to Jersey's own markets of New York and Philadelphia.

Milk cows replaced beef cattle as a prime source of income soon after the Civil War. Railroads sent their agents up and down the lines to encourage greater milk production and built receiving stations in the milk areas to speed dairy products off to the big cities. Farmers became interested in breeds that would give more milk, turning first to Guernseys, then Jerseys, and finally to the black and white Holstein that is still the standard milk cow in New Jersey. The quarter century between 1875 and 1900 definitely made Sussex, Warren, and Hunterdon important milk counties.

Chickens, once allowed to wander where they would to scratch for food, came into favor between 1880 and 1900. Breeding became as necessary to poultrymen as to dairymen, particularly after New Yorkers began erroneously to suspect that only white eggs were truly fresh. This made the stringy white leghorn a favorite; no chicken produced whiter eggs—and no chicken produced more. She was the favorite by the time poultrymen demanded membership on the State Board of Agriculture in 1889. The fact that the demand was honored paid tribute to the economic importance of the hen raisers (dirt farmers still felt much the same way toward poultrymen that cattlemen felt about sheepherders in the West).

More important than the leghorn herself was the emergence of the incubator, first demonstrated at a Newark show of the New Jersey Poultry Association in 1879. Many speculated that a chicken hatched that way would surely smell of kerosene all its life, but that year the world's largest incubating plant at Cresskill in Bergen County hatched 10,000 chicks weekly without a setting hen in sight.

Progressive farmers recognized that the old days of self-sufficient general farming, when a farmer grew everything possible, were gone. Now, to be successful, he had to specialize—in eggs, broilers, hatching, dairying, peaches, cranberries, green vegetables, tomatoes—in whatever the market demanded. Specialized societies sprang up between 1875 and 1900, organized to bring together major farm interests, whether poultry or flowers, milk or cranberries.

Farmers had to study and know their markets. Canning became big business in 1869 after Joseph Campbell and Abraham Anderson of Camden started to pack their noted beefsteak tomato ("so large that only one was packed to a can"). Wagonloads of tomatoes rolled to many South Jersey canneries in the late nineteenth century. They also went to railroad depots for shipment; the little town of Delanco in Burlington County daily sent as many as 1500 baskets of tomatoes to Boston in 1894.

Fruits and vegetables continued to sell well in nearby city markets, provided they were in the stalls crisp and sweet when shoppers came by in early morning hours. Refrigerated cars, introduced in the 1880s, brought even Boston and Washington market stalls close to the Jersey farmer. One Burlington County grower wrote in 1895 that New York had become only his third-best market, behind Newark and Boston. He did not even mention nearby Philadelphia.

A new agricultural day had dawned, but sometimes the new day simply brought new problems, undreamed of by grandfather. All the eggs in one basket, or, for that matter, all the bank balance devoted to fruit trees, could mean disaster.

Calamity struck Hunterdon County, for example, in the 1890s. Hunterdon's hills had grown thick with peach trees—more than two million by official 1890 Census count—and the county claimed it had become the world's prime peach region. Bad weather hurt the crop in 1890, but wonderful harvests in the next two years proved almost as bad. Fantastic overproduction in those seasons glutted the markets. Then, swiftly and without warning, a dreaded blight called "San Jose Scale" struck. Peach orchards withered pitifully; by 1909 Hunterdon growers had chopped down nearly all of their two million trees.

Specialization continued elsewhere; no farmer could believe that Hunterdon's problems could be duplicated in other products. White potatoes became the agricultural staple of Monmouth, Middlesex and Mercer counties, where the sandy loam suited their growth. But production varied wildly, between 1870 to 1900. A big potato crop one year meant low prices, followed by a radical drop in acreage the next. This would result in a shortage that would bring high prices and more acres planted the next spring. Each year, as a result, potato farmers found themselves a full season behind.

Sweet potatoes became a southern New Jersey specialty. A Hammonton minister, more in local pride than fact, in 1872 said Hammonton sweets were "unsurpassed the world over, both in quantity and quality." By then Gloucester County fields accounted for half of all sweets produced in New Jersey (more than two million bushels were harvested in the state in 1899).

Tastes had changed. The Madison area was proof of that. A newly risen carriage trade demanded ornamentation and Madison rose-growers moved to meet the demand. Judge Francis Lathrop shipped his roses to New York as early as 1865, but it took T. J. Slaughter, wealthy cotton broker, to put roses on the assembly line by sending more than 400,000 rosebuds to market in 1886. He was called "King of the Amateur Florists" that year and by 1900, dozens of rose ranges clustered in a small area between Madison, Chatham, and Summit. E. B. Ellwanger's authoritative book, *The Rose,* declared in 1898 that greenhouse roses "are nowhere brought to such perfection as in the neighborhood of Summit and Madison."

Roses, sweet potatoes, milk, specialization: the agricultural world had been turned topsy-turvy by science, a swelling population, and changing desires. The farmer of 1860 would have been completely dazed in 1890. More changes would come, but the pattern had been set as the nineteenth century neared its end. Never again could the farmer be as alone, as independent, as had been his proud boast in earlier and simpler times.

16

Ideas, Money, and Muscles

Visitors to the Philadelphia Centennial Exposition in 1876 probably were more out of touch with their immediate future than any people at any time. They stood amid the shiny splendor of new threshing machines, improved steam engines, and handsome buggies and assured themselves that man's inventive genius had gone just about as far as it could go.

One token of the future was there: An "electrical toy" exhibited by a Boston teacher named Alexander Graham Bell. Men would soon fight on Wall Street and in the courts for possession of Bell's "toy," but in 1876 the telephone received no more attention than a new "hog scalding tub" that won a Mt. Holly, New Jersey, maker a gold medal. The hot tub was closer to the hearts of most visitors than the hot line to carry a voice across the distances.

During that Centennial summer Thomas A. Edison moved into his "invention factory" on a hill at Menlo Park, overlooking the Pennsylvania Railroad tracks where excursion trains sped visitors to the Philadelphia Exposition. On that Middlesex County hill an incredibly new tomorrow was taking shape. Philadelphia could offer only yesterday.

Calling the last quarter of the nineteenth century the Age of Practical Ideas is entirely proper. Patent wars raged in the courts as mighty financiers raced to exploit inventions. Corporations sprang into being to let small, powerful groups control vast areas of wealth and production. Labor leaders advanced the then-strange notion that workers were an asset, not a deficit on company ledgers.

New Jersey had a wealth of men with ideas, and a combination of good location and unusually liberal chartering laws gained the state more than its share of big business. Many industrial combines came before 1900 to add their names to the New Jersey economy: Standard Oil, Tidewater Oil, United States Steel, United States Rubber, Westinghouse, General Electric, E. I. Du Pont de Nemours, and dozens more.

But in this period of economic boom, capital and labor widened the gulf between them. Once most employers worked side by side with their workers, always sharing the problems and sometimes sharing the rewards. After 1875, however, the owner all too often became an absentee figure behind a faraway desk, interested in his New Jersey factories only for their handsome dividends. Labor, to such owners, was simply another useful raw material. Inevitably, labor rebelled.

These, then, were the elements that would make the last quarter of the nineteenth century a time of advancement and a time of strife: men with ideas, men with money, men with clashing philosophies of the rights of labor.

Organized Search for Ideas

Thomas Edison, who would change his world more than any other man of his times, built his laboratory at Menlo Park for the frank purpose of pursuing patents. This horrified those who thought researchers should have blissful unconcern for profits. It must be recognized that one of Edison's greatest contributions to America was the research laboratory —the medium for organized pursuit of ideas.

Edison put together a team of chemists, engineers, model makers, theoretical scientists, mathematicians, and skilled mechanics at Menlo Park. His scoffed-at trial-and-error methods paid off in more than 300 separate patents between 1876 and 1882. Three of those Menlo Park patents—for the phonograph, the electric light, and the "Edison Effect" (forerunner of the radio tube)—etched Edison's name forever in the annals of achievement.

The phonograph came first, in August, 1877, quite by accident. Seeking a means of recording telephone messages, Edison first transcribed messages on a piece of paraffined paper, then drew plans for a machine which an aide, John Kruesi, built for eighteen dollars. Edison affixed a roll of tin foil to the completed model, turned a handle, and shouted into the machine: "Mary had a little lamb."

Edison rewound the tin foil and cranked again. Out came the sound, "almost perfectly" recognizable as the high-pitched voice of Thomas A. Edison himself. Kruesi "turned pale," and other onlookers "were dumbfounded."

Retired telegraph operators exhibited the phonograph in large cities and drew curious crowds. During one week in Boston, the operators took in $1800, but interest soon waned. One hearing satisfied the average listener that the wavering voices of a wandering troupe scratched on tin foil hardly represented good entertainment, even if it was a startling discovery.

Edison put the "Speaking Phonograph" aside when a group of New York capitalists persuaded him to work on a practical incandescent lamp in the spring of 1878. Edison had rejected the first offer to work on the light because so many others were working in that field. An arc light had been demonstrated in England as early as 1809; a British patent for an incandescent light had been issued in 1841, and by 1877 an electric arc light had been shown in Newark.

The Menlo Park researcher changed his mind and accepted the New York financial backing on October 18, 1878. Quickly, Edison and his aides made a workable lamp, using a prohibitively expensive platinum filament. They tried filament after filament (including a hair from Kruesi's beard), but all proved worthless—too unreliable, too fragile, too expensive. Finally, on Sunday, October 19, 1879, one year and one day after he began his quest, Edison tried a lamp with a filament of carbonized sewing thread. If it worked, it would be cheap enough.

The thread filament glowed beyond anything yet tried, then burned for forty hours, through the brightness of day, through the darkness of two nights and the brightness of all day Monday. On the afternoon of Tuesday, October 21, Edison stepped up the current to see how brightly the lamp could burn. It expired in an appropriate dazzle of brightness.

Someone prematurely leaked a story of "The Wizard of Menlo Park" to the New York *Herald*. The startled and unprepared Menlo Park team read on December 21 that there would be a public demonstration on New Year's Eve! Ten days later eager excursionists climbed the hill, to find incandescent lamps lighting the snow-covered street as well as the interior of the laboratory, office, and library. Edison recognized the value of a good show, even if it took every available light bulb. Visitors expressed astonishment at Edison's youth, expecting a "wizard" to be at least decently aged and wizened. Some of the souvenir seekers pocketed eight of the precious lamps.

POWER FOR CHANGE

Lamps without easy means of utilization could not make money, so Edison created sockets, switches, generators, improved lamp bases, and small supplies of incandescent lamps. In 1882 he completed the notable Pearl Street generating station in New York, to supply current to 5000 lamps, and in the same year he built a 330-volt dynamo in Roselle, New Jersey, to make that town the first ever to be lit fully by electricity. Demand for the incandescent light forced a move from a shack on the Menlo Park grounds to a big new lamp plant in Harrison.

Discovery of the incandescent lamp was important, but someone else soon would have done it if Edison had not. More fundamental was Edison's perfection of the new source of power that soon would free manufacturers from bulky steam engines and unsightly coal piles. Industry didn't rush to utilize the new power. New Jersey's 1890 Census showed only 706 industrial horsepower by sources "other than steam or water"—a scant 0.39 per cent of all industrial force.

Edison had noticed in 1880 that a current of electricity could be made to flow between two unconnected wires. He had discovered an inexhaustible source of free electrons at a time when the world needed free electrons even less than it needed voices on tin foil. The inventor turned to other interests, but that so-called Edison Effect led to experiments by Heinrich Hertz in Germany, Guglielmo Marconi, in Italy and Lee De Forest, the young Yale graduate who in 1903 perfected in his Jersey City factory the Audion radio tube, the basis of modern electronics.

THE SILVER SCREEN

The "invention factory" left Menlo Park in 1887 to occupy new and much larger laboratories at West Orange. Once again Edison picked up where others left off. This time, in 1889, he perfected motion pictures (he didn't "invent" the movies; he made them practical). He had erected the world's first movie studio in 1893—a tarpaper-covered shack nicknamed "The Black Maria," where Buffalo Bill, John L. Sullivan, and a variety of song-and-dance men came to be filmed in the celluloid world that Edison had created.

Edwin S. Porter, who had brashly represented himself as "Thomas A. Edison, Jr." on a tour of the West Indies in 1897, joined the West Orange crew in 1899 and five years later made movie history with *The Great Train Robbery*, the first motion picture with a plot. The 740-foot film cost $400, but the Edison company found the expense justified; it became a hit, and it brought the new movie industry to New Jersey. Bergen County, within easy ferryboat ride of New York, was a movie center where aspiring actors and actresses eagerly grasped at the magnificent five dollars a day movie entrepreneurs would pay.

D. W. Griffith, one of moviedom's great directors, started in Bergen County, using the Palisades at Fort Lee as background for his romantic films. Mack Sennett, Mary Pickford, Pearl White, Norma Talmadge, Theda Bara, Irene Castle, Milton Sills, Warner Oland, Fatty Arbuckle, and a host of other old-time stars all began their careers in Bergen. Out of Edison's mind had come another vast new industry.

Edison eclipsed his contemporaries, but there were other Jerseymen with fertile minds.

DYNAMOS AND LIGHT METERS

Edward Weston in 1877 built the country's first commercial dynamo factory in an abandoned Newark synagogue and demonstrated an arc light at the corner of Washington and Market streets, probably the first public showing of such a light in America. Weston supplied the know-how in 1881 when Newark became the first American city to expend public funds for electric street lights. Mayor Fiedler and his cautious Common Council authorized "not more than $300" for the five arc lights in shady Military Park.

Success in the park brought Weston other orders, including four strings of lights across the newly opened Brooklyn Bridge in 1883. Weston's electrical inventiveness rivaled Edison's; by 1884 his patents covered the field from generators to fuses. Yet his place in scientific history rests mainly in the field of precise measurement.

Chance changed Weston's direction in 1886, when he journeyed to Philadelphia's Franklin Institute to test a dynamo. The day was one of extreme exasperation. Even the earth's magnetism made his delicate instruments uncertain, and his frustration was complete when the iron buttons on a passer-by's suspenders threw his measurements out of balance.

Weston set out to devise new measurement devices, but his task was like that of a man who wanted to make a wheelbarrow before the wheel was discovered. He first had to perfect two new alloys, which he named Constantin and Manganin, both still fundamental in electrical measurement. He then made a new copper-base alloy to use in the delicate springs of his meters.

Fame came slowly. Weston introduced a Normal Cell in 1893 as the first stable standard for the volt, the basic unit of electromotive force. It took fifteen years for the International Conference on Electrical Units and Standards to rule that Weston's Normal Cell was the world-wide basis for all measurement of electrical force. Actually, this Weston discovery was more radically new than many of Edison's much more acclaimed inventions.

Others added, more or less, to the good life of the nineteenth century. Ideas seemed to flow, one from the other.

John Wesley Hyatt, an Albany typesetter, used his landlady's kitchen in 1869 to combine pyroxylin (basically nitrocellulose) and camphor to form Celluloid, the first commercially successful plastic. He moved to Newark in 1873 to take advantage of better manufacturing conditions. Soon three nearby factories used Celluloid for kewpie dolls, harness trim, "tortoise shell" combs, hair ornaments, and collars and cuffs of such flammability that the wearers were always in danger of becoming human torches. Hyatt also made the first injection molding machine in Newark in 1878—the key machine in mass production of plastics.

From Celluloid to roller bearings is a major change, but Hyatt made it in 1885 when a sugar refinery asked him to design a bearing for its heavy machinery. He responded with his patented roller bearings. Eventually, in 1900, the newly founded Olds Company ordered 120 rear-axle roller bearings from Hyatt's new plant in Harrison for its Oldsmobile. Thus began a friendship that continued when General Motors used Hyatt bearings exclusively.

The Reverend Hannibal Goodwin of Newark experimented with Hyatt's plastic as a photographic medium after children repeatedly broke his glass slides of Bible stories. After some minor explosions in the parsonage attic, the minister in 1887 used Celluloid to record photographic images and thus invented flexible photographic film. The courts upheld Mr. Goodwin's 1887 patent in a drawn-out legal suit that ended in 1914 with Eastman Kodak Company paying the minister's widow a substantial sum, a legal admission that the Newark parson had been first to make and use flexible film.

Another nonscientist who succeeded was an Irish-born schoolteacher from Paterson named John Holland, who constructed the first workable submarine. He took a fourteen-foot, cigar-shaped submarine to the bottom of the Passaic River in 1878. His real triumph came in 1881 when he piloted the thirty-one-foot *Fenian Ram* down a hundred feet off Staten Island and stayed submerged for a full hour. The Paterson teacher naïvely hoped the submarine would make war so horrible that no nation ever again would risk open conflict. He was half right; it *did* help to make war horrible.

Up From Medicinal Plasters

If Holland's dream of aiding mankind backfired, three New Jersey brothers named Johnson came along at about the same time to benefit humanity (and themselves) tremendously. They were Robert W., James W., and E. W. Johnson, who had made medicinal plasters as early as 1873 but whose meteoric rise began after they moved in 1885 to an old mill in New Brunswick. Two years later they acquired a corporate name—Johnson & Johnson.

Johnson & Johnson made its dressings sterile at a time when most doctors ignored cleanliness. They introduced their absorbent cotton in 1887, packing it in a blue box with a red cross, the same packaging that is still familiar. J.&J. educational booklets actually became pioneer textbooks in the teaching of antiseptic surgery; the accident kits introduced by the company in 1890 led to the widespread use of first-aid kits. The enterprise came to full flower in 1906 when the New Brunswick brothers supplied nearly 90 per cent of all surgical supplies used after the dreadful San Francisco earthquake.

Trenton's long-established potteries needed men with ideas, too. Thomas Maddock and Walter Scott Lenox were two who responded.

Maddock believed that sanitary ware for America's fine homes and hotels ought to be made in America rather than Europe. He loaded his Trenton-made washbowls and water closets in canvas bags, took them by train to New York and Brooklyn, and personally sold them. He cautiously labeled his wares "Best Staffordshire earthenware made for the American market." Conservatives were suspicious of American goods, but soon Maddock could label his products "Made in Trenton," as proudly as the city's finest makers of tableware. Thus began a new facet of ceramics manufacture in the capital city.

Walter Scott Lenox met similar conservatism in Trenton; capitalists who backed him in 1888 insisted that his original factory be so built that it could easily be converted into a tenement if, or when, the china venture failed. Dealers rebuffed Lenox until Tiffany's ordered $1000's worth of Lenox ware for their exclusive New York shop. But by 1908, Lenox still was $6000 in debt after twenty years of quality manufacturing. Blind when he died in 1920, Walter Scott Lenox lived to know that his china was placed in the White House by Woodrow Wilson in 1918. Since then, Lenox china has been the official White House dinnerware and is a standard of excellence throughout the world.

PARROT WITH A SORE THROAT

Another Johnson, no relation to the New Brunswick brothers, won a measure of fame in an entirely different area. He was Elbridge Johnson, a Camden machinist noted for taking the "bugs" out of the inventors' models. Emile Berliner, who was toying with improvements on Edison's phonograph, approached Johnson in 1896 with a phonograph that played flat disc records instead of the round cylinders used by others (including Edison). Berliner's squawking box sounded to Johnson "like a partially educated parrot with a sore throat," but he became enthusiastic.

Johnson cured the sore throat, improved the motor, made the turntable revolve at constant speed. He bought Berliner's patent in 1901 and founded the Victor Talking Machine Company. The company made both the machine and the records to play on it, hiring great artists, such as Enrico Caruso, to make records. The first year Victor realized $500 in sales; four years later the income was $12,000,000, a fantastic growth that makes even modern records pale. Johnson also discovered and used the painting of "Nipper," the little fox terrier immortalized as listening to "His Master's Voice." Originally, the canvas had "Columbia Graphaphone" painted on the horn, for the free-lance artist hoped to sell it there. Columbia said no, and so did Edison, but Johnson grabbed it. He had the artist substitute "Victor" for "Columbia" and one of the foremost American trademarks was born.

Money could be made in fields other than manufacturing, if a man had an idea. John Dryden of Newark announced in 1873 that he would sell insurance priced within the reach of the workingman, until then an unlikely subject for a financier. Dryden's Widows' and Orphans' Friendly Society began in the basement of the National State Bank of Newark and in 1877 changed its name to Prudential Insurance Company, with business already at an annual mark of $1,000,000 after only four years of existence. The company climbed out of the bank basement into larger quarters in 1878, by which time annual receipts had topped $4,000,000.

Dryden's dream was full-blown by 1892, when the Prudential moved into its new gray stone "castle" on Newark's Broad Street. The eleven-story Prudential home office was the biggest edifice in New Jersey. It had to be, for the company already had nearly 4000 employees. On dedication day, the company revealed telephones in every room, electric lights, and elevators capable of whisking people upward at 500 feet a minute. Newark had never seen the like—and the Prudential has never ceased to be New Jersey's most important financial center.

OIL BY THE HUDSON

Business slang of the day would have said that the Prudential had "struck oil," a tribute to the millionaires growing as the result of the increasing need for petroleum. John D. Rockefeller, Cleveland ex-book-keeper, topped them all. He did his prospecting with a steel pen point, gathering little Pennsylvania oil refiners together into his mushrooming Standard Oil Company. New Jersey loomed large in Rockefeller's plans, for kerosene and crude oil could be handled on Hudson County docks for export anywhere.

He had challenges. The little Tidewater Oil Company in 1878 threatened Rockefeller's claims on the Hudson River. Each bought a small refinery in Bayonne as an opening wedge, but Tidewater got the jump by contracting with Jersey Central Railroad to haul in Pennsylvania crude oil. Rockefeller countered with a 400-mile-long pipeline that snaked up and down some eighty hills, climbed the Appalachian Mountains, and spanned fourteen rivers and twenty creeks to join Bayonne's wharves and refineries with the oil fields in western Pennsylvania.

Bayonne had room for both Standard Oil and Tidewater. The two refiners continually enlarged their neighboring plants, filling blue wooden barrels with yellowish kerosene for export (saving the "white" kerosene for the fussy American market). Bayonne was *the* factor in the American oil trade of the 1890s, for three-fourths of all petroleum business was in kerosene for export. Standard Oil and Tidewater really had only one problem: what to do with the "gasoline" that remained after refining out the kerosene, sealing wax, and lubricants. Each day the rivals burned the useless gasoline, sending great clouds of black smoke billowing over Bayonne as a regretful symbol that refining was not *all* profit.

Horseless carriages might change that, but in 1900 only about one gallon in eight produced at Bayonne was "boulevard gas fuel." In that dawn of a new century, Standard and Tidewater employed a total of 3000 men at Bayonne and each day they refined 40,000 barrels of crude oil. Tidewater had its own pipeline, extending 1800 miles from Bayonne to just-opened oil fields in the Indian Territory of the Southwest. Soon, in 1909, Standard built a modern new refinery at Bayway in the Arthur Kill, where tankers came and went with ease. The modern Union County plant was known as "the kerosene factory," as evidence that gasoline was not yet the master.

The outlines of twentieth-century industry were emerging by 1900. Older industries were expanding—jewelry, leather, and beer in Newark; rubber in Passaic and Trenton; clay products near New Brunswick and in Trenton; canneries in Camden, Swedesboro, Salem, and Bridgeton; textiles in Paterson and Passaic; glass in Cumberland, Salem, and Gloucester counties; iron in Morris, Mercer, Passaic, and Essex; and apparel in every city where immigrants swarmed, from Vineland to Paterson, from Jersey City to Trenton. Yet the future rested not on the old but the new: electrical goods, automobiles, petroleum, telephones, chemicals, paint, phonographs, explosives, drugs, ships, paints, copper, and platinum.

Another major change had come to business—the little man of industry was hard pressed to survive. One study of rising costs showed that a farm implement factory could have been started in 1850 with a capitalization of $2674. By 1910, the same factory required $400,000 before opening the doors. Iron and steel manufactures of 1850 averaged $46,000 in capital, but sixty years later they would need more than $2,250,000 to start production.

Corporations were the obvious answer. But by the very nature of the ruthless competition they fostered they crushed and ground some businesses even as they built others. By 1888, both major political parties publicly discussed the evils of big money combines. The Republican presidential platform that year declared party opposition to "combinations of capital, organized as trusts or otherwise," and the Democratic platform said, "The interests of the people are betrayed when trusts and combinations are permitted to exist."

NEW JERSEY WELCOMES TRUSTS

Kansas passed the first antitrust law in 1889. Other states quickly followed suit until only New Jersey, Delaware, and West Virginia stood in favor of any kind of interstate money combines. Congress heeded Republican President Harrison's request to begin paying "earnest attention" to trusts in 1889, but New Jersey legislators looked away. While other states looked with distaste on "money combinations," New Jersey passed a law authorizing "holding corporations." Standard Oil promptly took advantage of the broad loopholes in the New Jersey law and in 1889 set up a state-based trust to include companies from coast to coast. The enabling law permitted Jersey Standard or any companies "domiciled in New Jersey" to hold stocks in any other companies, contrary to laws in nearly all other states.

The subsequent surge of scores of corporations to New Jersey merits more attention than can be given here. Many have speculated on why this state chose to ignore the powerful antitrust sentiment in the rest of the nation. Lincoln Steffens said the state's position as the terminus of great railroad systems made it responsive to corporate influence, but the nearness of Wall Street was also a factor, prompting Steffens to call Jersey City "West Wall Street." Mark Sullivan in his *Our Times* declared that "many of the ablest of the citizenry of New Jersey spent their working days in New York and had slight civic interest in the State in which they slept"—making it easy for politicians and "lawyers representing financial interest" to control the legislature to their advantage. Fees gathered from out-of-state corporations lightened New Jersey taxes, causing many to justify the easy laws on that ground.

At any rate, the state appeared in cartoons as "an exceptionally full-bosomed matron," calling "Come to mother," and gathering unto herself "trusts harried in other states and calling 'Help!'"

Fees were not high—twenty cents on each $1000 of capitalization—but mass production of corporate charters made the income mount and balanced New Jersey's budget painlessly. Hundreds of companies with no interest in New Jersey other than its liberality in trust matters established "home offices" in the state and held mock "annual meetings" on the west side of the Hudson River. Providing the "home offices" became a business in itself. One building in Jersey City had 1500 "home office" signs on its ample doors.

DOLLAR-DECORATED WELCOME HAT

Harassment of any corporation elsewhere was enough to cause the New Jersey legislature to amend the statutes to create a favorable situation for the offended trust. When the United States Supreme Court in 1892 dissolved Standard Oil Company as a trust, it simply reincorporated in 1896 under the Revised Act of the State of New Jersey. "New Jersey," concluded Lincoln Steffens, "was regularly in the business of selling not only indulgences, but absolution."

While the evils of a government's succumbing to external controls are evident, there were lasting dividends, too. The state established a reputation as friendly to industry that clings to this day—manufacturing enterprises gravitate to those places where they are wanted. Even when the state's antitrust laws came into agreement with national thought, that aura lingered.

As corporate ownership became increasingly impersonal, big management became ever more distant from those who made the machines run. Labor became bitter and dissatisfied, far beyond the normal labor-management friction that had been felt for nearly a century. One of the first factory strikes in the United States occurred in a Paterson mill in 1828, and by 1838 shoemakers had organized in Newark, Paterson, and New Brunswick. Hatters, harness makers, and curriers in Newark and construction workers in Trenton, Paterson, New Brunswick, and Newark were all organized at the same time. At first their grievances were easily attended to, for owners of small businesses needed the workers as much as the workers needed the jobs.

However, as cities became filled with young men in from the farms or with immigrants from Europe, the labor supply often exceeded demand and there was competition for jobs. As corporations grew, absentee ownership increased and the boss no longer worked side by side with his help. Grievances were more difficult to communicate, more difficult to mediate.

Newark's brewery workers called a major strike in 1886. The walkout spread to Elizabeth, Paterson, and New Brunswick, but conditions in the Newark breweries were the worst. One study said that beer makers "were always working except when asleep." Their work day began at 5 A.M. and lasted from fourteen to eighteen hours, with six to eight additional hours on Sundays. For this they received twenty to twenty-five dollars a month. The 1886 strike improved the workers' lot: their day was limited to ten hours, wages climbed 30 to 50 per cent, and Sunday work was discontinued.

Trenton's pottery makers warred less successfully with their employers. One walkout in the memorably cold winter of 1877–78 in protest against a wage cut was a failure. The men returned to their jobs after long suffering, feeling "beaten rather than convinced." That set the stage for a tougher strike in 1883–84. Once again the workers endured a hard winter and an even harder spring, when they took an 8 per cent wage *cut*. The pattern continued; an 1890–91 strike ended with another wage cut. Three strikes and three wage cuts as a result scarcely spelled success for labor.

Labor lacked organization: Joseph P. McDonnell, onetime friend of Karl Marx's, organized the New Jersey Federation of Trade and Labor Unions in Paterson in 1879 but gained few followers because of his emphasis on socialism. The Knights of Labor had enrolled 30,000 members in New Jersey by 1887, but the power of the Knights soon waned. Indeed, labor lacked even the *right* to organize in New Jersey until 1883. Before then, by common law, a worker was liable to indictment for criminal conspiracy if he "combined with his fellows for the purpose of changing conditions of employment."

Philip Charles Newman, in his *Labor Legislation of New Jersey,* wrote that the 1883 law granting workers the right to organize was "a Magna Charta for trade unionism." Labor had asked the legislature for, and was given, the right "to enter into any combination for organizing, leaving or entering into the employment of other persons."

Slavery in Glass Houses

While that seemed like a relatively minor concession, the situation in the southern New Jersey glassworks proved how desperately such basic laws were needed. More than fifteen years elapsed before the "Magna Charta" of labor reached down to the South Jersey pine forests, where company stores held workers in a strangling economic grip.

Company stores were necessary since the glass plants were miles from towns or cities, but the owners saw the stores as gold mines rather than convenience. Workers were compelled to buy in the stores, without cash (and with or without the knowledge that prices were usually 10 to 15 per cent lower elsewhere). On payday, envelopes were usually empty. An 1899 report spoke of 3000 glass-company pay envelopes containing not a cent in cash. Deductions included "store," "rent," "drawback," and the all-inclusive "alsos."

The glass worker's economic trap closed inexorably. Every purchase at the company store was in effect a cut in pay, since his dollar bought less. His pay became a debt and once in debt he didn't dare leave for leaving would put him on the industry's black list. He was, in short, an unofficial slave. His sons entered this bondage, too. Hired for five-year terms at low pay, they were usually eased out after completing their apprenticeships to make room for a new crop of underpaid apprentices.

There ensued a series of hopeless strikes in 1886, which lasted two years; in 1893, and in 1899, which practically shut down the glass industry. Legislators friendly to the glass industry watered down or pocketed bills which sought to end the company-store evil. Men of goodwill within the industry finally did. On August 15, 1900, manufacturers and glass blowers convened in Atlantic City and jointly abolished the system of forced purchases at the company store. The glass worker was far from well off, but at least he was no longer a slave at the crossroads emporium.

Labor at the Bottom

The turn of the century found that labor had made only minor gains, despite the 1883 "Magna Charta" and other improvements. Wages were low, hours long, working conditions often wretched. Immigrants flooding into cities tended to put labor at a constant disadvantage under the law of supply and demand, which exercised far greater influence than state or federal laws. The foreign workers spoke many tongues, inspiring employers to hire a variety of national groups to cut down interplant communication, and thus lessen organization. The immigrants were wary of organization and were satisfied with lower wages. Trade-union leaders scorned unskilled workers, and especially foreigners.

Soon bloody strikes, led by known left-wingers, would fester in the textile towns of Passaic County and in the oil refineries at Bayonne. Company officials, far removed from their employees, would counter with strikebreakers as callous and brutal as the professional labor agitators who raced to Paterson and Bayonne to foment trouble or to keep it going. Between these professional strike makers and breakers stood the majority of workers, helpless and hurt.

Somewhere, amid the progress and the promise of the last part of the nineteenth century, the principle of men working together for the advancement of all had been temporarily set aside. Yet, for all its flaws, America was the land of opportunity. The land where a man—of any nationality—might dream. It was a beckoning "open door" to success, a place of excitement for capital and labor alike, and to this world flocked the foreigners, reaching for the liberties which those already on the land often forgot existed.

17

The Huddled Masses

Swarms of newcomers hastened down the gangplanks at Hoboken and Jersey City in the 1880s and the 1890s, bright hope in their faces belying the heavy loneliness and doubt within their hearts. These were the "huddled masses yearning to breath free," as poetess Emma Lazarus idealized them in her lines inscribed on the Statue of Liberty. Most Americans, conveniently forgetting their own immigrant traditions, were not so idyllic; they saw more meaning in another, less quoted line from Miss Lazarus's poem: "the wretched refuse of your teeming shores."

However these new arrivals were viewed, they were simply an extension of the immigrant tides that had begun when the first New Amsterdam Dutch crossed the Hudson River to Bergen County in the 1620s. But these late nineteenth-century settlers were "different." They were not the traditional Anglo-Saxons, Germans or Scandinavians; they were Italians, Poles, Hungarians, Slavs, and Russians, come to change forever the face and voice of America and New Jersey.

These people with the differing complexions, exotic foods, and strenuous dances swarmed into every city or crossroads hamlet where industry needed their strong arms, their love for the soil, and their willingness to work for low wages in exchange for the privilege of someday becoming Americans.

Hoboken, Newark, Jersey City, Paterson, Passaic, Trenton, and Camden became rallying points for most of these "new" immigrants. Industrialists surrounding Perth Amboy and New Brunswick needed the Hungarians and Poles to labor in the clay pits. Madison, Morristown, Summit, and scores of other towns attracted Italians to work in greenhouses or to tend estate gardens. Poles gathered in Bayonne to man the oil refineries; Wharton and Franklin used Hungarians in mills and mines. Passaic and its environs lured the Slovaks to take jobs in textile factories.

Immigrants tackled whatever offered opportunity. Russian Jews stalked the countryside peddling wares from packs on their backs or from pushcarts. They opened little shops or began small farms in the sandy wastes near the seashore. Italians turned the thin soil near Hammonton and Vineland into rich gardens. Poles used the black muck at Great Meadows to grow lush vegetables. Poles, Russians, Hungarians, Slovaks, and Italians aided Manville in its industrial growth. Every major city in the state had its Greek shoeshine boys. Where there was a need, where there was housing and a day's wages, there the immigrants flocked.

THE ROOTS OF IMMIGRATIONS

This was in the solid American tradition. New Jersey had been a melting pot since colonial days. First came the Dutch, Swedes, and Finns, followed by the English, Irish, and Scotch, all before 1700—and the early British were varied in their beliefs, representing Puritans, Quakers, Anglicans, and Presbyterians. Germans and French Huguenots arrived before the Revolution. The colonial wilderness needed every talent, and liberal early charters welcomed foreigners.

Men from Rotterdam blew glass in Salem County in 1738. John Jacob Faesch, a Swiss, made Mt. Hope iron mines boom. Scots gave Perth Amboy its early charter and strength. Dutch founded New Brunswick, established Rutgers University, and gave early Bergen County a distinctively conservative nature.

John Witherspoon, Scottish-born president of the College of New Jersey at Princeton, was the spirit behind New Jersey's Revolutionary War stature. Elias Boudinot of Elizabethtown, a Huguenot descendant, was president of the Continental Congress from 1782 to 1784. English and Scotch started Paterson on its way to industrial vitality. French Royalist refugees taught dancing, drawing, fencing, and music in Elizabethtown between 1792 and 1815, giving the staid old town a temporary picturesqueness and foreign flavor.

New Jersey for a time even was called "The Foreign State" and "The Spanish State," because Joseph Bonaparte, onetime King of Spain and older brother of Napoleon, found haven in Bordentown in 1816. E. M. Woodward, in his story of Bonaparte at Bordentown, said: "King Joseph of Spain, settling in our state, and building the magnificent dwellings, which he adorned with rare paintings, statuary, etc., and spending his money with great profusion, caused persons residing in other states to call New Jersey 'Spain' and Jerseymen 'Spaniards.'"

"Fond of women, the fine arts and literature," Joseph lived well at beautiful Point Breeze overlooking the Delaware River, where exiles from France came to join him. Distinguished Frenchmen and such esteemed Americans as Henry Clay paid him calls. A delegation of Mexicans came to Bordentown to offer to him the crown of Mexico, but Joseph refused the new chance to be royal.

POTATO FARMERS AND REVOLUTIONISTS

Others not so well blessed with material things followed Joseph. Repeated failures of potato crops in Ireland between 1845 and 1848 and failure of the German Revolution in 1848 made American horizons beckon brightly to somewhat different immigrants.

Many of those Irish farmers reached Jersey City between 1845 and 1860 and never went much farther. The city needed them, to build railroad yards and dock facilities and to work in the new steelworks and tobacco plants. Others from Ireland came to group near the factory complex abuilding in Newark or to toil in Trenton ironworks and potteries.

Although they had been potato farmers in the "Ould Country," most of the Irish chose to seek their American fortune in industry—thus establishing the pattern which agricultural immigrants from Italy and Eastern Europe would follow fifty years later. This penchant of immigrants fresh off the farms for city life was—and is—a major problem of immigration. The Irish clung together: poor, untutored, proud, often sustained only by their Roman Catholic churches. Yet when they wrote home, they told of the greatness of America and the wonders of New Jersey, ignoring the hardships.

Germans who arrived in New Jersey in the 1840s and 1850s were generally well-educated, restless people who had been foiled in the abortive 1848 attempt to found a German Republic patterned on America. The Germans liked busy, cosmopolitan Newark particularly, but they also established themselves in a dozen or more towns in Hudson and Bergen counties—and far down in Atlantic County, at a place called Egg Harbor City.

German colonies in Hudson and Bergen arose from building associations organized by New York immigrants. They founded Guttenberg and Union (in Hudson County) in the 1850s, bought a thousand Weehawken acres for homesites in 1852, and swept into Hudson County's Union Township to live within sight of their *Zion Kirche*. A German Democratic Land Association bought 140 acres of land in 1854 and founded Carlstadt (Carl's City), named in honor of Dr. Carl Klein, the association leader.

Philadelphia Germans eagerly bought small farms from the Gloucester Farm and Town Association after the Association bought 30,000 acres in 1854 and founded Egg Harbor City. They laid out the "city" with broad avenues named for principal cities of the United States and

Europe and cross streets named for men famed in the arts and sciences. This town of, by, and for Germans soon became known for the wines made from grapes grown in the sandy soil.

Hoboken, Jersey City, and Newark kept the flavor of the Fatherland. They had German-language newspapers, beer gardens, brass bands and orchestras, singing societies, *Turnvereins* (gymnastic clubs), and a love of Sunday games and picnics. They observed Christmas as a holiday complete with Christmas trees and gaiety, a practice only grudgingly accepted by rigid descendants of the Puritans.

The miserably poor Irish also had fun wherever they stopped. In Lambertville, where several hundred were clustered in their "Dublin," an 1859 account tells of an Irish picnic: "They had a merry time, the lassies bedizened in their finest trimmings and the laddies with their new corduroys, going through the double quick motions of the Dannybrook [sic] jig." The loud St. Patrick's Day celebrations rocked many cities every March 17, irritating many. The simple fact that the Irish were predominantly Roman Catholic also irked many old-line Protestant families.

Bitter feeling against both Germans and Irish was spearheaded in the 1850s by the American or Know-Nothing Party, an "America for Americans" movement directed against so-called "German infidels" as well as the Irish Catholics. Two acts of violence illustrate the temper of the day.

In September, 1854, a parading mob descended on Newark, destroyed the altar, organ, pews, and doors of little St. Mary's Church. They killed an "inoffensive Irishman in Shipman Street," then went home, "without being molested in the slightest by the police." Three years later a "number of New York roughs" attacked a German athletic festival in Hoboken. Amply prepared, the Germans turned on the visitors, killing three of them and seriously wounding several others.

Some of the nationalistic bias faded with the Civil War, when Germans contributed 7300 and the Irish 8880 men to the New Jersey regiments. Thousands more Irish and Germans joined out-of-state regiments. Captain Owen Murphy of Orange and Captain John Toler of Newark took all-Irish companies to New York to sign with the Excelsior Brigade, while Captain A. M. Weyer and his Newark German Turner Corps enlisted as a unit in a New York regiment.

BOUND FOR FRISCO—AND VINELAND

Hoboken's German population spurted after the Hamburg-American Line established its American terminus there in 1863, while Jersey City received swelling influxes of immigrants eager to reach the Erie

Railroad's westbound "Emigrant" trains. The Erie's cumbersome, flat-bottomed ferry picked up Germans and Swedes in New York and took them across the Hudson for herding into the simple wooden cars bound for Wisconsin, Minnesota, Missouri, and on to San Francisco.

By Civil War time, there were faint indications of a new day in immigration. Italians gathered on the edges of Vineland, which was laid out in 1861 by Charles K. Landis, a Philadelphia lawyer. Landis envisioned a planned business and industrial area run by New Englanders, who would appreciate his wide streets, shade trees, and the rigid control of buildings and property. Beyond, in the piny woodlands, industrious Italians would best develop the farms needed to feed the New Englanders.

Landis sent printed blandishments to Italy to tell of Vineland's opportunity, and by 1873 the first of Vineland's Italians had been coaxed from the North of Italy. An Italian Catholic mission was started in the Vineland railroad station in 1874 and seven years later large numbers of Italians were settled in East Vineland, where a visitor noted that "they raise good crops and are well pleased with their new homes." They cleared the land of scrub oaks and pines and surprised their neighbors from New England with the sight of father, mother, and all the children working together in the fields in pursuit of a family income to buy the goods of American ease. New Englanders forgot that their own ancestors had worked in similar family fashion nearly 250 years before.

America desperately needed the muscles and eagerness of Europeans. Governor George B. McClellan's 1879 annual message asked that information on New Jersey's soil, taxes, climate, and nearness to good markets be brought to the notice of immigrants, "so that they may perceive the advantages offered to settlers in our state."

WHY GO TO MINNESOTA?

In 1880 the state's Bureau of Statistics sent a broadside to Southern Europe, asking among other things: "Why should the immigrant go to Minnesota, where the climate is like Sweden, when he can secure a home in the southern part of New Jersey, where the climate is more like the south of France or the shores of the Mediterranean?" That picture drawn by the Bureau was so attractive the wonder is that any immigrants went elsewhere than South Jersey.

The great tide of immigration had begun and the Bureau of Statistics had done its work well. When increasing numbers of Russian and Polish Jews reached New York City without friends, funds or skills in the late 1870s, the Hebrew Immigrant Society decided that southern New Jersey's inexpensive land and "climate like the south of France" might be an answer. The society founded the village of Alliance in

Salem County in 1881 as a planned agricultural colony (augmented by garment making and handicrafts). Alliance succeeded so well that soon similar towns—Norma, Brotmanville, Rosenhayn, and Carmel—were established nearby.

Ten years later, a noted colony was begun in Cape May County in a roadless, pine-covered section far off the beaten track. The region had only one obvious merit: land was cheap—and that pleased trustees of the modest Baron de Hirsch Fund, established by a wealthy French banker to aid European Jews. The trustees set aside $50,000 and in August, 1891, founded Woodbine in the wilderness of northwestern Cape May. Within a year South Russian Jews had cleared 650 acres of farmland and built twelve miles of farm roads.

Professor Hersch L. Sabsovich, colony supervisor, stressed both manufacturing and agriculture. The settlement attracted twelve small factories and the professor's school annually instructed nearly 100 students in agricultural science. The school sent Jacob Goodale Lipman to Rutgers College as a raw young schoolboy in 1894; seventeen years later, Dr. Lipman became director of the Rutgers Experiment Station. He also became the first dean of the College of Agriculture in 1915 and served Rutgers and New Jersey with distinction until his death in 1939. If Woodbine deserved to be known for nothing else, Jacob Goodale Lipman would be achievement enough.

Waves of people from Italy, Poland, Austria, Hungary, and Russia swept into America in the 1890s, and, for a time, America lent them a helping hand. There was ample room; industrialists favored the importation of cheap labor, and growing factories absorbed the successive boatloads of newcomers.

Inevitably, this "new" type of foreigner began to irritate the descendants of foreigners who had arrived several generations earlier. He was uneducated, unskilled, unused to the ways of cities or factories. He was a man of the soil settled in the city. He spoke in unfamiliar accents. He ate garlic and spices. His women pierced their ears. He learned his "English" from a factory foreman or dock boss and often said the wrong, profane things at the wrong time. He accepted low wages and saved strenuously to bring his family and friends to this land of opportunity.

This tide of immigrants was rushing outward from Europe for many reasons. Russian Jews sought to escape the brutal anti-Semitism of the Czar. Poles fled their divided land because of German demands that their children be taught German and because sons were conscripted into the German, Russian, and Austrian armies. Peasants in Southern Italy and Sicily found that their eroded farm regions could no longer sustain them.

More than twenty million immigrants came to the United States between 1880 and 1920, and about 517,000 of them settled permanently in New Jersey. The state ranked fifth among all the states in total number of immigrants in 1910, trailing only New York, Pennsylvania, Massachusetts, and Illinois. In concentration of immigrants the state ranked first, with eighty-two immigrants a square mile, compared to fifty-six in New York. The 1910 Census showed that for the first time New Jersey had fewer native-born than foreigners. Of the state's 2,517,000 people, only 39.8 per cent were "native" (both parents born in the United States).

Immigrants attuned to the plow were sadly lost in the cities—"where the money is." A 1911 study showed that of 47,000 newcomers to New Jersey, only 7300 had any demonstrable skill; 85 per cent knew nothing but the soil and 30 to 50 per cent of them (depending on country of origin) were illiterate *even in their native languages.*

Every city had its Little Italy, Little Hungary, or Little Slovakia and some cities had a bit of everything. A section of West Hoboken became known as the Dardenelles, because within a five-block section lived Armenians, English, French, Germans, Greeks, Italians, Spanish, Turks, Syrians, Romanians, Polish, Russians, Chinese, Japanese, Austrians, Swiss, Jews, Belgians, and Hollanders. West Hoboken's five blocks exemplified the nation's reputation as a melting pot.

Passaic woolen mills, founded in 1880 by German immigrants, attracted swarms of migrants from the plains of Slovakia and Hungary and the mountains of Carpathia. The staid little town of 6500 (in 1880) swelled to a crowded 54,700 thirty years later. Newcomers spilled over into Garfield, Wallington, Lodi, East Rutherford, East Paterson, and Fair Lawn.

They built their churches, both Roman Catholic and Greek Catholic, with its three-barred cross, and they manifested their love of athletics in their Sokol clubs. Never had Passaic been so lively, so confusing, so jammed with humanity, and by 1910 the city had a higher per cent of foreign born (52 per cent) than any other major America city.

Emily Greene Balch, Wellesley College professor, wrote in 1910 in *Our Slavic Fellow Citizens:* "From a purely aesthetic point of view, no one need wish to see a prettier sight than a Passaic handkerchief factory full of Polish girls in kerchiefs of pale yellow and other soft colors, the afternoon sun slanting across the fine stuff on which they are working."

Miss Balch also praised the neatness of Slavic homes in Jersey City, "where the most striking feature is the excess of decoration, for the household gods of the Slavic house are orderliness and decoration."

But the Slav, like many immigrants, did not dissolve easily in the melting pot. What Miss Balch said of the Slovak might fit all of the newly arrived:

The immigrant sees less of America than we think. He comes over with Slovaks, goes to a Slovak boarding house, a Slovak store, a Slovak saloon and a Slovak bank. His "boss" is likely a Slovak. He deals with Americans only as the street car conductor shouts, "What do you want, John?" or when boys stone his children and call them "Hunkies."

FLOCKING TOGETHER

Americans complained that the new groups "stick together so much." But the early Irish also had gathered near their churches and the Germans chose to live close to their rathskellers and turner halls. The Dutch, Swedes, Puritans, and Quakers long before had lived near one another through second and third generations. Immigrants needed one another to ward off loneliness, lest they be submerged in a land as foreign to them as they were to it.

Every city had its foreign sections, but no city had them chronicled so explicitly and sympathetically as Trenton, where in 1908 John S. Merzbacher published an artful little work, *Trenton's Foreign Colonies*. The particulars of Merzbacher's Trenton could be applied to virtually any city.

Merzbacher wandered through the immigrant lands of South Trenton, "a place where the American language is scarcely heard."

Hungarians occupied most of thirty-five streets and for six blocks on South Broad Street all store signs were exclusively Hungarian. By 1908 there were 6000 Hungarians in Trenton, most of them employed in heavy work in the iron mills. Merzbacher told of good-looking girls and strong boys dancing the Hungarian *csárdás,* in which "the spirit with which the young man and his partner dance is measured by the amount of love he bears for her."

Trenton's 5000 "sober and serious" Poles were the least clannish of the newcomers. Merzbacher saw them as dedicated to music, marching groups, athletics, but said that "even in their dances their sober state of mind finds expression." The city's 4000 Russian Jews "with their dark features and heavy beards portray a former condition of harsh, cruel, terrible subjection to tyrannical oppression in their Fatherland." In Trenton most of them ran small shops and lived quiet, charitable lives.

"Trenton surely has Italy transplanted!" exclaimed Merzbacher. He found "amazing numbers of dwellers" in all houses in Little Italy. "The Italian considers children his greatest blessing," the Trenton writer said, "and in this respect they are certainly very much blessed." The city's multiplying Italians worked on the trolley lines, on the streets, and in factory jobs.

Steadiness in their jobs and faithfulness to their religion marked the Trenton Italians of Merzbacher's time. Still, as he contrasted their life in incredibly crowded Trenton tenements with the farm huts they had left near the "tranquil waters of the Adriatic," Merzbacher was moved to ask: "Is it any wonder that so many of them emigrate back to their native homes when they once have acquired a competency here?"

Trenton's 3000 Slavs impressed the author with their skills and their intelligence. They were expert factory mechanics. Their gay daughters worked in the stores. Their boys readily learned trades. They joined the Sokols, went to church, and when the occasion moved them, could "engage in a wild cake walk (the *verbunk*), much more violent than Americans can imagine."

FLEECED AT THE DOCKSIDE

Merzbacher looked for, and found, the bright side of the immigrant picture. There was a drastically different side, presented in a 1914 report of the N. J. Commission of Immigration. Appointed three years earlier by Governor Woodrow Wilson, the commission received no state funds for the study, but its report was one of the frankest official documents ever prepared in New Jersey. The commission looked dubiously at Hoboken and Jersey City, where four of the country's largest railroads and four of the largest steamship companies had terminals. The report said:

> The sum total of their [immigrants'] assets when they enter the country are, first, a good physique; second, an average of $50 in money, and third, hope. . . . Many, however, are robbed of their last two assets [money and hope] before they have passed beyond a New Jersey terminal.

Steerage passengers were lucky: they went directly to Ellis Island and from there were guided by officials to their trains and friends. Second-class passengers (56,000 of them arrived in Hudson County in 1911 alone) had no such protection. They faced systematic and cruel fleecing within sight of the Statue of Liberty.

Every variety of con man met the ships. "Licensed" porters, who borrowed or lent badges with equanimity, conspired with hotels, cabbies, and employment agencies to bilk the trusting immigrants. There "seldom were trains to the West" on any day, according to porters, so they charged immigrants for a hotel reservation. Baggage was "weighed" or "checked" by self-appointed "agents." The commission noted one cabbie who charged four arrivals sixty dollars for a one-mile trip from dockside to the Lackawanna Railroad.

Bewildered, frightened, and scantly protected by the law, the immigrant dared not talk back. Unofficial threats of deportation rang constantly along the docks or in the hotels by agents flashing colored cards. The "tired," the "poor," the "tempest toss'd" couldn't complain that they were ignored, but they would have been less tired and poor if they had been. Encouragingly, in the midst of the rampant corruption, Wilson's commission found railroad employees, at least, uniformly honest and helpful to the immigrants.

Once past the docks and into the land of the free, the immigrant continued to face exploitation and abuse. Employers used newcomers for the dirtiest jobs. Labor groups saw them as unfair competition. Frank Julian Warne, in a smug study of immigration in 1916, said: "That they have many virtues there is no denying; still they are simply rough, unskilled, illiterate, unimaginative, hard-working laborers, and even in America, with all its opportunities, they will never be anything else."

Warne proved to be in error, but in 1916 he had lots of believers. The immigrant was fair game for almost anyone, including, far too often, his own countrymen who had preceded him by a few years or a few months.

Those who crowded into the northeastern city belt of New Jersey either moved in with friends and relatives or paid high rents. A Passaic study in 1912 showed that as many as eight unmarried immigrants boarded in a three-room apartment with a Slovak family. Sometimes fourteen or fifteen lived in three rooms (which the family rented for eight or nine dollars per month, then sublet to boarders for a dollar and a half per month each, plus two dollars a week for cooking privileges).

Hastily organized "foreign" banks became social and business centers for immigrants. Their banker was a man who did "practically any conceivable task which might be demanded of him by his more ignorant neighbors, not the least of which is the safeguarding of their money and sending it abroad," according to the commission. New Jersey in 1912 had seven Italian, five Hungarian, one Polish, and one German bank, plus sixteen Italian and nine Hungarian licensed "money transmitters." The astonishing total of $10,000,000 was sent abroad annually by immigrants.

For every authorized banker or transmitter, "often six unauthorized operated," the report said. Fraud was rampant. One unauthorized banker issued no passbooks but instead issued promissory notes to depositors. His greed got the better of him; he had the depositors themselves sign the promisory notes, which he then discounted in a bank. When his "bank" collapsed, the immigrants not only lost their money, they owed for the notes as well.

Bankruptcies in Jersey City, Perth Amboy, Woodbridge, and Passaic cost foreigners an estimated $200,000 in 1911. In Jersey City the same year, there was not one authorized money transmitter—but seven were found operating illegally.

The Commission on Immigration found other exploiters: justices of the peace, notaries public, employment agencies, and self-appointed foreign leaders. The exploitation of foreigners by Jersey notaries public became so flagrant that in 1912 eight foreign consulates refused to honor a document sworn to by any New Jersey notary public. "Employment agencies" charged heavy fees, bullied workers, and often sent immigrants traveling far on railroads to nonexistent jobs.

Padrones (leaders of Italian sections or families) led workers out of the cities every spring and summer to pick berries and vegetables in South Jersey. The *padrone* dealt directly with the farmer and paid his peons as little as he wished. The Italian workers lived in barracks at the bogs. Nineteen families shared one building on an Ocean County farm— with each family occupying a room only six feet by eight feet, where they cooked as well as slept.

Still, said the investigating commission in partial forgiveness, farm conditions "were probably more healthy than in the tenements," and families often took $150 to $200 in cash back to Philadelphia from the Jersey bogs.

LAND SWINDLES AND SHOE SHINES

Land swindlers advertised in foreign-language newspapers to urge Italians, Hungarians, Russians, and Poles to buy their own little plots of land. One trick was to get prospects to solve a puzzle. The correct solution would subtract $200 an acre from the cost, leaving a charge of fifty to ninety dollars an acre, on land worth ten dollars at most. The commission sent in four-puzzles, two deliberately incorrect, and received back congratulations and "discounts" on all four.

Perhaps the most depressing plight was that of the Greek shoeshine boy. Interviews with seventy-six of them in every major New Jersey city showed that seventy-three worked a minimum fifteen-hour day and that seventy-five worked a seven-day week. Their bosses took all tips, supplied greasy food and dirty beds and gave their legal slaves fifteen dollars per month. Often a boss cleared $300 to $500 a year per boy.

Shut off from schools, friends, and society, the Greek boys nevertheless saved money; every one of the seventy-six interviewed had a bankbook. Nearly all were sending money home. The boys worked their way out of their shoeshine parlors, sent for relatives, and opened their own little shops or restaurants. They made it the hard way, as hard a way as anyone who ever came to America.

Help was on the way. Many "foreign" bankers worked strenuously to upgrade their people. Tightening labor laws helped check exploitation. Small state grants encouraged formation of evening schools for foreigners. Second-generation "foreigners" were demanding, and getting, better things, including schools for their children. Many groups, including the DAR, the YWCA and local women's clubs, interested themselves in Americanization classes.

AMERICANS AT LAST

Settlement Houses and Neighborhood Houses in many towns helped immigrants live in friendship and neighborliness. Day nurseries run by dedicated women helped foreign children. The strong influence of the Catholic Church on its people helped keep the bulk of immigrants within the law. Parochial schools helped educate the young Italians, Poles, and Hungarians. The Public Library Commission of New Jersey in 1911 began studying ways of supplying books in foreign languages.

The immigrant began to believe in himself. He saw that Americans liked his spaghetti, his bagels, his noodles, his goulash. American boys liked pretty girls of any nationality. Powerful muscles proved as useful on the football fields as in the clay pits or ironworks. World War I hastened the assimilation, particularly since it permitted young soldiers to become naturalized quickly.

The problems, the segregation, the animosities, the misunderstandings, the smoldering hatreds would continue, but they were lessening. The melting pot simmered slowly; still, it simmered. Eventually, to be Italian or Hungarian or Polish or Russian was no worse than to be German or Irish, just as fifty years before being Irish or German was no worse than being English or Dutch. The words on the Statue of Liberty *did* mean something after all. This was a place for the tired, the poor, the tempest-toss'd.

18

Victorian Interlude

Now came the passion to forget workaday cares, and rich and poor alike responded according to their tastes and their pocketbooks. Wall Street's powerful lords, confident that money assured social position, established estates on the slopes between Short Hills and Far Hills, New Jersey. Games and sports absorbed rich and poor alike: baseball in every town and village, polo on the fields at Morristown, genteel lawn tennis at Newark's Branch Brook Park, cycling on every road and lane, crew races on the Passaic, and horse races in Monmouth and Camden. Seaside resorts enticed crowds to forget their cares in wildly exciting one-day excursions on fast trains.

Most call the nineties "gay" or "Victorian" (as if Queen Victoria had something to do with it), but they have also been called the "molting nineties," in proper recognition that old ways were being shed for new. They also might well be called the "in-between nineties," for therein lived a generation midway between the horrors of the Civil War and World War I that would shake America loose from old insular notions. They could afford their self-indulgence.

POPULATION UPWARD AND OUTWARD

Much happened as an old century gave way to new. The population expanded sharply enough to concern sociologists. The graduated income tax law of 1913 caused Morris and Somerset Hills millionaires to express grave doubts about "money-mad" government. Trolleys, then the automobile, pierced the hills west of Newark and the pinelands east of Camden. Women's fashions changed (and women attended college and demanded the vote). Princeton University turned to buildings of expensive Gothic, the supreme manifestation of a showy era.

New Jersey in 1890 had 1,444,000 residents; in 1915 the total had jumped to 2,844,000, almost a doubling in twenty-five years. Eighteenth in population in 1890, the state was tenth in rank by 1910. Essex, Hudson, Mercer, Middlesex, Passaic, and Union counties more than doubled their population. Bergen County jumped 300 per cent, converting its corn-fields to homesites at a bewildering pace.

So, as people came to play, they also came to stay. In either case the railroads accommodated them, coaxed them, and served them.

Railroads created the suburbs, encouraging those who worked in Newark or New York City to settle outward on the hills and plains. The Lackawanna vigorously advertised the beauties beside its route, and the Jersey Central organized the New Jersey Central Land Improve-ment Company to build up a strip south of the Watchung Mountains. The Erie urged prospects to locate in Bergen County, that "mecca of suburban dwellers." Such a move, the Erie promised, would make "your children and your children's children rise up and call you blessed."

Commuters, including the wealthy summer visitors on the Morris and Somerset hills, ruled wherever they settled. They made the suburbs solidly Republican and protected them against "outside" influences such as the trolley interests bound on easing travel. They enjoyed the restful pace of their restricted towns on weekends.

In the cities, on the other hand, multitudes saw Sunday as the chance to cut loose. Railroads acted quickly to accommodate these Sunday revelers. Long trains packed with humanity wheeled off to the North Jersey lakeland and to the South Jersey seashore. Those "Sunday spe-cials" democratized New Jersey's resorts, transforming them from wealthy retreats into playgrounds for millions.

True, the North Jersey lakeland long had known occasional visitors. Fishermen and campers, plus a rare cottager, had frequented Lake Hopatcong even before the Civil War. Thomas Gordon in 1834 said Green Pond was "much resorted to for its fish and beautiful scenery" and he saw Budd's Pond as a place where visitors "resort hither for amuse-ment." Greenwood Lake's charms were extolled as early as 1845 by Frank Forester (Henry William Herbert), noted Newark sportsman, author, and artist. During the Civil War and just after, landscape painter Jasper Cropsey captured Greenwood Lake's beauties on dozens of his canvases.

Thousands of weekend visitors learned firsthand about Greenwood Lake after the New York, Montclair & Greenwood Lake Railroad reached there in 1876. Excursion trains took two hours and twenty-seven stops to make the run from Jersey City to that "Switzerland of the East." The one-day excursionists fished, ate, rode steamboats around the lake, and raced back to the waiting train. It required four hours, fifty-four stops, and a dollar and a half for the round trip—with a four-hour stay at the lake—but it was sheer heaven while it lasted.

The Jersey Central carried equally enthusiastic Sunday throngs to Lake Hopatcong. Gustav Kobbé, who wrote about adventures beside the tracks, detailed the wonders of the Hopatcong day trips in his *Jersey Central*, published in 1890.

Kobbé's happy wanderers (some 50,000 of them in 1890) saw much real estate for their dollar round-trip fare from Jersey City to Hopatcong. The tracks meandered westward to High Bridge, then up German Valley (Long Valley) to Nolan's Point on the northeast shore of the lake. Excursionists enjoyed chartered boats and flying swings, a dance pavilion, and a hundred other joys ranging from gaping at the famous and wealthy visitors at the nearby Hotel Breslin to a hot lunch for fifty cents. Kobbé credited the Hotel Breslin for Hopatcong's boom, "for it brought to the lake the element of wealth and fashion in the wake of which everything else flows."

The Lackawanna (Morris & Essex) almost missed the excursion trade, since it ran no Sunday trains until 1899 (causing wags to insist M.&E. stood not for "Morris and Essex" but for "Methodist and Episcopal"). After the ban was lifted, the road ran specials to Lake Hopatcong, the Poconos, and other spots, but particularly to Cranberry Lake. Cranberry's little red station welcomed so many visitors between 1900 and 1919 that "old residents were aghast at the hordes unloaded on our erst-while peaceful shores."

Northern New Jersey railroads also whipped down to the Jersey Shore on the Sabbath, reaching into Atlantic Highlands, Long Branch, Asbury Park, and a few lesser resorts willing to let visitors share the sands. Atlantic Highlands was the most hospitable, and Ocean Grove the least, for Ocean Grove, then as now, permitted no levity on Sundays. The Grove clung tenaciously to its enduring camp-meeting code in the face of what it considered wickedness everywhere else.

Fortunately for the workers of Camden and Philadelphia, Atlantic City saw no reason to roll up the Boardwalk on Sunday. By 1885, trains regularly sped across the flatlands between Camden and Atlantic City, carrying on Sundays a crowd whose prudent habit of carrying sand-wiches earned the nickname "The Shoe Box Lunch Set."

Wealthy seaside cottagers sniffed at this loud-talking, flashily dressed, pleasure-bent mob. But the railroads had no such class consciousness. The city's promoters, for their part, shrewdly reckoned that you never could tell when today's one-day visitor might be back for a week or a summer. Atlantic City grew in permanent population from 8000 in 1885 to 37,500 in 1905, and practically all of the year-rounders depended on visitors for a livelihood—making Atlantic City the first major American city devoted to amusement.

Down the coast, Wildwood also threw its wide sloping beach open to the weekend train riders and added a dimension by creating "Fisher-men's specials" to lure pleasure-seekers to its strand. These one-day, one-dollar trains regularly pulled into Wildwood with so many fishing poles sticking out the windows that they looked like steam-drawn porcupines.

How to Have Fun Without Really Paying

A dollar in 1890 was a very big dollar. A family of six going from Camden to Atlantic City, or from Jersey City to Hopatcong, spent six dollars on fares alone and for many families six dollars represented more than a full week's wages. Jerseymen and Jerseywomen needed cheaper ways to expend the usual day of rest. Sports were the answer, for all levels of society.

Football, inaugurated in an historic match between Rutgers and Princeton in 1869, caught on so rapidly that by 1900 a Princeton-Yale "classic" found the road between Morristown and Princeton filled with carriages bound for the game. Stevens Institute of Technology carried football to supreme heights in Hoboken, winning eleven and losing none in 1883 and slaughtering City College of New York in 1885 by a merciless 162–0 score. In that same year, Newark (later Barringer) High School and Newark Academy instituted a gridiron rivalry.

Baseball, a so-so game at first, had been given a boost when Civil War soldiers learned to play in camp. By 1890 every town had a team and many industries hired stars to play for factory teams on Saturday or Sunday afternoons. Teams of doctors, lawyers, firemen, factory workers, college students, and little boys in knee pants abounded, and newspapers began giving wide attention to the exploits of young men with a "good eye" or a powerful pitching arm. Big Leaguers strode majestically into towns and villages to compete in exhibitions against awestruck local boys. Baseball became the great American pastime.

Horses were the pleasure of the elite, particularly at the fine annual horse show at Morristown in the 1890s. Others interested in improvement of the breed enjoyed tracks at Monmouth, Camden, Guttenberg, and a half-dozen other commercial raceways, and betting became so flagrant that laws were passed in 1894 to end the sport. New York bookmakers also relieved millionaires of part of their wealth every year at Morristown's society-sponsored racing meets. To escape the betting fraternity, red-coated millionaires took to riding behind baying hounds on weekends, first in Essex County and later in the Morristown to Far Hills area.

Cricket teams played at Newark, Hoboken, and Paulsboro; soccer attracted big crowds among Kearny's Scots; croquet and lawn bowling provided a chance for young ladies to compete in a polite and gracious sport. German and Slovak gymnasts competed energetically in Newark, Passaic, Hoboken, and many other towns. Boat clubs abounded along the Passaic River, at Bayonne, Elizabethport, along Arthur Kill and along Raritan River and Bay as well as at Barnegat Bay and along the Delaware River. A few males and fewer females played tennis; no well-bred young Ivy Leaguer was without a suit of tennis flannels and the Essex County Park Commission had lawn-tennis courts in its public parks. Golfers toured links at Morristown and Baltusrol (Summit) as early as 1894.

ON A BICYCLE BUILT FOR . . . A WHOLE STATE

Still, of all the popular sports, nothing equalled bicycling. For the twenty-year period between 1890 and 1910 cycling reached the proportions of a national craze, largely because the old high wheeler (also called "bone shaker") was superseded by a rubber-tired, low-slung safety bicycle. Riding was no longer a challenging, dangerous balancing act. Anyone could learn to ride in a few minutes, and soon it appeared that everyone had.

Cycling offered an escape from dreary city flats and young people clogged the roads leading to amusement parks and picnic groves surrounding Camden, Newark, Paterson, and Hoboken. When dusty, rutted roads threatened their sport, the cyclists helped pressure the legislature into appropriating $75,000 in 1891 for road building, thus making New Jersey first in the nation to consider better roads a matter of state concern. Do-it-yourself cyclists of the Cape May Bicycle Road Improvement Association spent thousands of dollars to build gravel roads and bike paths from Cape May to Millville.

Speed-mad cyclists flocked shoreward, causing Cape May in 1896 to set a limit of eight miles per hour. Some Cape May ladies formed the Anti-Bicycle Club to let immodest, fast-riding, bloomer-clad female cyclists know that in Cape May, at least, there *still* were some ladies left. The girl cyclists struck back in county newspapers, scoffing at the "Antis" who "affected waspwaists, high necks and trailing skirts." One eminent doctor gave the "bloomer girls" a decided lift by growling in print that "corsets fill more graves than whiskey."

The event that excited all cyclists between 1890 and 1910 was the annual Decoration Day Millburn–Irvington race, acclaimed as the leading bicycle contest in the country. Hundreds of wheelmen pedaled for such top prizes as new Iver Johnson or Wolf American bicycles and for the edification of 10,000 to 15,000 spectators. Hotels at Millburn and Maplewood and saloons in Irvington stayed open late for verbal re-runnings of the races.

THE HORSECAR'S LAST STAND

The mad dash of the cyclists began just as the electric trolley arrived on the scene. They first ran on April 24, 1889, at Atlantic City, where free rides were offered anyone daring enough to climb aboard on opening day. Cars ran up Atlantic Avenue from the Inlet to Kentucky Avenue, giving the city a service it first cherished, but came to rue in an automobile age. Intertown service began in the summer of 1890 when the Passaic, Garfield & Clifton Railway ran a three-car electric train to link the three towns.

Electric-powered travel didn't excite all towns. As neighbors in Passaic, Paterson, and Clifton prepared for the new service, Paterson's Board of Trade published an elaborate brochure in 1890 to detail the city's "advantages for manufacturing and residence." Town fathers boasted "it is extremely doubtful whether there is a city in the country in which more money has been spent on horse railroads." No city contested the claim.

Newark, the state's largest city, clomped along at the speed of horse-drawn trolleys until October 4, 1890, when the state's first continuous streetcar operation on a large scale opened between Newark and Irvington. Newspapermen reported opening-day fears that riders might be electrocuted, but within three weeks the city had accepted the new mode of travel. Ten years later only Phillipsburg among major towns clung sentimentally and economically to its horse-powered street railway.

Many towns bitterly fought the trolleys at first. In 1893 the Woodbury trolley to Camden was condemned as a "road to hell" because the line facilitated traffic to the race tracks and gambling dens at Gloucester. The classic case of opposition was Montclair's. That town smothered an application for a trolley franchise in 1890 but permitted a public hearing on the matter two years later. One speaker told the assemblage that he did "not propose to make Montclair a dumping ground for Dutch picnics and sick-baby excursions." Caldwell's contention that Montclair's stubborn attitude held up Caldwell's progress forced a capitulation in 1898. It was not unconditional surrender: *twenty-seven pages* of town regulations told trolley operators what would not be tolerated in Montclair.

Trolleys gave the masses a mobility they had never known. Skilled workers could live across town or even outside of town and still get to work on time. Newark's "lace-curtain Irish" moved out of the East Side and up to Vailsburg on the West Side to better their status. Others edged into the suburbs surrounding Newark, Elizabeth, Trenton, Camden, and other crowded cities. Gradually the suburbs began to build and to change.

Newark's industrial and business opportunities rose with its skyline (buildings towered as high as twelve stories by 1900), creating more jobs for the trolley riders. Merchants in the cities began decorating store windows to catch the eyes of shoppers coaxed into the city by trolleys.

The influence of the trolley broadened, by bringing people in to cities from nearby suburbs and by taking city crowds out to see green grass and tall trees in the open country on Sundays.

SMALL TOWNS APLENTY

Trolley lines served to increase urbanization in the areas where it had always been. Except for tracks to Lake Hopatcong, a run from Phillipsburg to Port Murray, a series of short runs along the shore, and a line winding from Vineland to Bivalve (via Millville and Bridgeton), all trolley rights-of-way were in the corridor between Bergen and Camden counties, where the population already had settled. Trolleys served an *existing* population; they didn't spread people.

Thus, in the face of sharply rising population, New Jersey remained a state of small towns. By 1905, only fourteen of the 455 municipalities had populations exceeding 25,000 and thirteen counties didn't have a single city of more than 25,000. Nearly two-thirds of the state's municipalities had fewer than 2000 people in 1905.

This was a state filled with crossroad settlements, where a few houses clustered about a store, a church or two, and a blacksmith shop. The village store sold everything from penny candy and salt mackerel to shoes and Sunday-go-to-meeting dresses. The sophistication, glitter, and new styles displayed in the big city newspapers and magazines didn't affect the farm towns.

Rural villages of 1900 enjoyed little of the alleged comforts of the "Victorian Age"; they were only slightly removed from colonial days except for kerosene lamps, coal stoves, and "store-bought" brooms. Electricity, sanitary plumbing, automobiles, and electrified trolleys were not for these people. Sometimes minstrel troupes or the Chautauqua shows would stop by, or a revivalist might set up a tent, but generally farmfolk satisfied themselves with church socials, taffy pulls, auctions, baseball games, weddings, christenings, and funerals, and maybe a talk by an aging Civil War veteran on Decoration Day. Children left school at an early age to work on the farms; college was almost as far away as the moon.

Medium-sized towns, such as Flemington, Newton, Hackettstown, Mt. Holly, Mays Landing, Bridgeton, Millville, Vineland, Somerville, and Woodbury assumed importance far out of proportion to their size. Villagers came in from time to time on critical errands, for those were the bank towns, the hotel towns, the depot towns, the link with the fast, confusing world beyond. Yet even in those relatively advanced spots the streets were unpaved, street lights (if any) used gas, and community sanitation was primitive.

THE MONEY ROLLS IN

The times were ripe for making great fortunes. Occasionally one of the small-town leaders made it in a big way, such as John I. Blair in Warren County or George G. Green in Gloucester.

Born in Foul Rift in 1802, Blair made his modest start in a country store at Gravel Hill (which saluted him in 1839 by changing its name to Blairstown). He founded a little school called Blair Academy in 1848, helped nominate Abraham Lincoln in 1860, and went west to make a fortune putting together railroad empires. Blair always returned to his simple home in Blairstown and there he died in 1899, leaving his heirs an estimated $70,000,000.

George G. Green of Woodbury made his money in patent medicines. Young Green took over his father's moribund business in 1872 and pushed such homemade nostrums as Boschee's German Syrup and August Flower into world-wide prominence. He eventually hired forty-four persons ("plus twenty-eight young ladies filling bottles") owned a hotel in Pasadena, California, an estate at Lake Hopatcong, and a private Pullman car that took him wherever he willed. His nineteen salesmen convened at a yearly conference in Woodbury, resplendent in high silk hats and swallowtail coats. Like Blair, Green never forsook his home town, although he did put on more of a show.

The rich who settled on the Morris and Somerset hills after making their fortunes in life insurance, the stock market, or railroads were millionaires of another sort. Generally, they talked to no one but other millionaires (that is, if their society-conscious wives were speaking). They ruled their areas with regal splendor and aloofness, but few left any lasting impact on their towns. They were respected or held in awe, not loved.

Most of these men of wealth maintained show places in New York for winter use, but they turned to New Jersey for surcease from the city's summer heat. They built fine cottages at Deal, Elberon, Rumson, Spring Lake, and Lakewood or they enjoyed the cool nights of readily accessible Summit and Morristown.

Those who fled to the Morris and Somerset hills were usually New Yorkers, for New Jersey's cities had their own aristocracies, pleased with their handsome old homes and their traditions. Hundreds of Newark families still traced their beginnings back to those who had founded the city in 1666.

The center of Newark continued as a first love of old and wealthy families living near the beautiful parks along Broad Street. Gustav Kobbé wrote in 1889: "These fine residences belong to people who have business as well as family interests in Newark, are thoroughly identified with the city's progress, and are proud to hail from it."

Newark's prominent people—its industrialists, its financiers, its editors, its educators, its elite—had not yet deserted the city where they made their fortunes for the "better life" along the railroads to the south and west. Newark's wealthy were "thoroughly identified with the city's progress," Kobbé pointed out. Few could believe then that their city would one day no longer be a fashionable place in which to live, but would become only a place to make a living before fleeing at night to the suburbs.

The outward move had begun subtly. Essex County hilltop farms were being cut into estates after the 1860s: General George B. McClellan bought in "The Ridge" above West Orange when he chose New Jersey for his home after the Civil War; Llewellyn S. Haskell had created exclusive Llewellyn Park on the Orange Mountain in 1875, and Stewart Hartshorn had founded Short Hills in 1877.

MORRISTOWN: JERSEY'S GRANDE DAME

Queen of all wealthy centers was Morristown, where soaring life insurance sales and the rampaging stock market enabled wealthy summertime visitors to create their own aristocracy. Morristown had genuine elegance: by 1874 Morristown was called "favorable in comparison with Newport" and by 1879 distinguished gatherings were being held in the Lyceum on South Street. By 1890, scores of millionaires were settled in the mountains surrounding Morristown, their dwellings ranging from cottages (thirty rooms or so) to full-fledged and ostentatious castles built in imitation of European originals. Cost was no concern.

Money attracted more money, until ninety to a hundred men of fabled fortune resided within three miles of the old Morristown Village Green. One reliable source, which listed them by name and net worth, said ninety-two persons worth at least $1,000,000 each called Morristown home (or at least a home away from Fifth Avenue or Newport). That source listed the aggregate means of these ninety-two Morristonians at $404,000,000. Forty-nine had only the basic qualifying million: another fourteen could boast only two million each, but fourteen had assets of $10,000,000 or more apiece.

Heading the list were Mr. and Mrs. Hamilton McK. Twombly, whose combined assets added up to at least $70,000,000. Contrary to often-told stories that Twombly was a rather poor boy when he married Florence Vanderbilt, favorite granddaughter of Commodore Vanderbilt, the truth is he had made millions from sulphur mines. He was in "modest circumstances" only in compariosn with Mrs. Twombly's holdings, which were in excess of $50,000,000.

The Twomblys lived in the grand and showy manner of self-styled American royalty. One of their "barn dances" in 1891 required $6000 just for electric lights. They called their 900 acres "Florham" (for "Florence and Hamilton") and urged the little village of Afton in which they dwelled to change its name to Florham Park. Afton, with an obedient eye on the tax ledger, complied in 1899.

Although the Twomblys had a mansion on Fifth Avenue and a villa at Newport copied after the Palace of Versailles, they loved their 100-room country house in Morris County. They modeled it after Hampton Court Palace in England at a reputed cost of $2,000,000. Each year Mrs. Twombly invited all residents of the area to the estate, where the curious could gape at the trimmings, the grounds, and the fifteen cars (including five Rolls-Royces) all trimmed in Twombly maroon. Chauffeurs, footmen, butlers, and servants wore the same maroon, and it was a matter of gossip that the chef received $25,000 a year.

The names of the other wealthy in and near Morristown included Dr. D. Leslie Ward, D. Willis James, Otto Kahn, John I. Waterbury, Robert Dumont Foote, Luther Kountze, Gustav E. Kissel, Robert H. McCurdy, Charles Scribner, Richard A. McCurdy, John Claflin, and Charles F. Cutler. In the Somerset hills to the southwest were such names as John F. Dryden, Frederic P. Olcott, C. Ledyard Blair, Percy R. Pyne, Walter G. Ladd, James Cox Brady, and James Buchanan Duke. The strip from Morristown to Far Hills was literally a *Who's Who* of the financial world.

While these people took themselves seriously, a writer for *World Magazine* in 1905 saw them with something less than unstinting respect:

> If you chance to be at the railroad station at Morristown, N. J., at about 5 o'clock of any weekday afternoon, you will see one of the comedies of real life—a comedy of almost pathetic seriousness to the participants, yet absorbingly interesting and almost mirth provoking to the spectator.

He told of hundreds of handsome equipages filling nearby streets, scores of automobiles lined up on the station grounds, and dozens of public hacks crowded along the curbs. Liveried servants were everywhere, "many sitting stiff and unseeing on the tiger's seat of a fashionable trap; others standing like automatons beside the emblazoned doors of heavy broughams."

When the "Millionaire's Express," arrived in late afternoon, the station and its grounds burst into excitement. The *World* reporter recorded the scene:

> From the forward coaches an indiscriminate mass of humanity pours forth, but from the club coaches at the rear emerge in leisurely fashion a silk-tied and usually corpulent host—men who, perhaps, have spent

the day considering the fate of nations, the financing of a new transcontinental railway or the funding of a dog show or a monkey dinner.

Hamilton McK. Twombly makes his way to the drag-and-four where his daughter, Miss Ruth Twombly, awaits him, surrounded by a coachman, two footmen and a postillion. Richard A. McCurdy walks slowly to his splendid victoria, where awaits Mrs. McCurdy, a coachman and a footman. Luther Kountze enters his eight horse power Panhard, to be whirled away to his palace on the Mendham Road. Robert H. McCurdy hurries to his pale blue motor car; William Stark Letchford to his trap; Otto H. Kahn to his saddle horse; John I. Waterbury to his brougham, and in a few minutes they are all speeding away to nearby homes.

For Morristown is the city of millionaires, and there is not another community like it in the United States—possibly not in the world. Here are gathered together in one little circle, within a radius of three miles, more men of millions than can be found elsewhere in many times the area the country over.

Inevitably chinks showed in the armor of this kingdom of wealth.

The ladies who had founded the Morris County Golf Club in 1894—as the country's first country club run by women—had never forgiven the men who had boldly taken control from them in 1896. The town's social leaders engaged in a struggle for power in 1903, and when Newark and New York papers headlined the social war, wounds were permanent. Furthermore, lawyer-investigator Charles Evans Hughes, in uncovering scandal in the New York insurance world, had included some well-known Morristown area names in his scathing 1906 report. Most important, the world was rushing toward a war that would make Morristown's gilded horse stables seem foolish and inconsequential.

The long, bittersweet sleep was coming to an end. The rich would suffer in a world turned topsy-turvy, but so would the poor. Towns would emerge from their isolation to depend, for better or worse, on other places. The often lovely if occasionally overdone gingerbread of Victorian architecture, which had replaced simple colonial lines, would in turn be scorned by a new breed of architects bent on only the simplest of geometric forms.

That Roar on the Highway

Two things in particular helped speed the "Victorian Age" to its end: the automobile and a deepening sense of social responsibility.

The automobile was making loud noises in the direction of the Jersey back country by 1900, in the hands of young men of means or mechanical inclination (sometimes both). Two young scions of noted families, Thomas A. Edison, Jr. and Edward R. Hewitt, bought steam-powered "locomobiles" on the same day in 1899, at a time when New Jersey law demanded that a man with a flag walk 100 yards ahead of any steam vehicle.

One memorable, daring trip by Hewitt and his wife illustrates the adventures of early New Jersey motorists. The Hewitts, against all sound advice, decided in 1899 to drive the twenty-eight miles of rough, narrow roads from the Hewitt estate at Ringwood to Morristown, and then head for New York—all in one day! Halfway to Morristown the spokes on the wire wheels began to snap, but Hewitt repaired the damage with ribs from an umbrella that he borrowed in Whippany. The couple reached Morristown and true to their boast, proceeded to New York. They made it, too, all before darkness.

Farmers protested automobiles speeding ten miles and more per hour on country roads. Unwelcomed in the farm areas, racers by 1905 had to head for the wide, hard sand at Cape May to indulge their passion for speed. Nearly all the esteemed figures of the automobile world competed in the July and August Cape May races that year, including Henry Ford in his six-cylinder "Wonder." Ford trailed such competitors as Christie, Campbell, and Chevrolet, but all of them thrilled "the greatest crowd of spectators ever visiting the resort."

Criticism of the wild automobilists came from pulpit, editorial office, and helpless wagon drivers forced into roadside ditches. The young Princeton University president, Woodrow Wilson, who was beginning to command wide attention, told the North Carolina Society in 1906 that "nothing has spread socialistic feeling in this country more than the automobile." He explained: "To the countryman they are a picture of the arrogance of wealth, with all its independence and carelessness."

Wilson probably blamed the automobile too much for the socialistic feeling. Other and greater forces were at work—women's clubs, conservation groups, "New Idea" politicians, dedicated social workers, independent newspapers, millionaires with consciences, labor leaders, and college professors. Reform was in the air, whether it be called progressivism, socialism, muckraking, radicalism, or just simple awareness that the goods of America ought not to be reserved for the few.

19

Of the People

The unmistakable stirrings of progressive thought were felt in America by 1893, but not in the New Jersey legislature. Indeed, the gathering of the Democratic-controlled legislature that winter seemed more like Old Home Week for the chiselers, the gamblers, and the race-track touts. As William Edgar Sackett has written, "everything that was venal or corrupt or offensive in the management of public affairs was largely reflected in the Legislature."

Speaker of the Assembly was Thomas Flynn of Passaic, distinguished as a "starter" at Billy Thompson's notorious race course at Gloucester. Billy himself sat in the Assembly, surrounded by as openly corrupt a band of legislators as the state has ever known. Cynically nicknamed the "Jockey Legislature," the politicians moved to garb their gambling activities with the silks of law, but in the midst of the mock debate, Democratic Assemblyman Thomas F. Lane of Union County rose to demand a public hearing on such bills.

Lane pointed to the powerful opposition already rising against the tainted legislation. Whereupon Speaker Flynn (according to Sackett) "curled his lip contemptuously" and made a sneering reference to the protestors as "old women and dominies." Stunned, Lane labeled this as a "gratuitous insult at the honest mothers and sisters and daughters of the Commonwealth." He added melodramatically, "The speaker will remember that the hand that rocks the cradle rules the world!"

CORRUPTION AND CONFLICT

Ignoring the warning, the legislature rushed through the infamous race-track bills and sent them to Governor George T. Werts. The governor, heeding the cries of indignation, vetoed the measures. The legislature overrode the vetoes, and Jersey Justice stood for the moment at a starting gate ready to be opened by Flynn, Thompson, and their assorted friends and touts of the paddock.

An inflamed battalion of ministers, priests, lawyers, and others stormed into Trenton on Washington's Birthday in 1893. Five thousand of them took possession of the Assembly chamber to cheer impassioned speeches against the race-track interests. The bills weren't repealed in that session, but the public had been heard as never before. The Democrats were swept out of legislative control that fall, and in 1896 John Griggs became the first Republican governor in twenty-seven years.

Replacement of the flashy race-track crowd by businessmen and lawyers did not bring immediate good government. Shorn of the horse players, the legislature found itself gripped by a combination of corporate powers that ruled as it willed. This too, would be swept away, for a great change had come to America: the once-silent man and woman in the street demanded that they have some say in "government by the people." Their strength could not be turned aside.

This period from 1895 to 1915 rightfully has been called the Progressive Era, a time of governmental reform. The progressives fought for conservation of natural resources, elimination of political bosses, decent labor laws, better education, an end to corporation abuses, humane prisons, control of utilities, repeal of scandalous election procedures, and aid for unfortunate women and children. They fought evil wherever they found it, against odds and against entrenched power.

Woodrow Wilson, Princeton president, governor of New Jersey, and President of the United States, is generally credited with leading the progressive movement in the state. Yet his essential contribution was to tie together a package that many others had assembled. Long before Wilson joined the fray, young figures and a few old ones in both major parties hammered away at the blatant cooperation between big money interests and easily bought politicians. A few independent newspapers took up cudgels against corruption. Church leaders of all faiths spoke out against entrenched political machines. High-minded millionaires joined the fight, to the horror of their fellows in exclusive clubs. It seemed, indeed, a vigorous reaction to injustice and moral decay.

THE WEAKER SEX RALLIES

A sweeping moral force was joined when women began to raise their voices openly against evil. Women by natural inclination always worked for "local uplift," on their own initiative or in "female charitable societies." Theirs was a devotion to the beauty of their surroundings, to the welfare of others, to betterment of schools and libraries. Now they began to speak out and to band together.

Here and there aggressive voices were raised. Lucy Stone of Orange refused in 1858 to pay taxes unless she could vote, indignantly citing "taxation without representation." The tax collector promptly sold Mrs. Stone's furnishings, including her baby's crib. Elizabeth Cady Stanton vainly tried to vote in Tenafly in 1875. The Reverend Antoinette Brown Blackwell of Newark and Elizabeth, the first woman to win ordination as a minister in an organized church, actively worked for women's rights from the 1860s to 1920—even as she bore six daughters, a supreme irony for one so cognizant of the difficulties faced by her sex.

Strength came in organization, sometimes in seeming subterfuge. New Jersey's first women's club, founded in Orange in 1872, earnestly debated questions like "Do the women of the middle and upper classes do their share of work in the world?" and "Would it be more advisable to civilize the Indians or to compel them to live upon their reservations?" Between times, they busied themselves with a careful study of the public schools—submitting a detailed and critical report in 1876, for example, on heat and ventilation. That was bold action. Fittingly, when a national organization, the General Federation of Women's Clubs, was founded in 1890, its first president was Charlotte Emerson Brown of the Orange club.

Other clubs organized, discussing literature and conditions in Africa but also looking sharply into matters close to home. They came together as a state-wide force in 1894 to found the New Jersey State Federation of Women's Clubs. Another Orange leader, Mrs. Margaret Tufts Swan Yardley, became first president.

Thirty-six clubs joined the State Federation in the first year, many of them boasting the most vital and energetic women of their day. The Jersey City Women's Club, founded in 1895, included the first woman lawyer in New Jersey, a physician, a college vice-president, the principal in the city's manual training school, and other distinguished citizens.

Jennie Cunningham Croly, national women's club historian, wrote in 1898 that the clubs represented "part of the great educational movement which is sweeping like a tidal wave over the country, and of which Chautauqua, summer schools, night schools, university extensions, etc., are all manifestations." She saw the clubs as "not an echo, not the mere banding together for a social and economic purpose, like the clubs of men," but as a "purely altruistic and democratic activity."

Women dared rush in where men urged caution. The New Jersey Federation found its first public cause and exhibited its first public strength over the beautiful—but rapidly disappearing—Palisades overlooking the Hudson River in Bergen County.

Legislators watched complacently as quarrymen crumbled the Palisades into trap rock. When the federal government failed in 1894 in efforts to create a military reservation atop the rocky bastion, all seemed lost. The State Federation decided to take action. Mrs. Yardley, "in an urge to show women's organized strength to the legislators on the Palisades question," led 300 club members to Trenton when the legislature convened in March, 1896. Blasting went on, but for the first time an effective counteraction had been taken and New Jersey women prevailed.

Governor Foster M. Voorhees in 1899 appointed Miss Elizabeth Vermilye of Englewood and Miss Cecilia Gaines of Jersey City to a commission to study the Palisades issue. A year later New York and New Jersey created the unique Interstate Park Commission to acquire the land, but only after the Federation of Women's clubs out-lobbied ardent quarry lobbyists. Women saved the Palisades—and won national acclaim for the feat—but neither New York nor New Jersey found room for a woman member on the commission.

Clubwomen pushed on many fronts. They sought home economics in the schools, urged establishment of kindergartens, and sought legislation to protect women factory workers. A historian cites the period between 1902 and 1904 as the time when women began to "make a mark all over the state," and it is evident that their aims were the aims of all progressive: greater chances and more protection for more people. They demanded improved sanitation, civil-service reform, child-labor laws, clean railroad stations, pure-food regulations, and a state reformatory for women with "intellectual and physical training provided." They urged the legislature to abolish night labor for boys in glass factories—"thus placing our state with those that favor boys over bottles."

Those were dedicated women seeking to improve their world and their country. As if the above list isn't comprehensive enough, here are other things sought by women: compulsory school laws, well-built, well-equipped schools, better pay for better-prepared teachers, abolition of billboards beside the railroad tracks, child-labor laws, licensing of midwives, smoke abatement, tuberculosis control, special instruction for handicapped children, laws forbidding white slavery, slaughterhouse inspection, "a less commercial Christmas," and minimum-wage bills.

These were women without party allegiance, without hope of political favor, without debts to political parties, neither liberal nor conservative, Republican or Democratic. They fought for principle, for they saw things as good or evil, right or wrong, outside the pale of politics. Many of the clubwomen became prominent figures of the day.

NAMES IN THE NEWS

Mrs. Emily E. Williamson of Elizabeth, president of the State Federation from 1898 to 1900, worked ceaselessly for prison reform and child welfare. As secretary of the State Charities Aid Association, she helped a young associate, Frances Day, enter the Hudson County Almshouse in 1897–98 as an inmate. Miss Day's shocking report of the exploitation and mistreatment of children shamed the state into formation of the State Board of Children's Guardians, whose original purpose was to place welfare children in foster homes rather than almshouses. It has since grown to include wide protection for children.

Mrs. Williamson served in 1908 on the Dependency and Crime Commission, created to "investigate the causes of dependency and criminality." One of Mrs. Williamson's co-workers was Mrs. Caroline B. Alexander (later Mrs. Otto H. Wittpenn, wife of a progressive Jersey City mayor). Mrs. Alexander pushed persistently for a separate women's prison and saw her plan started in 1910 on "a picturesque and salubrious site" at Clinton. It was opened three years later as the New Jersey Reformatory for Women.

There were others in the fore of the movement: Mrs. Stewart Hartshorn of Short Hills, concerned with improved conditions for women factory workers; Miss Mary McKeen of Moorestown, dedicated worker for conservation; Mrs. Henry H. Dawson of Newark, interested in betterment of public schools; and Mrs. Mabel Smith Douglass of Jersey City, who between 1912 and 1918 stumped the state for the New Jersey College for Women, and became its first dean in 1918. (The college was renamed Douglass College in 1955 in her honor.)

Miss Alice Lakey of the Cranford Village Improvement Association, carried her crusading spirit far beyond New Jersey's borders. She heard Dr. Harvey Washington Wiley, implacable foe of the entrenched food and drink trusts, tell the Cranford Club in 1902 of the harm that could befall mankind from the uncontrolled injection of chemicals into food, drink, and patent medicines. This advocate of pure-food laws found in Miss Lakey a willing disciple.

Out from Cranford went Miss Lakey to persuade the State Federation, the General Federation, and the National Consumers' League to take action. She lectured up and down the state and across the land before women's clubs, "transforming the suspicious disquiet of the women into outraged resentment and strenuous action." Women pressured Congress relentlessly and without partisanship. The canners and packers and the liquor trust could not resist that kind of opposition. President Theodore Roosevelt signed the Pure Food bill into law on June 20, 1906.

Mark Sullivan wrote in "Our Times":

> These women, by the support they gave Doctor Wiley, by the pressure they brought on Congress—without votes, without even thinking they needed votes, did a work greater than anything that women accomplished or attempted during the eight years after women got the suffrage in 1919.

Many males, probably most of the sex, viewed these reform-bent women with alarm. Ex-President Grover Cleveland from his home in

Princeton wrote in the April, 1905 *Ladies' Home Journal* that women should not join clubs except those with "purposes of charity, religious enterprise or intellectual improvement. . . . Her best and safest club is in her home." Six months later, the *Journal* carried Cleveland's fatherly philosophy that "sensible and responsible women do not want to vote. The relative positions to be assigned to man and woman in the working out of our civilization were assigned long ago by a higher intelligence than our own."

The women did not answer the aging ex-President. They were much too busy to heed the suggestion that they return to the nostalgic and predictable time of Cleveland's youth.

THE BATTLE IS JOINED

The women were not alone in their fight. Men of many social strata of both major political parties also fought to rid themselves of domination by powerful and selfish interests. It was the age of reform, of muckraking journalists, and of enlightened political newcomers. It was the time of Teddy Roosevelt and Woodrow Wilson.

Ransom E. Noble, Jr., chronicler of New Jersey's role in the era, observed:

> Probably no part of the Union offered more impregnable defenses to the onslaughts of progressivism than did New Jersey. The domination of politics by corporation-machine alliances had reached its full flower in the little state lying between the cities of New York and Philadelphia. . . . Politically corrupt and boss-ridden, "home of the trusts" and happy hunting ground of railroad and utility interests, New Jersey seemed fully committed to her role as sponsor and protector of "the system" against which reformers inveighed.

Democrats had fallen swiftly from public favor after their abject surrender to the race-track crowd in the 1890s. Republicans controlled both houses of the legislature (save the 1907 Assembly) from 1893 to 1910 and elected five successive governors before Woodrow Wilson broke the string in 1910.

Republicans proved subservience to bosses is often a matter of kind, not degree. General William J. Sewell, U. S. Senator from 1881 until his death in 1901, ran the Republican Party with an iron fist, championing the causes of both the GOP and the Pennsylvania Railroad. After his death, Republican bosses in Hudson, Essex, and Middlesex counties vied for control against Camden's big David Baird, who had South Jersey in his grip. Democrats, in turn, looked for leadership from flamboyant ex-U. S. Senator James Smith Jr. of Newark and Hudson County's shrewd Bob Davis. The state was held tightly, regardless of who succeeded at the polls.

For their part, the bosses of both political stripes jumped when big business cracked its whip, for every boss had powerful connections with corporations or utilities. Both of New Jersey's U. S. Senators in 1903 were heavily interested in utilities: Senator John F. Dryden, president of the Prudential Insurance Company, was a director of the North Jersey Street Railway, and his insurance firm was the major financial backer of the newly formed Public Service Corporation. Senator John Kean was president of the Elizabethtown Gas Light Company.

When Thomas N. McCarter resigned as State Attorney General in 1903 to head the new Public Service combine, no one in political power questioned the propriety of the legislature's approving as his successor his brother, Robert H. McCarter. Nor did anyone suggest possible additional conflict of interest in Robert McCarter's continuing as counsel for the D.L.&W. and Lehigh Valley Railroads. The question was not ability—for the businessmen *were* able—but whether such interlocking control was good for the public.

Mark M. Fagan, a young Jersey City undertaker, threw the first sand into the works of the smoothly operating machinery run by the small knot of Republican bosses. He was a Republican himself and at first he fought only Democrats. Then he swung at bosses of either party.

Outraged by conditions in his city's slums, Fagan accepted the Republican nomination for Hudson County freeholder in 1896 although Democrats long had "owned" his district. Fagan campaigned through the tenements, where Italian immigrants loved the hard-working, sincere man they called "Marka de Fage." He won an amazing upset victory and the party organization in 1901 backed him in his successful bid for mayor of Jersey City. The Grand Old Party loved this young man with the vote appeal, and for a while Fagan returned the affection. But he soon began to disturb his bosses. He advocated better schools, elimination of foul sewers, a new building to replace the old leaky, vermin-filled hospital, better parks, and public concerts.

Fagan chose a maverick Republican, George L. Record, as his corporation counsel. Maine-born Record, originally a Democrat, liked to compare himself with Abraham Lincoln (he *was* tall and lanky) and his political credo called for curing economic ills by eliminating monopoly privilege. Record influenced Fagan deeply, guided the later Republican "New Idea," and made significant contribution to Woodrow Wilson's conversion to progressivism. Historian Noble wrote that Record's hand "can be seen in every major move of progressive nature in the state from the 1890s on."

The Fagan-Record program needed money and the handiest sources were the railroads and utilities, the darlings of the political hierarchy. Some 30 per cent of all Jersey City land was railroad-owned and taxed by the state at rates designed to keep the state budget in balance. The gain to the rest of New Jersey was great; the loss to Jersey City and Hudson County crippled them. Fagan promised to carry the fight for local taxation of railroads to Trenton if re-elected mayor in 1903. He was, and promptly sought the aid of the legislature and of Republican Governor Franklin Murphy, millionaire Newark varnish maker.

Spurned by the lawmakers, Fagan dispatched a wrathful open letter to Governor Murphy in March, 1904, charging that the "Republican legislature is controlled by the railroad, trolley and water corporations, and the interests of the people are being betrayed. As a member of the Republican party, I deplore its subservience to corporate greed and in-justice."

Party bosses made some tax concessions—not enough to satisfy Fagan and Record, but enough to show that Fagan's open attack in the news-papers had accomplished far more than argument in secret Republican caucuses. Railroad taxes jumped 70 per cent in a year.

Fagan took on the Public Service Corporation with far less success. The corporation won a fifty-year franchise in Fagan's own city in 1904 despite the mayor's strenuous opposition. Republican bosses decided the mayor must go, but despite their undercutting he won his third straight term in 1905 and carried twelve Hudson Republicans with him into the State Assembly. The challenge to the bosses was unmistakable.

THE "NEW IDEA" PROGRESSIVES

Meanwhile, a group of insurgent young Essex Republicans, including wealthy Alden Freeman and brilliant lawyer Frank Sommer, mounted their opposition to a perpetual trolley franchise in the Oranges into a full-fledged campaign against all entrenched interests. Their chief foe was redoubtable Republican boss Carl Lentz, one-armed Civil War veteran, who said he preferred "to crush opposition rather than face it." Lentz found this tactic did not stop the progressives, whose proposals at first had been sneeringly labeled as a New Idea by party regulars.

The Essex progressives gained support from the Newark *Evening News* and by 1904 had their leader: Everett Colby, aristocratic, good-looking, and very rich. Colby received Lentz's warm endorsement when he ran successfully for the Assembly in 1902, but his independence soon angered Lentz's business backers. They refused to back Colby's bid for the Assembly speakership in 1905. Aroused, Colby fought vigorously for a law forbidding perpetual utility franchises, and succeeded in get-ting the legislature to appoint another of its innumerable investigating commissions.

Colby became the darling of the progressives. He won an impressive victory to the State Senate in 1905 despite the opposition of Lentz's forces. A New Idea sweep seemed imminent in the wake of the Fagan-

Colby triumphs. Their liberal policies forced even the sternest old-line regulars to accept progressive theories. That acceptance ruined the New Idea as such. With the regulars so progressive (on the surface, at least), young insurgents found difficulty in gaining election.

New Idea enthusiasts asked Colby to run for governor in 1907; his refusal ended the movement, but not the philosophy. Fagan suffered stunning defeat that year from Otto H. Wittpenn, but Wittpenn was also a liberal. Colby himself lost his bid for re-election in 1908, but his Democratic adversary, Harry V. Osborne, backed liberal causes with all of Colby's intensity. Hudson's young Democrats also followed Joseph P. Tumulty in demanding progressive legislation. While the New Idea was dead in name, its influence survived.

A Jersey Triumvirate

There has been a tendency on the part of historians interested in the progressive era to overlook the fact that New Jersey had a series of sound Republican governors between 1896 and 1910. At least three of them, Foster M. Voorhees, Franklin Murphy, and John Franklin Fort, helped establish the liberal base on which Woodrow Wilson operated so effectively.

Voorhees encouraged the battle to save the Palisades, backed Mrs. Williamson in her investigation of almshouses, approved creation of the Board of Children's Guardians, completed Rahway Reformatory and made it a prison for "less-hardened" criminals, urged studies of the Hackensack meadowland, and supported creation of the State Mosquito Extermination Commission.

Millionaire Franklin Murphy, in his turn, showed strong public consciousness. As president of Newark's Common Council he had pioneered a program of improved streets and pavements, parks, and electricity for street lighting. In 1895 he was a leader in establishment of the Essex County Park Commission, first county-park body in the country.

Once in the State House in 1902, Murphy continued to act like a businessman, to the consternation of many bosses and lesser politicians who long had felt business and politics did not mix, except at contribution time. He moved into a house in Trenton, disturbed the political hacks by demanding that everyone on the payroll show up for work on time, and took state funds out of favored banks which paid no interest and redeposited them in savings accounts bearing interest (earning $60,000 the first year). He ordered an annual audit of all departmental accounts.

Murphy began action to clean up the foul, sewage-clogged Passaic River, a fight he continued after he left Trenton. He backed a law setting up school boards independent of local politicians, with power to ask local government for money (for the first time, in many towns, teachers had some assurance they would be paid). He threw the weight of his office behind primary-election reform and strong child-labor laws.

Primary elections were brazenly fraudulent and open to cynical manipulation. The 1903 law endorsed by Murphy set up regular registration and election boards and provided for the use of official ballots and uniform ballot boxes (to supplant the cigar boxes that had served so many towns). Significantly, the new law established the principle that nomination in the primaries was a proper subject for public control as well as party concern.

Murphy also took up the cudgels for strong child-labor legislation, thus allying himself with the reformers. Studies had proved that children were being ill treated in hundreds of New Jersey factories. Tobacco makers hired children for two dollars a week to do jobs for which men were paid eight dollars.

South Jersey glassworks had a notorious reputation as low-paying places where boys, living away from their families, "learned drunkenness and profanity at an early age." Consumers League Secretary Helen Marot, attempting to investigate child-labor conditions at a Paterson mill in 1901, was refused admittance on the grounds that so many children were employed that her presence would distract them from their work.

Murphy forced the grossly incompetent state factory inspector, a former Salem County State Senator, out of office. The governor then sent his private secretary into the Passaic County textile mills and within six weeks he had recorded more than 200 violations of child-labor statutes.

The governor pressed for, and won, a new law, despite the well-financed opposition of textile-mill owners and glass makers. Under this regulation a child under fourteen could work only in stores, on streets, or on farms; fifty-five hours was set as the maximum week in mines and factories; and heavy penalties were set for infractions. The law called for a paid staff of thirteen persons, including two women, and made employers responsible for proving a child's age. Murphy ordered strict enforcement; this was not just for show.

Finally, on the eve of Woodrow Wilson's spectacular entrance into New Jersey politics, Governor John Franklin Fort tried valiantly, and vainly, for most of the governmental changes that Wilson later advanced as his political guidelines.

This was where Fort stood as he embarked on his term in 1908:

He favored a strong public-utilities control law; abolition of county tax boards—which he felt favored railroads; banning diversion of New Jersey drinking water to other states; a civil-service law; motor-vehicle and inheritance-tax departments; deepening of the inland waterway along the Jersey coast; construction of an ocean highway; and power to remove state and local officials found guilty of malfeasance.

Fort's liberal leanings frightened the Republican bosses, who in 1909 set up a committee to "assist" lawmakers. Something had to be done, they felt, to keep the Republican members of the legislature in line and to check the activities of Governor Fort. This reactionary Board of Guardians frustrated Fort, prevented him from pushing his legislative program, and thus cleared the way for Wilson's ascendancy.

New Jersey could not stand still. The population had soared to 2,537,-167 in 1910; manufacturing had doubled since 1900, and taxable property had tripled in value. Progressive legislation was critically needed in this urban state.

"Our state is growing fast," said Fort repeatedly. "It must spend more."

But he realized with ill-concealed bitterness that he could only nudge the state along the progressive trail. After Wilson's election Fort declared: "My only regret is that the legislation I advised was not enacted, and I believe that the result of the election evidenced that the people joined me in that regret. They have forcibly expressed their opinion."

Woodrow Wilson was elected governor in the fall of 1910 by a majority of 49,000 votes, but it was less a victory over Fort policies than a repudiation of boss-ridden, *laissez faire* Republicanism.

A CRUSADER ON CAMPUS

In his earlier days Virginia-born Woodrow Wilson seemed a man unlikely to lead a progressive state. Scholarly, politically and economically conservative, and withdrawn from public affairs, he had devoted himself to Princeton University since becoming its president in 1902. That was as high an honor as could be paid the scholar who had been graduated from Princeton in 1879. Wilson at first was adored on campus. Biographer Arthur Link says he "had taken a backward college with ancient traditions and transformed it almost overnight into one of the leading educational laboratories in the nation."

But he antagonized the alumni by proposing in December, 1906, that the hallowed social eating clubs be abolished as undemocratic. He suggested instead grouping students for "academic and intellectual reasons." Frustrated in that proposal (the clubs live on at Princeton, although considerably less revered than they were in 1906), Wilson turned in 1909 to acrimonious debate with Professor Andrew Fleming West over location of a proposed graduate school. Wilson wanted the buildings as part of the academic complex on the old campus, arguing that both graduate students and undergraduates would benefit by being together. West favored an isolated location on a golf course about a mile away from the main campus.

West had his way when a multimillion-dollar gift from a Massachusetts donor created the graduate school and stipulated the golf-course site. Wilson had his choice: accept the setback or resign, and many among both alumni and the trustees would have accepted a resignation with delight. Outwardly accepting the West triumph, Wilson inwardly seethed. There is ample evidence that if Wilson had prevailed in his fight for the graduate school he would not have left the campus.

ON TO THE STATE HOUSE

Meanwhile, powerful forces were interested in a political career for Wilson. Among them were George Brinton McClellan Harvey, conservative editor of *Harper's Weekly*, and James Smith Jr., Democratic boss of Essex County. They had vainly urged Wilson to be the Democratic nominee for the United States Senate in 1907. Harvey and Smith both saw the erudite Princetonian as a potential vote getter, and they kept after him.

Boss Smith felt the "Professor" was ready in 1910. Link says Wilson had moved in political philosophy, "from the right of center to center; he generally accepted most of the progressive premises." Still, he seemed safe enough for Smith. The Democratic leader rammed Wilson's name through a bitterly antiboss convention in 1910 and secured him the Democratic nomination for governor.

Wilson accepted the nomination at the Taylor Opera House in Trenton, where he moved a sullen audience to cheers by an impassioned declaration that he was pledged to no one. He accepted the progressive platform, promised a vigorous campaign, and "his earnest eloquence moved some of his more emotional and less sober audience to tears."

Liberals were charmed by Wilson, party regulars found him acceptable, and even Republican suburban commuters recognized his impeccable background of Virginia birth and Ivy League education. The suburbanites loved him even more when late in the campaign the railroads dealt a financial blow to their long-time Republican protectors by raising commuter fares 20 per cent. Legions of indignant commuters, long complacent about state affairs, rose up to demand a strong utilities commission, or *any* kind of commission with ability to lower fares. They also voted for Wilson.

Wilson's one-sided triumph made him master of New Jersey. Quickly he rebuffed the bid of his political mentor, James Smith, to become U. S. Senator, thus redeeming his pledge that he would not be bossed. Smith denounced Wilson as an ingrate and Hudson County boss Robert Davis sympathetically withdrew his machine backing from the governor. James Nugent, Smith's son-in-law and Democratic State Chairman, broke with the governor over patronage. Nugent loudly told Wilson he was "no gentleman." "You," Wilson riposted, "are no judge."

With the bosses put down, Wilson achieved nearly all the reforms that progressives of both parties had been pursuing for twenty years. The fine hand of George L. Record, most unswerving of New Jersey reformers, was apparent in much of the legislation, although Record, a nominal Republican, was not an official member of the Wilson political family.

Wilson tied his administration to four principal legislative measures: election reform, a corrupt-practices act, a strong public-utilities commission, and a decent workmen's compensation act. All four passed in his first months in office.

Under the new election laws, citizens now could vote in the primary on party nominations for all state offices. Official ballots replaced the old easily manipulated party ballots. Delegates to presidential conventions could be elected in the primary. Local election boards became bipartisan. This law solidified the power of the ballot; newspapers across the land hailed it as the death knell of boss rule.

The corrupt-practices act sought to eliminate the outrageous fraud and bribery that had become a hallmark of New Jersey politics. There was much evidence of the need for the law, in city and country alike. When sample ballots were sent in 1911 to registered voters in Newark, 11,000 were returned, unclaimed by phantom voters. In Republican boss Louis Kuehnle's Atlantic City, an investigation that same year showed districts where the vote was four-fifths fraudulent. "Repeaters" imported from Philadelphia voted often in Atlantic City, at two dollars a ballot.

The public-utilities law created the long-sought three-man board of public-utilities commissioners, with explicit powers. The board could appraise and evaluate public-utility properties, fix "just and reasonable rates," set standards of service, and, in general, give the word "public" as much weight as the word "utilities."

Last of the four major Wilson achievements was enactment of the workmen's compensation law. The old law had been called by the editor of the Newark News "the most ancient and unjust of any employers' liability laws in the country." Senator (later twice governor) Walter E. Edge of Atlantic County wrote the new law, which abolished old common-law principles of "assumption of risk by worker" and made employers legally liable for the injuries incurred while at work.

WASHINGTON CALLS

Amid a growing national acclaim during the summer of 1911, Wilson felt less and less at home in Trenton. It was clear his eye was on the White House. The Republican-controlled legislature criticized him for prolonged absences from New Jersey on speaking tours in 1912 and Wilson tartly replied that "no important matter of business has been allowed to fall in arrears in my office."

Progressivism ruled American thought, as the Presidential elections of 1912 proved beyond doubt. Breaking with Republican conservatives, Theodore Roosevelt ran as the candidate of the Progressive Party, created specifically for his talents. Roosevelt actually did not offer a clearcut Republican choice between conservative and progressive; William Howard Taft's term as President indicated his willingness to sponsor reforms, although with none of Roosevelt's showmanship.

Democrats faced internal dissension, their views ranging from followers of ex-President Cleveland's conservatism to backers of William Jennings Bryan, whose reform ideas centered on Western farming and silver mines. Threatened with a bitter split, the party met in Baltimore to choose its nominee.

Wilson's name rose to the fore. His New Jersey record proved his ability to get things done. His progressive views—tempered by his philosophy that federal government ought not to usurp new powers—endeared him to many Democrats. Southerners found his Virginia birth pleasant although they backed Oscar W. Underwood of Alabama. When Underwood proved unable to win, Southerners threw support to Wilson and he became the nominee on the forty-sixth ballot.

Voters gave Wilson more support than any other candidate, but he did not win a majority of votes cast. He received 6,296,547 to 4,188,571 for Roosevelt and 3,486,720 for Taft. New Jersey followed the national trend by giving Wilson its fourteen electoral votes, but only 178,289 votes out of 462,289 cast, about 38 per cent. Wilson's victory over Taft was beyond doubt; whether he might have downed Roosevelt in a face-to-face contest must always be problematical.

Nationally, Wilson swept 435 out of 531 electoral votes, and helped carry Democratic majorities into both houses of Congress. He faced nationally the same enthusiasm and support that he had previously enjoyed as governor of New Jersey.

Governor Wilson held on to his state office until four days before his departure for Washington in order to finish his New Jersey work. During his lame-duck days he induced the legislature to adopt the so-called Seven Sisters Acts of 1913, seven laws that severely limited the privileges of corporations in New Jersey. These forbade holding companies, curtailed interlocking directorates, and provided for revocation of charters for infractions of the laws.

The Seven Sisters Acts came far too late to aid New Jersey. By 1913, other states, envious of New Jersey's success in attracting new corporations (and thus gaining ratables), had liberalized charter laws. The net affect of the Wilson-backed legislations was to drive the lucrative trust business into other states imitating previous New Jersey's open-armed welcome. All seven laws were repealed by 1920.

RETURN OF THE BOSSES

Reformers were in full sway as Wilson headed for Washington. It was an era brighter for the average citizen, particularly those in industrialized states. For a time, too, it seemed that the bosses had been routed.

But they had not been; they had simply become smarter. In a few cases there were new faces in their ranks. A young Jersey City Democrat named Frank Hague began fastening a steel vise on Hudson County, where Republican progressivism had first reared its head. It is interesting to speculate on how solidly Republican Hudson County might be today if GOP bosses had backed Republican reformers Mark Fagan and George Record in 1907. Democrats might never have risen by the banks of the Hudson. Hague's start also rested ironically on the Wilson-inspired Walsh Act, which permitted municipalities to adopt the commission form of government. Hague ran in the commission elections, won, and started immediately to build an unmatched political empire.

Bosses were back in power by 1915, and now their chief concern was to keep women from winning the right to vote. This threat to bossism had been growing for years, and when it threatened to flower in 1915 in a constitutional amendment, bosses went to work in bipartisan unity.

James Nugent of Newark, ranking Democratic boss, summoned all bosses—of both parties—to a meeting in Asbury Park in May, 1915, to warn them of the evils that ensued when women went to the polls. The bosses, Republican and Democratic alike, circulated word that the proposed amendment must be defeated. Votes were bought openly (the going rate in Newark was "five dimes for votes against suffrage"). Nugent issued an open letter on election eve alleging that an "exhaustive study" (his) showed that whenever females voted, "freak laws" came into being. That man who stood staunchly against such evident threat concluded:

> New Jersey citizens through all history have stood for fidelity on contracts, the preservation of personal and property rights, unquestioned integrity of the courts, stability of government and above all, the purity, privacy and loving unity of the home.

Keep the women out of polling places, Nugent pleaded, and all will be well. Some fervent antisuffrage editors must have choked over that and it is likely that even some of the "five dimes for a vote" takers chuckled. But they all backed Jim Nugent.

The women campaigned valiantly for the constitutional amendment. They held 2000 meetings, traveled thousands of miles, wrote stacks of letters, and faced jeering crowds in the streets. But they saw once-friendly newspaper editors turn their columns into publicity media for the antisuffragists and they couldn't match the dollars, or dimes, of the bosses. On October 19, they lost their bid in an all-male election, 184,000 to 133,000, and politicians hailed the "wisdom of the electorate."

Yet, in an era that had seen much social and political evil swept away or lessened in three decades, women's suffrage would come to New Jersey, as it did in 1920. It was as logical as child-labor laws, control of utilities, welfare legislation, improved education, and all other things dear to leaders of the progressive movement. This new feeling of concern for government by the people couldn't stop short of votes for all.

Woodrow Wilson moved from the Princeton University campus to the State House and finally to the White House to inaugurate a vibrant twentieth century. New Jersey became a supply shop, a storage depot, and a port of embarkation in two world wars. It fought the powers of prohibition and the crippling effects of depression, and strengthened itself as one of America's prime industrial areas. Yet, surprisingly to visitors, the "good life" lingers—on the wide beaches, on the many farms, and in the upstate hills. Millions travel its highways and turnpikes; in the twentieth century, as in the seventeenth, New Jersey is the main road.

Woodrow Wilson, Virginia-born president of Princeton University, reviewed the State Guard on horseback after he became governor in 1910.

When he ran for President of the United States in 1912 and 1916, he voted as usual at his Princeton polling place.

Newark, foremost among the state's industrial centers, led the state in making war materiel, and its girls proudly marched to show their support.

Between wars, prohibition agents smashed kegs of illicit beer in the Newark meadows.

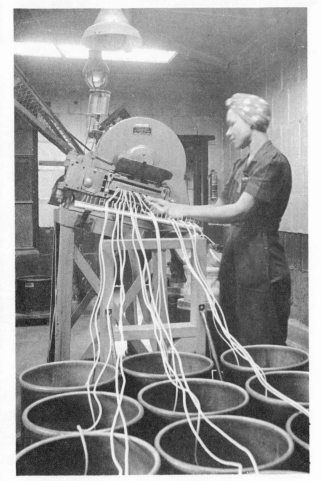

ABOVE, *World War II saw the state again making munitions, led by Picatinny Arsenal near Dover.* BELOW, *Picatinny workers made everything from giant shells to mile after mile of spaghettilike strands of smokeless powder.*

Signs of the twentieth century:
sprawling modern refinery at Paulsboro in Gloucester County, ABOVE,
shows the industrial emergence of
southern New Jersey, while micro-
wave instruments at Nutley, BELOW,
hint at the state's leading role in today's research complex.

Solitude or turmoil: the Jersey Shore offers both. ABOVE, old Barnegat lighthouse towers over Long Beach Island and Barnegat Bay as one of the seashore's chief photographic targets. BELOW, Atlantic City, famed the world round, offers the excitement of a genuine city overlooking the rolling ocean.

Unusual view shows the many new buildings in an evolving Newark, all of them surrounding the eighteenth-century tower of Trinity Church.

In contrast, the fields of Cumberland County stretch far beyond the freezing plant of Seabrook Farms, said to be the largest such operation in the world.

The view west from Staten Island reveals the densely settled metropolitan area near New York. In the middle foreground is Bayonne, between two strips of water. Westward are the port area of Elizabeth and Newark, Newark Airport, and the fully settled suburbs that roll to the hills.

Point of exit, point of entrance: Lincoln Tunnel at Weehawken. Each day hundreds of thousands of vehicles enter these portals to reach New York, or exit to begin the roll across New Jersey.

20

The Yanks Are Coming

An obscure Serb killed the Austrian crown prince and his wife in a town called Sarajevo in Bosnia on June 18, 1914, and struck a flame that would die only after nearly eight million gave their lives. Mighty Austria-Hungary immediately declared war on tiny Serbia, and within six days Germany declared war on Russia and France. Great Britain entered on the side of Russia and France.

World War I had begun, and, for the moment the United States saw it as something far away. Woodrow Wilson, up from the State House at Trenton to the White House in Washington, calmly called for Americans to be "impartial in thought as well as in action." Theodore Roosevelt, for once mild, said: "We must remain entirely neutral." It was easy to believe predictions for a short war, three months at the most.

THE WAR "GAME"

Most German-Americans thrilled to the Fatherland's move; a German-language newspaper in Hudson County set a mood with a big black headline that, translated, read, ALL GERMAN HEARTS BEAT HIGHER TO-DAY. Saloonkeepers in Newark, Hoboken, and Hudson County towns on the ridge of the Palisades boasted of the Kaiser's early triumphs. They backed their feelings with money, too; the Steneck Trust Company in Hoboken announced a spirited buying of German War Loan bonds. German influences were strong in many towns and villages; in Egg Harbor City, 80 per cent of the residents still spoke German.

It seemed like an exciting, distant game, and a prosperous one for a time. War meant jobs, higher wages, and good profits.

Most Americans tended to side lukewarmly with the Allies from the start. The fact that England and France quickly turned to New Jersey for quantities of war material boosted their popularity. The only lack of enthusiasm for the booming economy was among farmers, who expressed alarm when farm wages rose from fifteen cents to twenty-five cents per hour in 1915 (and rose all the way to five dollars per day in 1918).

Industry retooled for war. The Singer Sewing Machine Company in Elizabeth started making intricate recoil mechanisms for French cannon. Textile plants in Passaic County turned out woolens for Allied blankets and uniforms. Oil refineries in Bayonne and Bayway worked to float the Allies to victory "on a sea of oil." Middlesex County's copper refineries stepped up production. Newark's multitude of factories hummed with war work. New chemical plants were founded to make up for the threatened cutoff of German supplies.

Allied agents searched the northern hillsides and the southern vegetable patches for horses and mules, for their armies still functioned on genuine horsepower. Farmers sold willingly: prices upwards of $250 for an animal were too good to resist. Then came spring plowing time in 1915 and the farmers found themselves in turn at the mercy of horse traders from the West. They blamed the Allies for the high horse prices, forgetting how wonderful they had seemed the previous fall.

Nearly all of the Jersey ponies and mules trotted off the farms and up to the French Remount on the old Ho-Ho-Kus race track. There they joined animals from all over the land being unloaded daily at Nagle's Coal Yard. Quiet old Ho-Ho-Kus thrilled to the gallant French officers in town to dicker for the steeds. War was romantic, rewarding—and remote.

Feeding the War Machine

The state's vaunted powder-making know-how, built up since the 1870s, quickly attracted Allied buyers after England, Russia, and France entered the war. New Jersey munitions makers took rather a broad interpretation of Wilson's injunction to remain impartial. Their "neutrality" favored England, Russia, and France, largely because these nations at first controlled the shipping lanes.

Explosives manufacture boomed, and before the ringing bells tolled the new year of 1915, agents of the Russian Czarist government were testing shells at a new range at Lakehurst. Plants at Kenvil, Haskell, Pompton Lakes, and Parlin, all with long histories of explosives pioneering, stepped up production. Du Pont opened a giant new powder plant in the marshes of Carney's Point in Salem County. Explosives began to roll from new factories in Kingsland and Morgan and from an installation named Black Tom in Jersey City. Picatinny Arsenal at Dover expanded its lines to produce everything from .30-caliber bullets to sixteen-inch shells. Seldom has so much powder and shell making been jammed into such a limited region as in New Jersey during World War I.

Du Pont expanded most of all. At the end of 1916, its facilities in Haskell, Pompton Lakes, Parlin, Carney's Point, and Repaupo had more than tripled the company's production at the beginning of the war.

This pell-mell dash to feed Europe's war machine had its disasters, large and small.

There were small blasts at Haskell, at Pompton Lakes, and at Repaupo as warnings of things to come, but the first intimate brush with the horrors of war came for New Jersey on July 30, 1916, when disaster struck the Black Tom powder depot in Jersey City. Smashed clocks in the city's Journal Square established 2:08 A.M. as the hour and minute that Black Tom changed from an economic asset to a thing of terror. Fear gripped the entire metropolitan area while flaming barges filled with exploding shells floated loose in New York Harbor. Shrapnel from the Black Tom yard peppered the Statue of Liberty and the lower Hudson County shoreline. Chain-reaction explosions split the night and by morning nearly $40,000,000 damage had been done over a twenty-five-mile radius.

Only three persons died in that January disaster, despite the fact that the plant sat amid the most densely populated section of America.

Less than six months later there was a further calamity. This time a "deep-seated roar" at the Canadian Car & Foundry Company explosives plant threatened to wipe Lyndhurst off the map. Lyndhurst residents in 1915 had vigorously opposed construction of munitions plant to turn out $83,000,000 in shrapnel and shells for Russia, but the Canadian company nevertheless gained permission to erect its plant in Lyndhurst's Kingsland section on the edge of the meadows. The company attempted to calm the fear of the townspeople by taking out a $100,000 insurance policy. It proved to be a paltry gesture.

On January 11, 1917, a small fire broke out in Building 30 in the Kingsland marshes. Employees fled in screaming panic, fighting one another in an effort to reach the gates. A newspaper account told of mobs racing toward a barbed-wire fence surrounding the plant: "through this, though it tore them cruelly, they plunged, like so many cattle in a stampede." Minutes later, the first blast detonated. A half million exploding shells cannonaded the area for the next twelve hours, causing $16,750,000 in damage. Miraculously, there were no fatalities, but the Black Tom and Kingsland horrors gave evidence that war was not all a matter of good wages.

Although many suspected the Black Tom and Kingsland blasts were the work of German saboteurs, four weeks after the Black Tom explosion the courts found four officials of the Jersey City plant guilty of "criminal and gross negligence." A generation later, on the eve of another war, the German-American Mixed Claims Commission in 1939 found Germany guilty of both the Black Tom and Kingsland blasts.

Suspicion of sabotage in the two New Jersey explosions helped inch United States sentiment closer to war, but intervention had been inevitable since the German *Unterseeboot* 20 sank the unprotected *Lusitania* on May 7, 1915, taking 1198 lives. Revulsion was in no way lessened when German sympathizers pointed out that Germany *had* taken an ad in *The New York Times* to warn passengers not to take the *Lusitania*.

President Wilson urged calm. Three days after the *Lusitania* sinking he termed the United States "too proud to fight," and he campaigned for re-election in 1916 on the slogan "He kept us out of war." Wilson ran quietly for a second term, seldom venturing from the broad porch of Shadow Lawn, his summer White House in West Long Branch. He ignored furious voices, particularly that of Theodore Roosevelt, who called for action against Germany. The President campaigned as he saw fit, not sure himself of the mood of the nation.

Wilson went to bed at Shadow Lawn on election night believing that Charles Evans Hughes had defeated him. Three days after the election the issue was resolved; the ex-Princeton professor had won by the slim margin of 277 electoral votes to 254—scarcely a mandate either to fight or to stay neutral. Germany made the next move by arrogantly announcing unrestricted submarine warfare in February, 1917, and soon afterward it was learned Germany had promised Mexico to help reconquer her lost territory in Texas, New Mexico and Arizona if America entered the war. Wilson's patience was at an end.

The *Lusitania*, Black Tom, Kingsland, and unrestricted submarine warfare had stirred New Jersey. Even the farm village papers turned from church socials and agricultural hints to war reports. Disclosure of a powerful German radio station at Tuckerton in Ocean County enraged the public, who readily believed the unverified story that the 840-foot-tall radio tower had aided in the *Lusitania* sinking.

THE "GAME" OVER

When Congress declared war on April 6, 1917, New Jersey joined the nation in a wild wave of enthusiasm for the conflict.

Unfortunately, America was ready only in spirit. The fervor of the nation far transcended its ability to wage war. Everything had to be done: an army raised, leaders found, training camps established, supplies gathered, ships built, enemy agents controlled.

This war seemed the event that New Jersey had been moving toward in the nearly 300 years since the first Dutch had crossed the Hudson River to the province. New Jersey's capable, dedicated Woodrow Wilson sat in the White House. The railroads of America converged on the Hudson County piers. The state's shops and mills had the skills for mass production, and virtually all the explosives experience in the land was here. It appeared New Jersey's destiny was to be a vast arsenal of war, a training ground, a shipping point.

It had been a long time between wars. Nearly four months elapsed after the declaration of war before New Jersey sent off its first soldiers.

National Guardsmen were America's only reservoir of armed strength beyond the pitifully small regular army, and Guard experience beyond the parade ground and summer camp was slight. The war with Spain had scarcely stirred New Jersey in 1898, although the 5501 National Guard volunteers who fought in Cuba, the Philippines and in the mud of New Jersey camps saw it as a major effort (as did the families of the forty men who had died). Mexican border incidents in the summer of 1916 had brought the National Guard into brief but insignificant action again. Men returned with deeply tanned skins but precious little in the way of useful training.

The unconcealed scorn of the Regular Army for Guardsmen who served along the Mexican border caused Guard ranks to fall well below the authorized strength of 4288. The rush toward war with Germany reversed that trend and on July 25, 1917, New Jersey sent 9285 National Guard troops to maneuvers at Sea Girt.

Villages and towns turned out in the July heat to give their young Guardsmen an earnest farewell. Camden's contingent left their armory singing "Auld Lang Syne," but before they even reached the railroad station many had fallen victim to the heat and unaccustomed exercise and had to be carried to the trains. Once aboard all became undaunted soldiers; grinning faces shone above a legend chalked on the departing cars: "Battery B off to give the Kaiser hell!" Their immediate destination was Sea Girt, but they felt themselves ready for Berlin. Behind, on the platform, their women wept.

Jerseymen flocked to 106 local draft boards on opening day, June 5. Trouble had been expected throughout the nation, for officials remembered the Civil War draft riots, but none developed. On the contrary, men between the ages of twenty-one and thirty-one literally rushed to get in line. Some stood three hours waiting for the doors to open.

Three hundred thousand young Jerseymen registered that first day. They came out of the mines of Dover and Franklin. They came off the dairy farms, the vegetable farms, the potato fields. They left their bank desks and factory lathes in the cities between Jersey City and Camden. They came from the shad fisheries of the Delaware, the oyster fleet at Bivalve, the trawlers of Point Pleasant and Long Beach Island, the clay pits of Middlesex. Never before had young men been so eager to offer themselves for a military draft. Eventually, 762,000 registered from New Jersey and 72,946 found their way into uniform.

By September, cheered by pretty girls and orating politicians, the first

of the nation's drafted men headed for camps. Farmhands rubbed
shoulders with bank officials in a truly democratic army. The men were in
hand, or at least in sight. Where to train them, how to ship them? Again,
New Jersey provided many answers.

An army of hastily recruited carpenters, plumbers, electricians (and
many a farmer-turned-carpenter in view of the four-dollar-a-day wages)
constructed military camps: Dix, in the forests of Burlington; Wissahickon, within sight of Cape May town; Merritt, at Cresskill; Vail, at
Little Silver; and several others. By war's end New Jersey had sixteen
military establishments, most of them more miracles of haste than
monuments to good architecture.

Camp Dix: The Lost Woodland

Camp Dix grew from a woodland, starting in May, 1917, when the
property was acquired, to a training area capable of handling 70,000
men. Workers assembled 200-men barracks in ten hours, a fact never
doubted by the men who lived in the crude, drafty, yellow-pine quarters.
Within a year Camp Dix had 1600 buildings. Stables housed 7000 horses
and mules. Thousands of soldiers swarmed over the 6800 acres, learning
to shoot and to crawl under barbed wire by day, and dancing and
laughing away the lonely nights in social "huts" built by the Red Cross,
the YMCA, and the Knights of Columbus.

Outside the military reservation, in Wrightstown and other villages,
the sleepy Burlington County countryside was invaded by entrepreneurs
eager to trade their services and goods for the pay of soldiers.

Wrightstown in May, 1917, had forty-two dwellings, a seldom-fre-
quented hotel, a gristmill, two general stores, three blacksmith shops,
a barbershop, a hay press, and 250 residents. By December, thousands
of Camp Dix soldiers stalked its crowded streets seeking amusement.
Nearby Pointville, still getting its water from a village pump, catered to
demands for hot dogs, ice cream, and other amusements ("not all innocent," one soldier wrote).

Relatives and friends arrived from across the country to visit their
soldiers at Dix. The local people turned host, offering accommodations
complete with outside privies shared by many. Alarmed, the State
Department of Health set up a controlled five-mile zone completely
encircling the camp and enforced relatively rigid health rules in ten
towns and a score of villages.

Across state in Cape May, the Camp Wissahickon Naval Training
Barracks became the major source of armed guards for merchant ships,
troop carriers, and submarine chasers berthed in nearby Cold Springs
Harbor. Often 15,000 men crowded the base. Up the coast, artillerymen
kept vigil on Sandy Hook, and Signal Corps units trained at Camp Vail

on the old Monmouth Park race track. Three airships caused a Monmouth County sensation when "flying cowboys" flew the planes in from Kelly Field, Texas, for communications drills at Camp Vail in the spring of 1918. But the most-used and least-remembered New Jersey installation was Camp Merritt at Cresskill, completed in October, 1917, as an embarkation camp.

Merritt was the last stop this side of the Hoboken docks for briefings, equipment checks, and sick calls. On any given day as many as 40,000 men would be in the Bergen County barracks. Next morning nearly all might be gone. The young ladies of Bergen came to dance but there really was no reason to get chummy. These Merritt dancers were scheduled for France, and soon.

Nearly 600,000 men left Camp Merritt for overseas duty (and another half million passed through on the way home after the Armistice). As they rolled away from Cresskill the somber men whispered the camp slogan, "Hoboken, here we come."

THE WAR AND HOBOKEN

Hoboken, most "German" of all New Jersey cities, came under government control within hours after the United States declaration of war. Secret Service men swept in on April 6, arrested known German agents and seized the North German Lloyd and Hamburg American docks and vessels. The German vessels, including the proud *Vaterland,* were seen as the heart of a flotilla to carry the Yanks to Europe. German crews had other ideas; their sabotage in the engine rooms kept the ships at dockside until June.

Hoboken remained the center of ship movements for the duration: all transports on the East Coast (except those at Newport News, Virginia) were controlled from the Hudson city. Forty per cent of all soldiers sent to Europe went through Hoboken.

Military control never relaxed in Hoboken until peace had been signed. Soldiers guarded the piers, enforced saloon closings, patrolled the city streets to keep an eye on German sympathizers. Hoboken became a city of marching, of sailings, of tears, of love. Chaplains performed as many as forty marriages a day.

The first ships to depart Hoboken were fourteen vessels that left on June 14. Aboard were 11,991 Regular Army officers and men, a few nurses and 103 "casual civilians." The scene was described in a memoir, "With the Army in Hoboken":

> Along River Street, where the old bock beer signs of the German occupation still marked the Deutsch gardens and Kursaals, tramped the men of San Antonio and Rio Grande. So silently and efficiently was the work

done that few of the millions across the water knew that the eastward tide of American soldiers had begun.

There was none of the glamour and glory of war in their going. No crowds lined the Battery, no bands or citizen committees sped them on their way. Silently the big transports were warped out of their docks and silently they put to sea. Perhaps along the Staten Island shore commuters wondered as the big gray ships slipped through The Narrows to the sea. Perhaps next morning the off-shore fishing boats drew up their nets to watch the great convoy with attending destroyers come over the western rim of the sea.

But back in the city none knew of their going. The six millions in New York little guessed that the job of breaking the Kaiser's Army had begun in Hoboken.

Simultaneously, the job had begun elsewhere—on the farms, in the factories, in the shipyards, and in hundreds of thousands of homes.

Everyone Joins the Big Push

Patriotism ran high. New Jerseyans passionately joined fellow Americans in collecting for Liberty Loan Drives and the Red Cross. Some spoke before patriotic gatherings, others led community sings to lift morale. Week after week villagers marched in the streets—to boost fund drives and Red Cross campaigns and to say good-by to troops. Those left behind sewed bandages, canned fruits and vegetables, collected "smokes" for the "boys," entertained at camps, and conscientiously tried to follow the words of the song that admonished them to "Keep the Home Fires Burning."

Organizations sprang into action. Some had been long established, such as the Red Cross, Knights of Columbus, YMCA, and Salvation Army. Some were of short duration, "The Peach Stone Savers" (who gathered peach stones for use in gas masks) and the "Stenographers for Uncle Sam" being classic examples.

The Woman's Land Army of America sought to fight the Hun by planting seed and pulling weeds. No glory, no uniforms, no singing: just work. The New Jersey Department of Agriculture in its 1917 annual report said the Land Army had done "good pioneering work, demonstrating the value of girls" (on farms, presumably). The report admitted, on the other hand, that practical farmers doubted the value of the Land Army.

By the summer of 1917, 5000 high school boys had joined the Junior Industrial Army of New Jersey to work on farms. Attractions included the right to leave school early in the spring without loss of credit and a summer on the farm at fifteen to thirty dollars a month, plus board.

Younger boys and girls helped, too, being among the best of "Peach

Stone Savers" and collectors of bits of coal in ash piles. Grammar school boys and girls planted home gardens, and during the summers of 1917 and 1918 the youngsters at the Essex County Park playgrounds gave up basket weaving and ball playing to make simple articles for the Red Cross. Their ball playing would have been limited anyway, for the Essex County Park Commission in 1918 plowed up the park lawns in Belleville and Caldwell and planted corn.

Misguided Patriots

There were those, too, who displayed their patriotism in other ways. These self-appointed and nonuniformed guardians of America hunted down "spies" or accosted young men on the streets and accused them of draft-dodging. In July, 1918, Hoboken witch hunters conducted a "study" of "the Huns entrenched in City Hall," but another and less impassioned check revealed that Mayor Patrick R. Griffin's staff was predominently Irish. Amid the tension, Mayor Griffin found his own "statistics" that enabled him to proclaim on August 12 that the city was "30 per cent more American than a year ago."

Restaurants stopped offering sauerkraut; serving instead something that tasted the same but went under the name of Liberty cabbage. Hamburger, weiner, and wurst were dropped from menus, although their replacements looked and tasted the same under different labels. Newark changed Hamburg Place to Wilson Avenue, and the High Bridge Imperial Band called itself the High Bridge Liberty Band (with no noticeable change in its music).

In western Morris County, German Valley became Long Valley and the people of New Germantown in Hunterdon County poured out in plebiscite to change the town name to Oldwick. Only one brave citizen voted to keep the old name that had historic meaning. That single, defiant vote took courage. Only weeks before, a pathetic old tramp had set fire to a few oat stacks in a nearby Hunterdon County field and received a stiff, four-year prison sentence. He was a Slav; ergo, a dangerous saboteur in the minds of misguided "patriots."

Shells, Ships, and Planes

Fortunately, most people were far too busy and sensible to bother with such nonsense. They worked instead, and there was work aplenty.

The New Jersey plants hummed. Middlesex County refined more than half the copper turned out in the United States. Thousands of factories made blankets, tents, sweaters, uniforms, tools, harness, machines, electrical goods, chemicals, automobiles, wire, shoes, machine parts, and signaling equipment. But above all, New Jersey made ammunition and ships.

Calls from England, France, and Russia had prepared the powder and shell makers long before America officially joined the Allies. Of fourteen plants in the country in 1918, with a daily loading capacity of 284,000 shells, New Jersey had six, with a daily capacity of 216,000 shells. Thus the state had 75 per cent of the nation's shell-loading manufacture, most of it in Middlesex County. One exception was Bethlehem Steel Company's loading operation on the edge of Mays Landing, where more than 6500 men worked (the shells were tested off the beach just north of Cape May town). Du Pont and the Hercules Company boosted their smokeless powder output more than 1500 times over the 1914 level of production.

Shipbuilding increased astonishingly on both sides of the state.

New York Shipbuilding Company, established in 1899 at Camden, had the only big operation in the state before the war. The firm had surprised the Navy early in the century by finishing the cruiser *Washington* ten days ahead of schedule, an unheard of feat for a shipyard. Other orders followed: the Navy asked for seven battleships in pre-World War I days, plus destroyers, cruisers, and transports. "New York Ship," as it has always been known, took the war production in stride. The Navy ordered thirty destroyers betweeen July and December, 1917, but the yard's crowning achievement was building of sixteen transports, all over 500 feet in length, for the nation's "bridge of ships."

The marshlands of Kearny and Newark were converted to feverish emergency shipbuilding activity, and the Bethlehem Steel Corporation took over an old Elizabethport yard in 1917 to turn out more than thirty cargo ships, tankers, and oceangoing tugs. These shipbuilders on Newark Bay were blessed with a large labor market, excellent rail facilities to bring in raw materials, and deep-draught water for floating completed hulls.

Submarine Boat Company of Port Newark owed its success to Henry R. Sutphen's belief that giant ships could be fabricated, a notion that met with much criticism. The Newark yard's performance stilled the critics; its 118 freighters, started in 1918, were completed in January, 1920, a full year before the Hog Island Yard near Philadelphia finished its much publicized 122 freighters. Thanks to Submarine Boat Company, Newark led American cities in shipbuilding tonnage in 1919. That year New Jersey also led the nation in shipbuilding value, with $238,015,000 to Pennsylvania's $237,325,000.

Eastward in Kearny, Federal Shipbuilding Company, a U. S. Steel Corporation subsidiary, built an extensive permanent plant in contrast with the temporary nature of both the Port Newark and Hog Island facilities. Federal contributed thirty steel freighters to the emergency program, giving New Jersey three of the nation's top ten yards (Federal, Submarine Boat, and New York Ship).

Overseas, daring young men soared aloft in crude little planes to engage in a new type of aerial warfare. It didn't take New Jersey contractors long to learn to make airplanes; after all, they were scarcely more than automobile engines with wings.

Four builders in the state took advantage of the demand for flying machines. First of these was Inglis M. Uppercu, who in 1914 began taking orders for allied seaplanes at his Aeromarine Plane & Motor Corporation in Keyport. Soon Aeromarine covered sixty-six acres, used sixteen buildings to make hydroplane trainers and a "flying boat" for the Navy.

Standard Aero Company of Plainfield and Linden, backed by the Japanese Mitsui interests, had seventy-five people on its first payroll at Plainfield in 1916 and grew beyond the wildest dreams of both its Oriental and American backers. Standard enlarged its Plainfield plant, then expanded into the old Stevenson Car Works in Linden and by war's end employed 6500 people in the making of seventeen different kinds of aircraft, including the Italian Caproni and the English Handley-Page. Standard could finish a Handley-Page in ninety days and the company made 1033 planes before the Armistice ended its boom.

Desperately needed airplane engines caused Wright-Martin Aircraft Corporation and the Simplex Automobile Company of New Brunswick to merge in 1916 to build 450 of the famed eight-cylinder, 140-horsepower Hispano-Suiza (Spanish-Swiss) engines. Orders totaling $2,000,-000 in 1917 grew to $50,000,000 by October, 1918. When peace came, Wright-Martin was envisioning making 1000 engines a day.

Severance of relations with Germany had forced this nation into chemicals manufacture, and several small concerns began an industry that in time would grow to be New Jersey's biggest.

No state missed German organic chemicals more than New Jersey. Passaic County's textile industry needed German dyes. Production of TNT by Du Pont and Hercules in New Jersey faced collapse because of the critical shortage of toluene. The shortage of coal tar medicines became acute. Either this nation must develop its own chemicals or be perilously near disaster. Chemists learned as they went along. Twenty-three new chemicals firms started operations in New Jersey in 1917, every one of them using German textbooks as their guide.

A SHORTAGE OF HOUSING

Industry's meteoric growth changed the face of New Jersey. Factories rose in open fields, in marshlands, in wood lots by the rivers. Pressures unheard of before the war began to hit city and county alike.

Workers seeking wartime prosperity spilled into the cities. In the Newark area, the Submarine Boat Company alone employed 13,000 men in a newly founded shipyard. The city attracted between 50,000 and 75,000 new residents, causing serious complications in housing, health, transportation, amusement, and crime. Apartments became so scarce that crowds gathered outside newspaper offices every day to get classified-ad sections. House seekers rode trolleys to outlying sections, jostling one another to get off first in the race for an accommodation, like so many mechanized homesteaders.

Camden's housing troubles increased with the influx of 19,000 workers at the New York Shipyard, plus 6500 others at a new shipyard across the creek in Gloucester. The government fashioned hundreds of rapidly built, rickety homes at Noreg Village in Gloucester and at Yorkship Village in Camden to house the ship workers and their families.

Even more telling was the impact of new workers in the rural areas. The consequences of two plants built in the farmlands of Atlantic and Salem counties were most severe.

The first of these, a shell-loading plant outside Mays Landing, expanded beyond anything ever imagined in those Atlantic County hinterlands. Mays Landing's population had been below 2000 until the construction of Bethlehem Steel Company's new plant. By war's end the facility employed 6500 persons, and triple that number of dependents sought living quarters in the surrounding countryside. A settlement named Belcoville sprang up. Two years after the war, Belcoville was a ghost town, returning to the pine wilderness from which it had sprung.

Du Pont's new smokeless powder plant at Carney's Point created a similar upheaval. By 1916, the company's Salem County holdings had spread southward to the Deepwater Canal, and by 1918, 20,000 workers milled through the giant plant. Penns Grove zoomed in population from 2000 to 10,000 and the overflow spilled into the towns of Pennsville, Woodstown, and Salem, creating conditions of noise and conflict that reminded many of the old Klondike camp tales. Crime jumped to disturbing proportions, and for miles around farms and little industries suffered cruelly as men left plows and anvils to head for the Du Pont bonanza.

LUXURIES . . . AND PRIVATIONS

Money was plentiful. Paterson's mills were busy supplying silk shirts to workers who before the war had been lucky to own even a "Sunday shirt."

With the luxuries, however, came the suffering and privation of war, some of it occasioned by battlefield news, but much of it also brought on by shortages in everything from sugar to coal, from razor blades to wheat.

The winter of 1917–18 was especially harsh. Howling winds swept snow across the state (twenty days of snow in January alone), forcing temperatures down below freezing most of the winter and even down to thirteen degrees below zero in Essex County. Compounding the freezing weather was an unparalleled shortage of coal, so serious that people begged, borrowed, or stole the precious fuel. Starting on January 21, 1918, every Monday was designated as "heatless"; this was followed by "lightless" nights to conserve fuel.

Often coal cars reached Camden or Phillipsburg nearly empty, their cargoes pilfered at Pennsylvania stops. Most New Jersey towns and cities set up depots where coal could be purchased a bushel at a time, if the buyer could show a ration card. Families huddled together in one room to save heat.

Sugar also was short and so was meat. People grew increasingly weary of "sweetless, heatless, wheatless, and meatless" days as the excitement of April, 1917, gave way to the ugly reality of war. Off the coast booming guns could be heard, telling of submarine warfare within earshot of American soil. Newspapers carried the lists of dead and wounded along with reports of battles won. The docks at Hoboken began to receive the caskets of the fallen.

The Kaiser's armies gradually retreated, in the Argonne Forest, along the Meuse River, at St. Mihiel, at Belleau Woods, at Armentières. Battle accounts did not detail the doings of New Jersey's troops, except where special dispatches or letters to the newspapers identified state individuals, for the state's units had been incorporated into larger units. The New Jersey National Guardsmen who went off in July, 1917, for example, merged into the celebrated "Blue and Gray" 29th Division. New Jersey's Selective Service draftees in 1917 became part of the noted 78th Division. Other New Jersey soldiers were spread through a score of fighting units, on land and sea.

By summer's end in 1918 it was clear the war would soon be over. Only a startling reversal on the battlefield could save the German cause. Even the farmers, worried by inflation and irked by the inauguration of Daylight Saving Time, became optimistic.

AT HOME: THE NEW ENEMY

Then, without warning or precedent, a fate worse than bullets befell the world. Influenza struck, insidiously and terrifyingly.

The disease came silently and slowly, touching a home here and there in mid-September, scarcely enough to serve warning. It appeared to subside late in September, and people even joked about the "flu." Then it returned in October with a vengeance. At least 300,000 New Jersey cases were reported in October, November, and December of 1918. The influenza epidemic defies description in brief space. At least 10 per cent of the population was officially reported sick and many thousands more became ill and recovered without notifying doctors. Some fifty-five towns in the state set up emergency hospitals in barns, factories, sheds, or other vacant dwellings. Hundreds of nonresident doctors were summoned to the state, but they could do little in the face of this killer.

The death rate jumped five to six times normal during October. In Newark alone, seventy-nine deaths were reported on one day, October 26. Bodies piled up in cemeteries awaiting burial. At some cemeteries in Newark, the largest and therefore most savagely hit city, teams of horses plowed trenches and the dead were interred in rows.

Seventeen thousand died in the state from the flu or its complications (usually pneumonia)—five times the number lost in battle. The State Department of Health, summing up, said "no city, town or hamlet escaped its ravages; the hillsides of every community are dotted with newly made graves."

The flu struck down young and old alike in a mysterious and incomprehensible manner. By contrast, the explosion that tore apart the Middlesex County town of Morgan on October 5, 1918, could more easily be understood in spite of its tragedy.

The first small blast at the T. A. Gillespie plant in Morgan on a Friday evening was followed by a series of shocks and explosions that erupted through fourteen hours. Everyone in neighboring South Amboy fled, wheeling baby carriages, pulling weeping children, carrying bundles of personal belongings, causing observers to liken them to European refugees fleeing battlefront gunfire.

The detonations broke windows in a twenty-five-to-thirty-mile radius of Morgan; the streets of Perth Amboy and South Amboy were littered with glass. It could have been worse—thousands of tons of TNT lay deep in underground vaults. The flames never reached that awesome source of danger. The toll was bad enough: property damage exceeded $25,000,-000 and about a hundred dead were counted. No exact total of fatalities ever was made, since the first blast destroyed the company records even as it blew many workers into unidentifiable bits.

JOHNNY'S MARCH HOME

The Morgan blast and the flu epidemic brought the dying and the suffering close to home, but victory was in the air as October's bright weather turned into the first chill days of November. The nation awaited the news, and it came, prematurely, on November 7, when newspapers carried banner headlines:

GREATEST WAR IN HISTORY ENDS!

The flash had been cabled by a newspaperman; its authenticity could not be doubted, could it? The spirit of celebration spread like wildfire as civilians heard the news—from newspapers, from telegraph offices, from conductors riding trains into town. Workers left their jobs; teachers and children raced out of schools, housewives abandoned their chores, old and young danced in the streets. War-weary folk marched and countermarched, all through the day and long into the night. Although newspapers announced that the war continued, the wild celebrations merely picked up in intensity. People believed what they most wanted.

"It was a lovely party while it lasted; two such celebrations simply can't happen," a Newark newspaper said on November 8 in summing up the "false Armistice."

That writer was proved wrong in three days. The pandemonium that followed the real Armistice on November 11 made the November 7 fete look like a Sunday-school picnic. The news reached New Jersey at 2:45 A.M. By 5 A.M. city streets were packed, and by 8 A.M. Newark streets were so jammed with celebrants that traffic could not move, and no one cared.

Governor Edge was hunting rabbits in Hunterdon County when he learned of the Armistice. He hastened to Flemington, where a crowd of 10,000 danced in the streets. The governor pushed through the howling mob, mounted the Court House steps and promised that "soon all Jerseymen will be home." That set the crowd to screaming with joy.

Governor Edge estimated that day that 200,000 New Jersey men were under arms. Actually, about 150,000 New Jerseyans served in the armed forces between April 6, 1917 and November 11, 1918. Of this total, 3836 died. Those were the ones for whom lights would dim and voices cease at 11 A.M. on Armistice Days to come.

Happiness ran high for months, buoyed by each returning detachment heading through Hoboken and Camp Merritt before heading for another home-town parade. Wars always end that way, when Johnny comes marching home to those weary of battles. Everyone understood Governor Edge when he said:

"They fought our battles of war for us; now let us fight their battles of peace for them."

Those battles would come—in unemployment, in a tragic falling out between Woodrow Wilson and Congress that doomed hopes of a lasting peace, in Prohibition, and in depression. The high ideals of the war, fought to "make the world safe for democracy," would sink in the quicksand of words that follow any peace.

For the nonce, New Jersey celebrated. It was "over, over there."

21

Safe for Democracy

New Jerseyans joined all America at Philadelphia's Sesquicentennial Exposition of 1926, to commemorate the 150th anniversary of the signing of the Declaration of Independence. For a bit, New Jersey reveled in its own proud Revolutionary War history: the crossing of the Delaware, the bitter winters at Morristown, the Battle of Monmouth. Speeches, parades, essay contests, and newspaper attention made the Revolution live again. Sometimes it seemed much closer in thought than the late war waged to "make the world safe for democracy."

Eight years had slipped past since Armistice Day, 1918. Veterans still marched on Decoration Day or Armistice Day, but their uniforms were too snug at the waist and their hair was flecked with gray.

The world had not been made safe for democracy; Congressional opposition to Woodrow Wilson's hopes for a dynamic League of Nations ensured that. In Europe an Italian named Mussolini and an Austrian named Hitler were making noises, but they appeared harmless.

A New Amendment Is Cheered

Americans enjoyed newfound liberties, only vaguely related to the Declaration of Independence. Prohibition seemed to make liquor more cherished. Women were free—or at least entitled to vote, to smoke, bob their hair, and look as much like John Held, Jr.'s cartoon flappers as their figures and sense of modesty permitted.

"The vote," once only the dream of a tiny band of militant suffragists, had come in 1920—after New Jersey political leaders in bipartisan alignment had dared delay it no longer. Just before 1 A.M. on February 10, 1920, the Assembly voted on whether New Jersey would ratify the Nineteenth Amendment, which said no citizen should be denied the right to vote "on account of sex." But long before Republican David

Young of Morris County ended the roll call (by voting against the amendment), the packed galleries buzzed in awareness that the completed tally would place New Jersey beside twenty-eight other states which already had ratified the amendment. Only eight more states were needed to make the Nineteenth Amendment a law.

Ratification touched off a noisy, unladylike demonstration. Suffragists in the balcony waved purple, white, and gold banners and pummeled one another on the backs. Speaker Glover pounded his gavel, more in tradition than in any expectation of quieting the outburst. This moment had been too long coming.

Amid the pandemonium Mrs. Robert Patterson Finley of Camden County calmly sewed a twenty-ninth gold star on the freedom flag she kept to symbolize the advance of women's rights. Newspapermen dubbed her "The Betsy Ross of Suffrage"; Mrs. Finley gladly accepted the title.

Next morning Democratic Governor Edward I. Edwards expressed pleasure that "one of my first pledges to the people of New Jersey has been carried out."

A New Amendment Is Ignored

The governor worked even harder at keeping the Democrats' major pledge: to make New Jersey "as wet as the Atlantic Ocean." Politicians in both parties ignored the fact that the Eighteenth Amendment—Prohibition—had become law on January 16, 1920. The Republican-dominated legislature eventually became the forty-sixth and last state to ratify Prohibition (Rhode Island and Connecticut refused to adopt a law that they had no intention of enforcing). Ratification achieved, Republicans and Democrats alike openly identified themselves with lawlessness.

Thus, seven score and ten years after the signing of the Declaration of Independence, the nation found itself at the mercy of bootleggers, corrupt courts, and dishonest politicans—worse than anything devised by King George III.

But in the midst of the always cited lawlessness of the Roaring Twenties, the state grew as never before in peacetime.

The population soared from a war-inflated 3,155,900 in 1920 to 4,041,-334 in 1930, giving New Jersey ninth rank nationally, compared to eighteenth in 1890. Industry expanded. By 1926, the state stood sixth nationally in value of its products. Regardless of what people did at night—the state also ranked near the top in number of speakeasies—they worked by day.

By this time the automobile had begun to take over the pathway between New York and Philadelphia. New Jersey was being dubbed "The Corridor State."

The bistate Port of New York Authority, created in 1921 by New York and New Jersey to coordinate the terminal, transportation, and other facilities of commerce in, about, and through the Port of New York, quickly became enamored of automobiles, bridges, and tunnels. True, it dallied for a time with the railroads, seeking voluntary cooperation in the tangled web of tracks in the Hudson County marshlands and waterfront. The railroads, powerful and profit-filled, ignored the Port Authority efforts. Rubber tires, not steel wheels, would be the means on which New Jersey rolled; both ends of the New York-Philadelphia corridor stirred with bridge and tunnel construction.

OVER AND UNDER THE RIVERS

President Calvin Coolidge dedicated the new Delaware River Bridge between Camden and Philadelphia in 1926, in time to afford South Jersey motorists easy access to the Sesquicentennial grounds. The span, longest suspension bridge in the world, was seen as a short cut to South Jersey prosperity.

Property along the shore shot up in price as soon as work began on the bridge. There ensued a "Gold Coast" boom, not as fantastic as Florida's, but widespread enough to cause bitter seaside woe when it collapsed. Brick hotels rose above aging wooden boardinghouses in Asbury Park, Brigantine, and Cape May. Atlantic City saw hotel towers rising along the famous Boardwalk, as owners learned it was cheaper to build upward into the air rather than outward on high-priced land. Everyone waited for the golden stream of customers to roll across the Delaware River Bridge.

It did, for a while. But before 1926 was over, inflated real estate prices along the shore collapsed. Brigantine's speculators were bankrupt. The entire Cape May County beachfront suffered: one piece of property in Sea Isle City, bought for $75,000 early in 1926, sold for $750 within the year. Long before the Wall Street collapse, many parts of the Jersey Shore had their Black Fridays.

The automobile-oriented prosperity rolled on elsewhere, and the twenties became the era of tunnels and bridges. The Holland Tunnel under the Hudson River was built by New York and New Jersey commissions at a cost of $50,000,000 and collected its first fifty-cent automobile toll in 1927. Within a year, 8,744,000 vehicles had used the tunnel, and when the Port of New York Authority acquired it in 1931, more than 12,000,000 half dollars were being poured annually into tunnel toll booths. The silver stream has never stopped.

It was the time of bridges. The Port Authority in 1928 opened both the Goethals Bridge at Elizabeth and Outerbridge Crossing at Perth Amboy to link New Jersey and Staten Island. Three years later, the Authority collected its first tolls on the Bayonne Bridge over the Kill von Kull to Staten Island. Within the state, other bridges were built without Port Authority financing. The Pulaski Skyway rose 145 feet above the Passaic and Hackensack rivers near Newark, giving motorists a fast ride above the soggy, garbage-strewn meadows. The Victory Bridge spanned the Raritan River at Perth Amboy to provide fast, easy access to seaside resorts.

None of the bridges surpassed the George Washington in gracefulness or impact. Curving cables held the 3500-foot-long main span high above the river, joining the Palisades at Fort Lee with the cliffs of upper New York City. Six lanes of traffic scooted across the bridge after its opening in 1931—eight months in advance of schedule and $2,000,000 less than the estimated cost of $60,000,000.

The new river crossings changed the travel patterns of northern New Jersey. In 1926, 13,680,000 vehicles had crossed the Hudson River, every one of them loaded on ferries. Six years later, 28,500,000 vehicles traveled over or under the Hudson. Ferriage stayed high, at 11,600,000 vehicles, but the Holland Tunnel collected 11,400,000 tolls and the George Washington Bridge booths picked up another 5,500,000 half dollars in the same year. Within six years, therefore, 15,000,000 new annual crossings of the Hudson by bridge or tunnel had been added, all accounted for by the new accommodations for automobiles and trucks.

NEW PLANTS LINE NEW HIGHWAYS

Aware that it must improve its internal road system or become a state with fine bridges on either end and chaos between, the legislature in 1926 set out to spend $300,000,000 for a highway network within the state, to be spread over a twelve-year period. Thus a road expansion program begun modestly by Governor Edge in World War I neared fruition. New Jersey by the mid-1930s would enjoy a nation-wide reputation for its good highways.

Predictably, new industry chose to settle in the corridor beside the highways, just as it had previously located beside railroad tracks. Industry had rebounded from a postwar slump that saw New Jersey's industrial output drop more than a billion dollars in the two years from 1919–21. Slowly, the volume had come back, until by 1925 some 8000 plants were producing in excess of $3,500,000,000 annually, almost the volume of the wildly inflated war period.

Petroleum refining at Bayway and Bayonne and copper smelting and refining in Middlesex County together accounted for about 14 per cent of the total 1925 output, making the waterway region from Bayonne to Perth Amboy the state's most prosperous strip. Threading through the region was the brackish Arthur Kill, whose volume of industrial water traffic exceeded tonnage through the Panama Canal. Elsewhere in the state, electrical equipment, silk, chemicals, and machinery were the only other manufacturing categories with high dollar volume. The state was already blessed with industrial diversity, spread through hundreds of commodities, an evidence of good economic health.

Chemicals and silk were of special interest: chemicals because they were on the way up; silk because it was on the way out.

Lessons learned during World War I were paying off for chemicals makers. Almost nonexistent in this country in 1910, chemicals were fifth from the top in state industrial income in 1925. The Du Pont plant at Deepwater, where $43,000,000 had been invested in ten years, was humming. Once-modest chemical plants beside the Passaic and Raritan rivers, along the Kill von Kull, the Arthur Kill, and the Hudson County waterfront were enlarged greatly. Chemicals were big business, and getting bigger.

On the other hand, all was not well by the Great Falls of the Passaic. Paterson had depended heavily on silk for seventy-five years and by 1920, two-thirds of Paterson's families depended on the silkworm. A drop in demand that year threw 30,000 people out of work and cut weekly payrolls by $200,000. Silk was back in favor by 1925, but while other silk makers throughout the East began converting to looms using a new synthetic fiber called rayon, Paterson stood aloof. By 1934, there were 47,000 rayon looms in the United States. Paterson had none. There, in few words, was the story of an industrial suicide.

Paterson had always been a boom-and-bust city. Locomotives in the 1830s had been a boon after the decline of cotton making. Silk was dominant after locomotive manufacture moved elsewhere. Now, as the demise of silk making cast a dark shadow, Paterson found a new source of vigor—airplane engines, transferred to Paterson at the end of World War I when Wright Aeronautical Company found itself rattling around in a New Brunswick factory which had become "twelve sizes too big" after the end of war orders.

Wright received a tremendous boost in 1927 when Charles A. Lindbergh flew his "Spirit of St. Louis" nonstop to Paris in thirty-three hours and thirty minutes. Wright justly credited the 3600-mile hop to more than luck: Lindy had trusted in a Paterson-made Wright "Whirlwind" engine. Demands for Whirlwinds poured into the city, and within a year the company occupied seven times its original space.

THE BOOTLEGGER

Incoming and outgoing governors praised the state's rising economy, but none dared mention the biggest industry of all—bootlegging.

Who knows how many lived off the alcoholic flood? No one kept records, but on the "payroll" could be counted gangsters, their body-guards and their henchmen. There was also the small navy of Jersey Shore fishermen who found cases of scotch a far better haul than a load of cod or porgies. There could be added operators of illicit speakeasies and their bartenders, waiters, hostesses, and cooks. Others profited, too: crooked politicians, cynical judges, bribed policemen, and such specialists as the bridge tenders along the shore who developed an ability for rais-ing bridges for rum-filled boats and lowering them in the face of Coast Guard pursuers.

One bootlegging operation, controlled by a powerful short wave radio station atop the Atlantic Highlands, imported 10,000 illegal cases of liquor a week, valued at between $50 and $100 a case (upwards of $35,000,000 annually). Speakeasy patrons generally received drinks cut by a third, so estimated retail sales of the Atlantic Highlands supply alone totaled more than $100,000,000 a year! Since every inlet, bay, sound, and pier had its operators, the amount of illegal business was staggering, in more ways than one.

With so much at stake, and in the face of widespread cynicism, it is no wonder that lawyers, judges, politicans, and police generally failed to find evidence for convictions in a rash of gangland murders.

Some 325 persons were victims of New Jersey bootleg warfare between 1920 and 1934. The killings were not as spectacular as those in Chicago or New York, but they were nearly as steady. While most of the deceased were gangsters, victims of their profession, some innocent bystanders perished too. A baker in Passaic complained about bootleggers in 1928 and was killed. A caretaker on the Morrow estate in Englewood stumbled onto a liquor hijackers rendezvous in 1929 and was gunned down. Such murder of the innocent was condemned, but the power of the bootlegger was great.

The police seldom arrested the illicit traders. When they did, judges and juries usually listened sympathetically to the well-paid lawyers for the defense.

One Prohibition agent led a raid on the former Oscar Hammerstein house atop the Atlantic Highlands on October 16, 1929, and found a powerful radio station. Sixteen men on the premises denied knowledge of the station and its cellar arsenal of submachine guns, automatic rifles, revolvers, and ammunition. Those apprehended, plus forty-three others, went on trial in June, 1931. None was found guilty. During the trial it often appeared that the Prohibition agents and the Coast Guards-men were on trial rather than the bootleg ring.

Happily, at a time when Prohibition agents across the land often succumbed to bribery, the fifteen head agents who served in New Jersey earned reputations for honesty. But the agents could satisfy no one. Former Assemblyman Adrian G. Chamberlain served fourteen months as head agent in 1924 and 1925, smashing breweries and speakeasies at the rate of fifteen a day (4982 in one year). He resigned under heavy criticism—*from the Anti-Saloon League,* which thought him "lax." National Prohibition Administrator James M. Doran said in 1929, ". . . we regard New Jersey as one of the hardest spots to handle in the entire country."

ARRIVALS AND DEPARTURES

Actually, the times were so dynamic and prosperous that most people weren't aware of the evils of bootleggers. Newcomers crowded into the cities. Downtown Newark, Jersey City, Elizabeth, Trenton, and Camden gained genuine skylines, with Newark skyscrapers climbing as high as twenty-five stories along Broad Street. Stores attracted suburbanites who rode trolleys or autobuses into town.

Newark's leaders gave renewed attention to the swamplands on the eastern edge of the city. The city's seaport, begun in 1915, slowly advanced and, on April 1, 1928, trucks dumped the first load of fill for nearby Newark Airport. Ashes and garbage gradually covered the bogs and smoldering dumps, and commercial planes made 4000 passenger flights from the field in 1929. Two years later, with 120 daily trips in and out of the facility, Newark claimed to be the busiest airport in the world.

The old order changed even as its manifestations lingered. Thomas A. Edison grew more deaf and his shaggy head grew steadily whiter. Civil War veterans at the Soldiers Home in Kearny, or in scores of towns where they lived as private citizens, grew more infirm as their ranks thinned. Spanish-American War veterans lost the quick step of youth. Old landmarks fell to open the way for new highways and skyscrapers. In the forests, giant old chestnut trees, killed by a mysterious blight a decade before, began to turn silvery gray. And across northern New Jersey, the Morris Canal came to a dismal end.

Long-standing discontent with the outmoded canal between Jersey City and Phillipsburg culminated in its official abandonment in 1924. Newark created a trolley line in the canal bed, then made it a subway by paving its top with wide new Raymond Boulevard leading eastward to New York and westward to the suburbs.

Passing of the old canal filled thousands with nostalgia. These included the men who had opened and closed the locks, coaxed the mules along towpaths, and fed the canalers through the years. Many remembered swimming in the canal waters in summer and skating on the long ditch in winter. By 1930 the canal was largely an historical curiosity, its wooden bridges replaced by concrete and its bed occupied by roads or mosquito-breeding pools. At Lake Hopatcong, the old canal property brought another generation the pleasure of a state-owned park, complete with a spouting fountain.

The Delaware & Raritan Canal between New Brunswick and Bordentown died, too, but more slowly. Always more important economically than the Morris Canal, the D.&R. retained a few customers in 1924, although the two remaining "horse captains" along the waterway admitted their days were numbered. No boats passed through the locks in 1933, and in 1934 control passed from the Pennsylvania Railroad to the state. Canal days had ended forever in northern New Jersey.

THE "BACK ROAD" LIFE

Out in the country, north and south of the canals, time seemed to stand still. A life far different from that in the teeming cities was there for the finding. Newspapermen and photographers discovered and depicted a whole new world of people that "big city" readers found charming.

During those 1920s, oxen plodded along the roads in Pequannock and Green Village and blacksmiths hammered yet in scores of towns from High Point to Cape May. Motorists were either charmed or appalled by narrow dirt roads in the north and sandy ruts through the pinelands of the south. News photographers brought back pictures of white courthouses in Cape May and Mt. Holly, of mighty oaks at Salem, Crosswicks, and Basking Ridge, and of Miss America crowned casually at Atlantic City with small crowds watching. Little boys still swam in the Passaic River without benefit of bathing suits.

There were horses aplenty: horses tugging fishing boats off the surf at Long Beach Island; horses bringing milk to Warren and Sussex County depots; horses tied beside village stores in Hunterdon and Morris counties. Relatives and friends came from near and far for huge annual family reunions and big harvest home suppers. Barefooted boys fished blissfully in the Musconetcong River. Babe Ruth hunted and partied with friends in Sussex County. Shy Pinies picked blueberries and cranberries in South Jersey woodlands. Hordes of motorists became stuck on sandy roads as they tried to take in giant air shows at Lakehurst.

Actually, that life, not far removed from the nineteenth century, was only a few steps ahead of the oncoming motorist. More and more auto enthusiasts crowded out to the "country" or down to the shore as the 1920s ended, with the wise traveler putting extra "spares" on the tire rack and a tin of gasoline in the trunk. The tranquil rural world of the 1920s must disappear under the wheels of the automobile.

Behind the pastoral scenes lay rural drudgery—hand plowing, arduous hay gathering, poor schools, meager opportunity. Hundreds of one-room schools served rural needs in 1925, and by 1930 New Jersey still had

128,000 illiterates. Hundreds of villages depended on crossroads stores for everything from felt boots to mackerel in brine, with an evening checker game by the wood stove for "senior citizen" entertainment. Many thousands of families had neither bathtubs nor toilets in the house.

THE CRASH AND ITS IMPACT

Farmers at least lived in a world apart from Wall Street. Hence, when the Stock Market fell in October, 1929, the impact reached the far-out hills and pines less rapidly than the cities. But for the more than 75 per cent of the state's four million people who lived in the urban areas, the depression hit with tragic speed.

The Roaring Twenties, still wet and still corrupt, slipped into the so-called Tough Thirties with 55,000 New Jerseyans already on the relief rolls by December, 1929. Industry slowed down, with durable goods (motors, metals, machines) being hurt first. Lowered demands for copper hit Middlesex County refineries hard. Slack times slowed the Camden shipyards. Newark's diversified industries were not hit simultaneously, but before the fall of 1930 the city's payrolls had been pared drastically.

The depression overwhelmed the shore resorts, where heavy spending for "beautification" in the late 1920s had left budgets badly overextended. In Morris and Somerset's estate areas, relief rolls rose when domestics, small contractors, exclusive shops, and food suppliers felt the effects of collapsing fortunes. Carpenters, plumbers, and other skilled hands found little work. Only petroleum refining and food production weathered the crisis in fair fashion; people would drive and eat, come what may.

New Jersey acted more rapidly than most states to meet the emergency. Bergen in November, 1930, was the first county to hire unemployed men for public work, paying three dollars for a seven-hour day on county roads. Bergen had 5612 men seeking jobs but found funds to hire only 1000. Bayonne, Newark, and Trenton soon after also had "make work" programs.

There is a popular belief that such "made work" began with Franklin Delano Roosevelt's ascendancy to the White House in March, 1933. But the Emergency Relief Administration (ERA), created seventeen months earlier, in President Herbert Hoover's term, had 30,000 Jerseyans on emergency public payrolls. Top wages were paid in five industrial counties, where levels were twenty dollars a week for unskilled workers and twenty-seven dollars for skilled labor. Rural counties could pay eighteen dollars for unskilled and twenty-three dollars for skilled labor.

The economy continued to sag. In 1929 the average person's income in New Jersey was $839 a year; in 1932 it had dipped to $479, and a year later to $433. Thousands of families had no money and no likelihood of earning any. Government relief offered weekly food allowances of a dollar a person, with a maximum of eight dollars per family. Every county, city, village, and crossroads hamlet knew the hardship of depression. Fear haunted nearly every home.

PROGRAMS FOR RECOVERY

The economic collapse was near bottom by the time President Roosevelt was inaugurated. Dozens of New Jersey banks were bankrupt, dozens more were on the brink of failure. The dramatic "Bank Holiday" on the day that Roosevelt took office gave bankers a chance to breathe for a week while uneasy depositors stood in line to withdraw funds. Strangely, when the State Commissioner of Banking and Insurance submitted his report for 1933, his document made no mention of the Bank Holiday, surely the most important fiscal happening of the year—and perhaps of the century.

Per capita income edged up over $500 in 1935, but in 1936 there were still 700,000 Jerseyans on relief rolls. That was slightly misleading, for it included those employed in the numerous federal "alphabet" agencies— ERA, WPA (Works Progress Administration), CCC (Civilian Conservation Camp), NYA (National Youth Administration), and others.

"Relief" included a wide range of things. It included, by way of illustration, ERA junior colleges opened in the fall of 1933 in six towns and cities. Faculty members received fourteen dollars a week and 100 of them, many with advanced degrees, taught 2500 students in the first year. Classes met evenings in high school buildings. Hundreds of students used the courses to gain credits toward transfer to established colleges and universities. Some taxpayer groups protested that this was "boondoggling"; most educators felt the colleges were sound.

More maligned was the WPA. Many, including some newspaper editors, saw the WPA as a worthless gang leaning on shovels and drawing pay for no work. There was some basis for this, but for the 100,000 men and women who went on the WPA payrolls in 1936 the checks were desperately needed. What's more, accomplishments of the WPA workers in New Jersey belie the charge that they did nothing for their checks.

Here are some evidences that those on WPA gangs went to work with a vim:

They demolished the old Newark post office; turned thirty-one acres of swampland at Haddon Heights into a park; reconstructed the old Bradley Beach boardwalk and converted the Delaware & Raritan Canal bed in Trenton into the base for a highway through town. They built Roosevelt Stadium in Jersey City; constructed the Bacharach Home for infantile paralysis victims at Atlantic City, built a Greek amphitheater at

Montclair State College, and constructed an old-age colony in Cumberland County. They repaired Atlantic City's water mains and restored the Grover Cleveland House in Caldwell and built Speedwell Park in Morristown.

They improved county parks, built scores of post offices, dug mosquito ditches in swamplands throughout the state, installed sewer systems in many towns, constructed public schools, and provided sewing rooms where unemployed women made garments for the needy. In seven years the WPA in this state also built more than 6000 miles of streets and highways, constructed 326 new bridges and repaired 324 others, and built or improved more than 4000 culverts under highways.

Unquestionably some WPA workers rested on shovels or sat quietly in offices, but the record is clear that most of them worked—and worked hard.

Jerseyans took the depression in stride, finding that low wages were offset by twenty-five-cent admission to the movies, full-course dinners for fifty cents, gasoline for ten to twelve cents a gallon, and food budgets for newlyweds of six to eight dollars a week. A new car could be bought for $800, a fine apartment leased for thirty-five dollars a month, and a day at the shore or Lake Hopatcong enjoyed for little or nothing.

For a brief time people also learned to enjoy the pleasures close by. State and county parks were used by increasing numbers each year, and thanks to another government agency, the Civilian Conservation Corps, the parks were in top condition, better than ever. Shore communities found automobile "day trippers" increasing, and while the one-day tourists did not spend much, they enjoyed the surf and sand and built up a love for the seaside resorts that would be beneficial in prosperous times to come.

A Man Called Hague

Mayor Frank Hague of Jersey City dominated New Jersey politics in the twenties and thirties, despite the fact that both houses of the legislature were Republican between 1920 and 1940 except in 1932 and 1947. Most editorialists, and most Republicans, ignored the role of the Republican legislatures; Frank Hague was the perennial whipping boy for the low level of government in the state. Hague did not name Republican legislation, but he certainly had a say in electing governors.

Huge Hudson County majorities sent Democrats Edward I. Edwards (Hudson County), George S. Silzer (Middlesex), and A. Harry Moore (Hudson) to the governor's chair between 1920 and 1929. Republican Morgan F. Larson (Middlesex) served from 1929 to 1932, only to be succeeded by Moore. Another Middlesex Republican, Harold G. Hoffman, followed Moore, but Moore was back in the governor's chair for the third time between 1938 and 1941. Why only Hudson and Middlesex Counties could produce governors over a twenty-one-year period is a matter for speculation.

The occupants of the governor's chair or the legislative seats found that Frank Hague always exerted at least subtle influence. There existed what the editorial writers termed "Hague Republicans," a GOP group which seldom used its power to stop the mayor, no matter how much they might piously agree on his faults. Hague's story is long and involved, but clearly his manipulations and "deals" touched Democrats and Republicans alike.

Mayor Hague stood aloof from his detractors, appearing at times almost to be a legend. Jersey City employees knew he was not a legend on "Rice Pudding Day," the annual day for "contributions" to the Democratic machine. As the thirties began to wane, "His Honor" made himself available for the first time to interviewers. *The New Yorker* published a two-part profile and Marquis Childs of the St. Louis *Post-Dispatch* came east to study Hague in depth.

Childs was impressed with the mayor's immaculate attire and the uncanny budgeting ability of a man who never officially made more than $8000 a year, yet paid $7000 annual rent for his apartment in Jersey City, had a $125,000 summer home in Deal, and owned a handsome villa in Miami Beach. He lived like a millionaire on a Jersey City mayor's salary: he traveled only first class, spent big, and dazzled his followers with personal splendor.

Hague boasted that Jersey City "is the most moralest city in America." True, it had no red-light district and no burlesque houses, but gambling was rampant despite the fact the city had one policeman for every 300 residents. Hague was a "boss" in the time-honored traditions, and he outlasted most of the nation's big-city bosses. When federal largess made his Christmas and Thanksgiving baskets and his job handouts look like trifles, Hague's power began to wane. However, the electorate kept him in office from 1917 to 1947.

ONCE MORE: "OVER THERE"

Gradually Hague relinquished the headlines to bosses of another and far more evil kind: the men who had been making noise earlier, Adolf Hitler and Benito Mussolini.

The horrors of Hitler's pogrom against the Jews seeped into the newspapers, yet crowds poured out at Andover in Sussex County to hear an American Fuehrer named Fritz Kuhn harangue German-American Bund picnics with reports of Hitler's greatness. New Jersey's polyglot population had divided opinions in the thirties, but the German-American Bund's fervor for Hitler was soon matched by the bitter feelings of other groups. Slovak colonies cried out in anguish over the fall of Czechoslovakia in 1938 and the state's Poles wept at Hitler's overrunning of their homeland the following year. Hitler's entry into Poland launched World War II and when England and France declared war on Germany in September, 1939, sentiment ran heavily on their side.

War in Europe made America's economy surge. For the second time in three decades, New Jersey became an "Arsenal of Democracy." Once again the explosives makers near Dover and Kenvil added new shifts. Du Pont's several powder plants in the state resumed high output. Iron mines in the hills of Morris County regained activity. Middlesex copper plants received big orders. Railroad freight yards in Hudson County and docksides bustled with activity. Camden's shipyards benefited and petroleum refiners in Hudson and Union counties found Europe's needs demanding. The last vestiges of the depression disappeared in the rush toward war.

The end of 1939 saw 433,000 men and women on industrial payrolls, a twenty-year high. Value of products was only a shade below the inflated figures of 1919. New Jersey's manufacturing diversity showed; it could make radios, automobiles, ships, ammunition, uniforms, chemicals, machines, food, bridges, airplane engines, gasoline, copper, and hundreds of other things. New Jersey could supply the materials of war.

By June, 1940, France, Belgium, and the Netherlands had fallen and Great Britain had barely escaped disaster at Dunkirk. American munitions flowed eastward; adoption of the "lend-lease" policy in 1941 picked up the economic pace even more, but it also brought the war closer to home. Off to camp went the National Guardsmen in the summer of 1940 in a readiness move. Draftees followed in the early days of 1941, to drill with broomsticks in the kind of unpreparedness that shows between wars. Demands for munitions soared. Between June 1940 and June, 1941, the state received 9 per cent of all prime war contracts, trailing only California and New York.

It seemed like old times again: full employment, high wages, parades, humorous anecdotes about the dust and mud of the training camps. Gone were thoughts of bootleggers, who tested America's moral fiber in the twenties, and the depression, which disproved Communist claims that Americans would flock to the Red banner if the economy collapsed.

The year 1941 sped toward its close. Christmas shoppers filled the stores in the first week of December, grasping scarce goods. By Saturday, December 6, almost everything worth buying for a gift was gone. Americans ate hearty Sunday dinners on December 7, then sat down to listen to the football game on the radio or to doze. Abruptly in the midst

of the Sunday afternoon peace, radio announcers began to spout bewildering words: "Pearl Harbor," "Japan," "sneak attack," "emergency,"
"war."

Two decades had slipped by as if they had never existed. It *was* like
old times. War had come again.

22

Bullets, Babies, and Moving Vans

Governor Alfred E. Driscoll weighed his words carefully on the morning of June 12, 1947, after he rose in Rutgers University gymnasium to challenge the most important New Jersey gathering in at least a century. Before him sat delegates to the Constitutional Convention, chosen nine days earlier in a special election. The time had come to relegate the outmoded constitution of 1844 to the scrap heap.

The governor's first remarks set the tone: "It is only fair to say that a great work is expected of you. While this state has lived under the same constitution with but little change for over a century, its people, their life and work have undergone the effects of a Civil War, of two world wars, and of industrial and social revolution since our present constitution was adopted in 1844."

Still fresh in memory was World War II, when state and nation had been turned upside down. More than a half million New Jersey men (and 10,000 women) had gone to war and had seen the world in the process. A half million new jobs had been created in the state within three years. Hundreds of thousands of new people including thousands of "war babies" had come to live here permanently. The pressing need for schools, reservoirs, roads, sewers, colleges, and a new means of taxation, all contributed to problems in a state bursting its seams.

Delegates to the convention needed no reminder of the changes wrought the last five years. Here among them were industrialists who had supplied war material and parents of war veterans. Here, among the graying heads, were a few young veterans of the recent war; Morris County's delegation included Colonel Ruth Cheney Streeter of Morristown, wartime commander of the United States Marine Women's Reserve.

Outside the Rutgers gymnasium, as the balmy June days gave way to the sweltering heat and the shortening tempers of July and August, young veterans swarmed over the Rutgers campus, taking advantage of the GI Bill of Rights to resume or begin college careers. Beside many of them young wives walked and often pushed baby carriages.

Thus, in New Brunswick in the summer of 1947, the challenge of the future was stimulated by remembrance of tumultuous days just past.

THE WIDE FIELD OF VALOR

New Jersey's role in World War II was worth recalling, and its effects were fresh in mind. The total of New Jersey men who had enlisted (214,949) and those who had been drafted (345,552) added up to 560,501 men in uniform. That was about one-eighth of the total population of 1940. For 13,172 of those who had served, life had ended on muddy fields in Europe, in the sands of North Africa, on the beach of a Pacific atoll, or in service hospitals.

Seventeen New Jerseyans earned the Congressional Medal of Honor, rising for brief moments of glory above the ranks of the millions who slogged unsung through the mud and blood. Only seven of these survived to wear their medals in peace.

Marine Sergeant John Basilone of Raritan, son of immigrant parents, was the most famous hero. He won his Medal of Honor in a savage machine gun duel with the Japanese at Guadalcanal in 1942. Officials brought Sergeant Basilone home, paraded him up and down the land to sell war bonds as "The Hero of Guadalcanal." Appalled, the sergeant asked to be returned to active duty. He never came back. Sergeant Basilone died in one of the waves of Marines that waded ashore at Iwo Jima in February, 1945. He stands in memory in a bronze statue in his home town.

Another New Jersey Congressional Medal winner was Captain Thomas G. McGuire, Jr. of Ridgewood. He ranked second only to his commander, Major Richard Bong, as the outstanding Pacific area ace. McGuire had thirty-eight Japanese planes to his credit when he was killed as he sought to aid a fellow pilot who was trying to evade a Japanese fighter. McGuire Air Force Base at Fort Dix, world's largest military airport, was dedicated in his name in 1949.

A POWERFUL HOMEFRONT

The Basilones and McGuires and hundreds of thousands of other Jerseyans in uniform were armed by a multitude of war workers in factories back home. New Jersey ranked fifth among states in war contracts, filling one-sixteenth of all United States orders for military supplies. Nearly one million war workers were employed in fulfilling the twelve billion dollars in war contracts that came here. Nine billion went to just five counties—Hudson, Passaic, Camden, Essex, and Union, in order of total output.

New Jersey met nearly every conceivable type of war need: ships, airplane motors, explosives, radar, uniforms, radios, food, and a thousand other things. One major, unsung contribution was production of thousands of different components, or parts, to be fitted into larger, glamorous items of war. For this, New Jersey won still another nickname: "The Component State."

Shipbuilders again proved their versatility. At Camden's New York Shipbuilding Corporation, ships slid down the ways nearly every day, ranging from little craft for beach landings to huge aircraft carriers. The firm delivered $217,000,000 in new bottoms between March, 1942, and March, 1943, a record never exceeded by an American yard. Its 38,000 workers made twenty-nine of America's biggest fighting ships—cruisers, battleships, and aircraft carriers. Of all Camden achievements, "Old Nameless" (the *South Dakota*) and "The Sunsetters" are the most memorable.

Old Nameless or "Battleship *X*" (names stemming from the secrecy surrounding her) went into action in March, 1942, eleven months ahead of schedule. She steamed promptly to the Pacific to win glory in numerous engagements, particularly at the Santa Cruz Islands and Guadalcanal. In 1943, New York Ship delivered nine cruisers of the *Independence* class. Their exploits against Japan's Rising Sun earned them the nickname "The Sunsetters."

At Federal Shipyards in Kearny, 32,000 worked around the clock. Another 20,000 were on day and night shifts at an auxiliary yard at Port Newark. Six months after Pearl Harbor, Federal astonished the shipbuilding industry by launching four destroyers and four auxiliary vessels in one day. By 1943, Federal was building faster than any other American shipyard, delivering a ship every four and a half working days and cutting destroyer production time from eighteen months to less than five. Federal eventually made nearly a quarter of all United States destroyers.

Meanwhile, Curtiss-Wright of Paterson added more than 40,000 workers and in the five years between 1940 and 1945 and turned out 139,000 airplane engines, far more than any other American contractor. The Paterson engines took General James Doolittle's B-17 over Tokyo for his acclaimed daylight raid on April 18, 1942, and they powered the B-29 bomber, *Enola Gay*, that carried the atom bomb over Hiroshima on August 6, 1945.

New Jersey did not regain the powder-keg reputation it had in World War I, although Picatinny Arsenal at Dover continued as the chief Allied source of explosives know-how. More than 18,000 visitors came to Picatinny in 1942 to learn about munitions. They took their knowledge to private plants dispersed around the United States. Nearby, Hercules Powder Company in Kenvil produced just under two billion pounds of explosives.

New Jersey again became the "build-up" state, the staging and storage area for the big jump overseas, just as it had been in World War I.

Fort Dix alone handled 1,300,000 inductees. Camp Kilmer in Middlesex County, an open pastureland in 1942, became an encampment capable of clearing 100,000 troops a month for overseas duty. In all, Camp Kilmer funneled two million men to Europe.

Hudson County's train terminals and piers teemed with soldiers coming and going, and the Hudson dock workers each week forwarded hundreds of thousands of tons of material to the European theater. Earle Naval Ammunition Depot in Monmouth County each month sent nearly 130,000 tons of munitions eastward to help seal Hitler's doom. At times Earle stored enough explosives to blow all of New Jersey and New York City off the map; fortunately, it all went elsewhere.

Prelude to Victory

The ultimate blow was the atomic bomb. If nothing else served to make nineteenth-century ways fade, that bomb did. Many people in many lands contributed to that atom bomb, but New Jersey scientists played many roles. The "Father of the Atomic Bomb" was Albert Einstein, the German scientist who discovered the existence of atomic energy early in the century. He was lecturing in the United States in 1933 when the Nazis stripped him of his property and his citizenship because he was a Jew. He accepted the directorship of the School of Mathematics in the newly established Institute for Advanced Study in Princeton and remained there until his death in 1955.

Working independently, two scientists at Westinghouse Lamp Division in Bloomfield developed pellets of pure uranium in 1922 as they were searching for new lamp filaments. They put aside their discovery until twenty years later, when three tons of uranium were needed for the Manhattan Project (which built the bomb). Westinghouse scientists found ways to boost productions at Bloomfield from a few ounces to 500 pounds daily.

Concurrently, Professor Hugh Stott Taylor and associates at Princeton University "boiled" seventy-five *tons* of ordinary water down to ten *drops* of "heavy" water, each drop containing one part of heavy hydrogen, needed for the bomb. Dr. Enrico Fermi, Columbia University professor who was a top figure in the Manhattan Project, lived in Leonia.

Finally, on August 6, 1945, as the *Enola Gay* droned on its way to

Hiroshima, Captain Robert A. Lewis of Ridgefield Park sat as co-pilot in the fateful bomber, unaware of the destructive forces the plane's bombardier soon would unleash. Down went the device, bursting with a heat and force unknown before in history and leaving behind 60,000 dead, 100,000 injured, and 200,000 homeless. Three days later, Nagasaki perished under another A-bomb and on August 14 Japan sued for peace.

(As aftermath, it should be noted that J. Robert Oppenheimer, the physicist who is credited with much of the thought behind development of the bomb, became director of the Institute for Advanced Study at Princeton. Dr. H. D. Smyth, chairman of the physics department at Princeton University, wrote the official report on the A-bomb for the Atomic Energy Commission.)

The announcement of Japan's capitulation reached New Jersey and citizens went wild, screaming through a mad "V-J" night of relief and happiness. Once again the soldiers came home from Europe and the East. Nearly three million jammed through Camp Kilmer and another two million crowded into and out of Fort Dix as rapidly as possible. Amid the joy of homecoming, however, there seemed to be shadows ahead.

POSTLUDE TO WAR

Nearly a million men and women had worked in New Jersey war factories in September, 1943, with another million employed in other war-connected tasks within the state. The war-stimulated economy began to sag as early as October, 1943, and by October, 1945, some 300,000 war workers had lost their paychecks. Some of these were servicemen's wives, who had no desire to continue when husbands returned, but they were in the minority.

The loss of work was doubly bad, for paychecks had doubled in size—up from an average of twenty-six dollars a week in 1939 to fifty-two dollars a week in 1944.

Economists warned of depression, forgetting that even with the sudden drop in war demands, 1945 employment stood at a level half again as high as in 1939. They forgot, too, that, properly managed, the pent-up demand for automobiles, toasters, houses, diapers, schoolbooks, and a thousand and one other things would send the economy soaring again.

But it was a world turned topsy-turvy. Women worked in numbers never before known, and many a husband-and-wife working team enjoyed a heady living standard, even though it often meant neglecting the children. Young veterans and their enlarging families created unprecedented demands for housing and schooling. Automobile and appliance salesmen grew rich.

Spurred by the GI Bill of Rights, veterans overwhelmed college campuses. Many old-line professors doubted that ex-soldiers and sailors could succeed in the classroom (much less that such a high percentage of the populace should benefit from higher education). The veterans astounded them; they were serious, sober, and bright. Campuses grew in size as veterans crowded into Seton Hall, Fairleigh Dickinson, Stevens, St. Peter's, Upsala, Drew, Princeton, Newark College of Engineering, and Rider. They swarmed into Rutgers, The State University, and the six state teachers colleges. These early demands for college education grew; America quickly became accustomed to "education for all."

NEEDED: A NEW CONSTITUTION

There was much to be done. The words of Governor Driscoll, "a great work is expected of you," rang with telling clearness in the summer of 1947. New Jersey either had to move up with the times or move over. In a world awed by the A-bomb and a nation excited by education, a state using a constitution little changed since 1844 seemed as out of fashion as an industrialist using a team of oxen to deliver his wares.

Through the years efforts to change the constitution had been fruitless, despite some amendments in 1875. Agitation had swelled for decades for a new and modern constitution. Governors Charles Edison and Walter Edge both tried to update it during their terms; each failed as entrenched political forces fought any change. Voters had had a chance to act on a revised constitution in 1944, but they turned it down after a campaign of distortion mixed with pleas not to change the laws "while the boys are away."

The homefront constitutional battles of the early 1940s paved the way, however. They made clear, too, that politicians would fight changes in the makeup of either the Senate or Assembly. Reapportionment to give urban areas greater representation in the state legislature had been shunted aside in 1874 and not attempted since. New Jersey's stature as an industrial state was clear, but those eager for constitutional change knew better than to insist on open debate on such a touchy matter as realignment of the legislature. Changes in the makeup of either body of the state legislature specifically were ruled out of the Constitutional Convention, therefore. With that stumbling block removed, the Convention got to its task.

The delegates worked in harmony. They took one of the nation's most outmoded and wordiest constitutions, and cut it to 10,000 words (compared with New York's 19,000 and California's 46,000). New Jersey voters overwhelmingly ratified the new constitution in November, 1947; state government stepped into a new era.

The new constitution strengthened government at every level and liberalized official state philosophy.

The governor, once one of the nation's weakest chief executives, became one of the strongest. He can succeed himself once, serve four-year rather than three-year terms, have actual control over his department heads, and be on equal footing with the legislature. The latter, in turn, is stronger, for Senators serve four years instead of three and Assemblymen two years instead of one.

"Jersey Justice" is more than a slogan, possibly for the first time in the state's history. The old tangled complex of courts, based on old English law and bewildering to the public, was streamlined and simplified. The Supreme Court became truly supreme and the Chief Justice took over administration of the entire court system. The maze of old county courts, including the "Oyer and Terminer Court" (a name never understood outside the legal profession), was replaced by a single county court.

The new court system prompted Rutgers President Dr. Robert E. Clothier, Convention president, to comment: "The interests of judges and lawyers, important as they are, have been subordinated to the interests of the litigants."

Changes in the constitution's Bill of Rights brought the document into line with a philosophy that had ignored color, religion, or national origin when sending men to World War II battlefronts. In 1844, perhaps, it had been enough to forbid discrimination only for "religious principles"; the 1947 framers saw the need and the wisdom of removing race, color, sex, and national origin as bases for discrimination.

The expanded antidiscrimination clause brought quick repercussions. Many of the state's municipalities had to take immediate steps to integrate school systems, including such "northern" places as Asbury Park and Princeton. State National Guard units had to accept Negro enlistees—in defiance of a national Department of the Army policy that continued to declare that "local custom" (that is, opposition by Southern states to integration) made segregated Army units necessary.

Governor Driscoll's firm stand for integration in the New Jersey National Guard units had country-wide impact. New Jersey became the first state to desegregate its armed forces, despite rumors that federal money would be cut off. Integration at every level in all United States armed forces followed the New Jersey step.

Fittingly, since he had made an uncompromising declaration for the new constitution in his first campaign and then had proved his determination to enforce it, Driscoll was re-elected in 1949 as the first New Jersey governor to succeed himself in 105 years (prior to the 1844 constitution, governors could succeed themselves for an unlimited number of one-year terms).

THE "NEW" NEW JERSEY

As Governor Driscoll took office in the winter of 1950, U. S. Census takers began their nose count. This showed state-wide population had increased in a decade by nearly 700,000, up to 4,835,329. It also showed concrete proof of the move to "Suburbia," as newspaper writers and sociologists labeled the region outward from the cities. The automobile, combined with the GI Bill, which permitted veterans to buy or build houses on easy terms, was taking families out of the cities and into the countryside. This had happened before, but never in such magnitude.

This flight to open spaces would continue as would the mushrooming population. The 1960 Census showed the state with 6,067,412 people, 1,200,000 added since 1950—and close to 2,000,000 newcomers since 1940. An analysis of population shifts in those twenty years disclosed some reversals of long-standing tendencies.

For one thing, cities stood still or lost population. Hudson County's intensely urban complex lost more than 40,000 people in the two decades. Camden, Atlantic City, East Orange, Newark, Bayonne, Hoboken, Jersey City, Union City, Passaic, Elizabeth, and Trenton lost ground. Only Paterson, of the major cities, grew, and by a mere 4000.

Loss of populations coincided with the blight overtaking cities in all parts of the nation. Traffic-choked streets, inadequate parking, expanding slums, rising crime rates, soaring taxes, and fleeing industry beset practically every city. Newark, founded by Puritans in 1666, found itself on the downgrade as the 1940s merged with the 1950s. Then, in 1954, the Mutual Benefit Insurance Company announced it would stay in Newark and erected a new office building. Prudential Insurance Company followed with a new home office. The Port of New York Authority poured in millions of dollars to expand Port Newark and Newark Airport. The city was on the move.

Newark has changed dramatically since 1955. New buildings have risen along Broad Street. Housing for low-income and higher-income groups has been built. Port Newark's capacity has been doubled. Building continues on a "cultural area" to include new buildings for the Newark campus of Rutgers University and for Newark College of Engineering, as well as other facilities. Newark has a long way to go, but unlike 1940, when it was on the way down and didn't know it, the city in 1960 was on the way up and wanted to continue.

The renewal of its cities is as serious a long-range problem as New Jersey faces. Yet, in the decade of the 1950s, the growth of suburban towns and villages was unlike anything ever seen in the state. Developers cut up fields and built rows of look-alike houses, sometimes with little regard for anything beyond the down payment and the acceptance of a mortgage by the bank. Many of these settlements of new houses comprised 1200 to 2000 dwellings, new towns in themselves.

These developments follow an old trend: they are mainly in two semicircles centered on New York and Philadelphia. In the north, new homelands sprout within a twenty-to-twenty-five-mile arc of New York; in the south, in a slightly smaller arc east of Philadelphia, and spreading to Burlington, Camden, and Gloucester counties. The old New York-Philadelphia magnets are strong.

Unprecedented problems faced scores of onetime villages as the building rush of the 1950s picked up pace. New schools had to be built rapidly. Sewer systems had to replace septic tanks. Water-supply systems had to be enlarged. Taxes rose higher and higher. Often the country acres, which had looked so much greener from behind a city fence, seemed to take on the same coloration—at least the same tax coloration—as the cities. The "split-level trap" was as much a matter of economics as social condition. Local tax rates were—and are—high, since New Jersey has always depended heavily on local taxes to meet local problems.

Much of the population boom has been near two major toll roads, which crisscross in Middlesex County and lie like a flowing necktie along the Jersey Shore and down through the center of the state to Salem County. These are the 118-mile-long New Jersey Turnpike, fully opened to traffic in 1953, and the 164-mile-long Garden State Parkway, opened for most of its distance in 1954 and in full operation from the New York State line to Cape May three years later.

Traffic far exceeded expectations on both of these new roads. Within a year after opening, each had to be widened. Actually, each generates new traffic, thus creating new problems as it solves old ones.

Bergen County, at the north end of both the Turnpike and Parkway, added 140,000 new people between 1950 and 1960 to become the second county, behind Essex, in population. Middlesex County, the crossroad of the toll highways, added 169,000 people in the same decade. Shoreward, Monmouth County's position astride the Garden State Parkway accounted for a jump of 109,000 residents, while Ocean County, on the fringe of rapid commuting to the metropolitan area, nearly doubled its population.

The highways do a good job of moving people—the New Jersey Turnpike carries about one million automobiles every day—but only industry can make people stay. Here New Jersey has fared well, too, since World War II. The state is seventh nationally in industrial production.

Industry remains diversified; the battleships, airplane motors, and explosives of war have been replaced by the more prosaic needs of everyday life. New Jersey leads in the manufacture of chemicals. It also furnishes electronic supplies, apparel, rubber, paper, motorboats, automobiles, petroleum products, machinery, instruments, textiles, toys, beer, clay products, leather, food, jewelry, medicines, electrical and telephonic components, and a host of other products.

Despite economic ups and downs, shifts in political leadership, changes in buying habits, and departure of some industry to cheap-labor areas, New Jersey by 1960 still had jobs for more than two million people—including 800,000 in manufacturing. About 90 per cent of all the types of commodities made in the United States are made here.

Industrial progress in this state should occasion little surprise. After all, this has been an industrial state for more than 150 years. Two world wars proved its ability to rise to emergency. Since World War II, however, a dramatic change has occurred: industry has hastened to the country. Out there is cheap land, with plenty of room for sprawling plants and parking lots. Moreover, industry is now wanted—largely, it must be admitted, for the tax benefits it brings.

Industry is now plentiful in places where it seldom appeared before 1940—in the rural areas of Morris and Somerset, in outlying sections of Bergen, Passaic, and Union counties, and to some limited extent in Warren, Hunterdon, and Sussex counties. Downstate, the growth of industry in the Delaware Valley is an important aspect of the state's economic condition. Southern New Jersey's industrial spurt since 1950 has meant a transformation for an area where only agriculture had predominated for two centuries.

The New Jersey Turnpike and the Delaware Memorial Bridge at Deepwater were instrumental in southern New Jersey's industrial awakening, providing quick, convenient trucking links to great markets. Equally important is a quickened awareness that industrial development must go side by side with agricultural and recreational advancement if the economy is to remain healthy. The scores of new plants built or planned in the once-dormant southern counties attest to that awareness.

The economic future seems rosy: some 10 per cent of all United States research dollars are spent in nearly 700 research laboratories in New Jersey—and one of every eight American research employees pursues his work here. Nearly one-fifth of all research scientists are in residence in New Jersey.

Research has been a bright New Jersey chapter, ever since Thomas Edison began his work at Menlo Park almost a century ago. Since then, the state's researchers have pioneered in vitamins, miracle drugs, atomic energy, textiles, cancer research, transistors, television, radio, synthetic rubber, rocket motors, and space exploration, to mention only the major areas.

The fruits of research are being harvested. Surveys in 1960 showed that precision electronics research and manufacture added up to at least a billion dollars a year for New Jersey's economy. This is an entirely new billion dollars since World War II—and most of it is in the hands of young scientists and manufacturers inspired by World War II developments.

This space-age "baby" is growing in many places: in Bell Telephone Laboratories in Murray Hill, Whippany, and Holmdel; in a spate of thriving electronics firms surrounding Princeton and the Army Signal

Research and Development Laboratory at Fort Monmouth; in firms in Newark, Camden, Moorestown, Plainfield, Bedminster, and nearly a hundred other locations.

SUN LAND REJUVENATED

Back on earth, the state's economy has many facets, not the least of which is a continuing boom based on sand. The golden strand along the Atlantic Ocean makes cash registers ring. Prosperous visitors using the Garden State Parkway, the Atlantic City Expressway, and lesser highways bring millions of dollars into more than a half hundred resort towns along the 120 miles of shoreline. How many dollars is anyone's guess, but the total is estimated at near the two-billion mark each year.

Things are changing by the sea. Motels are replacing fading old hotels as automobile-attuned visitors replace the prewar type of sedentary hotel guest. Developers have put thousands of buildings atop dunes or along man-made lagoons, often to the dismay of buyers who watch in horror as the restless sea, spurred by a howling storm, rearranges things to her liking. One storm in March, 1962, tore the shore apart from Sandy Hook to Cape May, ripping down hundreds of buildings and causing tremendous dollar losses.

Regardless of the changes wrought by man, and recurrent alterations by the ocean, the seaside maintains its mystery and fascination—a precious asset for any state.

Up in the hills, the lakeland of Morris, Sussex, and Passaic counties is crowded as never before. Every foot of shoreline is dotted with cottages. Motorboats whine across lake surfaces in frightening numbers. Vacationists bring seasonal prosperity to these lake spas, and many former visitors now stay the year around, a change in living habit occasioned by wartime housing shortages.

In spite of the swelling population, booming industry and expanding research, New Jersey retains the nickname "The Garden State." Some consider this quaint; some political leaders vigorously, and unsuccessfully, opposed use of the phrase on automobile license plates. It may not be fully accurate, but it is not farfetched, either.

Agriculture is still here, but it is adapting to the times. Farmers in urban regions, caught in a spiral of rising land taxes and wooed by high offers, have sold out, often for $25,000 to $50,000 per acre. There were 300,000 fewer farm acres in 1959 than in 1950, but some 28 per cent of the state is still in farmland. Dairying is in a slow decline, despite its importance in the northwestern hills. Poultry and egg farmers in shore counties, in large measure victimized by their own wild expansion in the 1950s, have cut production drastically.

The farmers have adjusted to meet demands and have kept the state in first place in gross farm income per acre, a position maintained for nearly a century. Southern New Jersey's vegetable farms, tomato fields, and fruit orchards serve the nearby canneries and metropolitan markets. Blueberries have become a major summer crop, and the production of nursery products to meet demands of home developers and industries has become a big business. Many erstwhile potato acres in Monmouth County are now devoted to shrubs and landscaping plants.

A Political Unpredictable

New Jersey's varied economy is matched by varied political fortunes. No Republican or Democrat dares call New Jersey "safe."

When Dwight D. Eisenhower took New Jersey by 358,000 votes in 1952, the way seemed clear for Republican successes. But a year later, Democrat Robert B. Meyner captured the governor's chair by a comfortable margin of 153,000 votes. This amounted to an astonishing shift of a half million votes in one year. In 1956, President Eisenhower captured the state by 757,000 votes, but the next year Governor Meyner was re-elected by a margin of 204,000 votes! When Meyner's second term ran out, he was succeeded by another Democrat, Richard J. Hughes.

The political winds remained unpredictable when the state gave Democrat John F. Kennedy a slim margin of 22,000 votes in 1960. On the same ballot, it returned Republican Clifford B. Case to his U. S. Senate seat by a whopping margin of 332,000. Senator Case's colleague in the Senate is Harrison B. Williams, elected in 1958 by 84,000 votes and re-elected in 1964 by more than a half million votes in the landslide that saw Lyndon B. Johnson win the state by more than a million margin. Their Governor Hughes was re-elected by a wide margin in 1965, carrying with him Democratic majorities in both houses of the legislature for the first time in 50 years.

If anything can be read into the vagaries of election returns from the state, it must be that New Jersey has a wary, unpredictable public, voting for the man rather than the party.

This electorate is gradually coming to recognize the problems besetting any region where population has risen more than 50 per cent in twenty years.

The ability to face up to the problems and challenge of the twentieth century has increased greatly in the years since World War II. Since 1949, voters have approved a recurring series of bond issues to provide toll highways, to rebuild the six state teacher colleges, to greatly expand Rutgers as The State University, to construct reservoirs and mental and penal institutions, and to acquire land for recreational and conservation purposes. The total of more than $600,000,000 in bonds has indicated a willingness to pledge tomorrow rather than to pay today, but voters at least appeared aware of the problems caused by their own needs and numbers.

Challenges remain: urban renewal, the increasing Negro populations in the cities, water supply, inadequate highways, a deteriorating system of rapid transit, crowded higher educational facilities, sharply rising local property taxes, outmoded local schools in many areas, and green land disappearing rapidly beneath the "urban sprawl." These are the tests of twentieth-century living.

The legislature faced gingerly up to two major worries as the mid-1960s overtook the state: reapportionment of the Senate and Assembly to reflect the centers of population, and pressing demands for state income and/or sales taxes. Both have been on the agenda for years— reapportionment for at least seventy-five years, new state taxes for more than three decades.

THE VIEW FROM THE CORRIDOR

Against the challenges are the opportunities. New Jersey in 1960 still was 46 per cent forested, with some 1,200,000 acres of hardwoods in the north and 1,300,000 acres of pines in the south. Those are incredibly open lands in view of the widely held theory that the strip from Boston to Washington is one vast megalopolis, completely filled with homes, factories and highways. The Jersey Meadows, the aromatic stretch of real estate between Newark and Jersey City, once considered only a ghastly eyesore, are now recognized as a vital asset for the future of northeastern New Jersey. The open spaces of the Pine Barrens of Monmouth, Ocean, Atlantic, Burlington, and Cumberland counties also represent a priceless opportunity for planned growth.

The two great cities on either side of the state remain splendid market regions, excellent ports for movement into world trade, centers of culture, education, and opportunity. New York and Philadelphia often blur New Jersey's identity by tugging at opposite ends of the state, but without them the state would suffer more than diminished ego.

The role of a peninsula set between two fine harbors has been established. The corridor is busier and more crowded than ever, but this is a change of degree rather than kind. New people come, as they have since the Dutch and Swedes and English and French arrived in pre-Revolutionary days. As they come, they create problems as well as opportunity. Ready marketplaces lure new industry to the state, in continuation of traditions now a century and half old. Farmers still know that a fuzzy-cheeked Jersey peach with the warmth of the sun still on it will sell in New York or Philadelphia. The Jersey Shore and the North Jersey lakeland bear testimony that two centuries of experience in entertaining visitors has been passed on to eager hands.

Astride the main road of history, New Jersey has never been merely a spectator. It knew Indians, the marching and fighting of men in the Revolution, the exciting beginnings of railroads and industry. It played a self-doubting part in the Civil War, and was filled with the vigor of invention, immigration, and industry after the war. In the twentieth century, it has played key roles in war and in the frantic search for peace. Today it is keyed both to research and to the struggle of an urban civilization to succeed.

History has never passed New Jersey by. Whatever the word of the moment, the passion of the nation, it has been reflected here. The reason is simple: people passed this way—colonists, revolutionists, warriors, inventors, capitalists, workers, people of many nations and many races. They brought problems and they created answers. Perhaps more then anything else, New Jersey deserves the sometimes bestowed nickname: "The Typical State." Here, as much as anywhere, is a compound of all that makes America what it is.

Where to Find New Jersey

No state's history and spirit can be captured completely in one volume—or in many volumes, for that matter. Those whose interest in New Jersey is piqued by this one-volume history of the state will find ample material for further reading and study. The often-heard expression "There is so little available on New Jersey" is sheer fiction.

The best guide to further information is Nelson R. Burr's *A Narrative and Descriptive Bibliography of New Jersey* (Princeton: D. Van Nostrand Co., 1964), a detailed study of hundreds of books on every facet of the state's diversified past. A briefer guide is *This Is New Jersey, A Bibliography* (fourth revised edition; Trenton: Trenton State College, 1964).

However, even without those guides casual readers can find their own way into New Jersey history by seeking a relatively few books available in any well-stocked local library. Interest in local history has been manifested in many libraries within the past decade, stimulated in large measure by increasing demand from students and newcomers to the state.

Begin with the multivolume histories: Irving S. Kull (editor), *New Jersey, A History* (four volumes; New York: Lewis Historical Publishing Co., 1930–32); Francis B. Lee, *New Jersey As a Colony and As a State* (four volumes; New York: Publishing Society of New Jersey, 1902); William S. Meyers (editor), *The Story of New Jersey* (five volumes; New York: Lewis Historical Publishing Co., 1945). Lee's work is by far the most readable; it is bright, well written, and divided into short topical chapters, but it suffers because its publication date (1902) precluded any of the tremendous changes in the twentieth century. The volumes edited by Kull and Meyers move deeper into this century, but even the most recent of them stops with World War II not yet won.

Not a "set" in the sense of the Kull and Meyers works but nevertheless conceived and published as a unit are the thirty-one books in the New Jersey Historical Series that D. Van Nostrand Co. of Princeton began publishing during New Jersey's Tercentenary in 1964 and completed in 1965. These short books explore the state's historical periods (colonial, Revolution, Civil War, growth of urbanization, etc.) as well as its varied people, its culture, its industry and research, and its geological and geographical regions. Here is a compilation of detail not found elsewhere. This is a landmark of local publishing.

If detail is the key to history, then the place to look for that is in the many publications of the New Jersey Historical Society in Newark. The Society's *Proceedings* have appeared quarterly since 1845 and its forty-six volumes of *The Archives of the State of New Jersey*, published between 1901 and 1917, include original colonial documents, minutes of early state governing bodies, wills, and newspaper extracts. This is the bare stuff of history, reported almost as it occurred in the state's first century and a half.

But history is more than detail. It is an arrangement of those details. Samuel Smith made the first genuine effort to prepare such arrangement for this state in 1765 when he published *The History of the Colony of Nova Caesaria or New Jersey*. The original edition is extremely rare, but a reprint of 1877 is a standard in any library which has been able to pay attention to New Jersey history for more than thirty years.

Other "standards" found in most libraries are Thomas F. Gordon, *A Gazetteer of the State of New Jersey* (Trenton: Daniel Fenton, 1834) and John W. Barber and Henry Howe, *Historical Collections of the State of New Jersey* (Newark: Benjamin Olds, 1844; revised in 1853 and 1868.) These two works give an enlightening picture of the state in a time of tremendous change—when railroads and canals were being built, when the constitution of 1844 was being adopted and when industry and new towns were rising rapidly. The woodcuts in Barber and Howe have continuously charmed readers.

Also basic to a broad understanding of New Jersey is the meticulous volume compiled and written by a small battalion of WPA workers during the depression years, *New Jersey: A Guide to Its Present and Past* (Newark: New Jersey Guild Associates, 1939). The book must be used wisely. So much has happened in New Jersey since 1939 that descriptions of towns and cities can be hopelessly out of date, and the political philosophies expressed seem even a little quaint today. Still, this Federal Writers project stands as a monument to a group dedicated to giving New Jersey a proper place among states.

Beside the WPA guide must be placed *The New Jersey Almanac* (Upper Montclair: The New Jersey Almanac, 1963). This is undoubtedly the handiest compilation of information that New Jersey has ever enjoyed. It is not to be read in one sitting or in many sittings; its value lies in use to answer hundreds of specific questions and to find statistical data.

The *Outline History of New Jersey*, prepared in 1950 by a committee of State Teachers College professors and published by Rutgers University Press, is useful to students.

Now the reader interested in specifics can begin to narrow his quest for information. Here are a few of the books that can help:

Kemble Widmer, the state geologist, has pleasantly woven history and geology together in *The Geology and Geography of New Jersey*, (Princeton: D. Van Nostrand Co., 1964). An earlier but not nearly so enjoyable volume is Bulletin 50, *The Geology of New Jersey*, originally written in 1914 and revised in 1938–40 by Henry B. Kummel.

Dorothy Cross is the state's Indian authority; her *The Indians of New Jersey* (Trenton: Archeological Society of New Jersey, 1958) best serves to introduce the Lenni-Lenape. For a livelier account, see M. R. Harrington, *The Indians of New Jersey: Dickon Among the Lenapes* (New Brunswick: Rutgers University Press, 1963).

The ventures of Dutch and Swedish colonists are told by Adrian C. Leiby, *The Early Dutch and Swedish Settlers of New Jersey* (Princeton: D. Van Nostrand Co., 1964). Wesley Frank Craven's *New Jersey and the English Colonization of North America* (Princeton: D. Van Nostrand Co., 1964) details the inevitable conquest by the English in 1664, and Richard P. McCormick's *New Jersey from Colony to State*, another in the Van Nostrand series, very well sketches the history from 1609 to 1789.

Two Princeton University Press books are excellent for an understanding of New Jersey's role in the Revolution. Donald L. Kemmerer's *Path to Freedom: The Struggle for Self-Government, 1703–1776* (Princeton: Princeton University Press, 1940) gives ample evidence that New Jersey played a surprisingly active, if often quietly undramatic, part in events leading to war. Leonard Lundin's *Cockpit of the Revolution* (Princeton: Princeton University Press, 1940) is an absorbing, masterful treatment of the incomparable role that the state played in winning independence.

New Jersey's transformation from agricultural state to an industrial complex is a key story that is often overlooked in the glamor of the Revolution and the colonial period. Wheaton J. Lane has contributed the basic book on transportation, *From Indian Trail to Iron Horse* (Princeton: Princeton University Press, 1939). Unfortunately, for all its merit, Lane's book carries only slightly past the Civil War. John T. Cunningham's *Railroading in New Jersey* (New York: Associated Railroads, 1952) brings the story of the state's railroads to modern times. Another Cunningham book, *Made In New Jersey* (New Brunswick, Rutgers University Press, 1954), is the only compilation of industrial history.

Still sorely needed is a concise book on New Jersey's ambivalent role in the Civil War. Charles M. Knapp, *New Jersey Politics During the Period of Civil War* (Geneva, New York: W. F. Humphrey, 1924) and John Y. Foster, *New Jersey and the Rebellion* (Newark: M. D. Dennis, 1868) must be read in combination to give even a basic understanding, but neither is adequate. This phase of state history has been almost completely overlooked by academic—and popular—historians.

Agriculture has been reasonably well treated—in such books as Carl R. Woodward, *The Development of Agriculture in New Jersey, 1640–1884* (New Brunswick: Rutgers University, 1927) and John T. Cunningham, *Garden State* (New Brunswick: Rutgers University Press, 1955).

The excitement of the late nineteenth century and the twentieth century has generally been ignored by the state's chroniclers. Fortunately the Van

Nostrand Tercentenary series treated many hitherto-overlooked aspects—immigration, labor, urbanization, transportation, and the rise of progressive thought. Ransom E. Noble's *New Jersey Progressivism Before Wilson* (Princeton: Princeton University Press, 1946) makes it clear that liberal thought in the state did not begin with Woodrow Wilson. The role of Wilson in galvanizing action, however, is amply told in many books, most authoritatively in Arthur F. Link's *Wilson: The Road to the White House* (Princeton: Princeton University Press, 1947).

New Jersey's Tercentenary year generated a rash of local publishing in 1964—particularly county and town histories—in addition to books by Van Nostrand and Rutgers University Press. Now scores of town histories exist at last in regions from Sussex to Cape May, some of them well written and handsomely bound, others more pedantic but still useful.

County histories leave much to be desired, despite the publication of a few excellent works during the Tercentenary. Students of county history generally must go all the way back to the thick volumes of the 1880s, when enterprising publishers combined local biographies with some well-written and well-researched local history to permit publication of county histories.

Much used for the understanding of New Jersey counties is Cunninghams' *This Is New Jersey, From High Point to Cape May* (New Brunswick: Rutgers University Press, 1953). This tells the story of each of the twenty-one counties, amply illustrated by maps and photographs. *This Is New Jersey* remains the fundamental source in any start toward an understanding of the nature and history of county political subdivisions which are so important in New Jersey. (In this instance, and earlier, I have described my own works in the third person. This is neither affectation nor unqualified recommendation.)

No quest for New Jerseyana could ever be complete without a reading of the late Henry C. Beck's several entertaining books of folklore and history: *The Jersey Midlands, Forgotten Towns of Southern New Jersey,* and *Tales and Towns of Northern New Jersey,* among others published by Rutgers University Press. Henry Beck was the first author to give New Jersey a treatment of enthusiasm and wonder. His books deliberately intertwine fact and folklore, but his writings have a flavor and a feel unmatched in other New Jersey books. He is worth reading, for spirit as well as information tinged with imagination. In the same tone, Gustav Kobbé's two delightful little guide books, *New Jersey Coast and Pines* (1889) and *Jersey Central* (1890), written for the Central Railroad of New Jersey, are worth seeking.

Once past such basic books as those listed above, the researcher is led to the hundreds of documents and manuscripts in such places as Rutgers and Princeton University libraries, The State Library at Trenton, the New Jersey Historical Society, the Newark Public Library, and scores of local historical societies and public libraries. Then come the local newspapers, as they were or on microfilm. The beginnings of research are simple. The quest is endless.

New Jersey: America's Main Road

BY JOHN T. CUNNINGHAM

Index
